The Struggle for Understanding

SUNY SERIES IN CONTEMPORARY JEWISH LITERATURE AND CULTURE

EZRA CAPPELL, EDITOR

Dan Shiffman, *College Bound:
The Pursuit of Education in Jewish American Literature, 1896–1944*

Eric J. Sundquist, editor, *Writing in Witness:
A Holocaust Reader*

Noam Pines, *The Infrahuman: Animality in Modern Jewish Literature*

Oded Nir, *Signatures of Struggle: The Figuration of Collectivity in Israeli
Fiction*

Zohar Weiman-Kelman, *Queer Expectations:
A Genealogy of Jewish Women's Poetry*

Richard J. Fein, translator, *The Full Pomegranate:
Poems of Avrom Sutzkever*

Victoria Aarons and Holli Levitsky, editors,
New Directions in Jewish American and Holocaust Literatures: Reading and Teaching

Jennifer Cazenave, *An Archive of the Catastrophe:
The Unused Footage of Claude Lanzmann's* Shoah

Ruthie Abeliovich, *Possessed Voices:
Aural Remains from Modernist Hebrew Theater*

Victoria Nesfield and Philip Smith, editors,
The Struggle for Understanding: Elie Wiesel's Literary Works

The Struggle for Understanding
Elie Wiesel's Literary Works

Edited by

Victoria Nesfield and Philip Smith

Cover: "Rain in the Forest, Scarborough." Used by permission of the photographer, Mark Mullen.

Published by State University of New York Press, Albany

© 2019 State University of New York

All rights reserved

No part of this book may be used or reproduced in any manner whatsoever without written permission. No part of this book may be stored in a retrieval system or transmitted in any form or by any means including electronic, electrostatic, magnetic tape, mechanical, photocopying, recording, or otherwise without the prior permission in writing of the publisher.

For information, contact State University of New York Press, Albany, NY
www.sunypress.edu

Library of Congress Cataloging-in-Publication Data

Names: Nesfield, Victoria, 1984– editor. | Smith, Philip, 1983– editor.
Title: The struggle for understanding : Elie Wiesel's literary works / edited by Victoria Nesfield and Philip Smith.
Description: Albany : State University of New York Press, [2019] | Series: SUNY series in contemporary Jewish literature and culture | Includes bibliographical references and index.
Identifiers: LCCN 2018040458 | ISBN 9781438475455 (hardcover) | ISBN 9781438475462 (pbk.) | ISBN 9781438475479 (ebook) Subjects: LCSH: Wiesel, Elie, 1928–2016—Criticism and interpretation. Classification: LCC PQ2683.I32 Z886 2019 | DDC 848/.91409—dc23
LC record available at https://lccn.loc.gov/2018040458

10 9 8 7 6 5 4 3 2 1

Contents

Foreword   vii
    Peppy Margolis

Introduction   xi
    Victoria Nesfield and Philip Smith

Part I. Hasidic Origins

1. Between Fiction and Reality: Elie Wiesel's Memoirs   3
   Menachem Keren-Kratz

2. The Death of Humanity and the Need for a Glory Culture: The Existential Project of Elie Wiesel   25
   Yakir Englander

3. The Role of the Four Prophet Figures in *Night*   51
   Mary Catherine Mueller

Part II. The Other

4. Embracing Madness: Elie Wiesel's Madmen and Their Role in His Works   79
   Jennifer Murray

5. The Bystander in Elie Wiesel's *The Town Beyond the Wall*   97
   Christin Zühlke

6. Enduring Anti-Semitic Christian Scripts in Elie Wiesel's
   The Gates of the Forest   113
   Lucas Wilson

Part III. Theology and Tradition

7. Stories Untold: Theology, Language, and the Hasidic Spirit
   in Elie Wiesel's *The Gates of the Forest*   137
   Ariel Evan Mayse

8. Testifying, Writing, and Putting God in the Dock:
   Elie Wiesel and the Crisis of Traditional Theodicy   169
   Federico Dal Bo

9. The Importance of Memory: Jewish Mysticism and
   Preserving History in Elie Wiesel's *The Forgotten*   195
   Eric J. Sterling

Part IV. Later Works

10. Transcultural Networks of Holocaust Memories in
    Elie Wiesel's *The Time of the Uprooted*   219
    Dana Mihăilescu

11. Wiesel's Political Vision in *Dawn*, *The Testament*, and
    Hostage   239
    Rosemary Horowitz

12. Allegories of the Holocaust in Elie Wiesel's Late Fiction:
    The Forgotten, *The Sonderberg Case*, and *Hostage*   261
    Sue Vice

Contributors   283

Index   289

Foreword

Peppy Margolis

Eliezer "Elie" Wiesel (1928–2016) was born in Sighet, Romania, on September 30, 1928. In May 1944, when he was fifteen years old, the Nazis deported him, with his family, to Auschwitz. He was in Auschwitz at the same time as my mother. Women and men were separated, of course, but it is possible that Elie and his father, Shlomo, met my grandfather Rachmiel and my uncles, Perez and Zalmen.

On January 29, 1945, Elie and his father arrived on a transport to Buchenwald, where his father died before liberation. My father met Elie in Buchenwald, when they were together in Barrack 66. The Nazis were preparing to evacuate all prisoners from the camp when the American army arrived on April 11, 1945. My father, David Schwarzberg, and his cousin Joe Szwarcberg stood with Elie Wiesel at the gates when the US Third Army reached them.

When Buchenwald was liberated, most of the 904 children under the age of fourteen were orphans. The American army chaplains Rabbi Robert Marcus and Rabbi Herschel Schacter arranged for the offices of OSE (Oeuvre de Secours aux Enfants), the Jewish children's relief organization in Geneva, Switzerland, to help the children. On June 2, 1945, OSE representatives arrived in Buchenwald. The OSE sent 427 children to France with Rabbi Marcus; 250 went to England; and Rabbi Schacter escorted 280 to Switzerland. Elie Wiesel and my cousin Joseph were sent from Buchenwald to Ecouis, France. Of the children sent to France, a smaller group of about ninety to one hundred boys including Elie and cousin Joe went to a home in Ambloy, in Loir-et-Cher. This home, supervised by German-born Jewish social worker Judith Hemmendinger, offered its young residents kosher facilities and religious observances.

This group of boys called themselves "the Buchenwald Boys." The boys were subsequently moved to a home in Taverny near Paris that operated until 1947. Cousin Joe and Elie maintained a friendship even after Elie went to Paris to study at the Sorbonne. Joe, who now lives in Melbourne, Australia, maintains contact with many of "the Buchenwald Boys." He travels to see them where they scattered all over the world. He helped produce two films: *The Boys of Buchenwald* and *The Buchenwald Ball*, which tells the story of the "Boys'" yearly reunion in Melbourne to celebrate their survival, liberation, freedom, and friendship.[1]

It was at the Sorbonne that Elie learned French and studied literature, philosophy, and psychology. It was here that the lectures by philosophers Martin Buber and existentialist Jean-Paul Sartre reputedly influenced his later writings. While Elie studied in Paris, he became a journalist. For a decade he was silent about what he endured and atrocities that he witnessed during the Holocaust. After a meeting with French author François Mauriac, formerly a member of the French Resistance, and a Nobel Laureate in Literature, Elie was encouraged to set pen to paper. Mauriac, a devout Christian, remembers the young Jew with "the gaze of a Lazarus risen from the dead."[2] With Mauriac's guidance, influence, and persistence, *Night* was published.

Reading and rereading *Night* is an arduous task. I find myself searching for answers to the many questions Elie raises about human nature, especially good and evil. I ask how humans could allow and participate in this horrific event? Where was God's presence, kindness, and compassion during the Holocaust? Through *Night*, I began a journey into the darkness of the Holocaust—an event that both my parents endured. I try to comprehend the unimaginable struggle that Elie Wiesel and both of my parents lived through. I ask myself, how did they remain sane?

Elie said, "Only those who experienced Auschwitz know what it was. Others will never know. But would they at least understand?"[3] When we, as readers, enter the incomprehensible world of Auschwitz, we encounter the dark side of humanity. We learn about the suffering of the victims by executioners or perpetrators, plus that of bystanders, and the few upstanders or rescuers. After I read *Night*, I have to ask: What would I have done? Could I have behaved differently? What would I do when faced with choiceless choices? Would I have survived in the winter with no coat, hat, gloves, or shoes? Would I have withstood the starvation and the beatings? How did Elie, my parents, and other survivors manage to endure and survive this nightmare?

I traveled to Buchenwald, Auschwitz, and Majdanek, plus other concentration and death camps, on a trip with Holocaust educators. This trip had a profound impact on my life. I am named for my grandmothers who perished in Majdanek and Treblinka. By chance it was my birthday, July 19, when I arrived in Poland. The voices of my grandparents spoke to me, telling me to tell their story. I wondered if I was walking in the footsteps of my parents and Elie Wiesel. It was that day that I accepted my legacy.

At the end of their days, both my parents had Alzheimer's. The disease caused them to relive their horrific experiences. Since I look like my father's sister, he would take my hand and beg me to help him find his way back because he was lost. My father, David Schwarzberg, passed away four years ago on May 14, a few days after the sixty-eighth anniversary of the liberation of Buchenwald. He was eighty pounds and resembled the skeleton that was liberated on May 11, 1945. My father is finally at peace and reunited with his entire family.

My mother, Sara (Cederboim) Schwarzberg, survived two death camps: Majdanek and Auschwitz. She has not spoken, and cannot speak, about her traumatic experiences. Elie helped me better understand her unspeakable experiences. His writings have helped me to imagine the conditions and trauma that my parents experienced during the Holocaust. My mother, like my father, also has Alzheimer's. Since she too lives in the past, she hears noises of gunshots in the distance and people shouting. My mother packs blankets and coats so she can run away to find her family. She wraps food in tissues for an emergency. We hide in the corner and don't talk, fearing *they* will find us. I am not sure I will ever truly understand what she went through, but fiction offers a beginning. While reading *Night*, I enter, as much as those of us who came after can enter, the heart of darkness. I go there with my parents and Elie Wiesel.

Notes

1. *The Boys of Buchenwald*, dir. Audrey Mehler (Vancouver: Paperny Films, 2002); *The Buchenwald Ball*, dir. Danny Ben-Moshe, Uri Mizrachi, and Andrew Weisman (Melbourne: Pericles Films, 2006).

x / Foreword

    2. François Mauriac's foreword in Elie Wiesel, *Night* (London: Penguin, 2006), xix.
    3. Elie Wiesel's preface to *Night*, ix.

Works Cited

Ben-Moshe, Danny, Uri Mizrachi, and Andrew Weisman, dirs. *The Buchenwald Ball*. Melbourne: Pericles Films, 2006.
Mehler, Audrey, dir. *The Boys of Buchenwald*. Vancouver: Paperny Films, 2002.
Wiesel, Elie. *Night*. Trans. Marion Wiesel. London: Penguin, 2006.

Introduction

Victoria Nesfield and Philip Smith

On July 2, 2016, one of the most important voices to have emerged from the Diaspora after World War II was lost to us. Elie Wiesel lived through the Holocaust—an event of such terrible magnitude as to take the lives of most of his family members and to destroy the community where he was raised. It is remarkable not only that he survived and found a way to write about his experiences, but that when he did write it was with such elegance and profundity. Wiesel's works speak of silence, of loss, of frenzy, of madness, of community, and of faith. His writing is at once compelling, tragic, grotesque, and powerfully moving. He was not only a prolific novelist, but a teacher, chair of the US Holocaust Memorial Council, public speaker, activist, and recipient of the Nobel Peace Prize. He stands alone among those who have shaped the discourse on Holocaust memory, human rights, and modern Jewish culture.

Many of us who have had an ongoing relationship with Wiesel's work feel the tragedy of his loss all the more keenly because he passed away at a time when we needed him the most: in the six months that followed his death the world saw the acceleration of xenophobic politics on a global scale, a Holocaust Remembrance Day statement from the White House that made no explicit mention of Jewish victims or anti-Semitism, and the desecration of Jewish cemeteries in Philadelphia and New York. In August 2017, in Charlottesville, Virginia, many protestors at the violent Unite the Right march waved swastika flags and called out anti-Semitic chants, and on October 27, 2018, a man opened fire at the Tree of Life synagogue in Pittsburgh, killing eleven and injuring six more.

In a time when such issues seem as urgent as they have ever been, the questions of scapegoating, violence, the minority experience, memory, and memorialization remain at the heart of Wiesel's work, and they continue to yield insights. Over the course of commissioning chapters and working with our contributors for this collection, we were struck again and again by the ways in which the questions he raises felt, and continue to feel, more important, and more prescient, than they have ever been.

Wiesel Scholarship: An Overview

Elie Wiesel's life and literature has generated a sizeable canon of critical works, some dating back more than a decade. Such is the depth of his works that they will no doubt continue to attract new readers and produce an outpouring of scholarship for many decades to come. The recent publication of *Elie Wiesel: Messenger for Peace* by Alan Berger (2017) suggests that critical interest remains, and will continue to remain, high.

Biography

Some of the most significant early scholarship on Wiesel has been primarily biographical. John K. Roth's *A Consuming Fire: Encounters with Elie Wiesel and the Holocaust* blends Wiesel's biography with references to his literary works and with Roth's own personal responses to Wiesel's life, work, and religious identity.[1] His insights, bolstered by his personal relationship with Wiesel, represent one of the earliest interventions in Wiesel scholarship, and his work remains one of the most important points of reference for subsequent writing.

Irving Abrahamson's major, three-volume *Against Silence: The Voice and Vision of Elie Wiesel* remains a towering, authoritative source on Wiesel.[2] This collection of Wiesel's thoughts and commentary was gathered through his interviews, speeches, and articles, as well as his testimonial work. These volumes provide historical and contextual information. Frederick Downing's *Elie Wiesel: A Religious Biography*, similarly, is invaluable in its extensive research into Wiesel's origins and background.[3] As Wiesel's life, shaped by his religious upbringing and his faith, is retold by Downing, with his career and his literary responses to the world around him plotted alongside, this is a useful resource for any reader who wishes to understand the bibliographical context for Wiesel's fiction. Finally, of course, we have Wiesel's own memoirs, *All Rivers Run to the Sea* and *And the Sea Is Never Full*.[4]

As a further discussion of Wiesel's life, the focus of Margaret Taft's *From Victim to Survivor: The Emergence and Development of the Holocaust Witness 1941–49* is the development of a collective status for survivors–turned–public figures.[5] Taft challenges the notion that the Holocaust witness emerged largely from and after the 1961 Eichmann trial, uncovering the defiant and tenacious efforts of the first witnesses, some writing as early as 1941, to plot the first course from victim to survivor. The recurring themes Taft discovers in the experiences of these survivors, from indifference to hostile anti-Semitism, provide a solid literary and historical context for the scenes Wiesel sets in his novels, which so often feature a survivor coming to terms with the people and places of his past. Wiesel's own status as public survivor, of course, has informed the ways in which we must approach his works; while he has been instrumental in shaping Holocaust discourse, his name itself has accrued certain signifiers that he would not necessarily have chosen. Phillip Lopate contends: "Sometimes it almost seems that 'the Holocaust' is a corporation headed by Elie Wiesel, who defends his patents with articles in the Arts and Leisure section of the *Sunday Times*."[6] However fair we might consider such assertions to be, they unavoidably provide a context for our approaches to Wiesel's work.

Holocaust Fiction and Holocaust Testimony

The Holocaust is, of course, central to Wiesel's life and literary output, and Wiesel's oeuvre is, in turn, integral to discourse on Holocaust literature. Wiesel, famously, has argued against the fictionalization of the Holocaust and the reduction of a topic of such philosophical and material immensity to a simple three-act structure. Instead of reading fictional accounts, he asserts, we should look first to survivor testimony.[7]

At the same time, however, his own works often tread a careful line between what is remembered and what can be expressed. While this volume is primarily interested in Wiesel's novels rather than his life, it is often difficult to disentangle the two. Wiesel's biography is important to those who study his novels, of course, because of the dense relationship between his life and his literary works. While Wiesel himself described his trilogy *Night*, *Dawn*, and *Day* as memoir, the works shuttle between biography and fiction. Lawrence Langer writes of *Night*:

> Wiesel's account is ballasted with the freight of fiction: scenic organization, characterization through dialogue, periodic climaxes, elimination of superfluous or repetitive episodes, and especially an ability to arouse the empathy of his readers, which is an elusive ideal of the writer bound by fidelity to fact.[8]

Night, then, is too literary to be pure memoir but too committed to the ideal of testimony, and too autobiographical, to be read as fiction. Wiesel's works suggest that we lack a widely accepted vocabulary to discuss this kind of work. As editors of this collection we decided that, while a strong case can be made for *Night*, *Dawn*, and *Day* as memoir, the three texts contain sufficient novelistic elements to fall within the purview of this collection.

Tackling the challenging question of the discourse between historiography, biography, and literary invention, Ruth Franklin's *A Thousand Darknesses: Lies and Truth in Holocaust Fiction* considers well-known examples of both survivor testimony and Holocaust fiction, including Wiesel's *Night*.[9] Franklin, a literary critic and third-generation survivor, argues, counter to Wiesel, that fictional accounts of the Holocaust can serve an important role in public remembrance.

Beyond the question of the literary and the biographical, Rosemary Horowitz's edited *Elie Wiesel and the Art of Storytelling* contains some of the earliest interventions in Wiesel scholarship to identify some of the core thematic questions in Wiesel's fiction, among them being the role of silence.[10] The Holocaust, as scholars such as Berel Lang and Lawrence Langer and writers such as Primo Levi have argued, offers an apparent paradox—the Holocaust is beyond representation and yet, as Roger Luckhurst asserts, "silence is no option."[11] Wiesel himself argued that "Auschwitz is something else, always something else. It is a universe outside the universe, a creation that exists parallel to creation."[12] It is impossible to represent either the scale or the horror of the Nazi killing project, and yet, precisely because of its scale and its horror, it demands representation. Wiesel manages this paradox through the careful negotiation of different kinds of silence: Graham B. Walker argues that "there are at least two kinds of silence in Wiesel's novels: the silence of possibility, community, and creativity; and the silence of chaos, solitude, and destruction."[13] In Wiesel's work we encounter characters who use silence as an instrument of tragic defiance (in the vow taken by the community depicted in *The Oath*, for example), as a means to protect oneself (Gregor pretends to be mute to pass as a gentile in *The Gates of the Forest*), and in the terrible recognition of the impossibility of fully articulating the horror of genocide ("I feel unable to tell the story of this event, much less imagine it," says the narrator of *Day*).[14]

Wiesel's works, of course, have also informed the wider subject of Holocaust literature. Sue Vice, one of the United Kingdom's leading scholars on Holocaust literature and the first to establish an MA in Holocaust studies in the United Kingdom, published *Holocaust Fiction* in 2000, exploring, like Franklin, the often-controversial subject of fictional texts using the Holocaust as their context.[15] Vice's book is a scholarly analysis into the ethics of writing Holocaust fiction and the key academic debates that remain live. Aukje Kluge and Benn E. Williams's edited volume *Reexamining the Holocaust through Literature* covers discussion of a range of types of Holocaust literature, including survivor literature in the works of Charlotte Delbo and Wiesel, before broadening the scope to include works by second- and third-generation writers, including plays, novels, and comic books, across a range of national and cultural contexts.[16] Kluge and Williams's text, as Sara Horowitz identifies in her foreword, demonstrates the problem of attempting to isolate a definitive canon of Holocaust literature.[17] Vice's colleague Jenni Adams brings the field even more up to date, editing the *Bloomsbury Companion to Holocaust Literature* in 2014, a thorough treatment of a range of themes that arise in the broader field of Holocaust writing.[18]

Taking a transnational approach, the contributors to Alan Rosen's earlier edited volume, *Literature of the Holocaust*, offer considerations of the responses to and after the Holocaust in the literature of a number of countries, languages, and cultures.[19] Rosen's text showcases literature's special contribution to our understanding of the Holocaust and also its reach across the world, from the countries and languages of the victims' persecution to those of their refuge. The contributors of Rosen's volume note the interplay between history and literature but also the momentous points where the nuances of literature tell far more than historical facts can. The eight simple words uttered to arrivals at Auschwitz, directing men to the left and women to the right, is Rosen's case in point, as he illuminates how Wiesel brings this into sharp focus at the point he departed from his mother forever.[20] Rosen's volume recognizes that the war years yielded a rich source of Holocaust literature, several years before the likes of Wiesel took up the mantle and transformed it into the vast field we have today.

Steven Katz's edited *The Shtetl: New Evaluations* looks closely at the roots and representations of the shtetl and its significance in Jewish literature.[21] Although making a broader survey of this unique facet of Jewish life, one that reaches beyond its presence in literature, Katz and his contributors plot the representation of the shtetl through time and literature, without shying away from the less romantic realities of these Jewish worlds. Katz's volume identifies the shtetl's role in cultivating some key Jewish literary figures who emerge in Wiesel's fiction, such as the innkeeper—notably *The Trial of God*'s Berish. Wiesel's own chapter in the volume identifies the peculiar paradox of a community almost beyond the changes of time in the world outside the shtetl, and one whose religious influence dictates a fixation on the significance of time, place, memory, and looking to a better future. It is a world Wiesel returns to in his novels time and again.

Religions Belief and Tradition

Horowitz's volume also offers perspectives on the complex, and sometimes seemingly contradictory, role religion plays in Wiesel's writing. Wiesel draws heavily upon, and shows great reverence toward, the traditions of Talmudic scholarship while at the same time expressing a crisis of faith—not in the existence of God, but in the possibility of a loving God. This has been a recurring feature in Wiesel's writing throughout his career; in his foreword to the 2016 edition of *A Consuming Fire*, for example, Roth reflects on how in his later years, following emergency life-saving surgery and a subsequent book *Open Heart*, Wiesel's authorial tone and focus, although more conciliatory and less religiously rebellious than when Roth first encountered Wiesel, remained theologically challenging. The place for Jewish religious traditions in Wiesel's work arises once more in Carole J. Lambert's *Ethics After Auschwitz: Primo Levi's and Elie Wiesel's Response*.[22] Comparing the testimonies of Primo Levi and Wiesel with the specific focus on the survivors' approach to religious ethics, this ten-chapter volume is structured around the Ten Commandments. The premise illuminates some points of convergence between Levi and Wiesel's ethical and authorial voices. The fact remains, however, that on many issues of religion, faith, and ethics within and outside of the camps, Wiesel and Levi stand apart and often distinctly at odds.

Carole J. Lambert's *Is Man God's Friend? Theodicy and Friendship in Elie Wiesel's Novels* takes as a starting point the pained question of theodicy in a post-Holocaust world in conjunction with Wiesel's preoccupation with friendship.[23] Lambert considers the central characters of six of Wiesel's novels (*The Town Beyond the Wall, Twilight, The Gates of the Forest, A Beggar in Jerusalem, The Accident, The Judges*), and the values, faith, and goodness the characters might have hoped to find in God, but in the face of trauma and suffering, find instead in their friendships. Lambert further argues that Wiesel's novels deserve the same scholarly attention that his nonfiction work has so rightly achieved, recognizing that the reception of Wiesel's novels in the United States is a far cry from the acclaim they have received in France.

Steven Katz and Alan Rosen's edited *Elie Wiesel: Jewish Literary and Moral Perspectives* offers a further intervention in the role of religious belief and scholarship in Wiesel's writing.[24] It offers insights not only on Wiesel's novels but his nonfiction (particularly his commentary on his Hasidic writing), and his work as a teacher and activist. The volume is perhaps most insightful in its demonstration of the ways in which Wiesel's works act as a bridge between Jewish theological traditions of the past and Jewish culture today. Wiesel's writing, the volume convincingly demonstrates, is deeply infused with Talmudic and Midrashic traditions. The Bible, Talmud, Midrash, and Hasidism provide both Wiesel's recurring points of reference and, in a more structural sense, his propensity for drawing out conflicting and textured interpretations from a given story—his deep skepticism, in other words, of simplistic or seemingly transparent readings.

Elie Wiesel's Literary Works

Given the volume of work on Wiesel, then, one may ask why a new collection is necessary? One of the central motivating impulses of this work is to bring a scholarly apparatus to bear upon Wiesel's later novels. Such was Wiesel's output that, even as he has attracted the attentions of many of the most authoritative scholars to study Holocaust literature, he consistently outpaced his commentators. While there has been an outpouring of works on *Night* and Wiesel's Hasidic writings, his later novels such as *Hostage* have gone almost completely unrecognized in critical works. Several of the essays featured in this collection address these later novels.

This collection, then, seeks to engage with the existing critical work on Wiesel, to move forward certain debates, and to expand the conversation by offering interventions on works which, until now, have not received any significant critical attention. We have grouped these essays into four parts: Hasidic Origins, The Other, Theology and Tradition, and Later Works. These parts offer broad thematic groups and a very broad chronology of the fiction under consideration.

Hasidic Origins

For the purposes of this volume we define Hasidic origins as the traditions, spiritualism, and mysticism that characterize the culture of the specific branch of Orthodox Judaism that Wiesel grew up within and identified with. Menachem Keren-Kratz's essay opens this collection. He seeks to locate Wiesel in the literary and cultural environment of Sighet—the town in which Wiesel spent the first fifteen years of his life. Sighet, he contends, was not the isolated and culturally conservative shtetl popularly represented in Wiesel (auto)biography, but a thriving literary hub. Wiesel, he argues, was deeply influenced by the writers of his hometown. Their impact on Wiesel's authorial voice remained palpable throughout his literary career. Keren-Kratz raises challenging questions, such as why Wiesel appeared to willfully deny the literary scene he was surrounded by as a youngster, or the literature that he suggests Wiesel was influenced by. Our opening chapter further raises a broader question: as a human rights activist, theologian, figure of public admiration and political influence, is Elie Wiesel as a novelist held to higher standards than other authors of fiction in telling a faithful story? Keren-Kratz challenges the reader to not read Wiesel's fiction and novels passively, but to ask what agendas and motivations drove such a prolific output that started at such a young age and following such trauma to span, as Keren-Kratz identifies, a lifetime of literary, journalistic, and academic writing.

Following the literary scene setting of chapter 1, chapter 2 offers a Hasidic context to the themes that recur in Wiesel's fiction. As a corollary to scholarly work on Wiesel and God, Yakir Englander proposes that Wiesel's writing articulates a loss of faith in humanity. Englander argues that, just as the Holocaust led Wiesel to reexamine his relationship with God, his understanding of human beings, too, was irreparably shaped by the events he witnessed and was subject to. The tests—and failures—of human strength recalled in *Night*, are, as Englander asserts, "the moments that truly terrify Wiesel." Faced with the impossibility of faith in either the human or the divine, Englander argues, Wiesel's only recourse was to a theology grounded in Hasidic teachings, Wiesel's "spiritual mother tongue," in Englander's words. Wiesel's religious and philosophical position, then, which Englander sees as a deviation from the traditional ultra-Orthodox response to the Holocaust, can be understood as analogous to that of the tzaddik—one who lives among, and influences, those who do not understand him. The loneliness of the mystical figures in Wiesel's texts resounds with his own distance from any particular Hasidic community after the Holocaust, despite his clear attachment to Hasidism.

The question of Jewish, and particularly Hasidic, teachings recur throughout this volume. One prominent figure from Jewish theological traditions to appear in Wiesel's work, Mary Catherine Mueller argues in this volume, is that of the prophet. With *Night* as her focus, Mueller proposes that Wiesel uses various prophet figures—those who both see and proclaim—to grapple with the (perhaps impossible) task of experiencing and describing both the empirical and experiential truth of the Shoah. The prophet in his or her various guises, she argues, serves as a bridge between the world the reader occupies, and the "anti-world" of the Nazi death camps.

The Other

The authors in part 2 of the volume offer detailed readings of three groups of characters who feature in Wiesel's novels not as central protagonists, but as vital to the narratives in their "otherness" to the leading characters: the madmen (and women), the bystanders, and the Christians. The Other encapsulates the outsider figures that populate Wiesel's texts, those who stand apart from the protagonists and the mass, be they Jews who are spiritually or psychically "other" or non-Jews.

Jennifer Murray examines the "mad" characters who appear in *Night* and *The Town Beyond the Wall*. Each of these figures, she argues, represents a form of mystical madness—their insanity provides them with insights and revelations unavailable to either the reader or the other characters around them. Mueller and Murray's pieces can thus be read as two overlapping readings of a recurring figure in Wiesel's work, the messenger, whose eccentricity (etymologically "outside of the circle") belies a crucial insight into the nature of the world.

The tragedy of the messengers was that their visions and prophesies would not, could not be believed until the violence was already visited upon the Jews. For Wiesel, however, one of the greatest tragedies of anti-Semitic violence was not in the actions of the perpetrators, but in the lack of intervention from others. The bystander, by virtue of his or her failure to act, permits and even normalizes an act of violence. Christin Zühlke's chapter concerns the role of the bystander in Wiesel's *The Town Beyond the Wall*. The novel poses a central question—why would an individual who is perfectly capable of saving lives with little personal risk choose to allow an act of violence to occur? This question, of course, concerns both individual and geopolitical entities. It has far-reaching implications for both psychology and global politics. By way of an answer, Zühlke turns to studies of the bystander in psychology and social psychology. The bystander exists, Zühlke concludes, because, first, individuals typically do not feel responsible for those they consider to be outsiders, and, second, because they feel (perhaps artificially) that they are separate from, and thus not responsible for, the things they witness.

A recurring theme in Wiesel's work is the problem and question of anti-Semitism. In novels such as *The Oath*, which places two survivors—one of a pogrom, one of the Holocaust—in dialogue, Wiesel seeks to show that the Holocaust was not an aberration, but the culmination of a long history of blame, victimization, and explosive acts of mass violence. Two chapters in this volume document and examine the rhetoric and psychology that has facilitated and sought to justify violence against the Jewish people. Lucas Wilson uses the Passion play that occurs in *The Gates of the Forest* as a lens to understand certain forms of Christian anti-Semitism. Wiesel uses the Passion play, Wilson proposes, as a means to make explicit the invocation of Christian scripture in anti-Semitic rhetoric. The novel then, represents an injunction to "go off script" as it were—to find new forms of Christian-Jewish dialogue.

Theology and Tradition

In part 3 questions of Jewish theology and tradition are explored as they arise in a number of historical, geographical, and social contexts in several of Wiesel's novels. For the purposes of this work, Theology and Tradition relates more broadly to Jewish values and the relationship between God and the Jews. In chapter 7, Rabbi Ariel Evan Mayse seeks to intervene in the question of silence in Wiesel's works. Silence was for Wiesel, as discussed earlier, a theme of central importance, and one he returned to in literature and journalism. Mayse argues that a Hasidic philosophy of language offers a means to understand the role silence plays in Wiesel's *The Gates of the Forest*. Hasidism, Mayse argues, presents forms of utterance, including silence, laughter, song, and the absurd, which operate outside of and in concert with directly or transparently communicative forms. Where Englander identifies departures in Wiesel's approach from certain traditions, Mayse sees Wiesel's embrace of this distinctly Hasidic spectrum of language.

Federico Dal Bo takes up a recurring theme in the question of Wiesel's religiosity: the problem of reconciling belief in God with the Holocaust. This is a subject commentators and scholars of Wiesel have grappled with as much as the author, who negotiated a deeply personal faith with searching and pained theological questions, often utilizing his novels. Wiesel's works have taken a range of positions on God, at times separating a respect and deep affection for Jewish traditions from a belief in a Jewish God, at times declaring that the Holocaust represents the end to any possibility of belief, and at times proposing a misotheistic worldview—one that proposes a malevolent or criminally negligent deity. Dal Bo seeks to ground Wiesel's various approaches to belief in Jewish theology, arguing that Wiesel ultimately takes a position that requires us not to argue about God, but to argue *with* Him.

In chapter 9, Eric J. Sterling takes up the question of memory. Using *The Forgotten* as his focus, Sterling examines Wiesel's portrayal of Alzheimer's disease as a gateway to consider the profound importance of memory in Jewish tradition and among survivors. For Wiesel, Sterling argues, the act of remembering is a solemn duty placed upon the living by the dead and the divine. In the novel, Sterling argues, Alzheimer's and (more broadly) human frailty represent a threat to memory. The transmission of memory between generations, however, offers hope.

Later Works

Our final part, Later Works, considers those novels published after 2000, as the World Wars, the Holocaust, the creation of the State of Israel became events of the past century. Although earlier literature is brought into these chapters as points of comparison, this section considers the work of an aging yet ever-active Wiesel. A recurring theme in these chapters is the porous boundary between Wiesel's life and fiction; it can be no coincidence, for example, that many of his leading characters are writers of some kind themselves. His novels, as the chapters in this volume make clear, are deeply colored by Wiesel's political, religious, and philosophical views, none more so than his later works.

Dana Mihăilescu's chapter can be read as an intervention in the question of transnationalism and the Holocaust as highlighted by the contributors to Rosen's volume. Mihăilescu considers *The Time of the Uprooted* and affirms Wiesel's role in the trailblazing position of literature to intervene in discourses of transculturality, memory, and the politics of memorialization. She argues that the novel describes the effects of distance—geographical, generational, and temporal—on memory and the act of memorialization. The novel, she asserts, complicates and resists the easy assimilation of Holocaust narratives into US popular culture, a self-conscious reference on Wiesel's behalf, perhaps, to his own position as a writer in that culture.

Rosemary Horowitz seeks to place Wiesel's later works in dialogue with both his life and the emergence of political and religious Zionism. Seeing Wiesel's novels as a call to action on the central principles of his life, she offers a reading of *Hostage* through the lens of the captivity narrative. This framework not only provides a means to approach Wiesel's later fiction, but can inform our understanding of Wiesel's earlier works, namely, *Dawn* and *The Testament*. Horowitz presents these three novels as an ongoing discourse on Israel, charting the period of Mandatory Palestine under the British, armed resistance, communist Zionism, and the modern Israeli state.

In the final chapter, Sue Vice addresses *The Forgotten*, *The Sonderberg Case*, and *Hostage*. She seeks to draw connections between these texts, considering Wiesel's later meditations on the role of memory, autobiography, the relationships between different generations of Holocaust survivors, and the Israeli-Palestinian conflict. She argues that these novels can be productively read as a form of autofiction—literature that draws upon, and relies upon the reader's knowledge of, true events of a historical or autobiographical nature.

As anyone who has had the pleasure of reading Wiesel's works will attest, his fiction endures. It raises questions that demand answers and it lingers long after one has set the volume down, but, as Peppy Margolis attests in this volume's foreword, entering Wiesel's world *with* his literary works is a beginning. The events of the Holocaust—both during and after—remain close to the surface in Wiesel's novels, yet as the contributors to this volume demonstrate, Wiesel's literary themes are as expansive and prolific as his novels. Subjects that replay in novel after novel, such as how to meaningfully respond to genocide, or the place for God after atrocity, are questions to be struggled with rather than answered. His work will undoubtedly provoke reflection and debate for many years to come. This volume, then, should be read as a continuation of existing conversations and an invitation for further discussion.

Notes

1. John K. Roth, *A Consuming Fire: Encounters with Elie Wiesel and the Holocaust* (Eugene: Wipf & Stock 2016, originally published by John Knox, 1979), 3–4.

2. Irving Abrahamson, ed., *Against Silence: The Voice and Vision of Elie Wiesel* (New York: Schocken Books, 1985).

3. Frederick Downing, *Elie Wiesel: A Religious Biography* (Macon: Mercer University Press, 2008).

4. Elie Wiesel, *All Rivers Run to the Sea* (New York: Schocken Books, 1996); Elie Wiesel, *And the Sea Is Never Full* (New York: Schocken Books, 2000).

5. Margaret Taft, *From Victim to Survivor: The Emergence and Development of the Holocaust Witness 1941–49* (Elstree: Vallentine Mitchell, 2013).

6. Phillip Lopate, quoted in Michael Rothberg and Art Spiegelman, "'We Were Talking Jewish': Art Spiegelman's 'Maus' as 'Holocaust' Production," *Contemporary Literature* 34.4 (1994): 665.

7. Elie Wiesel, "Art and the Holocaust: Trivializing Memory," Iver Peterson trans., *New York Times*, 11 June 1989.

8. Lawrence L. Langer, "The Dominion of Death," in *Elie Wiesel's Night*, ed. Harold Bloom (New York: Infobase, 2001), 16.

9. Ruth Franklin, *A Thousand Darknesses: Lies and Truth in Holocaust Fiction* (Oxford: Oxford University Press, 2011).

10. Rosemary Horowitz, ed., *Elie Wiesel and the Art of Storytelling* (Jefferson: McFarland & Co., 2006).

11. Roger Luckhurst, *The Trauma Question* (London: Routledge, 2008), 5; Berel Lang, *Holocaust Representation: Art within the Limits of History and Ethics* (Baltimore: Johns Hopkins University Press, 2000); Berel Lang, *Act and Idea in the Nazi Genocide* (Syracuse: Syracuse University Press, 2003); Lawrence Langer, *Holocaust Testimonies: The Ruins of Memory* (New Haven: Yale University Press, 1991).

12. Wiesel, "Art and the Holocaust: Trivializing Memory."

13. Graham B. Walker, "Transfiguration," in *Elie Wiesel and the Art of Storytelling*, ed. Rosemary Horowitz (Jefferson: McFarland & Co., 2006), 162.

14. Elie Wiesel, *Day* (New York: Hill and Wang 2006), x.

15. Sue Vice, *Holocaust Fiction* (New York: Routledge, 2000).

16. Aukje Kluge and Benn E. Williams, eds., *Reexamining the Holocaust through Literature* (Cambridge: Cambridge Scholars, 2009).

17. Kluge and Williams, *Reexamining the Holocaust through Literature*, vii.

18. Jenni Adams, ed., *The Bloomsbury Companion to Holocaust Literature* (New York: Bloomsbury, 2014).

19. Alan Rosen, ed., *Literature of the Holocaust* (Cambridge: Cambridge University Press, 2013).

20. Rosen, *Literature of the Holocaust*, 3.

21. Steven Katz, ed., *The Shtetl: New Evaluations* (New York: New York University Press, 2009).

22. Carole J. Lambert, *Ethics After Auschwitz: Primo Levi's and Elie Wiesel's Response* (New York: Peter Lang, 2011).

23. Carole J. Lambert, *Is Man God's Friend? Theodicy and Friendship in Elie Wiesel's Novels* (New York: Peter Lang, 2006).

24. Steven Katz and Alan Rosen, eds, *Elie Wiesel: Jewish Literary and Moral Perspectives* (Bloomington: Indiana University Press, 2013).

Works Cited

Abrahamson, Irving, ed. *Against Silence: The Voice and Vision of Elie Wiesel*. New York: Schocken Books, 1985.

Adams, Jenni, ed. *The Bloomsbury Companion to Holocaust Literature*. New York: Bloomsbury, 2014.

Downing, Frederick. *Elie Wiesel: A Religious Biography*. Macon: Mercer University Press, 2008.

Franklin, Ruth. *A Thousand Darknesses: Lies and Truth in Holocaust Fiction*. Oxford: Oxford University Press, 2011.

Horowitz, Rosemary, ed. *Elie Wiesel and the Art of Storytelling*. Jefferson: McFarland & Co., 2006.

Katz, Steven ed. *The Shtetl; New Evaluations*. New York: New York University Press: 2009.

Katz, Steven, and Alan Rosen, eds. *Elie Wiesel: Jewish Literary and Moral Perspectives*. Bloomington: Indiana University Press, 2013.

Kluge, Aukje, and Benn E. Williams, eds. *Reexamining the Holocaust through Literature*. Cambridge: Cambridge Scholars, 2009.

Lambert, Carole J. *Ethics After Auschwitz: Primo Levi's and Elie Wiesel's Response*. New York: Peter Lang, 2011.

Lambert, Carole J. *Is Man God's Friend? Theodicy and Friendship in Elie Wiesel's Novels*. New York: Peter Lang, 2006.

Lang, Berel. *Act and Idea in the Nazi Genocide.* Syracuse: Syracuse University Press, 2003.
Lang, Berel. *Holocaust Representation: Art within the Limits of History and Ethics.* Baltimore: Johns Hopkins University Press, 2000.
Langer, Lawrence L. "The Dominion of Death." In *Elie Wiesel's Night*, ed. Harold Bloom, 3–16. New York: Infobase, 2001.
Langer, Lawrence. *Holocaust Testimonies: The Ruins of Memory.* New Haven: Yale University Press, 1991.
Luckhurst, Roger. *The Trauma Question.* London: Routledge, 2008.
Rosen, Alan, ed. *Literature of the Holocaust.* Cambridge: Cambridge University Press, 2013.
Roth, John K. *A Consuming Fire: Encounters with Elie Wiesel and the Holocaust.* Eugene: Wipf & Stock 2016, originally published by John Knox, 1979.
Rothberg, Michael, and Art Spiegelman. "'We Were Talking Jewish': Art Spiegelman's 'Maus' as 'Holocaust' Production." Contemporary Literature 34.4 (1994): 661–67.
Taft, Margaret. *From Victim to Survivor: The Emergence and Development of the Holocaust Witness 1941–49.* Elstree: Vallentine Mitchell, 2013.
Vice, Sue. *Holocaust Fiction.* New York: Routledge, 2000.
Walker, Graham B. "Transfiguration." In *Elie Wiesel and the Art of Storytelling*, ed. Rosemary Horowitz, 156–81. Jefferson: McFarland & Co., 2006.
Wiesel, Elie. *And the Sea Is Never Full.* New York: Schocken Books, 2000.
Wiesel, Elie. *All Rivers Run to the Sea.* New York: Schocken Books, 1996.
Wiesel, Elie. "Art and the Holocaust: Trivializing Memory," trans. Iver Peterson. *New York Times*, 11 June 1989. Accessed 9 August 2017.
Wiesel, Elie. *Day.* New York: Hill and Wang, 2006.

Part I

Hasidic Origins

1

Between Fiction and Reality
Elie Wiesel's Memoirs

MENACHEM KEREN-KRATZ

From Sighet to Paris via Auschwitz

Elie Wiesel was born in late 1928 in Sighet, Romania, which he describes as "a typical shtetl, a sanctuary of Jews."[1] He proceeds to describe it as a town submerged in Jewish ambience, in which, for example, all Jewish businesses would cease their activity on the Sabbath:

> Sighet, after all, was pretty much a Jewish town, and all our Christian neighbors knew that a Jew could not light a fire on Saturday, eat leavened bread during Passover, or touch impure meat. The opposite was not the case. I knew nothing of the Christian religion.[2]

Wiesel was raised in a traditional ultra-Orthodox family and as a child received mostly religious schooling.[3] He showed no interest in worldly matters, such as sports, and rarely watched a movie or visited the theater.[4] He did attend the state's general school but "was less concerned with secular studies than with holy books," which he continued to study in the afternoon heder.[5] In 1940, as Wiesel turned twelve, World War II descended and Sighet, along with the entire region known as northern Transylvania, was annexed to Hungary. This event threw the whole region into turmoil as Jews began to sense a growing wave of anti-Semitism that spread into the education system as well.

Despite the Hungarian occupation, Wiesel continued his high school studies and was even sent to study in other towns. Besides the basic curriculum, he also studied with private teachers who taught him Latin, mathematics, physics, and to play the violin.[6] Wiesel's father tried to introduce him to Hebrew-language authors such as David Frishman, Haim Nahman Bialik, and Shaul Tchernichovsky, but he preferred to immerse himself in the study of the Kabbalah.[7] Wiesel's life was abruptly thrown into turmoil in March 1944, when he was only fifteen. German troops entered Hungary—Sighet included—and, under Adolf Eichmann's command, commenced to implement the Final Solution. Soon thereafter all the Jews were forced into the ghetto and within a few weeks they were all transported to Auschwitz in cattle wagons.

After his release from Buchenwald, the sixteen-year-old Wiesel joined a group of several hundred children dispatched to Ecouis, France, where the French Children's Aid Society (Oeuvre de Secours aux Enfants or OSE) had opened a rehabilitation center. From there he moved along with a smaller group of boys from Orthodox homes to Ambloy, where they were housed in a home that served kosher food and maintained a religious lifestyle. This home was subsequently moved to Taverny and operated up until 1947.[8] A few months later, after spending a short time in Versailles, Wiesel moved to Paris, where he was admitted to the Sorbonne and studied French, literature, philosophy, and psychology.[9]

By the time he was nineteen, he had begun to work as a translator and a journalist with the Yiddish periodical *Tsien in Kamf* (Zion in Struggle), which belonged to a right-wing Zionist organization.[10] A few months later, having just turned twenty, he published his first literary piece, a story titled "A Meeting." This was the beginning of a lifelong career of literary, journalistic, and academic writing.

What's Missing?

According to Wiesel's testimony, in his youth he was barely exposed to literature, never read a newspaper, and spent his entire childhood studying religious, and especially Kabbalistic, texts. He did not graduate from high school and spent the crucial years of his adolescence in concentration camps and in orphanages. Wiesel also tells us that he was drawn to literature shortly after arriving in Paris, when he had barely mastered the French language.[11] The question at hand is how a young man with very little literary inclination, who had probably never read a serious work of literature and who had no practical experience in literary writing, could have become a professional writer in so short a time.

"A man is a mold of his childhood's landscape," wrote Shaul Tchernichovsky, whose poems Wiesel heard from his father. Following this line, I claim that Wiesel encountered both literature and journalism when he was still a boy. Sighet, I seek to demonstrate, was far from a backwater shtetl; it was a thriving literary hub. Wiesel was deeply influenced by the literary ambiance in his hometown, and he should be regarded as a spiritual successor of earlier generations of authors and journalists who operated in Sighet for many decades before him.

When Wiesel wrote his autobiography in 1995 and described his hometown as "a shtetl," he knew that only a handful of his readers knew what a real Jewish shtetl looked like. When most people, Jews and non-Jews alike, imagined a Jewish shtetl, they relied on literary images, such as those found in Isaac Bashevis-Singer's stories; or visual images, such as those created by the painter Marc Chagall; and above all on pseudo-realistic images to be found in plays and movies such as *Yentl* or *Fiddler on the Roof*.[12]

Sighet, however, was not a "typical," "Shalom Aleichem" sort of shtetl, with muddy streets and dilapidated wooden sheds, where God-fearing old Jews who know nothing of the world but the ancient sacred texts walked the streets carrying sacks on their bent backs. The truth is that Sighet was anything but the ordinary shtetl Wiesel sketches. It was, as we shall see in the following section, a town in which ultra-Orthodox Jews established a lively and modernist literary and journalistic center that became renowned throughout the Jewish world.

Sighet: A Town Like No Other

The Beginning

Since the early nineteenth century, when Jewish immigration to Hungary accelerated and brought with it the spirit of modernity, Jews became increasingly involved in nonreligious culture and especially in the writing of poetry. While this was true throughout Hungary, it was particularly true of the district of Transylvania.[13] Despite its conservative atmosphere, several groups of Jewish intellectuals, all raised in ultra-Orthodox and Hasidic homes, established a nonreligious cultural center in Sighet, then a small rural town in Transylvania. Various sources reveal that from the mid-nineteenth century onward several *maskilim* living in Sighet wrote poetry, while others penned reports and essays for leading Jewish newspapers.[14] In the mid-1870s the first Jewish newspaper, *Ha-Tor*, appeared in Sighet, and was the first Hebrew-language newspaper in all of Hungary.[15] Since that period and up until World War I a further fifteen Jewish newspapers appeared in the town, most of them in Yiddish.

In roughly the same period, Sighet became known for its Hebrew printing industry and for issuing dozens of books and newspapers as well as other printed materials, both in European languages and in Hebrew and Yiddish. Many Jews who either owned printing houses or were employed in them not only learned the relevant trades, but also grew to respect writing skills.[16] Consequently, prior to World War I Sighet's intellectuals published some forty nonreligious books on topics such as Jewish studies, history, philosophy, and Zionism. Hundreds of Jews, most of them ultra-Orthodox, constituting a significant portion of Sighet's Jewish population, were involved in the printing and newspaper industries, while others became authors, journalists, book dealers, and library owners. They and their extended families, as well as the town's intelligentsia, which included Wiesel's father, constituted the readership of Hebrew and Yiddish nonreligious books and newspapers.[17]

In the wake of its defeat in World War I, Hungary was dismantled and most of its former territories were annexed to other countries. Sighet, along with the southern part of Maramaros County and the entire region of Transylvania, was annexed to Romania, which controlled it until 1940. During that period, with a population of approximately eight hundred thousand Jews, Romanian Jewry became Europe's third largest, after the Soviet Union and Poland.

Sighet under the Romanian Regime

Unlike Hungary, Romania boasted a noteworthy history of Yiddish culture. It was one of the first East European countries to have a Yiddish newspaper, which was followed by dozens of daily, weekly, and monthly Yiddish publications.[18] These were subsequently joined by other literary and informational publications.[19] Added to this was the Yiddish theater scene, with its acclaimed playwrights and itinerant theater companies that disseminated and promoted Yiddish culture all over Romania.[20] This Yiddish cultural ambience exerted a marked influence on the small cultural center that was then just beginning to evolve in Sighet and its vicinity.

Another result of World War I was the occupation of Palestine by the British and the mandate given to Britain to rule the country by the international League of Nations. This development raised great expectations among Jews that the British would implement the Balfour Declaration that expressed support for a "national home" for the Jewish people. Consequently, the Zionist movements in Romania expanded their operations, reaching even the highly Orthodox region of Maramaros. It is therefore not surprising that Wiesel himself had a number of friends who were Zionists.[21] The Zionist activists did not merely resume and broaden their operation in Sighet, they also became a leading force in its cultural revolution.[22]

In 1921, only a few years after the war, Sighet's new Yiddish newspaper, the *Yidishe Tseitung* (The Jewish Newspaper), promoted and reported on a variety of nonreligious cultural activities. As Wiesel himself recalls, Yiddish plays were performed both by local amateurs and by professional traveling troupes. Jewish movies were screened at the local cinema and a Jewish choir began rehearsing and performing. Sighet's Jews also began to enter artistic professions and became painters, sculptors, and musicians, and even formed their own big band jazz ensemble named Keep Smiling. A Jewish soccer club named Samson was established in town and Jews played tennis in their own club.[23]

Crystallization of Sighet's Literary Circle

Sighet's literary circle was established and prospered in the 1920s. Among its founders was Dr. Eliyahu Blank (1887–1955), one of the first Zionist activists in the region. He published several newspapers in Sighet and, after migrating to Palestine, he continued to publish both newspapers and books. Another member was Joseph Holder (1893–1940), Sighet's most renowned poet, whose works were published in many literary magazines throughout the world. The author and essayist Shlomo Schwartz (1883–1944) and the poet Avraham Mordechai Hirsh (1906–?) were both involved in the publication of Yiddish newspapers. A few years later they were joined by a group of younger writers that included authors Yechezkel Ring (1913–2005) and Wolf Tambur (1916–1995), the poet Berl Schnabel (1909–1972), and some twenty other authors of whom only little is known.[24]

These men, and a few women, some of whom still adhered to Jewish religious practices while others had abandoned them, were all part of Sighet's literary milieu. They all took inspiration from their physical and spiritual surroundings, and this was manifested in their writings. Holder, for example, was inspired by the wild nature of the countryside of Maramaros. His poems bear titles such as "The Young Flowers," "A Pine," "The Autumn Wind," and "Under the Dying Acacias." He also wrote poems that referred to the Jewish calendar, such as "Shavuot Twigs" and "The Jewish New Year's eve of 1920."[25]

Wolf Tambur published a novella titled *Next to the Door*, in which he describes the clash between ancient Jewish tradition and the modern Zionist spirit.[26] In his collection of stories, titled *My Home*, Tambur portrays everyday life in the villages and townships of Maramaros.[27] In his book *The Miller's Street*, poet Berl Schnabel portrays the life of the poor non-Jewish villagers and their relations with the Jews. In the second section of this book, "Barefoot," he focuses on several Jewish personalities, while the final poem was named after the town of Sighet and dedicated to it.[28] The first section of Schnabel's book *Yeshiva Poems* contains a lyrical description inspired by his own experience in the local yeshiva, the same institution that Wiesel attended. It includes several love poems, some of which engage with the secret romantic admiration of the students for the rabbi's beautiful daughter.[29] In another section, titled "Maramaros," he portrays a series of typical figures such as "Sighet's street children," "The poor Jew from the mountains," and "The Maramaros girl."

One of the more active members of Sighet's literary circle was author Yechezkel Ring. His first book, *The Lost Melody*, is a Hasidic-style fantasy tale whose protagonist is a divine melody. The story is set on the eve of the festival of Shavuot, which has a special meaning in the Hasidic calendar, and ends as the melody enchants the entire village, Jews and non-Jews alike.[30] His second book, *A Turmoil in Heaven*, is another outstanding fantasy story. Based on Kabbalistic ideas, it is set both on earth, in a shtetl, and in heaven.[31]

During the 1930s Sighet's bustling literary scene realized it needed its own publication, and several activists got together to establish a monthly cultural magazine named *Maramarosher Bleter* (Maramaros's Pages).[32] This magazine was devoted exclusively to the cultural and literary life in Maramaros in general and in Sighet in particular. Its correspondents reported on local events, including Jewish movies, theater plays, sports events, art exhibitions, music performances, lectures, and public readings. It also promoted various cultural initiatives, such as the establishment of a Yiddish Writers Association in Sighet.[33] The magazine likewise published literary works, penned by both renowned international authors and by young local writers. Shortly after this magazine ceased to appear in 1932, the young poet Berl Schnabel founded a new and radical biweekly magazine named *Der Stern*. Unfortunately, since not a single issue of this journal has survived, we know very little about it. These literary magazines were just the topping on Sighet's extensive journalistic activity, which produced several weekly Yiddish magazines and a daily Jewish newspaper in Hungarian.

Sighet's most notable literary achievement was the publication of the literary magazine *Oyfgang* (Rising, or Sunrise), which appeared between 1933 and 1938. Despite being edited and printed in a remote town, far away from any significant Jewish cultural center, the magazine was distributed all over the Jewish world, including the United States and Palestine. Its publishers managed to convince the best-known Yiddish authors, poets, and essayists to contribute to the magazine. It likewise covered other cultural activities, such as theater, movies, music, and art. *Oyfgang* had a life span of five years, far longer than that of several similar magazines that were published in locations with a much larger Jewish population.[34]

To conclude, despite its small Jewish population, which barely reached ten thousand; its remote location; and its ultra-Orthodox character, Sighet became a leading and influential cultural center. From the 1870s to the Holocaust, dozens of its authors published over thirty different Jewish periodicals, including four literary magazines. In addition to more than 150 religious books, local authors produced more than seventy nonreligious books, including no less than twenty works of prose and poetry and hundreds of short pieces that were published in periodicals worldwide. While these numbers may seem small by today's standards, Sighet was one of the five major Jewish literary centers in the region, far outpacing much larger cities.[35]

Sighet's Literary Center and Its Influence on Wiesel's Writings

Sighet makes an appearance in many of Wiesel's novels as well as in his autobiography. Yet one would gain little sense of its literary output from Wiesel's works alone. To claim that he was not aware of what was going on in Sighet would be implausible. Growing up in such a small community, in which everyone knew almost everyone else, Wiesel could hardly have been ignorant, given his self-avowed curiosity and rebellious nature.[36]

Moreover, Wiesel's father was an educated and open-minded merchant, who introduced his son to modern Hebrew literature.[37] He was also a man of the world, as Wiesel tells us:

> I remember only feeble echoes of Franklin Delano Roosevelt's victory in the American presidential elections, the Reichstag fire, the first Stalinist purges, social and political convolutions in Spain, the war in Ethiopia, the death of the League of Nations: there was talk of all these things at the synagogue, and my father would discuss them with visitors at night.[38]

Wiesel's father was precisely the type of person who would have read both the local Yiddish newspapers and the books that were published by local authors, and who would have attended the numerous literary gatherings that took place in town.

Wiesel's autobiography is laced with dozens of authors' names and book titles. Yet it never mentions any of Sighet's authors or poets. Even when he tells us that he learned about a single book that was written in Sighet, he fails to disclose its title or the name of its author.[39] Wiesel even fails to mention Sighet's most renowned literary figure, Hirsch Leib Gottlieb (1829–1930). Gottlieb was an Orthodox Jew who worked as a professional jester and, in 1878, when he was almost fifty, published his first newspaper. He continued to involve himself in this field and published, alone or with others, no less than ten newspapers, mostly in Yiddish. He was known all over the region not only for his activism on behalf of social change, including a call for women's equality and social justice, and his support of Zionism, but also for his popular poems. All Sighet's Jews, regardless of their age or religious orientation, knew Gottlieb's name and were familiar with his works, some of which were already regarded as part of local folklore.[40]

Moreover, Wiesel tells us that as a teenager he sought to further his knowledge on religious matters and especially on Kabbalah and Jewish mysticism. The only place, however, where such books and manuscripts were available was Sighet's only library. This was not a public institution but was privately owned. Israel Weiss, an ultra-Orthodox businessman, opened his private collection of several thousand books to the public, and the library became a hub for Sighet's intellectuals of all sorts, from the most observant Hasidim who came to study the ancient versions of the Talmud to the town's secular Jews who wished to read the latest Hebrew and Yiddish books and newspapers. This library was the place where educated individuals such as Wiesel's father or inquisitive youngsters like Wiesel himself would have gone to meet with their peers or pass the time alone.[41]

Even if one accepts Wiesel's claim that this intellectual young man had somehow remained totally unaware of Sighet's bustling literary life, one may wonder how he failed to mention it in his autobiography, which appeared in 1995. Two books published in the 1970s, both by authors associated with Sighet, reviewed Romania's Jewish literary production. The first, written by Nathan Mark (1897–1988) that appeared in 1971, traces the history of Yiddish books that were published in Romania. Although he did not live in Sighet, he was an active member of the town's literary circle and published one of his books under *Oyfgang*'s auspices. The second was a book published in 1977 by Wolf Tambur, a native of Sighet, which reviews the dozens of Yiddish periodicals printed in Romania. Both books, which Wiesel must surely have come across, celebrate Sighet's outstanding contribution to Jewish literature. These facts were furthermore mentioned by other scholars, including Naftali Ben-Menachem, a prominent librarian at the Israeli National Library, and by the authors of the highly detailed Yizkor book commemorating the Jewish communities of Maramaros, the largest section of which is dedicated to the region's capital—Sighet.[42] Moreover, detailed information about Sighet's literary achievements appeared regularly in the monthly journal titled *Maramaros-Sziget*, which was published by the town's survivors between 1960 and 1974. Wiesel not only received it regularly, but also contributed a few articles of his own.

I therefore conclude that Wiesel deliberately ignored his hometown's literary history in his memoirs. He did so for two reasons. First, had he portrayed Sighet as a modern town, this would have discredited his grand narrative of the simple-minded, ultra-Orthodox, God-fearing Jews who were suddenly and unwittingly thrown into the turmoil of World War II and the Holocaust. And second, that far from being the lone, self-made author he portrayed himself to be, he was, I claim, yet another, highly distinguished, link in a chain of authors all influenced by Sighet's unique spiritual atmosphere.

I now offer several examples in support of the assumption that the young Wiesel was familiar with texts written by Sighet's authors before the Holocaust. It goes without saying that Wiesel did not seek to emulate or to imitate them; he was too talented and resourceful to have to resort to that. However, upon reviewing these examples, one may deduce that, like almost everyone, Wiesel absorbed ideas and concepts during his adolescence that had a great impact on his future life, even if he was not fully aware of this.

Criticism of God

Wiesel's questioning of God's role during the Holocaust appears in the early short stories he wrote for journals in the 1950s and is a constant refrain in many of his later novels.[43] In these books, as well as in his essays and memoirs, Wiesel claims that despite the Holocaust and the immense suffering it brought about, he never ceased to believe in the existence of God. In fact, it was this belief that led him to converse with God and to accuse Him of allowing such evil to prevail:[44]

> The suffering and death of innocent children inevitably places divine will at question and arouses men to wrath and revolt [. . .]. Theories of the idea that "God is dead" have used my words unfairly as justification of their rejection of faith [. . .]. I will never cease to rebel against those who committed or permitted Auschwitz, including God. The questions I once asked myself about God's silence remain open. If they have an answer, I do not know it. More than that, I refuse to know it.[45]

This ambivalent relationship with God, maintaining staunch faith in His existence on the one hand while harshly criticizing Him for the wrongs of the world on the other, is a not a new theme and has been widely addressed in literary works. In fact, it is indeed possible that Wiesel came across this debate even before the Holocaust during his high school years in Sighet.

In those years, Yechezkel Ring was a young and promising author, fifteen years Wiesel's senior. Much like Wiesel, he was raised in a Hasidic home with a father who was an open-minded yet fully observant Jew. Ring published his first book in 1937, his second in 1940, and his third in 1941. In the same year he likewise published the single issue of Sighet's last literary journal, *Ying Marmarosh*, which contained a collection of works by most of Sighet's young authors. Ring's second book expressed its author's feelings in the face of the atrocities committed during the Spanish Civil War. The book, which was printed in Sighet, was titled *Oyfen Himel A Yarid* (A Turmoil in Heaven). The book generated turmoil in earthly Sighet as well.

The book's protagonist is Satan. Having for centuries performed the role of purveyor of evil in the world, he begins to question his actions. This contemplation is triggered by three different elements. First is the daily routine in hell, which Ring describes in the most horrific detail, employing both Christian and Jewish motifs. The second is an episode in which all the world's dogs, which are generally considered to be faithful to men, rebel against their masters and attack them ferociously. The third and crucial element is an unremarkable episode in which a poor man is destined to die. The lamentations of his young children, who are about to become orphans, deter Satan, the angel of death, from carrying out the sentence. Coming face to face with such evils, the Devil rebels and informs the "clerks of Heaven" that he is no longer prepared to execute the commands of a God that is neither merciful nor compassionate.[46] The Devil is then brought to trial in God's heavenly court, which forces him to resume his horrible, yet unavoidable, duties.

The questioning of God's actions, however ruthless they may appear, and the idea of rebelling against Him, was intolerable in the ultra-Conservative society of Sighet, all the more so since this heresy was propagated by someone educated in a Hasidic home. Ring's book sparked mayhem in the town, and it is inconceivable that Wiesel, already a teenager when the story broke, could have remained oblivious of the episode even had he not read the book.[47] Ring's story appears to echo in Wiesel's writings, such as the play he wrote in 1979 titled *The Trial of God*, in which he takes up Ring's theme and holds God accountable for the horrors of the world. And in the words of one of the play's protagonists: "To mention God's mercy in Shamgorod is an insult. Speak of his cruelty instead!"[48]

The Particular Beadle, the Town's Madman, and the Child

Night is Wiesel's most important novel, on which he wrote: "if in my lifetime I was to write only one book, this would be the one."[49] It begins as follows:

> They called him Moishe the beadle, as if his entire life he had never had a surname. He was the Jack-of-all-trades in a Hasidic house of prayer, a *shtibl*. The Jews of Sighet—the little town in Transylvania where I spent my childhood—were fond of him. He was poor and lived in utter penury [. . .] physically he was as awkward as a clown. His waiflike shyness made people smile. As for me, I liked his wide dreamy eyes, gazing into the distance. He spoke little. He sang, or rather he chanted, and the few snatches I caught here and there spoke of divine suffering [. . .].[50]

Further into the narrative, as Wiesel describes how Sighet's Jews were transported to Auschwitz on freight trains, another awkward protagonist, Mrs. Schächter, enters the plot. She begins to hallucinate about fire and warns everyone of a danger that only she can see. These two strange characters are, in fact, the only ones who warn Sighet's Jews of the fate that awaits them, only to be ignored until it was far too late. The witness to their narratives is a child, obviously Wiesel himself, a boy of fifteen whose nonjudgmental observation allows him to detect the truth in their words.

In 1937, Yechezkel Ring published his first novel in Sighet titled *Farblondgeter Nigen* (The Lost Melody). It too begins with a description of the town's beadle:

> Simon the beadle learns a page of the Talmud. We say that he did, but he wasn't really learning. The left side of his face was cradled in his soft beadle'ish hand, his big blue eyes are wide open, dreamfully gazing at the silky petals of a rose that grew in the clay pot in the window, bathed in the golden light of spring.[51]

In the following passage the beadle's daughter, a fifteen-year-old schoolgirl, enters the scene and finds her father in an extraordinary state of ecstasy and confusion that she cannot comprehend. Frightened, the girl runs to her mother and tells her that her father has lost his sanity.[52] Like Moishe, Wiesel's protagonist who teaches him the secrets of the Kabbalah, Ring's Simon is also immersed in the Jewish mystical teachings. Both, as Jewish tradition tells us, are at risk of losing their sanity as a result of their interest in the covert and mysterious texts.

As the story unfolds, Ring introduces the town's fool: Avraham.[53] Like Mrs. Schächter, who cries "fire, fire," a warning that nobody on the train can understand until they arrive at the gates of Auschwitz and see the fire shooting out of the chimneys of the crematoria, Avraham alludes to things that no one can understand. He speaks of lust and desire between men and women, and of the link, according to the Kabbalah, between carnal love and the relationship between God and his people.[54]

The endings of these two stories also bear similarities. In the final passages of his book, Wiesel describes how, upon liberation from the camp, the survivors went on a spree of binge eating and sexual activity. The last sentences portray Wiesel's return to the "normal" world: "I had not seen myself since the ghetto. From the depths of the mirror a corpse was contemplating me. The look in his eyes as he gazed at me has never left me."[55]

Ring's ending likewise depicts a state of utter havoc from which the protagonist emerges to gaze at reality: "Both his eyes opened, wet, blue, like two crushed flowers. His cheeks were flickered by blood, which dribbled down to his beard. But on his pale face, marked with blue veins, a smile was spreading, the holy joy of the doomed melody."[56]

The Father and the Son

Jewish folklore places great emphasis on the Jewish mother, the *Yidishe Mame*, who, unlike the "Jewish father," features in numerous songs, especially lullabies.[57] In his memoirs, however, Wiesel's father receives far more attention than his mother. This becomes apparent already in the first chapter of his autobiography, titled "Childhood," which opens with the sentence "Last night I saw my father in a dream."[58] This is rather surprising, as most people tend to associate their earliest memories with their mother rather than with their father, because it is she who raises the child while the father spends most of his time at work. As Wiesel himself admits, "Shabbat (the Sabbath) was the only day I spent with him."[59] This too raises questions about how close Wiesel was to his father, given that both his parents perished during the Holocaust by the time Wiesel was sixteen years old and he would clearly have spent much more time with his mother than with his father, who was a merchant and a public figure and no doubt frequently absent from the family home.

Throughout the book Wiesel portrays his father as a far more dominant figure in his life than his mother. For example, he says, "I admired him, feared him and loved him intensely," yet never uses such superlatives to describe his mother.[60] His mother is mentioned only in passing, and the most he can say about her is, "My mother was my sole ally and support. She alone understood me. Yet I never gave her a present."[61] Reading his autobiography one realizes that, intentionally or otherwise, while Wiesel bestows many "presents" on his father in the form of warm and admiring words, he once again denies his mother such appreciation.

To understand Wiesel's favorable attitude toward his father, and in fact toward most of the masculine figures in his life, as opposed to his almost nonchalant treatment of female figures, his mother included, one may begin with one of his early stories, titled "Ten O'clock," which was published on December 10, 1948, when Wiesel was barely twenty. It appeared in *Tsien in Kamf*, the first Yiddish journal that employed him, under Wiesel's first pseudonym, Ben Shlomo (the son of Shlomo, which was, unsurprisingly, his father's name).

The story is set in Palestine in the years leading up to the establishment of the State of Israel. The protagonist is the father of a young child, who is critically ill, and is also the commander of an *Etsel* group (an underground movement that fought the British forces in an attempt to end Britain's occupation of Palestine). He is therefore torn between his fatherly obligation to look after the sick child (symbolically named Israel), who begs him to stay with him, and his commitment to the cause, to the establishment of the State of Israel. As the clock turns ten, the man decides to leave his child and to lead his troops, leaving the sorrowful mother alone with her dying son.

This story echoes at least three tales Wiesel might have come across in Sighet. The first, published in four parts in an ultra-Orthodox journal, was authored by Herzl Apshan (1866–1944) from Sighet. He was an observant Jew whose stories about the Hasidic courts were very popular. One of his stories, titled "The Clock Struck 12," speaks of a critically ill man who lies on his sickbed and is determined to live another day and to die only after the town's clock strikes twelve. In both Wiesel's and in Apshan's story the clock signifies both destiny and a firm resolution.

Nathan Mark, who did not reside in Sighet but was closely associated with its literary circle, wrote the second story. Titled "Velvel Shtroy" (Wolf the Straw), the tale was included in his book *Di Leimene Foyst* (Fist of Clay), which was printed and published in Sighet in 1937. The plot tells of Velvel, the town's strongest, yet a simple-minded man, who has just learned of his son's death at the hands of some anti-Semitic students after he, his father, sent him off to earn money for his family. In this story, as in Wiesel's, the father is torn between his concern for his son on the one hand, and his other obligations, in this case to provide for the whole family, on the other.

The third story, "Der Geshmadeter" (The Convert), was written by Dr. Naftaly Shternberg, who led the right-wing Beitar youth movement in Sighet, which was politically linked to the organization for which Wiesel worked in Paris. This is, once again, a story about a father so affected by his son's untimely death that he decides to rebel against God and convert to Christianity, to the amazement of all his friends and relatives.[62]

Conclusion

Besides the aforementioned examples, there are several additional indications that Wiesel was inspired by the literary atmosphere he absorbed in Sighet. For example, most of Wiesel's early novels either deal directly with Sighet or are inspired by it. In these texts the town is identified, and its image serves not only as a backdrop to the plot but sometimes plays an active role in it. Such use of Sighet as a "protagonist" was common among the town's authors. Several of them devoted poems, stories, and even books either to the town itself or to the region of Maramaros, of which Sighet was the capital.[63]

A further example: Wiesel's first job was with the journal *Tsien in Kamf*, which was issued by the right-wing movement Herut. There, in addition to performing the technical tasks of translator and editor, Wiesel wrote several short stories, all of which glorified the movement's ideals and deeds. When reading them, one senses Wiesel's passionate attachment to the movement's ideology. Although it is possible that Wiesel became acquainted with the movement's ideas only in Paris, it is more probable that he learned about them in Sighet.[64] From the late 1920s onward, the movement's youth organ, *Beitar*, ran a branch in Sighet and its leaders published a monthly literary magazine, *Maramaroshre Bleter*. Between 1933 and 1934 they also published a Yiddish language weekly titled *Yidishe Velt* (The Jewish World), which was the only Yiddish newspaper at the time. Wiesel's father, the intellectual merchant, was probably among its readers. The movement's leaders were also active in the literary scene, and some of them wrote short stories and poems for other local newspapers.

~

In my study on Sighet's literary history I employed an idea suggested by Shlomo Bickel, the renowned scholar of Yiddish literature, and sorted Sighet's authors into three "literary generations."[65] Authors belonging to the first generation were those who began publishing their works before World War I. This group comprised some fifteen authors, among them the journalist and poet Hirsh Leib Gottlieb, historian and essayist Rabbi Yekuthiel Yehuda Greenwald, and Avraham Ginzler, who published Sighet's first Jewish newspaper. The second literary generation included authors who began to publish their works immediately after World War I. Among them were the author Herzl Apshan, the poet Yosef Holder, the essayist Moshe Koppler, and the author and journalist Shlomo Schwartz.

The third generation began to publish its works in the 1930s. It was this generation, which comprised some twenty young men and women who were responsible for turning Sighet into a literary center, for publishing its literary magazines, and for producing some twenty books of poetry and prose. This group, I claim, inspired the young Wiesel and indirectly influenced his decision to become an author, an essayist, a playwright, and a journalist. This analysis indicates that, contrary to the impression that Wiesel sought to convey to his readers, he was not an entirely self-made author unconnected to any literary tradition. He was, in fact, one of the fourth generation of an established literary dynasty of which he was, apparently, not very proud. Other members of this group included, among others, essayist and playwright Israel Leib Bruckstein (1920–1988), author Eliezer Basch (1918–?), and journalist Hilel Danzig (1918–1992).

No one knows why Wiesel chose to downplay Sighet's extraordinary literary legacy. Perhaps he preferred not to be associated with a group of provincial authors, or perhaps he saw himself as a self-made man who had created his own legacy. Despite the fact that Sighet played a significant role in his work and legacy, Wiesel consistently denied any connection to its literary history. In 2013, I was close to completing my book *Maramaros-Sziget: Extreme Orthodoxy and Secular Jewish Culture at the Foothills of the Carpathian Mountains*. This is the first and as yet only academic work to review Sighet as a literary and journalistic center. I expected that Wiesel would be happy to write a foreword to the book, which was based on a Summa cum Laude dissertation, but he declined my request. I tried to approach him through other channels, as did the book's editor, a renowned professor of Yiddish at the Hebrew University, who also published the book. Wiesel's reactions, both orally and in writing, conveyed the same message—he had no wish to be associated with Sighet's literary circle.

More recently, and especially after Wiesel's death in 2016, the administrator of his archive, Dr. Joel Rappel, announced that he had discovered several unpublished manuscripts. Wiesel had stipulated that they were not to be published during his lifetime. At least two of them may shed light on how he truly perceived his hometown. The first is Wiesel's unpublished Hebrew adaptation of his book *Night*. This text, which was especially amended for the Israeli readership, was not published, and instead the Hebrew edition was merely a translation of the original French version. The second is the earliest manuscript of Wiesel's memoirs, a work nine hundred pages in length. This document, which was believed to be lost, formed the foundation for Wiesel's first book *Un di velt hot geshvign* (And the World Remained Silent). Perhaps once these texts are made public, they will offer some explanations as to the questions this chapter raises.

Notes

1. Elie Wiesel, *All Rivers Run to the Sea: Memoirs* (New York: Schocken Books, 1995), 4.
2. Wiesel, *All Rivers Run to the Sea*, 23.
3. Wiesel, *All Rivers Run to the Sea*, 9–12.
4. Wiesel, *All Rivers Run to the Sea*, 20.
5. Wiesel, *All Rivers Run to the Sea*, 23.
6. Wiesel, *All Rivers Run to the Sea*, 23.
7. Wiesel, *All Rivers Run to the Sea*, 34–37.
8. Wiesel, *All Rivers Run to the Sea*, 120–21.
9. Wiesel, *All Rivers Run to the Sea*, 154–56.
10. Wiesel, *All Rivers Run to the Sea*, 158.
11. Wiesel, *All Rivers Run to the Sea*, 343–44.
12. Dan Miron, *The Image of the Shtetl and Other Studies of Modern Jewish Literary Imagination* (Syracuse: Syracuse University Press, 2000).

13. Szonja Ráhel Komoróczy, *Yiddish Printing in Hungary: An Annotated Bibliography* (Budapest: Center for Jewish Studies at the Hungarian Academy of Sciences, 2011); Moshe Carmilly, "Hebrew Poetry in Hungary," in *Hungarian Jewish Studies*, vol. 1, ed. Randolph L. Braham (New York: World Federation of Hungarian Jews, 1966), 295–342; Moshe Carmilly, "Meshorerim Ivri'im Be-Transylvania," in *Memorial Volume for the Jews of Cluj-Koloszvár*, ed. Moshe Carmilly (New York: self-published, 1979), 28–112 (in Hebrew); Attila Gidó, *Úton: Erdélyi zsidó társadalom- és nemzetépítési kísérletek 1918–1940* [On the Way: Transylvanian Jewish Attempts at Society- and Nation-Building] (Csíkszereda: Pro-Print, 2009) (in Hungarian).

14. Menachem Keren-Kratz, *Maramaros-Sziget: Extreme Orthodoxy and Secular-Jewish Culture at the Foothills of the Carpathan Mountains* (Jerusalem: The Dov Sadan Publishing Project of the Hebrew University, 2013), 171–72 (in Hebrew).

15. Keren-Kratz, *Maramaros-Sziget*, 207–10.

16. Menachem Keren-Kratz, "The Newspaper Industry in Maramures: A Hungarian, Romanian and Jewish Joint Venture," in *Representations of Jewish Life in Romanian Literature*, ed. Camelia Craciun (Iasi: Alexandru Ion Cuza University Press, 2014), 377–90.

17. Naftali Ben-Menahem, *Misafrut Israel Be-Hungaria* (Jerusalem: Kityat Sefer, 1958), 100–287 (in Hebrew).

18. Volf Tambur, *Yiddish-Presse In Romeniye* (Bucharest: Kriterion, 1977) (in Yiddish).

19. Shlomo Bickel, *Rumenye: Geshikhte, Literatur-Kritik, Zikhroynes* (Buenos Aires: Kiyum, 1961); Nathan Mark (Avi Abir-Zion), *Yiddish Literatur In Rumenye: Fun Ir Onhoyb Biz 1968* (Tel Aviv: Ha-Levanon, 1971) (in Yiddish); Yitzhak Korn, *Yiddish In Rumenye: Eseyen* (Tel Aviv: Avuka, 1989) (in Yiddish).

20. Israel Berkowitz, *Hundert Yor Yiddish Teater In Rumenye 1876–1976* (Bucharest: Kriterion, 1976) (in Yiddish).

21. Wiesel, *All Rivers Run to the Sea*, 27, 37, 46, 54.

22. Avraham Nagari, *Desired Goal: Zionist Youth Movements in Romania as a Foundation for Jewish National Revival (1918–1941)* (Givat Haviva: Yad Ya'ari, 2007) (in Hebrew); Israel Klausner, *Hibat Zion Be-Romania* (Jerusalem: Hasifriya Ha-Tzionit, 1954) (in Hebrew).

23. Wiesel, *All Rivers Run to the Sea*, 18, 20, 25, 27, 29; Keren-Kratz, *Maramaros-Sziget*, 130–33.

24. Keren-Kratz, *Maramaros-Sziget*, 186–93.

25. Joseph Holder, *Oft Zingt Zikh* (Vilnius: Farlag Múlt és Jövő—Budapest, 1928) (in Yiddish).

26. Wolf Tambur, *Bay Der Tir: Dertzeilungen* (Cernăuți: Farlag Yiddish Vort, 1937) (in Yiddish).

27. Wolf Tambur, *Main Heim: Dertzeilungen* (Sighet: n.p., 1940) (in Yiddish).

28. Berl Schnabel, *Milner-Gas* (Bucharest: Farlag Shalom Aleikhem, 1936) (in Yiddish).

29. Berl Schnabel, *Yeshiva Lider* (Bucharest: Yidishe Bibliotek, 1942) (in Yiddish), 25.
30. Yechezkel Ring, *Farblondgeter Nigun* (Sighet: Centrala, 1937) (in Yiddish).
31. Yechezkel Ring, *Oyfen Himel A Yarid* (Sighet: Centrala, 1940) (in Yiddish).
32. Published between 1931 and 1932.
33. It was inspired by the PEN (Poets, Essayists, Novelists) association of writers founded in London in 1921.
34. Menachem Keren-Kratz, "The Social and Cultural Role of Small Jewish Literary Centers: The Case of Sighet, Romania," *Journal of Modern Jewish Studies* 16, no. 2 (2017): 179–97.
35. Keren-Kratz, *Maramaros-Sziget*, 124–25. In addition to the Jewish newspapers, over fifty non-Jewish newspapers were published in Sighet prior to the Holocaust, some of which were owned, edited, or sponsored by Jews. See Keren-Kratz, *Maramaros-Sziget*, 257–69; Keren-Kratz, "The Newspaper Industry in Maramures."
36. Wiesel, *All Rivers Run to the Sea*, 32.
37. Wiesel, *All Rivers Run to the Sea*, 36.
38. Wiesel, *All Rivers Run to the Sea*, 18.
39. Wiesel, *All Rivers Run to the Sea*, 32.
40. Menachem Keren-Kratz, "Hirsh Leib Gottlieb: A One-Man Newspaper Empire," *Kesher: Journal of Media and Communications History in Israel and the Jewish World* 46 (2014): 58–66 (in Hebrew). See also Hirsh Leib Gottlieb, *Lider Fun Main Leben*, vol. 1 (Seini: Jacob Wieder, 1933) (in Yiddish).
41. Menachem Keren-Kratz, "Libraries in Sighet as a Cultural Meeting Place," *On-line Magazine of the Jewish Librarians Association* 24 (2013) (in Hebrew), accessed November 13, 2017.
42. Shlomo Gross and Yitzkhak Yosef Cohen, eds., *Sefer Marmarosh* (Tel Aviv: Beit Marmarosh, 1983) (in Hebrew); Ben-Menachem, *Misafrut Israel*. This book contains a bibliographic description of more than two hundred books and some thirty periodicals that were printed in Sighet.
43. Elie Wiesel, "Dos Groyse Shvaigen" (Yiddish: The big Silence), *Der Teater Shpigel* 4 (1951): 11 (under the pseudonym of Elisha Carmeli. Elisha was Wiesel's father's middle name) (in Yiddish).
44. Wiesel, *All Rivers Run to the Sea*, 83–85. Wiesel consistently refers to God using masculine pronouns in his body of work. In discussing Wiesel's relationship with God, I use his terminology.
45. Wiesel, *All Rivers Run to the Sea*, 84–85. Here and following, brackets enclose the chapter author's omissions in quoted material.
46. According to Jewish tradition, these are two of God's thirteen Attributes of Mercy.
47. Wiesel, *All Rivers Run to the Sea*, 32.

48. Elie Wiesel, *The Trial of God (As It Was Held on February 25, 1649, in Shamgorod)* (New York: Random House, 1979), 43.

49. Elie Wiesel, *Night* (New York: Hill and Wang, 2006), vii. On the question whether *Night* should be regarded a novel or a memoir, and on the relationship between Holocaust testimonies and Holocaust literature, see Lawrence L. Langer, *The Holocaust and the Literary Imagination* (New Haven: Yale University Press, 1975); Lawrence L. Langer, *Holocaust Testimonies: The Ruins of Memory* (New Haven: Yale University Press, 1991); Lawrence L. Langer, "Whose Testimony? The Confusion of Fiction with Fact," in *Elie Wiesel: Jewish, Literary, and Moral Perspectives*, ed. Steven T. Katz and Alan Rosen (Bloomington: Indiana University Press, 2013), 201–10. A brief overview of this topic can also be found in the introduction to this volume.

50. Wiesel, *Night*, 3.

51. Ring, *Farblondgeter Nigen*, 5 (translated from Yiddish).

52. Ring, *Farblondgeter Nigen*, 7–15.

53. Ring, *Farblondgeter Nigen*, 51.

54. Ring, *Farblondgeter Nigen*, 54.

55. Wiesel, *Night*, 115.

56. Ring, *Farblondgeter Nigen*, 71.

57. Joyce Antler, *You Never Call! You Never Write! A History of the Jewish Mother* (Oxford: Oxford University Press, 2007).

58. Wiesel, *All Rivers Run to the Sea*, 3.

59. Wiesel, *All Rivers Run to the Sea*, 4.

60. Wiesel, *All Rivers Run to the Sea*, 5.

61. Wiesel, *All Rivers Run to the Sea*, 13.

62. *Maramarosher Bleter*, October 1, 1931, 4–5.

63. Hirsh Leib Gottlieb, "A Maramarosher Am'ha'aretz," *Lider Fun Mein Leben*, 74–75; Berl Schnabel, "Sighet," *Milner-Gas*, 60–61; Berl Schnabel, "Sigheter gasen Kinder," *Yeshiva Lider*, 75–76; Eisik Pollak, "Maramarosh," *Ying Maramarosh*, March 1941, 3; Yizhak David Izrael, "Maramaroshener," *Ying Maramarosh*, 7–14; Wolf Tambur, *Maramaroshener* (Bucharest: Kriterion, 1975).

64. Sholomo Shitnovitzer, ed., *Beitar Ve-Hatenuah Ha-Revizionistit Be-Romania 1925–1950* (Jerusalem: Berit Trumpeldor, 1992) (in Hebrew).

65. Shlomo Bickel, *Yahadut Romania: Historia, Bikoret Sifrutit, Zikhronot* (Tel Aviv: Hitahadut Yotzei Romania Be-Yisrael, 1978), 211 (in Hebrew).

Works Cited

Antler, Joyce. *You Never Call! You Never Write! A History of the Jewish Mother.* Oxford: Oxford University Press, 2007.

Ben-Menahem, Naftali. *Misafrut Israel Be-Hungaria.* Jerusalem: Kityat Sefer, 1958 (in Hebrew).

Berkowitz, Israel. *Hundert Yor Yiddish Teater In Rumenye 1876–1976.* Bucharest: Kriterion, 1976 (in Yiddish).
Bickel, Shlomo. *Rumenye: Geshikhte, Literatur-Kritik, Zikhroynes.* Buenos Aires: Kiyum, 1961.
Bickel, Shlomo. *Yahadut Romania: Historia, Bikoret Sifrutit, Zikhronot.* Tel Aviv: Hitahadut Yotzei Romania Be-Yisrael, 1978 (in Hebrew).
Carmilly, Moshe. "Hebrew Poetry in Hungary." In *Hungarian Jewish Studies*, vol. 1, ed. Randolph L. Braham, 295–342. New York: World Federation of Hungarian Jews, 1966.
Carmilly, Moshe. "Meshorerim Ivri'im Be-Transylvania." In *Memorial Volume for the Jews of Cluj-Koloszvár*, ed. Moshe Carmilly, 112–28. New York: self-published, 1979 (in Hebrew).
Gidó, Attila. *Úton: Erdélyi zsidó társadalom- és nemzetépítési kísérletek 1918–1940* [On the Way: Transylvanian Jewish Attempts at Society- and Nation-Building]. Csíkszereda: Pro-Print, 2009 (in Hungarian).
Gottlieb, Hirsh Leib. *Lider Fun Main Leben*, vol. 1. Seini: Jacob Wieder, 1933 (in Yiddish).
Gross, Shlomo, and Yitzkhak Yosef Cohen, eds. *Sefer Marmarosh.* Tel Aviv: Beit Marmarosh, 1983 (in Hebrew).
Holder, Joseph. *Oft Zingt Zikh.* Vilnius: Farlag Múlt és Jövő—Budapest, 1928 (in Yiddish).
Keren-Kratz, Menachem. "Hirsh Leib Gottlieb: A One-Man Newspaper Empire." *Kesher: Journal of Media and Communications History in Israel and the Jewish World* 46 (2014): 58–66 (in Hebrew).
Keren-Kratz, Menachem. "Libraries in Sighet as a Cultural Meeting Place." *Online Magazine of the Jewish Librarians Association* 24 (2013): n.p. (in Hebrew).
Keren-Kratz, Menachem. *Maramaros-Sziget: Extreme Orthodoxy and Secular-Jewish Culture at the Foothills of the Carpathan Mountains.* Jerusalem: The Dov Sadan Publishing Project of the Hebrew University, 2013 (in Hebrew).
Keren-Kratz, Menachem. "The Newspaper Industry in Maramures: A Hungarian, Romanian and Jewish Joint Venture." In *Representations of Jewish Life in Romanian Literature*, ed. Camelia Craciun, 377–90. Iasi: Alexandru Ioan Cuza University Press, 2014.
Keren-Kratz, Menachem. "The Social and Cultural Role of Small Jewish Literary Centers: The Case of Sighet, Romania." *Journal of Modern Jewish Studies* 16, no. 2 (2017): 179–97.
Klausner, Israel. *Hibat Zion Be-Romania.* Jerusalem: Ha-Hifriya Ha-Tzionit, 1954 (in Hebrew).
Komoróczy, Szonja Ráhel. *Yiddish Printing in Hungary: An Annotated Bibliography.* Budapest: Center for Jewish Studies at the Hungarian Academy of Sciences, 2011.
Korn, Yitzhak. *Yiddish In Rumenye: Eseyen.* Tel Aviv: Avuka, 1989 (in Yiddish).

Langer, Lawrence L. *The Holocaust and the Literary Imagination*. New Haven: Yale University Press, 1975.
Langer, Lawrence L. *Holocaust Testimonies: The Ruins of Memory*. New Haven: Yale University Press, 1991.
Langer, Lawrence L. "Whose Testimony? The Confusion of Fiction with Fact." In *Elie Wiesel: Jewish, Literary, and Moral Perspectives*, ed. Steven T. Katz and Alan Rosen, 201–10. Bloomington: Indiana University Press, 2013.
Mark, Nathan. *Di Leimene Foyst*. Sighet: Oyfgang, 1937 (in Yiddish).
Mark, Nathan (Avi Abir-Zion). *Yiddish Literatur In Rumenye: Fun Ir Onhoyb Biz 1968*. Tel Aviv: Ha-Levanon, 1971 (in Yiddish).
Miron, Dan. *The Image of the Shtetl and Other Studies of Modern Jewish Literary Imagination*. Syracuse: Syracuse University Press, 2000.
Nagari, Avraham. *Desired Goal: Zionist Youth Movements in Romania as a Foundation for Jewish National Revival (1918–1941)*. Givat Haviva: Yad Ya'ari, 2007 (in Hebrew).
Ring, Yechezkel. *Farblondgeter Nigun*. Sighet: Centrala, 1937 (in Yiddish).
Ring, Yechezkel. *Oyfen Himel A Yarid*. Sighet: Centrala 1940 (in Yiddish).
Schnabel, Berl. *Milner-Gas*. Bucharest: Farlag Shalom Aleikhem, 1936 (in Yiddish).
Schnabel, Berl. *Yeshiva Lider*. Bucharest: Yidishe Bibliotek, 1942 (in Yiddish).
Shitnovitzer, Sholomo, ed. *Beitar Ve-Hatenuah Ha-Revizionistit Be-Romania 1925–1950*. Jerusalem: Berit Trumpeldor, 1992 (in Hebrew).
Tambur, Volf. *Bay Der Tir: Dertzeilungen*. Cernăuţi: Farlag Yiddish Vort, 1937 (in Yiddish).
Tambur, Volf. *Main Heim: Dertzeilungen*. Sighet: n.p., 1940 (in Yiddish).
Tambur, Volf. *Maramaroshener*. Bucharest: Kriterion, 1975.
Tambur, Volf. *Yiddish-Presse In Romeniye*. Bucharest: Kriterion, 1977 (in Yiddish).
Wiesel, Elie. "Dos Groyse Shvaigen" [The Big Silence]. *Der Teater Shpigel* 4 (1951): 11 (under the pseudonym of Elisha Carmeli, in Yiddish).
Wiesel, Elie. *All Rivers Run to the Sea: Memoirs*. New York: Schocken Books, 1995.
Wiesel, Elie. *Night*. New York: Hill and Wang, 2006.
Wiesel, Elie. *The Trial of God (As It Was Held on February 25, 1649, in Shamgorod)*. New York: Random House, 1979.

2

The Death of Humanity and the Need for a Glory Culture

The Existential Project of Elie Wiesel

YAKIR ENGLANDER

Introduction

In 1986, Elie Wiesel was awarded the Nobel Peace Prize. The Norwegian Nobel Committee referred to him as a "humanist," that is to say one who believes in human uniqueness. The committee wrote that Wiesel is "one of the most important spiritual leaders and guides in an age when violence, repression and racism continue to characterize the world. Wiesel is a messenger to mankind; his message is one of peace, atonement and human dignity."[1]

Using tools from cultural theory and anthropology, I will argue that while Wiesel's perspective has deep implications for human relationships, his project is not humanistic either in its secular or in its religious inter-

---

I would like to thank the following readers of this chapter for their comments and ideas: Orit Kamir, Henry R. Carse, Sidra Dekoven Ezrahi, and Natalie Bergner; and to my editors, Ati Waldman, Jonathan Schild, Alexandra Weisse, and Henry R. Carse. Special thanks to the editors of this book, Philip Smith and Victoria Nesfield, for their comments. This piece was written mostly during my year as a visiting scholar in the Women's Studies Department at Harvard Divinity School and by the generous scholarship of the Ephraim E. Urbach Post-Doctoral Fellowship Grant, Memorial Foundation, and the Shalom Hartman Institute in Jerusalem.

pretations.² Instead, Wiesel's writings are an example of the longing of a man who has lost his faith in humanity. Wiesel subsequently struggles to overcome this loss of belief and attempts to restore the ability of people to have trustful relationships with one another, despite the fact that they cannot rely on the good nature of human beings as a foundation of trust.

Although, I argue, Wiesel shares his feelings about God and people in an ultra-Orthodox (more accurately Hasidic) Jewish language, his claims and descriptions of religion and the existential human situation are relevant not only for Jews. Wiesel's perspective can speak to any person who suffers from the same loss of faith in humanistic values, and who wonders how to create a healthy, just society, and on what foundation. My claim is that Wiesel's theology is not humanistic but connected to what I call "glory culture." The purpose of the theology of glory culture is to promote goals that other people reach by humanistic tools, for those who do not believe in the premise of humanism.

It is important to note the distinction between "humanity," "humanism," and "dignity"—terms including beliefs about the nature of human beings—and "humankind" or "humans"—meaning, people themselves, not ideas about them. Wiesel's desire to have a relationship with humankind does not imply positive assumptions about the nature of human beings. I will deal with these various concepts by focusing on the term "dignity" and the use of different Jewish responses to the Holocaust characterized by the term.

The devastation of War World II reopened fundamental questions about the nature of humans and their behavior. World War II marked the crisis of trust in humanity among theologians and thinkers who had tried to build a good world for centuries.³ Humanistic values and the trust in human goodness forms a discourse that was established over several centuries, especially after the great revolutions and World War I but was shaken after the unbearable events of World War II. Responses after the war can be loosely divided into three groups. The first was to hold to this discourse of humanism even more vigorously and to try to strengthen it. The United Nations' Declaration of Human Rights, for example, holds that "all human beings are born free and equal in dignity and rights." For the United Nations, especially after these two wars, dignity is the essence of humanism, is a human "birthright"; there is no need to acquire dignity, and it cannot be lost. The recognition of human dignity as an absolute value of every human life sets a strict boundary not to be crossed for any reason in human relations.

The second path is a withdrawal from humanistic universal values to particularistic systems of values drawn from both cultural and ethnic sources. I identify this response as connected to the values of honor, as I will explain in depth later. The third option is not to choose either of these two options, but to create an ethical system that is based in neither dignity nor honor. Creating a new ethical system is the unique contribution of Wiesel's theology. In my reading, Wiesel is a thinker who could not maintain the values of humanism after the war but who also refused to take the traditional path. Many who grew up in the ultra-Orthodox community, as Wiesel did, lost their belief in humanism and chose to create an honor theology and culture. Departing from this trend, Wiesel used his mystical Hasidic language to create a modern social theology that can include both the religious and the secular.

Honor, Dignity, and Glory Cultures and the Events of the Holocaust

The fields of anthropology and cultural studies have both described at length the cultural differences between dignity and honor cultures.[4] Therefore, I will not go into the details of the theory but will only summarize it in a simple way, focusing mostly on the characteristics most relevant to this chapter.[5]

In *honor societies*, honor correlates with an individual's social status and is perceived as property, assets, and possession. Honor (and its attendant social status) may be acquired during an individual's lifetime through compliance with social norms, for instance, by appropriate normative behavior. An individual may gain honor in a social community through behavior perceived as honorable. One person may also seize the honor of another, because living in an honor society is a zero-sum game: when one person or community gains honor, someone else must lose it. Notably, as Peter Berger wrote, "honor only applies among those who share the same status in the hierarchy."[6] Groups within an honor society often preserve their honor through the exclusion of certain "dishonorable" individuals, groups, and nations. However, there are also certain groups who are not considered to be part of the honor "game" at all: they neither gain honor nor lose it. In Europe, for example, during some periods and in different places, Jews were not considered an honorable community and were entirely excluded from the honor system. Other times, they were considered part of the honorable community but low on the honor ranking.

The fact that Jews were often excluded from the European honor culture, or at least had, as a group, very little honor, does not mean that they were not deeply influenced by this culture. And indeed, while they were excluded from the honor culture of the general society, they created an inner Jewish culture and theology of honor.[7] *Honor societies are not humanistic* since they do not teach, as humanism does, that all human beings are intrinsically equal and share some fundamental qualities with each other.[8]

On the other hand, dignity, opposed to honor, is understood as the universal value and worth of any and every human person, regardless of gender, race, age, class, or group affiliation.[9] As Orit Kamir defines it:

> Human dignity is the inherent value ascribed to the category "human." It is, therefore, inherent in the human nature of every human being. [. . .] We can think of it as a stamp of human quality that is imprinted in each of us. It is important to stress that as a value, dignity is an ethical *ought* and not an empirical, factual *is*; it is normative and not descriptive. Human dignity does not depict people's empirical value; it constitutes them as normatively worthy merely because they are human. [. . .] Because we believe that all humans are identical in their human nature and partake equally in the human category, they also partake equally in the inherent human value, i.e., Human dignity.[10]

Humanism as a philosophical and ethical category focuses on and sanctifies the notion of human dignity. Historically speaking, the concept of human dignity arose from the religious sphere, rooted in the scriptural description of humanity created in the Image of God; over time, however, the concept was transposed into secular language and no longer depends on belief in the existence of God.[11] Dignity culture is based on the premise that all human beings are entitled to basic rights unconditionally.[12] Thinkers who establish links between human dignity and the Image of God belong to dignity culture as long as establishing such links does not incline them to condition basic rights, limiting those rights only to certain humans and/or based on some of their actions.

One of the main differences between honor and dignity cultures is that "the concept of honor implies that identity is essentially, or at least importantly, linked to institutional roles. The modern concept of dignity, by contrast, implies that identity is essentially independent of institutional roles."[13] After the French Revolution, and into the twentieth century, European civilization oscillated between these two poles: on one hand, *honor culture* with its emphasis on earned (or assigned) exclusive rights and achievements for some, and, on the other hand, *dignity culture*, with its focus on unconditional and universal rights for all, especially as a counterpoint to and critique of the mechanical and existential alienation of post-industrial Europe. It can be assumed that all modern societies contain values of both dignity and honor cultures.[14]

Starting in the eighteenth century the European Enlightenment expanded notions of citizenship and brought more and more Jewish communities into the general European society. As a result, these European perceptions of dignity and honor sparked some Jewish reactions: first the Haskalah, and then Zionism. The Haskalah, the Jewish Enlightenment movement of the eighteenth and nineteenth centuries, advocated liberation and better integration for Jews into European society and culture. The Zionist movement, for its part, aspired to abolish the prototypical "Diaspora Jew" entirely and to create a "New Jew"—one connected both to the land and to the body. Both movements envisioned Jews with more dignity as well as more honor.[15]

The two World Wars disrupted the progression of European dignity culture. Still, many thinkers and theologians, including several Jews, claim that although humans display vicious cruelty toward each other, they still have the potential for goodness. These thinkers focus on the need to have an educational system focusing on humanistic values, to develop this potential.[16] For others, the Holocaust was proof of the lack of this human potential, so they decided to focus on honor values, instead. The majority of ultra-Orthodox rabbis interpreted the events of the Holocaust using an honor language.[17] The rabbis claim that the Nazis set out to destroy the honor of the Jewish God by hurting the Jewish people.[18] According to this narrative, although the Nazis wanted to exterminate all the Jews of Europe, their main campaign was against the religious aspect of Judaism. Their goal, first and foremost, was to kill rabbis, heads of yeshivas, and anyone who represented the Jewish God:[19]

> They forced [the Jews] to take out the Torah and the many [religious] books from the synagogues. [. . .] The Germans [sic] tried to force Rabbi Lifshitz to light the fire, but the rabbi

> adamantly refused to carry out their command. The proud behavior of the rabbi shocked the Germans. [. . .] They set fire to the holy books to make fun of the Jewish God. [. . .] They switched the hats of the rabbi and his wife. On the head of the rabbi—the wife's hat, and on the head of the wife—the rabbinical hat. With teary eyes and shocked hearts, the rabbi and his wife were forced to watch the *Chillul Hashem* [desecration of the name of God].[20]

According to this theology of honor, there are two interconnected struggles. The first is the visible and tangible assault of the Nazis in their effort to exterminate the Jews. The second, and more essential, is the cosmological battle between the *sitra achra* ("other side," for instance, Satan)[21] and (the Jewish) God, waged in the invisible sphere, expressed in spiritual terms and influenced only by the spiritual weapons of keeping faith in the Jewish God and observing Jewish religious law (*halakha*). The role of Jews, which the ultra-Orthodox community has taken upon itself, is to represent (the Jewish) God in this world. By keeping their loyalty to the Jewish God and by keeping the Jewish law even in the ghettos and the concentration camps, they gain honor from the Nazis.[22] More than that, by maintaining their belief that the "real" battle is not the one waged by the Nazis but the cosmological one, by focusing only on this combat, and not reacting to the Nazis by fighting against them physically, they gain honor and the Nazis lose theirs.[23]

Elie Wiesel grew up in the Hasidic (ultra-Orthodox) community of Vizhnitz and experienced the Holocaust when he was a teenager. But unlike the majority of ultra-Orthodox survivors, he refused to respond to the Holocaust by using the language of honor culture.[24] As Kamir details, following World War II, Western Europe tried to eradicate all elements of honor culture and to focus only on dignity culture.[25] This is one of the reasons for the welcome Wiesel's work received in the West. From his first work in French/English (*Night*) to the last interview he gave, Wiesel spoke only in language that alludes to the concept of dignity. Precisely because of his unique voice within Jewish theology, many therefore identify his work as humanistic and as seemingly relying on a dignity-based value system.[26] However, this assumption is flawed. Although Wiesel's work includes some language and values associated with dignity culture, his unique contribution is actually related to his loss of faith in humanistic assumptions. He does not trust the assumptions that create the definitions of human dignity and humanism. *Night* is a painful, existential testimony dedicated to this disillusionment.

Wiesel instead tries to create a society that would abide by principles and norms that constitute a dignity-based culture, despite the fact that the cultural foundations of dignity society and humanism do not exist for him anymore. To do this, Wiesel turns to the mystical roots of Hasidic theology, with *his* unique interpretation, and with this theology he creates a new foundation, neither dignity-based nor honor-based, and with this foundation he suggests a new possibility to restore relationships among people. I will call this paradigm a "glory culture."

Orit Kamir demonstrates the complexity of the Hebrew language, specifically in the various meanings of the Hebrew word *kavod*.[27] As Kamir notes, a word in one language may have several counterparts in another language, with different and even contradictory meanings. In the case of the Hebrew word *kavod*, there is no single equivalent in English, but rather several meanings that may sometimes conflict with each other. *Kavod* can be *honor* or *dignity*. But, *kavod*, according to Kamir, can be also another thing—*glory*.

In general, glory, when it is connected to humans and culture, means that human beings have a unique position in nature, since they were created in the "image of God," or because in adhering to certain religious belief, for example belief in Jesus, they acquire the "image of God." The language of glory—references to the divinity reflected in humans as the Image of God—can be found in both dignity and honor cultures, creating the impression that glory is nothing more than a borrowed concept used in both. In other words, the Image of God can be a theme with which some societies enrich their sets of values (honor/dignity), which themselves are predicated on the values of their general society, rather than as a fundamentally different culture.[28] Glory, I assert, can be not only a language to speak the values of dignity/honor cultures but a culture or a theology unto itself, which is different from both.

By contrast, and as I will elucidate in the next section, at the outset of his work Wiesel asserts that during the Holocaust he lost faith in humanity. He chooses, however, to continue to try engaging in human relationships, the practice of which is similar to the behaviors of dignity culture. Participants in a glory culture or a dignity culture may exhibit the same behavioral patterns, like a focus on repairing a broken world and combatting injustice. And yet, the theological basis for his choice is in a set of religious values that do not share the same basic assumptions as dignity models. There is a substantial and qualitative difference between belief in "the human family" and "embodying the Image of God." In "glory culture," God is always present as the *condition* and the mediator of any attempt to establish a way of life that corresponds essentially to the principles of dignity.[29]

The Death of Humanity in Wiesel's Theology

Wiesel has always insisted that his work includes two different genres: one historical (including his many interviews and *Night*),[30] and the other literary (all the rest of his writings).[31] Here I will focus on his insistence that *Night* is a historical memoir in literary form, and that the events recorded there really happened and comprise a historical testimony.[32]

According to Wiesel's narrative, his cultural background before the Holocaust was based in a religious context attuned to the European Jewish *dignity* culture. As Wiesel himself provides as an example, even after the German invasion in 1944, Hungarian Jews[33] did not flee, because they were embedded in their dignity-based value systems and therefore could not accept the reality of the reports from the concentration camps: "We were naïve. Innocent. So innocent that we refused to believe that evil exists. We were incapable of believing that human beings could fall so low."[34] Similarly, his Hasidic community knew that history is full of anti-Semitism and of Jewish suffering; however, in their opinion, this only showed that, empirically, many people had not behaved with dignity toward Jews. They did not think it taught them anything about humanity as a whole, nor certainly did it lead them to believe in the death of humanism.[35] Jews could not believe that an entire nation, particularly the German nation—the center of Western society, wanted to destroy the Jews in a systematic way: "Over and over the survivors tell us that one reason they did not resist was that, until it was too late, their 'faith in humanity' made the prospect of such monstrous inhumanity impossible to imagine."[36]

As we learn in *Night*, on his first night in Auschwitz, Wiesel, like many other Jews, starts losing his faith in humanity, and from that moment he could no longer rely on dignity values: "At Auschwitz, not only man died, but also the idea of man."[37] The death of belief in humanism is not only a Jewish problem, but also a human problem. Therefore, for Wiesel the implications of the Holocaust are relevant to all possible societies:

I have said here more directly than before that whatever happens to the Jews happens to all mankind. People thought they could kill Jews and remain alive, and they were wrong. When they kill Jews, they kill themselves. And that is what they have done: They have killed themselves.[38]

Wiesel describes this loss of faith in three interrelated ways: (1) the behavior of Nazis toward Jews; (2) the behavior of Jews toward each other (including, for Wiesel especially, the inner feelings he experienced in relation to his father); and (3) the indifference (not ignorance) of the world, in its shocking failure to intervene.[39] In other words, the kind of human behavior that Wiesel was exposed to during the Holocaust touched the essence of human nature and exposed the fact that humans are missing those fundamental elements that created dignity culture and humanism. For Wiesel, this understanding is not a logical, philosophical, or theological proof, but an existential one.

One of the most famous paragraphs in *Night* is the description of God, hanging in the dead child at Auschwitz. Some scholars have understood this as a description of the "Death of God."[40] Wiesel himself disavowed this explanation, arguing that even in Auschwitz he continued to believe in God. My argument is that it is not surprising that Wiesel refers to the dying of God when describing the child's death, "a child with a refined and beautiful face, unheard of in this camp. [. . .] He had the face of a sad angel."[41] What died that day in Auschwitz was Wiesel's belief in humanity and in *dignity culture*; a dignity culture that he, as a child, lived in, using religious language to express its values.[42] Until Auschwitz, in Wiesel's life, the glory of God meant human dignity. That day, however, the theological connection between humanity and God (the "child-angel") was destroyed by the Nazis. As Wiesel has declared, he continued to have faith in God, but the perception of God changed ontologically; what died was his previous understanding of God and his presence in the world of human dignity: "these days the tendency is to say no *of* God, rather than *to* God. The catch phrase is God is dead. Surrounded as we are by destruction, it is close to fact to say MAN is dead. It's not God's job but man's to keep mankind alive."[43]

Wiesel's journey offers a unique contribution to ultra-Orthodox post-Holocaust literature. It is almost impossible to find such despair from human beings in the Hasidic community, possibly because the leaders felt the responsibility to rebuild their community. Expressions of loss of faith in humanity appear on rare occasions in ultra-Orthodox sources. The Rabbi of Blazob, for example, confessed that after the Holocaust he desired to distance himself from human beings, including the ultra-Orthodox community, and to live alone:

> Even perhaps to settle far away from all human contact, in some distant colony, among trees and rocks, to weep there for the immensity of the shattering of myself and of all my family and people. Always, I loved humans and human companionship, but today I am finished with it. [. . .] Whoever did not live in Europe during the last six years, can never imagine what disgraceful creatures human beings actually are.[44]

In *Night*, Wiesel describes the cruelty of both Nazis and Jews toward Jews. However, there are moments when he shifts his focus from outer cruelty to his inner existential feelings. In these moments, Wiesel tries to describe changes in his ontological understanding of humanity that occurred in him in Auschwitz. During the journey from one camp to another, Wiesel met Rabbi Eliahou, who was "well loved by everyone in the camp [. . .]. Despite the trials and privations, his face still shone with his inner purity. [. . .] He was like one of the old prophets, always in the midst of his people to comfort them."[45] Rabbi Eliahou was a model of maintaining faith in humanity; for him, "glory" and "dignity" were still indivisible. During that journey, Rabbi Eliahou was looking for his only remaining son, whom he had lost along the way. Wiesel focused on the unique bond between this father and his son: "For three years they had stuck together. Always near each other, for suffering, for blows, for the ration of bread, for prayer."[46] The rabbi had a narrative to explain the fact that his son had disappeared: "We lost sight of one another during the journey. [. . .] I hadn't any strength left for running. And my son didn't notice."[47] Unfortunately, Wiesel knows that the rabbi's narrative is not true:

> His son had seen him losing ground, limping, staggering back to the rear of the column. He had seen him. And he had continued to run on in front, letting the distance between them grow greater. [. . .] He had wanted to get rid of his father! He had felt that his father was growing weak, he had believed that the end was near and had sought this separation in order to get rid of the burden.[48]

These are the moments that most terrify Wiesel. He constantly argues that even people who were close and loved each other, when they were pushed to their limits, behaved with no regard for dignity. By witnessing this, Wiesel discovered that his reliance on dignity had no foundation.[49] This was an existential experience, not a philosophical discussion. However, it is often the case that such experiences can shatter and transform personal perceptions of reality, and this is true for Wiesel. Wiesel's desire to act differently than Rabbi Eliahou's son failed. When his own father became sick, Wiesel felt a voice inside himself, "Don't let me find him! If only I could get rid of this dead weight! [. . .] Immediately I felt ashamed of myself, ashamed forever. [. . .] No better than Rabbi Eliahou's son had I withstood the test."[50]

A key point of my argument is that the role of the memoir *Night* is to describe the fact that Wiesel lost faith in human dignity, which automatically led to a crisis in his religious perception of God.[51] Before the Holocaust, his Jewish culture was the language by which he spoke and acted his faith in dignity culture, and therefore the death of humanity at Auschwitz was the death of this perception of God: "The most frightening aspect of our present world is not the horrors in themselves, the atrocities, the technological exterminations, but the one fact at the very root of it all: the fading away of any human criterion."[52] It was important to Wiesel to describe this existential crisis, and to let his readers know that it was an irreversible ontological upheaval in his own life. This he could never describe with historical tools, since *facts* cannot transmit an existential experience and therefore, Wiesel chose to write his memoir *Night* in a literary style.[53]

The final aspect of Wiesel's utter loss of faith in humanity does not appear in *Night* but at the end of the war. Like many Holocaust survivors, he painfully describes the dying wish of many of the victims: that the survivors will tell the victims' stories to the rest of the world.[54] The assumption behind this wish was that many European Jews believed that it was only the Nazis who wanted to kill them, and that the rest of the Western world was unaware of the Nazi plans. This is expressed in the journal entries of those who did not survive, in their repeated assertions that "the world" for whom they write will never believe their descriptions of the atrocities inflicted on them by the Nazis, for the simple reason that "the world" is human, while the events described are not.[55] In terms of dignity, the actions of the Nazis alone could not destroy the Jewish ontological belief in humanity as a whole. It was therefore imperative that the truth be told to, and preserved in memory by, people with dignity.

In his interviews, Wiesel agonizingly describes the moments when he and other survivors understood that the rest of the Western world (Jews and non-Jews) had the information[56] already in 1942 about the Nazi mission to exterminate the Jews of Europe.[57] And still, almost nothing was done, either to stop the atrocities, or at least to warn the Hungarian Jews so that they could flee before the Nazis invaded Hungary in 1944. The fact that the world knew of the "Final Solution," and still did so little to intervene, wounded the survivors no less than the actions of the Nazis themselves and confirmed their utter loss of faith in human dignity. If humans can be so immoral, then they have no special intrinsic value. Their humanness is not precious. Their worth is not a sublime, innate quality:[58]

> At a risk of offending, it must be emphasized that the victims suffered more, and more profoundly, from the indifference of the onlookers than from the brutality of the executioner. The cruelty of the enemy would have been incapable of breaking the prisoner; it was the silence of those he believed to be his friends—cruelty more cowardly, more subtle—which broke his heart.[59]

As a result, some survivors no longer had a clear understanding of what they should do with the memories and final wishes of those who had died. In Wiesel's opinion, the fact that so many Holocaust survivors committed suicide years after the end of the war should be attributed to their internalization of this brutal dilemma: "To live in a world where there is nothing anymore, where the executioner acts as god, as judge—many wanted no part of it. It was its own heart the world incinerated at Auschwitz."[60]

Wiesel indeed lost his faith in humanity; since this was his existential experience, he could not deny it. However, unlike some other survivors, Wiesel believes that realizing the nonexistence of innate human dignity does not mean that human beings are not capable of devoting their lives to forming relationships—both within themselves and with those around them. More than that, the terrifying introspection of Wiesel, free from any dignified masks, allows him to recognize not only the diabolical nature of others, but also of himself. This, for

Wiesel, is the starting point of human life after the Holocaust, from which it may be possible to create a new foundation for existence. In order to create relationships with others, Wiesel returned to the roots of his Jewish mystical Hasidic culture.[61] However, he no longer looked through the lens of dignity, but used his religious language in an effort to create a glory culture through which and in which he could seek a solution to the crisis of human existence.

Wiesel's Mystical Theology as a Vision of Glory Culture

In my reading of Wiesel, the Hasidic-mystical sphere is his safe zone where he can re-create relationships with people, precisely because it is an inner sphere that allows people to train themselves in taking leaps of faith beyond the given reality. The mystical sphere allows Wiesel to deal with his existential internalization of the death of the belief in dignity and humanism. Mysticism enables Wiesel to wish for healthy human relationships and to define the conditions for them.

This foundation of the new relationship is very different from those he had before the Holocaust, when he had faith in humanity. After the Holocaust, people who still desire to have relationships are aware of the fact that they take a risk, since they realized that the foundations for natural humanistic trust in the "Other" never really existed. However, the mystical sphere allows Wiesel not to surrender to this internalization, but rather to struggle to create a new set of tools enabling the reestablishment of human relationships: "It is possible, in spite of everything, to believe in friendship in a world without friendship, and even to believe in God in a world where God's face had been eclipsed. It is possible to see in fire a light, a light that will give man a new lease on his own future."[62] The mystic, in Wiesel's theology, must repeatedly practice seeing beyond the given, beyond social structures. Wiesel believes that this lifestyle helps the mystical Hasid to create a new kind of relationship with humans, too: the mystics are constantly training themselves to be attuned to the suffering of the "others," to see and feel their pain, especially when society ignores it.[63]

One of the major theological elements in Hasidic mysticism is "struggling with God as an act of love": "Abraham and Moses, Jeremiah and Rebbe Levi-Yitzhak of Berdichev teach us that it is permissible for man to accuse God, provided it be done in the name of faith in God."[64] The struggle with God means a struggle with the ultimate "given." These struggles occur primarily when the Hasid (who is not himself a mystic), turns for help to his tzaddik (mystical-Hasidic community leader) since his reality is too hard to bear.[65] The tzaddik examines whether the problem can be solved naturally. That is to say, if practical solutions do not work, such as with serious illness and infertility, then the tzaddik sometimes decides to use the element of "struggling with God as an act of love" as a tool to create a miracle:[66] "He is the one who says 'no' to God. He says to God: 'What you are doing is unjust.'"[67] To struggle with God means that the tzaddik sacrifices himself for his Hasid (his student). The ability of the tzaddik to prove his self-sacrifice is crucial. Sometimes this is expressed by God, who threatens the tzaddik that if he makes God alter natural forces, the punishment of the tzaddik will be that he will lose his place in Heaven or will lose his knowledge of Torah: "Was it a sudden attack of sadness, of depression? Was it his way of telling God, Either You save Your people or erase me from Your book? I no longer wish to go on living—unless You put an end to Jewish suffering?"[68] At the moment the tzaddik gives up his place in the next life, he thus proves his love for his community, and the miracle happens; there is a leap of faith beyond the given.[69] The ability of the mystic, of the tzaddik, to struggle with God in order to help other humans comes from the fact that God created humankind in His image. The image of God inside humanity gives humans the responsibility to care about each other, even if it means to struggle with the divine.

According to this Hasidic idea, the coming of the Messiah and of redemption may be identified with the very moment when a human being chooses—quite contrary to human nature—to look upon the world and upon other people with a compassionate gaze: "The Messiah [. . .] is that which makes man [sic] more human, which takes the element of pride out of generosity, which stretches his soul towards others."[70] This is the narrative Wiesel seeks to give to Western society after the horror of the Holocaust. The tzaddik is required to train himself to love his community and to sacrifice something in himself for the other. Likewise, after the Holocaust and "the death of humanism" people can choose to dedicate their lives' training to see beyond the loss of faith in human dignity, and to create new relationships between themselves and others. Wiesel and people who follow his beliefs know that people have the capacity to hurt them, but like the tzaddik, who knows that

God can punish him for struggling with God for the sake of the people, they choose to maintain sincere human relationships despite the risk.

As in the Hasidic stories, Wiesel's novels are dedicated to recreating relationships among people. Wiesel is not a historian; only rarely does he deal explicitly with the Holocaust in his novels. The heroes in his novels are facing the implications of the events of the Holocaust. They try to go back and live among people, but they have all lost their faith in humanity. However, they continue to try.

I opened this chapter with the distinction between "honor," "dignity," and "glory" cultures. For many theologians, honor and dignity cultures are both religiously practicable, despite their differences. For them, religious language embellishes their honor/dignity culture values rather than creating any existential contradictions. In glory culture, however, there is an inherent tension rising from the refusal to adapt to the honor/dignity cultures around them. Wiesel's theology is an example for such a way of living. Wiesel refuses to choose one or the other. He rejects Jewish interpretations invoking God's vengeance, or an honorable Jewish death in holy martyrdom (*Kiddush Ha-shem*). On the other hand, his lost faith in humanity prevents him from adopting the humanistic responses to the Holocaust. Instead, he uses the Jewish belief that all humans were created in the Image of God in order to offer humans a tool to re-create the relationships among themselves. As the mystic continues to struggle with God to help humanity, since he was created in the Image of God, we too can wish to have healthy relationships among humans, even if we have lost faith in humanity. It is this very complexity in Wiesel's theology, speaking of Glory mystical culture that allows him to resist the move from "glory" to "honor" language, which, as pointed out earlier, was adopted by most of the post-Holocaust ultra-Orthodox rabbis.[71] For those rabbis, the temptation to resort to honor culture was spurred by a combination of the unbearable pain of the Holocaust, their ongoing belief in the existence of God, and the incomprehensible trauma of God's actions (and inaction).

Wiesel is well aware of the difficulties posed by his radical theology. This is evident in his framing of his theology as intensely personal, being as personal and alienating as the mystic's. It is, therefore, not surprising that the community Wiesel imagines establishing in the world is a community of *individuals* who still wish to live together. This was, indeed, how he lived his own life—although Hasidic theology appeals deeply to him, he never actually joined any Hasidic community after the Holocaust, and the mystical figures in his stories are always lonely.[72]

My claim is that according to Wiesel, the sensitive balance of his theology can only be practiced individually, not communally.[73] His journey is by definition a journey into and within the inner life. It is not surprising that Wiesel focuses on the person of the Hasidic tzaddik, who in Hasidic theology is ontologically separate from his community.[74] The tzaddik, like the "madmen" in Wiesel's literature, lives among people who do not understand him, and this is exactly why his disciples admire him.[75] As a leader of a Jewish community, the tzaddik lives in constant conflict and tension: he desires to follow his inner journey, but also knows that he must shepherd a community of people who do not share that journey.

Epilogue

Elie Wiesel wrote for sixty years; his writings are first and foremost for his own spiritual survival. He fears any attempt to give reasons and explanations for the Holocaust without looking directly at the reality: his experience that the events of the Holocaust preclude continuing to believe in humanity or the traditional Jewish God. For Wiesel, the ultimate betrayal of the victims of the Holocaust is the attempt to paint the Nazi movement as the ultimate evil, an easy way to escape the radical understanding that we cannot continue to believe in humanity. The uniqueness of the Holocaust is not a "Jewish matter" but the universal fact that "the event robbed man of all his masks."[76] What is important is not to revert to the wearing of those masks, but to internalize the stark reality and then to create a new existential system that allows, once again, fragile but true human relationships.[77]

Only through the recognition of people's inherent evil, and only by constantly coping with natural and flawed human elements, can a healthy society be created. Society needs to appreciate those people who choose to live outside of the majority society, in a unique glory culture, whether they be the Hasidic tzaddik or the "madman": "In times like these madmen are our only friends. They do not kill us in the name of beliefs or ideas."[78] Wiesel tells us about the Hasidic tzaddik who sang while walking to his death. Singing to God was his way to express how a human being can see beyond the "given."[79]

Elie Wiesel chose Hasidic theology, not only because it is in some ways his spiritual "mother tongue," but also because its potential to create a glory culture shifts the human focus away from historical redemption and toward inner, spiritual, and psychological redemption. This is a theology that does not attempt to change the whole world but does demand that the individual try to change himself.

> And what do you expect of yourself? The Rabbi asked him. Very little. Almost nothing. I have only one purpose: not to cause others to suffer. [. . .] I'm no longer intent upon measuring myself against fate and saving humanity. I'm content with little; to help a single human being is enough for me.[80]

Notes

1. "Press Release—Peace 1986," Nobelprize.org, Nobel Media AB 2014, http://www.nobelprize.org/nobel_prizes/peace/laureates/1986/press.html, accessed 14 November 2017.

2. Although my essay focuses on literature, I employ a theory from cultural studies. This is because while Wiesel's writings begin with a personal dialogue between the self and God, they have implications for recreating the foundations of healthy relationships in society after the traumatic events of the Holocaust. As with any other writer, Wiesel himself does not exist in a vacuum, but rather his views on humanity and God are influenced by the culture in which he lives. See also, Peter Berger, "On the Obsolescence of the Concept of Honor," *European Journal of Sociology* 11, no. 2 (1970): 344.

3. There is considerable scholarly and existential writings on the change in the perception of humankind given the history of the first half of the twentieth century. See, for example, Primo Levi, *If This Is a Man?* (New York: Penguin, 1979); Giorgio Agamben, *Remnants of Auschwitz: The Witness and the Archive*, trans. Daniel Heller-Roazen (New York: Zone Books, 2002). For a summary of the Jewish perspective see, Amos Goldberg, "If This Is a Man: The Image of Man in Autobiographical and Historical Writing during and after the Holocaust," *Yad Vashem Studies* 33 (2005): 381–429.

4. For a few of the many important academic works on the subject, see J. G. Peristiany and Julian Pitt-Rivers, eds., *Honor and Grace in Anthropology* (Cambridge: Cambridge University Press, 1992); J. K. Campbell, *Honor, Family and Patronage: A Study of Institutions and Moral Values in a Greek Mountain Community* (Berkeley: Oxford, Clarendon Press, 1970).

5. There are many distinctions between types of societies and cultures, such as the distinction between shame- and guilt-based ones. In this chapter I focus on one such distinction, between honor- and dignity-based societies and

cultures. I am also aware that there are different uses of these words in English and many scholars do not distinguish between honor and dignity. However, in cultural studies, these everyday words become concepts that represent different types of cultures with distinctive ways of behaving. Here, I use these terms as concepts, and their definitions are important for the understanding of my argument.

6. Berger, "On the Obsolescence of the Concept of Honor," 340.

7. Yakir Englander, "The 'Jewish Knight' of Slobodka: Honor Culture and the Image of the Body in an Ultra-Orthodox Jewish Context," *Religion* 46, no. 2 (2016): 186–208.

8. I do not claim that from a humanistic perspective members of honor societies lack dignity or the Image of God. The argument here is that honor cultures, by definition, are not humanistic.

9. Bourdieu Pierre, "The Sentiment of Honor in Kabyle Society," in *Honor and Shame: The Values of Mediterranean Society*, ed. J. G. Peristiany (Chicago: University of Chicago Press, 1966), 191–214; Orit Kamir, *Israeli Honor and Dignity: Social Norms, Gender Politics and the Law* (Jerusalem: Carmel, 2004), 27–43.

10. Orit Kamir, "Dignity and Its Significant Others: Respect, Honor and Glory," forthcoming.

11. George Kateb, *Human Dignity* (Cambridge: Harvard University Press, 2011), 113–72. For the connections between dignity and religion and its history, cf. Beverly Eileen Mitchell, *Plantations and Death Camps: Religion, Identity and Human Dignity* (Minneapolis: Fortress Press, 2009), 39–53.

12. Rachel Bayefsky, "Dignity, Honour, and Human Rights: Kant's Perspective," *Political Theory* 41, no. 6 (2013): 811.

13. Berger, "On the Obsolescence of the Concept of Honor," 343.

14. On the nuance and changes of Europe from being an honor culture to more of a dignity culture, see Mika LaVaque-Manty, "Dueling for Equality: Masculine Honor and the Modern Politics of Dignity," *Political Theory* 34, no. 6 (2006): 715–40.

15. Todd Presner, "'Clear Heads, Solid Stomachs, and Hard Muscles': Max Nordau and the Aesthetics of Jewish Regeneration," *Modernism/modernity* 10, no. 2 (2003): 269–96.

16. For a summary of the different Jewish theological responses to the Holocaust, cf. Steven T. Katz, *Post-Holocaust Dialogues: Critical Studies in Modern Jewish Thought* (New York: New York University Press, 1983); Zachary Braiteman, *(God) After Auschwitz: Tradition and Change in Post-Holocaust Jewish Thought* (New Jersey: Princeton University Press, 1998); Steven T. Katz, ed., *The Impact of the Holocaust on Jewish Theology* (New York: New York University Press, 2005).

17. I will dedicate a separate research project to this subject.

18. Anonymous, *Ki Esh Kadcha Beapi Vatikad ad Sheol Tachtiya* (Jerusalem: Private, 1980), 6–8, 11; Mendel Piekarz, *Ideological Trends of Hasidism in Poland during the Interwar Period and the Holocaust* (Jerusalem: Bialik Institute, 1990), 393; *HaPardes: A Rabbinic Collection* (Adar: n.p., 1945), 14.

19. Anonymous, "Lezecher Alfei Batei-Kneset Shenehersu ba-Shoah," *Bet Yaacov* 27–28 (1961): 21–22; See also, Elie Wiesel, *Against Silence: The Voice and Vision of Elie Wiesel* (New York: Holocaust Library, 1985), 3: 106.

20. Yehoshuah Eybeschitz, "Hasefer Betkufat Ha-Shoah," *Chagim* 2 (1971): 1. My translation.

21. Anonymous, *Ki Esh Kadcha Beapi Vatikad ad Sheol Tachtiya* (Jerusalem: Private), 2–3.

22. Esther Farbstein, *Hidden in Thunder: Perspectives on Faith, Theology and Leadership during the Holocaust* (Jerusalem: Mossad Harav Kook, 2002), 133–58.

23. Tziporah Fayvlovitz, *Bematzok Ubitchiya* (Haifa: Private, 1994), 50.

24. See Harry James Cargas, "What Is a Jew? Interview with Elie Wiesel," in *Responses to Elie Wiesel*, ed. Harry James Cargas (New York: Persea Books, 1978), 154.

25. Orit Kamir, *Escape from Dignity: The Comeback of Honor and Shaming*, forthcoming.

26. Michael Berenbaum, *Elie Wiesel: God, the Holocaust, and the Children of Israel* (Millburn: Behrman House, 1974), 160.

27. Orit Kamir, *Israeli Honor and Dignity: Social Norms, Gender Politics and the Law* (Jerusalem: Carmel, 2004).

28. For an example of how the language of glory can be written in honor culture language, see: Zvi Kolitz, *Yosl Rakover Talks to God*, trans. Carol Brown Faneway (New York: Pantheon Books, 1999), 11.

29. Elie Wiesel and Richard D. Heffner, *Conversations with Elie Wiesel* (New York: Schocken Books, 2003), 121; Elie Wiesel, *A Journey of Faith: A Dialogue Between Elie Wiesel and His Eminence John Cardinal O'Connor* (New York: Donald I. Fine, 1990), 8.

30. Harold Flender, "Conversation with Elie Wiesel," in *Elie Wiesel: Conversations*, ed. Robert Franciosi (Jackson: University Press of Mississippi, 2002), 22.

31. Wiesel himself speaks only infrequently of the different genres of his own work; cf. Ekkehard Schuster and Reinhold Boschert-Kimmig, "Elie Wiesel Speaks," in *Elie Wiesel Conversations*, ed. Robert Franciosi (Jackson: University Press of Mississippi, 2002), 154–55.

32. Cargas, "What Is a Jew?," 151. Many literary scholars have grappled with the possibility/impossibility of any accurate literary representation of the Holocaust; cf., for example, Lawrence L. Langer, *Admitting the Holocaust: Collected Essays* (New York: Oxford University Press, 1995), 16–18; Michael Bachmann, "Life, Writing, and Problems of Genre in Elie Wiesel and Imre Kertész," *Rocky Mountain Review* 63, no. 1 (2009): 79–88. See the introduction to this volume for an overview of the debates concerning *Night* as literary memoir.

33. Wiesel was Romanian by birth in a territory that went over to Hungary and was part of the great Hungarian deportation between May 15 and July 8, 1944.

34. Elie Wiesel, *A Jew Today*, trans. Marion Wiesel (New York: Random House, 2010), 140.

35. Wiesel, *Against Silence*, 3: 110.

36. Terrence Des Pres, "The Authority of Silence in Elie Wiesel's Art," in *Confronting the Holocaust: The Impact of Elie Wiesel*, ed. Alvin H. Rosenfeld and Irving Greenberg (Bloomington: Indiana University Press, 1978), 51. See also: "Yes, we even doubted that he wanted to exterminate us. [. . .] there are your Germans! What do you think of them? Where is their famous cruelty?" Elie Wiesel, *The Night Trilogy* (New York: Hill and Wang), 18–19.

37. Elie Wiesel, *Legends of Our Time*, trans. Frances Frenaye (New York: Schocken Books, 1968), 190. In some of Wiesel's other books, he moves from the historical sphere (exemplified in *Night*) to the spiritual; in these works, he engages in an exact and almost cruel analysis of the disintegration of the "I" and of the human being's knowledge of self, for example, Elie Wiesel, *One Generation Later* (New York: Schocken Books, 1982), 52–59.

38. Lily Edelman, "A Conversation with Elie Wiesel," in *Responses to Elie Wiesel*, ed. Harry James Cargas (New York: Persea Books, 1978), 13.

39. Lawrence L. Langer, *Versions of Survival: The Holocaust and the Human Spirit* (Albany: State University of New York Press, 1982), 131–89.

40. John S. Friedman, "The Art of Fiction LXXIX: Elie Wiesel," in *Elie Wiesel Conversations*, ed. Robert Franciosi (Jackson: University Press of Mississippi, 2002), 88.

41. Wiesel, *The Night Trilogy*, 70. See also, Wiesel, *One Generation Later*, 41–44.

42. Alfred Kazin, *Contemporaries* (Boston: Little, Brown, 1962), 297–98.

43. Barry Hyams, "Witness and Messenger (An Interview)," in *Elie Wiesel Conversations*, ed. Robert Franciosi (Jackson: University Press of Mississippi, 2002), 14; Alan L. Berger, "The Storyteller and His Quarrel with God," in *Elie Wiesel and the Art of Storytelling*, ed. Rosemary Horowitz (Jefferson: McFarland & Co., 2006), 71–89.

44. Yisra'el Shapira, *Sefer Shufra De-Yisra'el al Ha-Torah* (New York: Private, 2001), 74. My translation.

45. Wiesel, *The Night Trilogy*, 96.

46. Wiesel, *The Night Trilogy*.

47. Wiesel, *The Night Trilogy*, 97.

48. Wiesel, *The Night Trilogy*.

49. Over the years, Wiesel's views softened, and at times he claimed that incidents of Jews acting in a manner that denied human dignity were rare, and that these did not decrease Wiesel's own faith in human dignity. In my opinion, this amounts to a change in his position, a change that does not correspond with the general tenor of *Night*; cf., for example, Bob Costas, "A Wound That Will Never Be Healed: An Interview with Elie Wiesel," in *Telling the Tale: A Tribute to Elie Wiesel*, ed. Harry James Cargas (St. Louis: Time Being Books, 1993), 140–41.

50. Wiesel, *The Night Trilogy*, 111–12.

51. See also, Wiesel, *One Generation Later*, 29–36.

52. Erich Kahler, *The Tower and the Abyss: An Inquiry into the Transformation of the Individual* (New Brunswick: Transaction, 1989), 224.

53. Cf. Wiesel's description of his writing of *Night*, in Harry James Cargas, "An Interview with Elie Wiesel," in *Telling the Tale: A Tribute to Elie Wiesel*, ed. Harry James Cargas (Missouri: Time Being Books, 1993), 15.

54. Elie Wiesel, "Why I Write," in *Confronting the Holocaust: The Impact of Elie Wiesel*, ed. Alvin H. Rosenfeld and Irving Greenberg (Bloomington: Indiana University Press, 1978), 202.

55. Wiesel, too, quotes these voices and writes: "I know you will not believe me. I know, but you must." Elie Wiesel, *Dimensions of the Holocaust* (Evanston: Northwestern University Press, 1977), 11.

56. Ever since Walter Laqueur's fine work *The Terrible Secret*, Holocaust scholars have distinguished between knowledge and information. See *The Terrible Secret: Suppression of the Truth about Hitler's "Final Solution"* (New York: Owl Books, 1980), 76–85, 95–100. Wiesel makes no such distinction in his writings.

57. Elie Wiesel, "When an Eye Says Kaddish," *Telling the Tale: A Tribute to Elie Wiesel*, ed. Harry James Cargas (Missouri: Time Being Books, 1993), 90. Wiesel, *Dimensions of the Holocaust*, 5. For his critique of the American and Palestinian Jewish communities, see: Wiesel, *A Journey of Faith*, 37; Wiesel, *A Jew Today*, 191–92. Over the years, Wiesel forged a distinction between the behavior of Jews and Christians. He blames, among others, the Roman Catholic Church, and especially the Pope, for an ambivalent relationship with Nazis who were members of the Church; cf. Wiesel, *Against Silence*, 1: 104.

58. Wiesel, *One Generation Later*, 37.

59. Wiesel, *Legends of Our Time*, 189. Cf. the harsh words of Wiesel in *Dimensions of the Holocaust*, 5–7.

60. Wiesel, *Legends of Our Time*, 190. Similar expressions of the bankruptcy of culture in Wiesel's view can be found in Wiesel, *A Journey of Faith*, 15. We should not discount posttraumatic stress disorder as also being a factor. See Bessel Van Der Kolk, *The Body Keeps the Score* (New York: Penguin Books, 2015).

61. Wiesel acknowledges that his description of Judaism reflects his own experience and not that of most of the Jewish world; compare, for example, Elie Wiesel, *A Small Measure of Victory: An Interview by Gene Koppel and Henry Kaufmann* (Tucson: University of Arizona Press, 1974), 11.

62. Wiesel, *Against Silence*, 3: 219.

63. Elie Wiesel, *Four Hasidic Masters and Their Struggle against Melancholy* (Notre Dame: University of Notre Dame Press, 1978), 7.

64. Elie Wiesel, *All Rivers Run to the Sea*, 84; Wiesel, *Against Silence*, 3: 112.

65. Concerning the responsibility of the tzaddik for his disciple, see Elie Wiesel, *The Town Beyond the Wall*, trans. Stephen Becker (New York: Schocken Books, 1982), 11; Elie Wiesel, *Souls on Fire: Portraits and Legends of Hasidic Masters*, trans. Marion Wiesel (New York: Random House, 1972), 125.

66. Wiesel, *Four Hasidic Masters and Their Struggle against Melancholy*, 19–21. See also, Yakir Englander, "Halakha as Praxis: The Body of the Zaddik in 20th-Century Hasidic Stories," *Mechkarei Yerusalim be-Safrut Ivrit* 27 (2014): 103–32.

67. Victor Malka, "Elie Wiesel: Joy and Light (an Interview)," in *Elie Wiesel: Conversations*, ed. Robert Franciosi (Jackson: University Press of Mississippi, 2002), 38.

68. Elie Wiesel, *Somewhere a Master: Further Hasidic Portraits and Legends*, trans. Marion Wiesel (New York: Summit Books, 1982), 137. See also, 104–5, 130–31; Elie Wiesel, *From the Kingdom of Memory* (New York: Schocken Books, 1990), 29–30; Wiesel, *Souls on Fire*, 4–5.

69. John S. Friedman, "The Art of Fiction LXXIX: Elie Wiesel," in *Elie Wiesel: Conversations*, ed. Robert Franciosi (Jackson: University of Mississippi Press, 2002), 88–89.

70. Elie Wiesel, *The Gates of the Forest*, trans. Frances Frenaye (New York: Holt, Rinehart and Winston, 1966), 33.

71. For Wiesel's own critique of religious society and its concept of "truth," cf. Wiesel and Heffner, *Conversations with Elie Wiesel*, 55–56.

72. Wiesel, *The Gates of the Forest*, 189–210.

73. Harry James Cargas, "Can We Bring the Messiah? An Interview with Elie Wiesel," in *Telling the Tale: A Tribute to Elie Wiesel*, ed. Harry James Cargas (Missouri: Time Being Books, 1993), 38.

74. For the connection between the tzaddik and his disciples in Wiesel writings, cf. Carole J. Lambert, *Is God Man's Friend? Theodicy and Friendship in Elie Wiesel's Novels* (New York: Peter Lang, 2006), 6–7.

75. On the admiration of the Hasidic leaders for madmen, see: Wiesel, *Souls on Fire*, 104–5. On the unique and inimitable role of the Hasidic tzaddik, cf. Berenbaum, *Elie Wiesel*, 47.

76. Wiesel, *Dimensions of the Holocaust*, 6.

77. Josephine Knopp, "Wiesel and the Absurd," in *Responses to Elie Wiesel*, ed. Harry James Cargas (New York: Persea Books, 1978), 92–101.

78. Wiesel, *The Gates of the Forest*, 13. See also, Edelman, "A Conversation with Elie Wiesel," 15.

79. Wiesel, *The Gates of the Forest*, 21.

80. Wiesel, *The Gates of the Forest*, 196.

Works Cited

Agamben, Giorgio. *Remnants of Auschwitz: The Witness and the Archive*. Trans. Daniel Heller-Roazen. New York: Zone Books, 2002.

Anonymous. *Ki Esh Kadcha Beapi Vatikad ad Sheol Tachtiya*. Jerusalem: Private, 1980.

Anonymous. "Lezecher Alfei Batei-Kneset Shenehersu ba-Shoah." *Bet Yaacov* 27–28 (1961): 21–23.

Bachmann, Michael. "Life, Writing, and Problems of Genre in Elie Wiesel and Imre Kertész." *Rocky Mountain Review* 63, no. 1 (2009): 79–88.

Bayefsky, Rachel. "Dignity, Honour, and Human Rights: Kant's Perspective." *Political Theory* 41, no. 6 (2013): 809–37.

Berenbaum, Michael. *Elie Wiesel: God, the Holocaust, and the Children of Israel.* New Jersey: Behrman House, 1974.

Berger, Alan L. "The Storyteller and His Quarrel with God." In *Elie Wiesel and the Art of Storytelling*, ed. Rosemary Horowitz, 71–89. Jefferson: McFarland & Co., 2006.

Berger, Peter. "On the Obsolescence of the Concept of Honor." *European Journal of Sociology* 11, no. 2 (1970): 338–47.

Bourdieu, Pierre. "The Sentiment of Honor in Kabyle Society." In *Honor and Shame: The Values of Mediterranean Society*, ed. J. G. Peristiany, 191–241. Chicago: University of Chicago Press, 1966.

Braiteman, Zachary. *(God) After Auschwitz: Tradition and Change in Post-Holocaust Jewish Thought.* Princeton: Princeton University Press, 1998.

Campbell, J. K. *Honor, Family and Patronage: A Study of Institutions and Moral Values in a Greek Mountain Community.* Berkeley: Clarendon Press, 1970.

Cargas, Harry James. "An Interview with Elie Wiesel." In *Telling the Tale: A Tribute to Elie Wiesel*, edited by Harry James Cargas, 11–18. St. Louis: Time Being Books, 1993.

Cargas, Harry James. "Can We Bring the Messiah?" In *Telling the Tale: A Tribute to Elie Wiesel*, ed. Harry James Cargas, 36–44. Missouri: Time Being Books, 1993.

Cargas, Harry James. "What Is a Jew? Interview with Elie Wiesel." In *Responses to Elie Wiesel*, ed. Harry James Cargas, 150–57. New York: Persea Books, 1978.

Costas, Bob. "A Wound That Will Never Be Healed: An Interview with Elie Wiesel." In *Telling the Tale: A Tribute to Elie Wiesel*, edited by Harry James Cargas, 137–63. Missouri: Time Being Books, 1993.

Des Pres, Terrence. "The Authority of Silence in Elie Wiesel's Art." In *Confronting the Holocaust: The Impact of Elie Wiesel*, ed. Alvin H. Rosenfeld and Irving Greenberg, 49–57. Bloomington: Indiana University Press, 1978.

Edelman, Lily. "A Conversation with Elie Wiesel." In *Responses to Elie Wiesel*, ed. Harry James Cargas, 45–57. New York: Persea Books, 1978.

Englander, Yakir. "Halakha as Praxis: The Body of the Zaddik in 20th Hasidic Stories." *Mechkarei Yerusalim be-Safrut Ivrit* 27 (2014): 103–32.

Englander, Yakir. "The 'Jewish Knight' of Slobodka: Honor Culture and the Image of the Body in an Ultra-Orthodox Jewish Context." *Religion* 46, no. 2 (2016): 186–208.

Eybeschitz, Yehoshuah. "Hasefer Betkufat Ha-Shoah." *Chagim* 2 (1971): 10–11.

Farbstein, Esther. *Hidden in Thunder: Perspectives on Faith, Theology and Leadership during the Holocaust.* Jerusalem: Mossad Harav Kook, 2002.
Fayvlovitz, Tziporah. *Bematzok Ubitchiya.* Haifa: Private, 1994.
Flender, Harold. "Conversation with Elie Wiesel." In *Elie Wiesel: Conversations*, ed. Robert Franciosi, 19–28. Jackson: University Press of Mississippi, 2002.
Friedman, John S. "The Art of Fiction LXXIX: Elie Wiesel." In *Elie Wiesel: Conversations*, ed. Robert Franciosi, 69–98. Jackson: University Press of Mississippi, 2002.
Goldberg, Amos. "If This Is a Man: The Image of Man in Autobiographical and Historical Writing during and after the Holocaust." *Yad Vashem Studies* 33 (2005): 381–429.
HaPardes: A Rabbinic Collection. Adar: n.p., 1945.
Hyams, Barry. "Witness and Messenger (an Interview)." In *Elie Wiesel: Conversations*, ed. Robert Franciosi, 9–15. Jackson: University Press of Mississippi, 2002.
Kahler, Erich. *The Tower and the Abyss: An Inquiry into the Transformation of the Individual.* New Brunswick: Transaction, 1989.
Kamir, Orit. "Dignity and Its Significant Others: Respect, Honor and Glory." Forthcoming.
Kamir, Orit. *Escape from Dignity: The Comeback of Honor and Shaming.* Forthcoming.
Kamir, Orit. *Israeli Honor and Dignity: Social Norms, Gender Politics and the Law.* Jerusalem: Carmel, 2004.
Kateb, George. *Human Dignity.* Cambridge: Harvard University Press, 2011.
Katz, Steven T. *Post-Holocaust Dialogues: Critical Studies in Modern Jewish Thought.* New York: New York University Press, 1983.
Katz, Steven T., ed. *The Impact of the Holocaust on Jewish Theology.* New York: New York University Press, 2005.
Kazin, Alfred. *Contemporaries.* Boston: Little, Brown, 1962.
Knopp, Josephine. "Wiesel and the Absurd." In *Responses to Elie Wiesel*, ed. Harry James Cargas, 92–101. New York: Persea Books, 1978.
Kolitz, Zvi. *Yosl Rakover Talks to God.* Trans. Carol Brown Janeway. New York: Pantheon Books, 1999.
Lambert, Carole J. *Is God Man's Friend? Theodicy and Friendship in Elie Wiesel's Novels.* New York: Peter Lang, 2006.
Langer, Lawrence L. *Versions of Survival: The Holocaust and the Human Spirit.* Albany: State University of New York Press, 1982.
Laqueur, Walter. *The Terrible Secret: Suppression of the Truth about Hitler's "Final Solution."* New York: Owl Books, 1980.
Langer, Lawrence L. *Admitting the Holocaust: Collected Essays.* New York and Oxford: Oxford University Press, 1995.

LaVaque-Manty, Mika. "Dueling for Equality: Masculine Honor and the Modern Politics of Dignity." *Political Theory* 34, no. 6 (2006): 715–40.
Levi, Primo. *If This Is a Man?* New York: Penguin, 1979.
Mitchell, Beverly Eileen. *Plantations and Death Camps: Religion, Identity and Human Dignity*. Minneapolis: Fortress Press, 2009.
Peristiany, J. G., and Julian Pitt-Rivers, eds. *Honor and Grace in Anthropology*. Cambridge: Cambridge University Press, 1992.
Piekarz, Mendel. *Ideological Trends of Hasidism in Poland during the Interwar Period and the Holocaust*. Jerusalem: Bialik Institute, 1990.
Presner, Todd. "'Clear Heads, Solid Stomachs, and Hard Muscles': Max Nordau and the Aesthetics of Jewish Regeneration." *Modernism/modernity* 10, no. 2 (2003): 269–96.
"Press Release—Peace 1986." Nobelprize.org. Nobel Media AB 2014. http://www.nobelprize.org/nobel_prizes/peace/laureates/1986/press.html. Accessed 14 November 2017.
Rosenfeld, Alvin H., and Irving Greenberg, eds. Confronting the Holocaust: The Impact of Elie Wiesel. Bloomington: Indiana University Press, 1978.
Shapira, Yisra'el. *Sefer Shufra De-Yisra'el al Ha-Torah*. New York: Private, 2001.
Schuster, Ekkehard, and Reinhold Boschert-Kimmig. "Elie Wiesel Speaks." In *Elie Wiesel: Conversations*, ed. Robert Franciosi, 146–59. Jackson: University Press of Mississippi, 2002.
Van Der Kolk, Bessel. *The Body Keeps the Score*. New York: Penguin Books, 2015.
Wiesel, Elie. *Against Silence: The Voice and Vision of Elie Wiesel*, vols. 1 and 3. New York: Holocaust Library, 1985.
Wiesel, Elie. *All Rivers Run to the Sea*. New York: Schocken Books, 1996.
Wiesel, Elie. *Dimensions of the Holocaust*. Evanston: Northwestern University Press, 1977.
Wiesel, Elie. *Four Hasidic Masters and Their Struggle against Melancholy*. Notre Dame: University of Notre Dame Press, 1978.
Wiesel, Elie. *From the Kingdom of Memory*. New York: Schocken Books, 1990.
Wiesel, Elie. *The Gates of the Forest*. Trans. Frances Frenaye. New York: Holt, Rinehart and Winston, 1966.
Wiesel, Elie. *A Journey of Faith: A Dialogue Between Elie Wiesel and His Eminence John Cardinal O'Connor*. New York: Donald I. Fine, 1990.
Wiesel, Elie. *Legends of Our Time*. Trans. Frances Frenaye. New York: Schocken Books, 1968.
Wiesel, Elie. *One Generation Later*. New York: Schocken Books, 1982.
Wiesel, Elie. *A Small Measure of Victory: An Interview by Gene Koppel and Henry Kaufmann*. Tucson: University of Arizona Press, 1974.
Wiesel, Elie. *Somewhere a Master: Further Hasidic Portraits and Legends*. Trans. Marion Wiesel. New York: Summit Books, 1982.

Wiesel, Elie. *Souls on Fire: Portraits and Legends of Hasidic Masters*. Trans. Marion Wiesel. New York: Random House, 1972.
Wiesel, Elie. *The Town Beyond the Wall*. Trans. Stephen Becker. New York: Schocken Books, 1982.
Wiesel, Elie, and Richard D. Heffner. *Conversations with Elie Wiesel*. New York: Schocken Books, 2003.
Wiesel, Elie. *The Night Trilogy*. New York: Hill and Wang, 2008.
Wiesel, Elie. *A Jew Today*. Trans. Marion Wiesel. New York: Random House, 2010.

3

The Role of the Four Prophet Figures in *Night*

MARY CATHERINE MUELLER

From earliest times of antiquity to the present day, the role of the prophet has been crucial to various religious teachings and exegetical writings. In Hebrew the most frequently used term for prophet is *navi* (pl.: *nev'im*), which relates to the verb "to call" or "to proclaim."[1] Two less common terms refer to the prophet as a "seer" or as "one who has a vision."[2] Douglas Knight and Amy-Jill Levine elaborate on these definitions, arguing that a prophet is one who proclaims the future. They also note that a prophet's message seems like "madness" to his or her audience. The notion of the prophet's call, message, and even proclamation is one that is rooted in the Jewish narrative and has branched into various testimonies and writings about the Holocaust. In the following, I will draw upon Knight and Levine's definitions of prophesy to address the role of the prophet figures in *Night*, highlighting key attributes and motifs of the prophet figure as he or she appears in Wiesel's writings. There are four prophet figures whose callings, warnings, proclamations, and sights are essential in *Night*. It is through the lens of these prophet figures that the reader acquires a glimpse into the skewed—what I call—anti-world (a world where any assumptions about humanity, rooted in living in a civilized world during the twentieth century, are inverted and distorted) of the Holocaust.

The Prophet Figure in Relation to
Jewish Teaching and Wiesel's Writing

Jewish traditions and teachings are rife with prophet figures. From the authorship of the Torah that was bestowed upon Moses, the message foretelling the messianic hope found on the lips of Elijah, the bold songs of justice sung by Deborah, and Jeremiah's narrative tangled with woe and hope, judgment and mercy, to countless others, the role of the prophet in Judaism is found in the very fabric of its teachings and traditions. To be a prophet, one does not merely utter words of wisdom or even predict the future, but rather one serves as a mouthpiece for God to the people. However, what means are taken to "voice" this message from God differs with each prophet and each situation, speaking "in public, speaking directly to the audience that most needed to hear their message—in the royal court, in the marketplace, in judicial contexts, in the temple, and in other public and private settings."[3] Knight and Levine argue that the prophet generally focused on the particular area or group of people to whom his or her message was addressed. The significance of the prophet's audience in *Night* is seen through the characters Moishe the Beadle (when he comes back from surviving the mass shooting in the forest to his town to tell his people of what he had witnessed) and Mrs. Schächter (when she relentlessly warns those traveling toward Auschwitz on the train with her about the fire). By including prophet figures in *Night*, such as Moishe, who bears witness to the suffering mankind is capable of inflicting on one another, and Mrs. Schächter, who foretells the atrocities that mankind is about to encounter, Wiesel follows the traditions of the Jewish teachings, which concentrate on and recount the actions man is capable of in this world.

In an interview with Robert Franciosi and Brian Shaffer, Elie Wiesel asserts, "I am a student of the ancient prophetic texts; every prophet usually had to be both a seer of pain and a consoler. I wish I had the power to console. I try, meaning I desperately seek hope. The emphasis is on desperate."[4] Wiesel places himself on the path of various Jewish exegetical teachings, specifically the teachings of the prophets. Later in this interview, Wiesel states, "I am not a prophet, but I am a student of Jeremiah and I love Jeremiah. [. . . O]f all the prophets he is the one whose writings I am closest to. He is the one who foresaw tragedy, lived tragedy, and remembered tragedy to write about it."[5] Once again, though he denies being a prophet, the characteristics that Wiesel claims to be typical of most prophets, mainly their being "both a seer of pain and a consoler," are characteristics that surface throughout *Night*. For instance, in his book, *Five Biblical Portraits*, Wiesel writes that Jeremiah was a prophet who "forces us to look at what we refuse to see" and through his experiences and warnings, "he [Jeremiah] is, in short, a survivor, a witness."[6] Wiesel's writings about the Holocaust are interwoven with warnings of wretched conditions to come, the foreseeing of fear, and the accompanying promises (and possible consolations) of prophets such as Jeremiah from the Bible and other prophets from various Hasidic and Talmudic texts. In many cases, the horrors to come are of such profundity that consolation is impossible: philosopher Martin Buber claims that the prophets "always aimed to shatter all security and to proclaim in the opened abyss of the final insecurity the unwished for God who demands that His human creatures become real."[7] Through writing *Night*, Wiesel enables a profound and, in turn, prophetic proclamation of how the security of the pre-Holocaust world was shattered when it was met with the realities of the Holocaust.

As with Wiesel's interviews, his private writings, and his other literary works, *Night* is a culturally and religiously vibrant text, which captures the horrors and atrocities that engulf the world of the young Eliezer Wiesel. *Night* follows Eliezer from the very moments he is spewed into the anti-world of the Holocaust to the moments when he survives only to see himself as a corpse—a corpse living as a witness. *Night* is not a coming-of-age novel or even a bildungsroman of Wiesel's life; rather, it is a literary memoir that, through the warnings of the prophet figures, unravels the very presupposed threads of humanity, society, and culture in order to uncover the fears, cruelties, and evils that rob a child of his youth, his community, his home, his family, his name, his voice, and even his faith.[8]

One tool that Wiesel uses to sculpt this anti-world is the voices of various prophets. Wiesel "had been completely immersed in Talmudic studies (in the time-honored manner of intelligent Jewish boys), presumably preparing for a life as a Talmudic scholar [and that] his world was that of Orthodox Judaism, governed in every detail by Jewish law, outside the mainstream of European culture."[9] It is of no surprise, then, that the prophet appears frequently in *Night*. The most visible of these prophet figures, of course, is "Moishe the Beadle," who appears at the beginning of *Night* and issues a warning, largely unheeded as to the coming destruction. In addition to Moishe the Beadle, three other prophet figures are ensconced in *Night*; Mrs. Schächter (the "mad" woman on the train during Eliezer's transport), Rabbi Eliahu ("the only rabbi whom nobody ever failed to address as 'Rabbi' in Buna" during their final march), and finally, Eliezer Wiesel (the teller of the story, the witness, the survivor).[10] I aim, in this close reading of *Night*, to demonstrate the significance of the "prophet figure" in the literature of the Holocaust. Each prophet represents a various layer of the anti-world that was molded across Europe during 1939–1945. Just as there are multiple meanings and connotations for the word "prophet," all four of the prophet figures in *Night* represent four differing dimensions of Eliezer's life during the Holocaust.

Traces of the Prophet Figure in Wiesel's Writings

For years, scholars of Elie Wiesel have examined, through different lenses, the "madman" or prophet figure that appears throughout his literary oeuvre. In this volume, Jennifer Murray argues that in Wiesel's work "madness reveals to others a truth that is hidden from sight." Seymour M. Finger, similarly, argues that "in *Twilight*, [Wiesel] tested the madness of faith as 'an answer to insanity,' stating in the preface that 'the world couldn't exist without madmen.'"[11] In "*Twilight*: Madness, Caprice, Friendship, and God," Robert McAfee Brown describes the mad or prophet figures in Wiesel's works as "those who see life in such a different perspective from the rest of us that the rest of us become uneasy in their presence and seek to incarcerate them or, if necessary, put them to death."[12] Like McAfee, Finger again explores this figure, asserting, "The 'threat' of Wiesel's madmen is that they may have a surer, saner corner on the truth than we do."[13]

In "Biblical Dimensions in the Work of Elie Wiesel," Albert H. Friedlander notes: "Wiesel cannot just be defined as a rabbinic commentator. He is a messenger-prophet-witness whose writings always struggle with the tradition and always constitute a direct or indirect reminder of the Holocaust."[14] In tandem with both Finger and Friedlander, in his "From *Night* to *Twilight*: A Philosopher's Reading of Elie Wiesel," John K. Roth examines the various themes inculcated into each narrative, including the role of the madman or his or her "madness," which serves as a connecting thread begun in *Night* and woven throughout Wiesel's works. Roth asserts, "*Twilight*, as well as *The Town Beyond the Wall* and some thirty more of Wiesel's books, follows *Night*. In one way or another, all of *Night*'s sequels explore how the world might be mended."[15] Yet, the madness of the prophet figures in *Night* is a different kind of madness than that which appears in his works such as *Twilight* or *The Town Beyond the Wall* or even the madness in *The Gates of the Forest* and *A Beggar in Jerusalem*.

In his *The Vision of the Void: Theological Reflections on the Works of Elie Wiesel*, Michael Berenbaum further notes the differing connotations of madness that Wiesel inculcates though his narratives. Berenbaum writes:

> In *Night* Wiesel described madness as a correct perception of reality in a world gone mad. Only the mad person could truly perceive or express the horrors of reality. Sanity becomes insanity in a mad world. Moishe the Beadle, the man who had been to the camps and returned to tell the tale, was labeled mad. Madame Schächter, the woman on the train who correctly foresaw the flames of the crematoria revealed a truth prior to its time and was consequently considered mad. The dedication of *The Town Beyond the Wall* begins with a quote from Dostoevsky, "I have a plan—To go mad." Again, Moishe appears, and this Moishe knows: "I am a madman and in this base world only madmen know. They know that everything is false." [. . .] Varady goes mad, and his madness allows him to imagine the power to endure and impose his will upon reality. [. . .] Pedro's madness is not Moishe's madness or Madame Schächter's. His madness is not a correct perception of reality; rather it is an act of freedom that allows the individual to transcend his fate and alter his destiny.[16]

Concomitant with Berenbaum's observations regarding the different characteristics of madness among the characters Wiesel weaves throughout his works, I also agree with his observations regarding the madness of both Moishe the Beadle and Mrs. Schächter. However, my analysis extends beyond their individual association with madness. Rather, when considering these two particular prophet figures—or figures associated with madness—one must note how these are not two isolated figures, but rather two of the four prophet figures in *Night*, who sequentially play a role in ushering Eliezer into the anti-world of Auschwitz-Birkenau. Thus, these four prophet figures differ from all other prophet-like or madman-like figures of Wiesel's works, for like four corners on a door, these four figures join together in ushering Eliezer into different phases of the anti-world—the world of "Planet Auschwitz."[17]

Elie Wiesel also writes about this role of the prophets in his book *Five Biblical Portraits*. In this book, he claims that "when we are struck by misfortune, we turn to him [the prophet Jeremiah] and follow in his footsteps; we use his words to describe our struggles."[18] Wiesel may not use the exact words of Jeremiah to describe his struggles, but when surrounded by darkness, he looks to Jeremiah's words as a guiding light:

> Then the word of the Lord came unto me, saying, "Before I formed thee in the belly I knew thee; and before thou camest forth out of the womb I sanctified thee, and I ordained thee a prophet unto the nations." Then said I, "Ah, Lord God! Behold, I cannot speak: for I am a child." But the Lord said unto me, "Say not, I am a child: for thou shalt go to all that I shall send thee, and whatsoever I command thee thou shalt speak. Be not afraid of their faces: for I am with thee to deliver thee, saith the Lord."[19]

In the preceding passage, Jeremiah is called to be a prophet. Concomitant with the biblical prophets' call to deliver a message, the prophet figures in *Night* share the weight of the message they must voice. Therefore, similarly to the hesitation, dread, and despair voiced by Moishe when he says, "I no longer care to live. I am alone. But I wanted to warn you. Only no one is listening to me," and the impetus for the constant, continual, recoiling shouts of Mrs. Schächter that enable her to break "free of her bonds and [shout] louder than before," the prophet figures carry the burden of being called to speak of what they had witnessed, what they will witness, and what they lived to witness.[20] Though a shadow might seem to veer away from its original source, it is nonetheless always connected and tied to that which gives it form. Similarly, we see the shadow of the prophet Jeremiah's words in Wiesel's prophet figures in *Night*. There are a plethora of prophets and of prophecies, just as there are moments in time; nevertheless, there are a few commonalities that are found in the four prophet figures in *Night*, such as isolation, silence, and madness. One aspect of the prophet figure is their story—their ability to tell a story, their story, and the story of others. In his essay "The Maggid of Sighet: Jewish Contexts for Wiesel's Storytelling," David Patterson addresses the power and place of storytelling throughout the Jewish tradition. Patterson writes:

> For the Hasid Elie Wiesel, the tales of the Hasidic masters are far more than legend, folklore, or "literary influences"—they are manifestations of Torah, modes of prayer, and ways of connecting with the Holy One. Wiesel makes it clear that he sees his storytelling as a form of prayer when he refers to a teaching from the thirteenth-century Hebrew poet Eleazar Rokeah, who maintained that God is not silent—He is Silence. "It is to this silence that I would like to direct my words," says Wiesel.[21]

Patterson's point is that Wiesel's "story" is not merely words of testimony, but prayer-like words—words written for all those who were silenced in the Holocaust, words written to bring out the Silence of God. Like most prophet figures, Wiesel relates the "story" of the past to warnings of the future—what happened in the Holocaust and what evil could happen if mankind were again to turn their backs on one another. Thus, it is in the midst of the chilling "Holy Silence" and in the aftershock of post-Holocaust silence that Wiesel's *Night* equips its readers with the testimonies concerning an atrocious assault on mankind that enables readers to bear witness, as well.

Moishe the Beadle

Moishe the Beadle represents the first dimension of the Holocaust and the anti-world for Eliezer: the spiritual *gate* that Eliezer must cross to enter into the anti-world. Within the first few pages of *Night*, Wiesel gives his readers this prophet figure, who seems to embody the "prophet of doom"—his words, his experience, and the "story" that he so ardently tries to tell does not merely foreshadow what might come, but rather describes what has come and what will come again. The opening lines of *Night* begin, like several Midrash and other exegetical texts, by evoking the prophecy (or warnings) of the prophet: "They called him Moishe the Beadle [. . .]. He was the jack-of-all-trades in a Hasidic house of prayer [. . .]. Moishe the Beadle was the exception. He stayed out of people's way. His presence bothered no one. He had mastered the art of rendering himself insignificant, invisible."[22] This first passage regarding Moishe the Beadle's very physical presence in Eliezer's village foreshadows how his verbal warnings of the horrors he witnessed would be dismissed as the words of a madman. Moishe the Beadle, the "exception," as he was so gently described in the opening paragraph, would once again be considered the "exception" when he would return from his near death—he escapes execution in the Galician forest—to warn the villagers of what awaits them.

Wiesel emphasizes the transformative effect of the act of witnessing: "Moishe was not the same. The joy in his eyes was gone. He no longer mentioned either God or Kabbalah. He spoke only of what he had seen."[23] In tandem with the Judeo-Christian tradition of prophets, as described throughout the Bible, the instant Moishe witnessed the horrors of what he had seen and acknowledged the power of the message he must tell others, his life and his words were consumed with the telling of his story to all. These warnings seemed "mad" to those living in a civilized world, where "love your neighbor as yourself" was a governing concept. In regard to this attribute of "madness" engulfing the prophet figure, Knight and Levine write:

> Although this role of delivering messages is central, the prophets have other functions and characteristics as well. For example, ecstatic prophecy appears both in the Hebrew Bible and in other cultures. In this type of activity, the prophet is so grasped by God or so possessed by a spirit that behavior becomes frenzied.[24]

Wiesel writes, "day after day, night after night, [Moishe] went from one Jewish house to the next, telling his story [. . .]. But people not only refused to believe his tales, they refused to listen. Some even insinuated that he only wanted their pity, that he was imagining things. Others flatly said that he had gone mad."[25] Moishe the Beadle finds himself wandering among his own town, from home to home, person to person, only to realize that the horrors and atrocities of which he speaks seem not only foreign to the ears of those who hear but absurd. "Even I did not believe him," young Eliezer states.[26] Although, according to this text, it appears that Moishe's warnings are ignored by his fellow townspeople, in reality, people living in villages, towns, and cities all across Nazified Europe could not leave their homes or escape anywhere. Moishe has a message that he cannot deliver—the story of his own death: what he witnessed, experienced, and escaped from—which makes him appear to be mad.

Perhaps the most profoundly affected among Moishe's audience is young Eliezer; the act of seeing, while transformative, is a continuation of Moishe's earlier role of mentor in the book. Like most prophecies from Jewish teachings, Moishe inducts his student into a demented world where fellow humans murdered masses of innocent people. The image of Moishe as "possessed" with a message he must tell, and "frenzied" by the burden of telling that message to others, is reflected for the reader in the description of Moishe the Beadle within the first few pages of *Night*. Wiesel begins this novel by introducing the reader to Moishe as a calm man who serves in ecstatically molding Eliezer's own spiritual knowledge of the teachings of the Kabbalah and the world of mysticism:

> From that day on, I saw him [Moishe] often [. . .] the poorest of the poor of Sighet, spoke to me for hours on end about the Kabbalah's revelations and its mysteries. Thus began my initiation. Together we would read, over and over again, the same page of the Zohar. Not to learn it by heart, but to discover within the very essence of divinity.
> And in the course of those evenings I became convinced that Moishe the Beadle would help me enter eternity, into that time when question and answer would become ONE.[27]

Moishe's teaching to Eliezer about how "to discover [eternity] within the very essence of divinity" may be prophetic in nature, but it harbors a prophecy that Eliezer could never fathom at the time.

Moishe's teachings become prophetic in his ability to usher Eliezer into a gate unlike anything he had imagined in this world—a *gate* that he must pass through in order to enter the realm of mysteries and understanding, a gate that leads to the anti-world:

> After a long silence, he said, "There are a thousand and one gates allowing entry into the orchard of mystical truth. Every human being has his own gate. He must not err and wish to enter the orchard through a gate other than his own. That would present danger not only for the one entering but also for those who are already inside."[28]

Here, too, Moishe the Beadle first utters words that announce the other world, the anti-world, to Eliezer. However, his words are quickly transposed from words of instruction and guidance to words of warning—words that sound distorted to those who hear. According to some religious and Kabbalah teaching, the gate in the orchard (*pardes*) represents the upper, unearthly realms of encounter with the divine.[29] Yet, Eliezer's gate is not a gate of ascension toward the Divine; rather, it is a gate marked "Arbeit Macht Frie," and it is through this passageway that he enters into an unearthly realm of Auschwitz—the realm where he collides with the absence of the divine's presence and, correspondingly, with the assault against the divine. Moishe's words are those that only the mad could truly believe. They are words that speak of the killing and murdering of innocent children, women, men, and the aged: "You cannot understand. I was saved miraculously [. . .]. Life? I no longer care to live. I am alone. But I wanted to come back to warn you. Only no one is listening to me . . ."[30] Traditionally characteristic of the prophet figure, in the end, Moishe the Beadle is not concerned with his own life but instead is living to carry his message and warning to the lives of others. He is alone, alive, and burdened to tell what he had witnessed—the very same predicament in which Eliezer will find himself at the end of *Night*, when he looks into the mirror for the first time since life before the ghetto and sees death gazing back at him. Parallel to the warning of Moishe the Beadle, Elie Wiesel's memoir is not merely a warning of the atrocities and assaults mankind is capable of, it is the story of his stolen innocence and his death: "From the depths of the mirror, a corpse was contemplating me. The look in his eyes as he gazed at me has never left me."[31]

Within these first pages of *Night*, the reader witnesses the transformation of two characters, Moishe the Beadle and Eliezer. Moishe, the silent, forgotten man who once stuck to the outskirts of town, now is shouting and disturbing the peace of homes, synagogues, and houses of prayer in order to "warn" and "tell his story" by urging all, "Jews listen to me!"[32] Elie, the young boy who would "run to the synagogue to weep over the destruction of the Temple [the dwelling place of the Shekinah and the body of Israel]" and who studied and listened to every word that Moishe the Beadle would teach him, now found himself also not believing the warning of Moishe the Beadle.[33] Moishe's story (of what took place in the Galician forest) seemed like warnings from a madman, absurdities that, once spoken and heard, seemed foreign and incongruous to a cultured, ordered, civilized world. It is within these first pages that Wiesel crafts the prophet figure who foretells the future for Eliezer and his family by proclaiming a warning of what he had witnessed and experienced. The warnings of this prophet figure serve as the first steps toward the anti-world for Eliezer: a world where the home and the Temple (the Jewish people) will be destroyed and a world where the young and the aged will be carted away like cattle.

Mrs. Schächter

The second prophet figure that appears in *Night* is Mrs. Schächter. The eight prophetic warnings of "fire" proclaimed by Mrs. Schächter while riding on the train to Auschwitz serve to usher in the second dimension of the Holocaust for Eliezer: the religious aspect. As with the introduction of Moishe the Beadle, Mrs. Schächter is introduced with the simple sentence: "There was a woman among us, a certain Mrs. Schächter."[34] However, unlike Moishe the Beadle, she is immediately associated with madness: "She was a woman in her fifties and her ten-year-old son was with her [. . .]. Her husband and her two older sons had been deported with the first transport, by mistake. The separation had totally shattered her [. . .]. I knew her quite well [. . .]. Mrs. Schächter had lost her mind."[35] This notion of a "shattered" person seems to evoke, once again, the notion of the "frenzied" prophet whose alteration in life reflects madness rather than reason. The response of the people in the cattle cart toward Mrs. Schächter's eight prophetic cries echoes the townspeople's reactions to Moishe the Beadle's prophecies. As argued earlier, the narrative of the Jewish people includes several mad or ecstatic prophets. The "mad" prophets are typically those whose message is so inconceivable, burdensome, and critical that the tellers of those prophecies seem mad to all who hear and see them.[36] Knight and Levine argue that in such cases the "ecstatic prophecy must be observed or experienced; there will not necessarily be a verbal message."[37] This theory of the prophet describes Mrs. Schächter, who embodies the mad, ecstatic, and eventually silent prophet. Already garbed in madness for the reader, Mrs. Schächter seems mentally and emotionally crazed. Her apparent madness does not preclude her from accessing the truth; she issues eight "piercing" warnings of "Fire!" during the train transport and is thus the second character that Wiesel includes in his story that directly warns and foretells of the impending fate awaiting all caged in the cattle car heading toward Auschwitz. Wiesel does not merely have this character "warn" the others a few times of the looming fate waiting at the next train stop; rather, Mrs. Schächter loudly, piercingly, painstakingly (even upon the threat of "lethal blows" and beatings) speaks prophecies of the "Fire" eight times:

"Fire! I see a fire! I see a fire!" [. . .]

"Look! Look at this fire! This terrible fire! Have mercy on me!" [. . .]

"Fire! I see a fire! [. . .]

Jews, listen to me," she cried. "I see a fire! I see flames, huge flames!' It was as though she were possessed by some evil spirit" [. . .]

"Look at the Fire! Look at the flames! Flames everywhere . . ." [. . .]

"The fire, over there!" [. . .]

"Look at the fire! Look at the flames! Over there!" [. . .]

"'Jews, look! Look at the fire! Look at the flames!' And as the train stopped, this time we saw flames rising from a tall chimney into a black sky."[38]

The passage evokes *Devarim Rabbah* 3:12 in which the Torah is associated with fire. The Midrash says that the Torah is black fire on white fire. It also says that it is the prophet's task to reveal and transmit the Torah, since every Jewish soul is tied to a letter of the Torah. Here, woven through Mrs. Schächter's prediction of fire, is the very fire that consumes the Torah; it is the pillar of fire kindled by the Jewish people going up in flames.

The significance of Mrs. Schächter's warnings is not found in her poignant prediction of fire but in her warning of it eight times. Eight is a number that evokes the uppermost realm of spirituality for the Hassidic and mystic teachings, a number whose significance Eliezer would have known. This number invokes the eight days of observing Passover, the eight days of the celebration of lights (Hanukkah); however, more importantly, these *eight* warnings call to mind the "uppermost realm." As Ori Z. Soltes states, "this is the realm associated with the three uppermost *heikhalot* of *merkavah* literature. Above all, it is referred to as the 'dwelling' of God's *Shekhinah* 'aspect'—that aspect of Godness that dwells among us even as God is so ungraspably beyond us."[39] Soltes's commentary about the Shekinah's presence being associated among God's people is one that echoes the notion of how God's Presence "dwelt" among Moses and the Israelites, even when they were exiled in the wilderness. Thus, upon her utterance of the prophetic image of "Fire" eight times, Mrs. Schächter transitions from embodying the persona of "madness" to embodying the persona of "divinity" and, in a sense, "holiness." She is a prophetess whose divinely given foresight suggests that of the Shekinah—the female aspect of God, the feminine divine presence that is inculcated and quite prevalent in various Jewish Kabalistic teachings. As Knight and Levine write, "in the Jewish tradition, Wisdom is associated with *Shekhinah* (from the Hebrew root meaning 'to dwell, to camp,' related to the *mishkan*, the 'tent of meeting')."[40] Shekinah goes into exile with her children—the Jewish people.[41] In the case of Mrs. Schächter, she not only goes with the Jewish people (in the train cart), but she goes before them, entering into the insane world that they, too, will soon witness. Her insanity reveals itself through the actions of her silent, soundless presence in the cart, the moment Eliezer and the others see the "fire" for the first time. It is during the transport and upon the fulfillment of Mrs. Schächter's prophecies that Eliezer and the others are instantly sealed into the camp: the place where the world becomes an anti-world—a world governed by death rather than life, by individuality rather than community, by numbers rather than names, by hate rather than love, and by evil rather than good.

Consequently, the eight warnings of this prophet figure are not merely cried out to the Jews in the train going from one world to another, but they resound as an attempt to reason with the incomprehensibility of a world whose wind smells of burning flesh:

> Mrs. Schächter had fallen silent on her own. Mute again, indifferent, absent, she had returned to her corner. We stared at the flames in the darkness. A wretched stench floated in the air [. . .]. Strange-looking creatures, dressed in striped jackets and black pants, jumped into the wagon [. . .] they began to strike at us left and right [. . .]. We jumped out. I

> glanced at Mrs. Schächter. Her little boy was still holding her hand. In front of us, those flames. In the air, the smell of burning flesh. It must have been around midnight. We had arrived. In Birkenau.[42]

Mrs. Schächter allows the prophecy to speak itself into fulfillment. Her silence is a prophetic one that signals the second dimension of the antiworld for Eliezer. Moishe the Beadle's silence was heard the instant Eliezer stepped into the train cart; likewise, Eliezer hears Mrs. Schächter's silence the instant he steps into Birkenau. Mrs. Schächter's silence reveals how "the prophets' effectiveness lies not just in their message, but also in the power of their rhetoric and actions."[43] It is through the actions of Mrs. Schächter sitting silently in the cart that her prophetic message was fully voiced. Mrs. Schächter signals the world that Eliezer and the others pass through before being faced with the world of extermination, the world of "Fire!" and the world of burning flesh—Birkenau and Auschwitz.

Mirroring these eight warnings of Mrs. Schächter, were the eight words: "'Men to the left! Women to the right!' Eight words spoken quietly, indifferently, without emotion. Eight simple, short words" pull Eliezer out of the comprehendible world of life before the transport and into the incomprehensible world of Auschwitz-Birkenau.[44] Though separated from all the women (mothers and sisters, wives and daughters), Eliezer and his father were not yet separated from the feminine aspect of God—the prophetess, Mrs. Schächter. When Eliezer's father asks him, "Do you remember Mrs. Schächter, in the train?" Eliezer's response to his father is not one of outward expression but rather an inward prayer, an inward plea to himself to never forget that night, the night Mrs. Schächter's cries became silent.[45] The night God became silent:

> Never shall I forget that night, the first night in the camp, that turned my life into one long night seven times sealed.
> Never shall I forget that smoke.
> Never shall I forget the small faces of the children whose bodies I saw transformed into smoke under a silent sky.
> Never shall I forget those flames that consumed my faith forever.
> Never shall I forget the nocturnal silence that deprived me for all eternity of the desire to live.
> Never shall I forget those moments that murdered my

God and my soul and turned my dreams to ashes.
Never shall I forget those things, even were I condemned to live as long as God Himself.
Never.[46]

With these eight "Nevers," Eliezer enters the anti-world where the invocation of the uppermost sacred realm, to the Shekinah, the female aspect of God, the Holy Spirit, and Wisdom is met with silence. The silence of Mrs. Schächter mirrors the silence of the prophet Jeremiah, "Now it came to pass, when Jeremiah had made an end of speaking all that the Lord had commanded him to speak unto all the people, that the priests and the prophets and all the people took him, saying, Thou shalt surely die."[47] The silence of both Jeremiah and Mrs. Schächter has been sounded.

This silence in the camp represents the silence of Mrs. Schächter, other prophet figures, mothers, children, and the aged, whose cries seem to forever echo in the smoke and ash. Whereas God may have been present in the piercing prophecies of Mrs. Schächter, He is now present as the Silent One, in the snapping sound of the boy being hanged in the camp:

> But the third rope was still moving: the child, too light, was still breathing [. . .]. And so he remained for more than half an hour, lingering between life and death, writhing before our eyes. And we were forced to look at him at close range. He was still alive when I passed him. His tongue was still red, his eyes not yet extinguished. Behind me, I heard the same man asking: "For God's sake, where is God?" And from within me, I heard an answer: "Where He is? This is where—hanging here from this gallows . . ." That night, the soup tasted of corpse.[48]

Through this hanging of the child, all source of redemption was hanged. The silence of Mrs. Schächter is heard in the silenced death of the child, and in the unspoken prayer of eight "nevers" by Eliezer. According to Judaic-Christian teachings that stem from the Bible, children are a gift from God to mankind, and through the blessing of a child, man and woman are able to participate in divine creation.[49] It is through children that mankind's legacy continues. It is for children that wisdom is passed on and traditions are taught. As François Mauriac notes, Wiesel was a child who "from the time he began to think, he lived only for God, studying the Talmud, eager to be initiated into the Kabbalah, wholly dedicated to the Almighty" and thus, he would have understood the Jewish teachings that children are a source of redemption, they are the essence of holiness, and are walking testimonies of divine gifts.[50] For Eliezer, when the only remaining child is hanged, the divine Presence of God—the Shekinah—is suddenly absent from the camp and from Eliezer. Yet, it is due to this absence of the Shekinah, that Eliezer forces himself to remember the child and bear witness to the child's life for,

> while the child remains nameless, the Holy Name speaks through the words of the witness, often despite the witness. The Testimony of the witness places the lost child on another shore, over *there*. Thus the disturbances of the witness situate the child in all the "theres," which is the literal meaning of the Hebrew word for "heaven," *shamayim*, the abode of the Holy One whom tradition associates with the child.[51]

As Patterson notes, it is through the witnessing of the child and the acknowledgment of his or her existence that the testimony of the witness is molded. Through Mrs. Schächter's prophetic vision, Eliezer first hears of the flames that would consume the world as he knew it and spew him into a world where his prayers would become inward cries, a world where a child would hang in the presence of the Silent Holy One.

Mrs. Schächter's prophesy of "Fire!" ushers Eliezer into a world where he is forced to see that fire produces only darkness and where children, and any notion of innocence and youth, are stolen and hanged. In the preface to the new (English) translation of *Night*, Wiesel notes that the original Yiddish version of *Night* begins with "We believed in God, trusted in man, and lived with the illusion that every one of us has been entrusted with a sacred spark from the Shekinah's flame; that every one of us carries in his eyes and in his soul a reflection of God's image."[52] The boy's eyes are extinguished when he is hanged and all sparks of the Shekinah disintegrated to darkness: to a place where "days resembled the nights, and nights left in our soul the dregs of their darkness," to a place where "no one recited Kaddish over [the dead]. Sons abandoned the remains of their fathers without tears," to a place where Elie "ceased to pray [. . . for he] was not denying His [God's] existence, but doubt[ing] His absolute justice."⁵³ It is in this second dimension of the anti-world that the prophet figure's silence speaks for the Silence of the Holy One, who is hanging with His child on the gallows. It is through this second prophet figure that Eliezer enters into the anti-world, where the very notion of being alive seems like an assault on any presuppositions of his religion, his faith, and his God.

Rabbi Eliahu

On his march out of (or perhaps further into) this anti-world of darkness, death, and doubt, Eliezer encounters the third prophet figure—Rabbi Eliahu. Unlike Moishe the Beadle and Mrs. Schächter, Rabbi Eliahu does not embody the prophet whose teachings, warnings, and prophecies foretell a world to come; instead, he represents the world that was—the world before the transport, the chimneys, the camp, and the march. Eliezer writes,

> Despite the ordeals and deprivations, his face continued to radiate his innocence. He was the only rabbi whom nobody ever failed to address as "Rabbi" in Buna. He looked like one of those prophets of old, always in the midst of his people when they needed to be consoled. And, strangely, his words never provoked anyone. They did ring peace.⁵⁴

The strangeness of Rabbi Eliahu is not his embodiment of peace, but rather his representation of the "prophets of old"—of faith, teachings, prayers, and rabbis before Eliezer's entering of the anti-world. His very name, "Eliahu," is derived from the messianic prophet Elijah, a name that seems synonymous with the messianic prophecies that foretold the hope of the Messiah's return, His fulfillment of the Law, and His bringing of peace. Rabbi Eliahu does not speak any particularly prophetic words or messages to Eliezer; instead, Rabbi Eliahu serves as prophet figure for Eliezer at the moment when Eliezer realizes that he had witnessed Rabbi Eliahu's son abandon his father. Watching and hearing Rabbi Eliahu search for his son causes a prayer to spring from Eliezer's lips: "And in spite of myself, a prayer formed inside me, a prayer to this God in whom I no longer believed. 'Oh God, Master of the Universe, give me the strength never to do what Rabbi Eliahu's son has done.'"⁵⁵ It is through this prophet figure that Eliezer's relation with his own father is revived. It is through this relationship between Rabbi Eliahu and his son that the reader is given a glimpse of one of the greatest attacks against the "family" during the Holocaust: the death of the patriarch, the priest of the home, the leader of the house—the death of the father.

In his book *The Shriek of Silence*, David Patterson highlights the power lurking in the anti-world, where all sense of relation between father and son is distorted and destroyed:

> Operating in the absence of the father, of course, may breed not only a longing for the father but also a rebellion against the father. As the bearer of the word, the father bears a promise; when the word is emptied of its meaning, the promise goes unfulfilled. The effort to regain the word of the father, who harbors the seminal seed of life, may take the form of a struggle with the father, to wrestle from him what death has swallowed up.[56]

The breaking of relation between father and son not only prowls throughout *Night* but throughout testimonies of the Holocaust. By constructing an anti-world where the father is no longer able to pass on the "word" and "promise" of his teachings to his son, the Nazis created a foundation on which the assault of the family and relations was built. It is through the prophet figure of Rabbi Eliahu and his beckoning for his son (his relation) that Eliezer is reminded, however fleetingly, of a world before the Holocaust—a world where a son would respond to the call of his father, a world where fathers and sons could exist. Upon Eliezer's entry into the anti-world surrounded by the barbed-wire electric fence, where he is immersed in death, everything about the world before the "eight spoken words" becomes not merely a soft echo, but a distorted one. Patterson describes this world as, "a world without the father—the world from which the Holocaust novel emerges—is a world without God and man."[57] It is inside the camp—"the world without God and man"—that a spoon held more value than a life, a bread ration thwarted a threat of death selections, and a dying father's cry to his son would be ignored. Through the third prophet figure, Rabbi Eliahu, Wiesel reveals how inside this anti-world, death became a dance rehearsed constantly and the "prophet of old" became the forgotten foreigner.

Eliezer Wiesel

The fourth prophet figure in *Night* is Eliezer Wiesel, himself—the protagonist of the novel. He represents the fourth dimension of the Holocaust: survival and the shattering of the anti-world. Patterson contends that the protagonist of *Night* "is a teller of tales not because of any 'literary' aspiration or even any 'artistic' endeavor. In his own words, he tells the tales 'in order not to go mad. Or, on the contrary, to touch the bottom of madness.'"[58] With this linking of storytelling to madness, Wiesel's words connect with those of the prophets. His urge and necessity to madly "tell" what he has witnessed mirrors the role of Moishe the Beadle, as well as that of prophet figures. Wiesel does not see himself as a prophet, yet the very narrative and message he tells through *Night* seems to earn him his place at that table. Wiesel described Jeremiah as one "who foresaw tragedy [like Mrs. Schächter], lived tragedy [like Moishe the Beadle and Wiesel], and remembered tragedy to write about it [like Wiesel's *Night*]."[59]

Like Jeremiah, the teller of the story of the destruction of the Temple during the early biblical age, Wiesel tells his story of tragedy and atrocity in *Night*: the child who had wept over the destruction of the Temple now tells the tale of the destruction of the Temple embodied by the people of Israel. Wiesel, like Jeramiah, is able to reflect on his life inside the anti-world of the Holocaust. Jeremiah saw and spoke of the world as it was and the world as it would become: "Then the Lord put forth his hand, and touched my mouth. And the Lord said unto me, Behold, I have put my words in thy mouth. See, I have this day set thee over the nations and over the kingdoms, to root out, and to pull down, and to destroy, and to throw down, to build, and to plant. Moreover the word of the Lord came unto me, saying, Jeremiah, what seest thou?"[60] Correspondingly, Wiesel's writing of *Night* is not merely a book of reflection; instead, it serves as a message issued from a world to which we, who were not there, otherwise have no access.

Night is a message given to its readers in hope that the atrocities and horrors mentioned in its pages might never, ever happen again. In the very act of writing his memoir, Wiesel evokes the role of the prophet whose message is a warning of what came and what could come again. Wiesel writes, "Having lived through this experience, one could not keep silent no matter how difficult, if not impossible, it was to speak."[61] On multiple occasions, Wiesel has referred to himself as a "storyteller," and

David Booth contends that "Elie Wiesel turn[ed] to storytelling as a way of finding meaning in the modern world. This conception of storytelling as a meaningful act comes from Hasidism's conception of storytelling as a religious act, as well as from earlier Midrashic traditions."[62] Booth's theory of religiosity is reflected in the various prophet figures in *Night*. Patterson further argues, "the storyteller himself enters into Aggadah, a messenger who entrusts the listener with a message to deliver and a truth to attest to."[63] Both Patterson and Booth tie this notion of Wiesel's storytelling to that of his religious background. For Wiesel, to bear witness is to write of his people, their experiences, and trials during the Holocaust. To be a witness is to "tell" their story.

Therefore, much like a prophet of old, Wiesel brings his message as a survivor, a witness, and the author of *Night*. The shattering of this anti-world—a world where a son (Elie) does not respond to his dying father's call for him: "Eliezer"—is essential to a return to the world where the prophet would readily answer, "*Hineni*—Here I am," when called by God, the heavenly Father. This anti-world will forever, as a corpse looking back from a mirror, confront the storyteller, and the reader, with the Horrors of what was done. Thus, like the other three prophet figures, Wiesel serves in warning all that hear his cry—a cry that is sounded through the words in *Night*—of the maliciousness that man is capable of inflicting upon other fellow human beings. As a prophet figure, Elie is burdened to tell his story of life inside the anti-world as a warning that if such atrocities and assaults on humanity took place in a "civilized" world of the twentieth century, then such atrocities and assaults might take place once again. His cry is one that enables the reader to join in telling the story, so that they may never bear the burden of the transformation of the prophet—the transformation that Eliezer recognized only in the "depths of a mirror" when he saw "a corpse [that] was contemplating [him]."[64]

Elie Wiesel's book *Night* is rife with religious and exegetical allusions; however, through his inclusion of these four prophet figures, he places his testimony and his narrative and his witnessed prophecy into the Jewish tradition. By creating these prophet figures, Wiesel evokes the prophets of the Bible, the prophets of his faith; he evokes the past and the present. Through the process of "telling a story," Wiesel does not merely allude to the authors of the previous centuries or even the authors whose Midrash and commentary have been passed down through the ages, but he evokes the very Word of God: "In the beginning God created the heaven and the earth . . . ," the story of the creation of the world—a world that became an anti-world and a world that could become an anti-world yet again.[65] Patterson contends "the aim of [Wiesel's] storytelling, however, is not to paralyze us [the readers] with fear but to enable us to live—by transforming us [the readers] into messengers."[66] Within this written narrative and the messages of the four prophet figures, Wiesel unravels the anti-world for his reader. Through Moishe the Beadle, Wiesel captured the prophet figure whose words of warning seemed like "madness" to all who heard him (those still living and believing in a world of humanity, justice, and mercy). Through Mrs. Schächter's cries and silence, Wiesel captured the prophet figure whose words of warning were wrought with confusion and disbelief to all who heard her (those in the train who were caught between the illusion of the world as it was and the soon-to-be anti-world it would become). Through Rabbi Eliahu, Wiesel captured the prophet figure whose very existence reminded those living in the anti-world about their faint memory of a world that was governed by community, humanity, and family. Finally, by bearing witness to the atrocities of the Holocaust, through his writings and storytelling, Eliezer Wiesel stands as the prophet figure whose words warn all who read them of the evil that man is capable of.

In *Five Biblical Portraits*, Wiesel discusses the burden of the story and being the witness when he writes:

> And what are we doing, we writers, we witnesses, we Jews? For over three thousand years we have been repeating the same story—the story of a solitary prophet who would have given anything, including his life, to be able to tell another kind of tale, one filled with joy and fervor rather than sorrow and anguish.[67]

It is with the weight of the storyteller and bearing the tale of "sorrow and anguish" that Wiesel writes *Night*. Like hands molding clay, these four prophet figures' warnings come together to shape an underlining narrative that is woven throughout *Night*—one that captures the physical, mental, and spiritual aspects of the Holocaust. It is through these prophet figures that *Night* becomes more than another memoir, more than a survivor's account of a specific time in his life, and more than a witness's account of the crimes. It is through the four prophet figures that *Night* becomes *the* Holocaust memoir for readers. *Night* is not a memoir about Elie Wiesel's life, but rather, it is an inverted memoir about Elie Wiesel's death—and the death of millions of others. Furthermore, characteristics and attributes of these prophet figures found in *Night* can also be seen in other works by Wiesel, as well as in other narratives of Holocaust literature. Through the prophecies and warnings of the four prophet figures, *Night* becomes a memoir that unravels the horrors, atrocities, and realities of Elie's life inside the anti-world of the Holocaust.

Notes

1. Douglas A. Knight and Amy-Jill Levine, *The Meaning of the Bible: What the Jewish Scriptures and Christian Old Testament Can Teach Us* (New York: HarperOne, 2011), 414.

2. Ludwig Koehler and Walter Baumgartner, *The Hebrew and Aramaic Lexicon of the Old Testament* (Leiden: E. J. Brill, 1994–2000), 661–62.

3. Knight and Levine, *The Meaning of the Bible*, 417.

4. Robert Franciosi, Brian Shaffer, and Elie Wiesel, "An Interview with Elie Wiesel," *Contemporary Literature* 28, no. 3 (1987): 289.

5. Franciosi, Shaffer, Wiesel, "An Interview with Elie Wiesel," 290.

6. Elie Wiesel, *Five Biblical Portraits* (Notre Dame: University of Notre Dame Press, 1981), 109, 100.

7. Martin Buber, *The Eclipse of God: Studies in the Relation of Religion to Philosophy*, trans. Maurice Friedman et al. (New York: Harper & Row, 1957), 73.

8. There is some debate over the classification of *Night* as memoir. See the introduction to this volume for an overview.

9. Josephine Knopp, "Wiesel and the Absurd," *Contemporary Literature* 15, no. 2 (1974): 212.

10. Elie Wiesel, *Night* (New York: Hill and Wang, 2006), 90.

11. Seymour M. Finger, "Elie Wiesel: Between Memory and Hope," *American Foreign Policy Newsletter* 13, no. 4 (1990): 14.

12. Robert McAfee Brown, "Twilight: Madness, Caprice, Friendship, and God," in *Elie Wiesel: Between Memory and Hope*, ed. Carol Rittner (New York: New York University Press, 1990), 180.

13. Finger, "Elie Wiesel," 14.

14. Albert Friedlander, "Biblical Dimensions in the Work of Elie Wiesel," *European Judaism* 12, no. 1 (1978): 20.

15. John K. Roth, "From *Night* to *Twilight*: A Philosopher's Reading of Elie Wiesel," *Religion and Literature* 24, no. 1 (1992): 62.

16. Michael Berenbaum, *The Vision of the Void: Theological Reflections on the Works of Elie Wiesel* (Middletown: Wesleyan University Press, 1979), 103–4.

17. Ka-tzetnik, *Shivitti: A Vision*, trans. Eliyah De-Nur and Lisa Herman (New York: Harper & Row, 1989), xi.
18. Wiesel, *Five Biblical Portraits*, 101.
19. Jer. 1:4–8 (King James Version).
20. Wiesel, *Night*, 7, 26.
21. David Patterson, "The Maggid of Sighet: Jewish Contexts for Wiesel's Storytelling," in *Elie Wiesel and the Art of Storytelling*, ed. Rosemary Horowitz (Jefferson: McFarland & Co., 2006), 102.
22. Wiesel, *Night*, 3.
23. Wiesel, *Night*, 7.
24. Knight and Levine, *The Meaning of the Bible*, 414.
25. Knight and Levine, *The Meaning of the Bible*, 7.
26. Knight and Levine, *The Meaning of the Bible*, 7.
27. Wiesel, *Night*, 5.
28. Wiesel, *Night*, 5.
29. Louis Jacobs, "The Doctrine of the 'Divine Spark' in Man in Jewish Sources," in *Studies in Rationalism, Judaism and Universalism*, ed. Raphael Loewe (London: Routledge and Kegan Paul, 1966), 87–114.
30. Wiesel, *Night*, 7.
31. Wiesel, *Night*, 115.
32. Wiesel, *Night*, 3.
33. Wiesel, *Night*, 7.
34. Wiesel, *Night*, 24.
35. Wiesel, *Night*, 24.
36. Hos. 9:7 (King James Version).
37. Knight and Levine, *The Meaning of the Bible*, 415.
38. Wiesel, *Night*, 24–28.
39. Ori Z. Soltes, *Mysticism in Judaism, Christianity, and Islam: Searching for Oneness* (Lanham: Rowman & Littlefield, 2008), 119.
40. Knight and Levine, *The Meaning of the Bible*, 150.
41. Patterson, "The Maggid of Sighet," 107.
42. Wiesel, *Night*, 28.
43. Knight and Levine, *The Meaning of the Bible*, 415.
44. Wiesel, *Night*, 29.
45. Wiesel, *Night*, 34.
46. Wiesel, *Night*, 34.
47. Jer. 26:8 (King James Version).
48. Wiesel, *Night*, 65.
49. Gen. 1:28; Ps. 127:3–5 (King James Version).
50. François Mauriac, "Forward to 'Night' by François Mauriac," The Night Holocaust Project, http://thenightholocaustproject.com/elie-wiesel/francois-mauriac-forward/ n.d., accessed 29 November 2018.

51. David Patterson, *Wrestling with the Angel: Toward a Jewish Understanding of the Nazi Assault on the Name* (St. Paul: Paragon House, 2006), 80.
52. Wiesel, *Night*, xi.
53. Wiesel, *Night*, 100, 92, 45.
54. Wiesel, *Night*, 90.
55. Wiesel, *Night*, 91.
56. David Patterson, *The Shriek of Silence* (Lexington: University Press of Kentucky, 1992), 54.
57. Patterson, *The Shriek of Silence*, 70.
58. Patterson, "The Maggid of Sighet," 108.
59. Robert Franciosi, ed., *Elie Wiesel: Conversations* (Jackson: University Press of Mississippi, 2002), 290.
60. Jer. 1:9–11 (King James Version).
61. Wiesel, *Night*, x.
62. David Booth, "The Role of the Storyteller: Sholem Aleichem and Elie Wiesel," *Judaism: A Quarterly Journal of Jewish Life and Thought* 167.42, no. 3 (1993): 304.
63. Patterson, "The Maggid of Sighet," 116.
64. Wiesel, *Night*, 115.
65. Gen. 1:1 (King James Version).
66. Patterson, "The Maggid of Sighet," 112.
67. Wiesel, *Five Biblical Portraits*, 127.

Works Cited

Berenbaum, Michael. *The Vision of the Void: Theological Reflections on the Works of Elie Wiesel*. 1st ed. Jaffe Holocaust Collection. Middletown: Wesleyan University Press, 1979.

Booth, David. "The Role of the Storyteller: Sholem Aleichem and Elie Wiesel." *Judaism: A Quarterly Journal of Jewish Life and Thought* 167.42, no. 3 (1993): 298–312.

Brown, Robert McAfee. "Twilight: Madness, Caprice, Friendship, and God." In *Elie Wiesel: Between Memory and Hope*, ed. Carol Rittner, 177–90. New York: New York University Press, 1990.

Buber, Martin. *The Eclipse of God: Studies in the Relation of Religion to Philosophy*. Trans. Maurice Friedman et al. New York: Harper & Row, 1957.

Finger, Seymour M. "Elie Wiesel: Between Memory and Hope." *American Foreign Policy Newsletter* 13, no. 4 (1990): 13–14.

Franciosi, Robert, ed. *Elie Wiesel: Conversations*. Jackson: University Press of Mississippi, 2002.

Franciosi, Robert, Brian Shaffer, and Elie Wiesel. "An Interview with Elie Wiesel." *Contemporary Literature* 28.3 (1987): 289–300.
Friedlander, Albert. "Biblical Dimensions in the Work of Elie Wiesel." *European Judaism* 12, no. 1 (1978): 19–23.
Friedman, Maurice. "Elie Wiesel's Messianism of the Unredeemed." *Judaism: A Quarterly Journal of Jewish Life and Thought* 38.3, no. 151 (1989): 310–19.
Jacobs, Louis. "The Doctrine of the 'Divine Spark' in Man in Jewish Sources." In *Studies in Rationalism, Judaism and Universalism*, ed. Raphael Loewe, 87–114. London: Routledge and Kegan Paul, 1966.
Ka-Tzetnik, 135633. *Shivitti: A Vision*. Nevada City, CA: Gateways/IDHHB, 1998.
Knight, Douglas A., and Amy-Jill Levine. *The Meaning of the Bible: What the Jewish Scriptures and Christian Old Testament Can Teach Us*. New York: HarperOne, 2011.
Knopp, Josephine. "Wiesel and the Absurd." *Contemporary Literature* 15.2 (1974): 212–20.
Koehler, Ludwig, and Walter Baumgartner. *The Hebrew and Aramaic Lexicon of the Old Testament*. Leiden: E. J. Brill, 1994–2000.
Mauriac, François "Forward to 'Night' by François Mauriac." The Night Holocaust Project. http://thenightholocaustproject.com/elie-wiesel/francois-mauriac-forward/ n.d. Accessed 29 November 2018.
Patterson, David. "The Maggid of Sighet: Jewish Contexts for Wiesel's Storytelling." In *Elie Wiesel and the Art of Storytelling*, ed. Rosemary Horowitz, 102–22. Jefferson: McFarland & Co., 2006.
Patterson, David. *Shriek of Silence*. Lexington: University Press of Kentucky, 1992.
Patterson, David. *Wresting with the Angel: Toward a Jewish Understanding of the Nazi Assault on the Name*. St. Paul: Paragon House, 2006.
Rittner, Carol. *Elie Wiesel: Between Memory and Hope*. Jaffe Holocaust Collection. New York: New York University Press, 1990.
Roth, John K. "From *Night* to *Twilight*: A Philosopher's Reading of Elie Wiesel." *Religion and Literature* 24, no. 1 (1992): 59–73.
Soltes, Ori Z. *Mysticism in Judaism, Christianity, and Islam: Searching for Oneness*. Lanham: Rowman & Littlefield, 2008.
The Holy Bible: King James Version. Iowa Falls: World Bible Publishers, 2001.
Wiesel, Elie. *Five Biblical Portraits*. Notre Dame: University of Notre Dame Press, 1981.
Wiesel, Elie. *Night*. New York: Hill and Wang, 2006.

Part II

The Other

4

Embracing Madness

Elie Wiesel's Madmen and Their Role in His Works

Jennifer Murray

In the preface to the Hill and Wang 2006 edition of *Night*, Wiesel ponders his purpose for writing the memoir, saying, "Did I write it so as *not* to go mad or, on the contrary, to *go* mad in order to understand the nature of madness, the immense, terrifying madness that had erupted in history and in the conscience of mankind."[1] Here Wiesel evokes World War II, complete with the immense, terrifying, and largely hegemonic madness of Nazism and the Holocaust the Nazis perpetrated. Whether his writing was a protection against his own madness or a way to safely explore the madness mankind experienced during and after the Holocaust, all of Wiesel's books—fiction and nonfiction alike—address the question of madness.[2] Wiesel's exploration of mad characters begins in *Night* and carries on into his fiction, where the theme of madness remains present throughout much of Wiesel's oeuvre.[3] Wiesel explores madness in far more detail in his novel *The Town Beyond the Wall* than perhaps in most, employing a large cast of characters plagued by various forms of madness. Still, many more of Wiesel's texts provide additional pieces of the puzzle of meaning behind his use of madmen in his literature. *The Time of the Uprooted*, *The Forgotten*, *Twilight*, and "Zalmen, or the Madness of God" join many others in featuring mad characters in one form or another. In this chapter I will first offer an understanding of the forms of madness represented in Wiesel's texts. Then, I will explore in more detail Wiesel's specific representations of madness and madmen in

The Town Beyond the Wall. By offering readers a look into the mind of a central character, Michael, who narrates the world around him through the prism of madness, *The Town Beyond the Wall* provides an ideal starting point for identifying the many varying roles fulfilled by madmen in Wiesel's body of work.

Madness

In order to properly evaluate the representation of madness in Wiesel's works, we must first establish an understanding of madness. Whether it be mad characters in a text, or authors writing because of (or in a desperate attempt to avoid) a slip into madness themselves, madness and literature have enjoyed a long, well-documented history together. Thus, for the sake of space, I will not undertake a comprehensive study of the history of madness here as this has been done extensively elsewhere. Instead, I will point to the few key features of madness that inform my own definitions and proceed from there.

Shoshana Felman discusses madness in terms of its relationship to psychoanalysis, philosophy, and literature, each in its turn. She first provides a framework for understanding madness as a function of philosophy. Much of this framework is based on Michel Foucault's first major work, *Madness and Civilization: A History of Insanity in the Age of Reason*, which exhaustively traces and defines the cultural, political, and even literary history of madness through the eighteenth century. Though Foucault's historical study makes clear that madness being "released from its 'physical chains'" and "reduced to the diminished status of 'mental illness'" in the late eighteenth century was simply substituting one form of confinement for another, Felman suggests that what was at truly at stake was "the philosophical search for a *new status of discourse*, [. . .] a discourse which would obliterate the line of demarcation and the opposition between Subject and Object, Inside and Outside, *Reason and Madness*."[4]

The coexistence of madness and literature is especially prevalent in literatures of the Holocaust. Despite this prevalence, however, the representations are far from monolithic. Carole J. Lambert positions the figure of the madman as a citizen of "a dark world," situated within the "hate, despair, violence, injustice, [. . .] falsity, and indifference" of the post-Holocaust world.[5] This description lends an air of desperation and hopelessness to the madman; Wiesel's approach to madness is far more generous. He utilizes madness in a manner that illuminates and reveals what is hidden by the shadows of the dark world Lambert describes. In "Darkness That Eclipses Light," a chapter from his 1994 book, *Elie Wiesel: Messenger to All Humanity*, Robert McAfee Brown introduces us to three basic categories of madness. Brown describes the first as "being so out of touch with one's surroundings as to be unable to function within them, cut off from the ability to respond or communicate" and notes that this type of madness is sometimes referred to as "clinical" madness.[6] Brown then points us to "moral madness," a term coined by Abraham Heschel, which refers to "the madness of the Hebrew prophets."[7] Finally, the madness Wiesel has termed "mystical madness," which is characterized by Brown as being embodied by "those whom the world calls 'mad.' [. . . those who] live by a different vision and challenge the existing order in the name of that vision. They are spokespersons for the divine and purveyors of a truth all persons need to hear."[8] Each type of madness holds different impacts and applications. For example, for his own purposes, Wiesel is careful in his definitions and clearly distinguishes mystical madness from the moral madness that became necessary in the Germany of 1943 by saying: "When hate and indifference are the norm in society, one must become morally mad to protest against society's inhumanity. [. . .] One had to choose moral madness to avoid being swallowed up by the prevailing 'sanity.' "[9]

Drawing on Foucault's historical work, Felman argues that historically, "literary knowledge mirrors psychiatric knowledge and in many ways competes with it," alternatively seeming to position the author as psychiatrist and antipsychiatrist."[10] This chapter will not, however, seek to position Wiesel as either psychiatrist or antipsychiatrist but rather will look to his reliance on certain psychological norms in building his characters. Despite the complex history of madness, using solely the definitions of madness that Wiesel himself has provided, it seems clear that madness is a condition of protected interiority, imposed, if not fully constructed, from within, that is based at least in part on an unwillingness or inability to comply or conform to the conditions or expectations of one's surroundings. Often, and especially in the case of Wiesel's mad characters, this condition of madness reveals to others a truth that is hidden from sight. Felman further states that the literary madman is "most often disguised as a philosopher: in literature, the role of madness, then, is eminently philosophical."[11] For Felman this clarifies the problematic relationship between the two disciplines of literature and philosophy. Madmen figure centrally in Wiesel's texts, but he does not employ madness in the same way across his canon. Indeed, he represents each type of madness defined earlier at various times and in various texts, particularly in *The Town Beyond the Wall*, which is not only populated by mad characters but also narrated by a character who is fighting madness himself. In a 2009 interview with the *LA Times*, Wiesel explains his affection for mad characters by saying, "These were the first people to be taken away [. . .]. Children, old people, madmen. I give them shelter in my books; there is always a place for them. They haunt my universe and I say, 'Come in.'"[12]

In an interview for PBS with Gary Henry, Wiesel uses a Hasidic tale to reiterate his belief in the long-standing existence of a mystical madness—"the madness of an individual who has seen things inaccessible to others."[13] As Henry notes, "this is the position that a Holocaust survivor finds himself in when he tells his tale."[14] This state of mystical madness was indeed the position that Elie Wiesel found himself in when he began to tell his tale in the memoir *Night*. Wiesel's experience in the camps is relayed autobiographically in *Night*, placing the author in the position of mystical madman, tasked with finding the words to express an experience inaccessible to others. As noted by Mueller elsewhere in this volume, there are two primary characters in *Night* who exhibit symptoms of madness: Madame Schächter and Moishe the Beadle. By including these characters, Wiesel clearly represents his long-held assertion that the mad often reveal the truth.[15] Moishe came back to his village with warnings of the danger that awaited the Jews. His warnings were ignored and he was considered mad. Many years later, Wiesel would reiterate the sheer inability of the people of Sighet to believe the stories Moishe told upon his return to the village, saying "people thought he was crazy."[16] Wiesel reminds us that the villagers, even then, had no idea what was happening in the deportations and even though Moishe spoke the truth it was simply too inconceivable to believe. Similarly, in *Night*, Madame Schächter shouted prophetic warnings of fire and flame to the Jews on the train.[17] Again, in the face of their circumstances, they dismissed her warnings and thought her mad, although she was, in fact, revealing the truth.

Over the course of the next several decades, Wiesel continues to write and continues to incorporate madness in his tales. Despite the concern he expresses for his own sanity in his preface to *Night*, Wiesel carefully warns against the flippant ascription of madness to others by reminding us that sometimes in the "dissent from the 'collective neurosis' of [a] society [gone mad], the sane person will be judged mad, even though it is society and not he that suffers from skewed vision."[18] His warning, however, does not restrict him from incorporating madness into his narratives. In *The Forgotten*, for example, Wiesel twists the idea of madness into the shape of Alzheimer's by dissolving memory and creating a desperation to recall in the character of Elhanan.[19] In *Twilight*, Wiesel combines mysticism with madness to shape the storyworld of the protagonist, Raphael.[20] Raphael is both a teacher and a student of mysticism who moves into an asylum with schizophrenics—many who imagine themselves to be biblical figures—in order to study the link between mysticism and madness.[21] Although Raphael eventually begins to question his own sanity, Wiesel's affection for madmen can even be seen to figure into his characterization of non-mad characters. *The Time of the Uprooted*, for example, introduces us to Gamaliel, who, though not mad himself,

> delight[s] in madmen. I love to see their crazed, melancholy faces and to hear their bewitching voices, which arouse in me forbidden images and desires. Or rather, it's not the madness itself I love, but those it possesses, those whose souls it claims, as if to show them the limits of their possibilities [. . .]. Some fear them, and so put them away where no one can hear them cry out.[22]

In addition, one of Wiesel's two dramas, "Zalmen, or the Madness of God," features a rabbi who is not considered mad but who holds the mad character Zalmen in high affection, offering him shelter within the synagogue. Ultimately, it is Zalmen who "rekindles in the [rabbi] a prophetic fire."[23] These examples comprise a small fraction of Wiesel's corpus but distinctly reflect his stated desire to invite the elements of madness in his writing.

It is clear the madmen in Wiesel's texts are not fragile and weak, passively receiving the benefit of shelter by Wiesel; they are doing important work. Wiesel has often forged a connection between madness and God, using madmen as the conveyers of divine wisdom and knowledge inaccessible to others as in "Zalmen." Further, Wiesel often ties the madman with the unheard witness, as he does with Moishe the Beadle and Madame Schächter in *Night*. Are the madmen in his novels, then, meant to be representative of God and faith, or are they simply the literary "other" meant to represent one of the defining principles Wiesel concluded through his *din torah*: If we can't dialogue with the "other," what business have we approaching God?[24] Alternatively, Wiesel has said we are most truly human when we are weak and when we try to overcome weakness, so could it be that in embracing the madman in his novels he is showing through their presumed weaknesses their basic humanity?[25] Or is it quite simply, as Colin Davis notes, that "the madmen of Wiesel's novels are captivating storytellers, and as such they serve to represent the storytelling impulse of the novelist himself"?[26] The answer to these questions of authorial intent can never be completely clear to the reader—indeed, they may not even be entirely relevant—and yet, as Wiesel so often notes, asking questions often reveals more than answers. For our purposes, the questions remain alongside the fact that Wiesel has quite intentionally made a path in his storyworlds for both the madmen and the madness itself.

Often, and in varying ways, the madness and the madmen serve to uniquely advance the narrative and to provide a framework for exploring these various roles, often conveying unconventional wisdom that is easily overlooked. The inclusion of madness and madmen is clear in *The Town Beyond the Wall*, perhaps clearer in this text with its large cast of mad characters than in most. Before examining the characters, however, we must situate ourselves within the narrative itself.

The Town Beyond the Wall

In *The Town Beyond the Wall*, Wiesel is building on the foundations he established in his previous novels toward an understanding of humanity in the post-Holocaust world and is beginning to form a new realization: that man cannot be truly alone. Everything before *The Town Beyond the Wall* has focused on the internal, the self. His writing thus far has centered on the darkness, the pain, the brokenness of the self, and being alone in the world (or what's left of it). In *The Town Beyond the Wall*, Wiesel begins to move to the external: truly observing, evaluating, and engaging the "other." In *The Town Beyond the Wall*, Wiesel begins to turn toward light and healing and a chance at finding community again, and he does so through the veil of madness.

The opening paragraph of *The Town Beyond the Wall* briefly places the reader in a twilight scene that we quickly learn is little more than a memory evoked by the narrator, Michael, a Hungarian Jew who survived the Holocaust only to later be subjected to imprisonment and torture by Communist occupiers in Hungary after he illegally crossed the border back into his hometown of Szerencsevaros, twenty years after the war ended. As a method of interrogation and torture, the Communist occupiers in Hungary force prisoners, particularly Jewish prisoners, to stand facing a wall for "a day, two days, three [. . . until] in the end, they talk."[27] This torture technique is referred to as "The Prayer," and it "consist[s] of breaking the prisoner's resistance by keeping him on his feet until he pass[es] out. The torture [bears] the name of prayer because the Jews pray standing."[28] Despite being frequently accosted by the guard on duty demanding he speak and harshly warning "most prisoners break within twenty-four hours,"[29] Michael commits to himself that he will last three days because that is the time it will take to save his friend, Pedro. Throughout the text, narration fluidly shifts between the present time in the prison and a revisiting of scenes from Michael's past. From the beginning, the narrator refers to these analeptic moments as "Michael [going] back to his city," or "return[ing] to his pictures."[30] In these moments, the reader meets many of the novel's mad characters.

While perhaps the Silent One and the Impatient One, two of the three mad characters who appear latest in the novel, are the easiest to be recognized as mad, Robert McAfee Brown carefully draws our attention to several other mad characters deserving of attention: Martha, Old Varady, Kalman, and Moishe. First, Old Martha, the town drunk who lives her life "in submission to impulse," and, as Brown tells us, under an "organizing principle [of] chaos."[31] Old Martha is the first character to whom we are introduced, even before Michael himself. Indeed, she is not only the first character introduced; she is the first *clearly mad* character. She returns again and again in a flurry of drunkenness, nudity, and shrieking. She is a frightening and sad character who is perhaps most representative of the dark madness Lambert describes. She frightens Michael, even as he is entranced by her.[32] Martha easily represents the other—so unlike Michael that she is incomprehensible.

The reader must wait a mere ten pages before being introduced to the next mad character. Moishe, the village's crazy man who is the highly coveted guest for Shabbat, joins Michael's family for dinner. He introduces himself as "Moishe the Madman" and asks Michael if he is afraid of crazy men. When Michael answers "no," Moishe responds: "That's good. [. . .] You should never be afraid of other people, even if they are crazy beyond the pale. The one man you have to be afraid of is yourself."[33] This warning is passed over as the ramblings of a self-proclaimed madman and nearly forgotten, despite the ominous "Who says the others aren't you? Who says Moishe the Madman isn't you?"[34] Michael's father describes Moishe in terms of the mystical madman: "He sees worlds that remain inaccessible to us. His madness is only a wall, erected to protect us—*us*: to see what Moishe's bloodshot eyes see would be dangerous."[35]

In his brief examination of Wiesel's mad characters, Brown also points to Old Varady. Old Varady is described by Stanford V. Sternlicht as a "slightly mad [neighbor], who greatly influences Michael in his adolescence. Varady claims to be immortal [. . . ,] sees other men as weak[,] and admires other men only when they, like him, are willing to challenge even the universe."[36] And finally, Brown draws our attention to Kalman, the town's mystic teacher, who "renounces reason at the start in order to find it later, embellished and vigorous, at the heart of madness," and to whom we will later return, along with his three students who are notably absent in Brown's list of mad characters in this novel.[37]

It is not only mad characters who display unpredictable and divergent characteristics in *The Town Beyond the Wall*, however. It is necessary, therefore, to examine the narrative techniques of the text that contribute to the theme of madness. As noted earlier, the narration itself shifts unpredictably in perspective, time, and place, with few cues initially apparent to the reader apart from certain italicized portions, which represent the first-person narration of Michael's conversations with Pedro. In a discussion of narrator authority, Seymour Chatman notes that even omniscient narrators are limited by questions of space and time. Limitations of space contend with whether the narrator is "allowed to report only one scene at a time [. . .], shift freely back and forth between scenes in an attempt to convey simultaneous actions [. . .], [or] spatially summariz[e] what has happened."[38] Limitations of time may restrict the narrator to "the contemporary story moment, retrospectively seen, or [. . . to allow him] to range into past or future, either through specific scenes, or through summaries, speaking of events of long duration or iteration in only a sentence or two, or, contrarily, expanding events in such a way that it takes longer to read about them than it took them to occur."[39] Michael's narration of events covers the entire spectrum of limitations that Chatman describes. Certain moments in the narrative present Michael as a character-narrator, self-aware and referring to himself as "I" while talking to Pedro. This limits the narrative to Michael's perspective in the place and time of the moment the conversation takes place. However, even in the third-person narration the reader is limited to what Michael knows, what Michael remembers, and what Michael understands, effectively revealing him to be the exclusive point of view character throughout all diegetic levels. Eventually, despite the extensive character list and the shifts in narratorial perspective, the reader comes to realize that the narration has been exclusively provided by Michael, who continues to serve in the capacity of a homodiegetic narrator with varying degrees of focalization. Just as Chatman suggests, Michael is limited by time and space, although the degree to which this limitation applies often varies. Furthermore, the narration's frequent shifts often seem to conflate these features as well. This divergence from the expected limitations of narration begins to give the reader an indication of Michael's state of mind. The influence of madness has begun to affect the limits of narrative.

As the story progresses, it becomes increasingly important to remember that the narrator is still Michael, whether in memory or imagination, explaining the events of the storyworld: We never see what is happening in other parts of the prison or get the interiority of any other characters—neither the guards, the other prisoners in the present, nor the people who exist in the many recalled vignettes of Michael's past—we only see what is in Michael's head. At a certain point in the narrative Michael recalls the feeling "that if he were to live another life he would like to be a teller of tales."[40] Indeed, through the narration of *The Town Beyond the Wall*, Michael has become a captivating teller of tales, though the reliability of his narration must be called into question.

Hence, with this understanding of Michael's role and his limitation as a character-narrator, we can begin to position Michael as a lens for analysis of the text. Before we begin, however, it is important to remember the framing we have already been given for the syuzhet: we are in the mind of a man under torture trying to survive *three* days to save his friend. The number three is not insignificant. As an adolescent, Michael studied religion and mysticism with Kalman, the town mystic who taught his disciples lessons from the *Mussar*, the Talmud, and the *Zohar*.[41] It is reasonable to expect that those studies would include the

88 / Jennifer Murray

study of gematria, the Jewish system of numerology in which "numbers are used to reveal messages in texts."[42] Through gematria it is understood that the number three corresponds to the third letter of the Hebrew alphabet, *gimel*, and thus signifies "bestowal/reward" of a kindness.[43] An examination of the text reveals a repetition of threes that reflect the concept of bestowal of kindness or reward.

Threes

Beginning with Michael's desire to survive three days of prayer, threes recur early in the text and become fewer as we progress further into the narrative. The desire to survive three days is representative of a kindness paid to Pedro in return for his friendship. After the introduction of Mad Moishe in the chapter entitled "First Prayer," Michael narrates his first encounter of actually talking with the madman. During this encounter, Michael offers Moishe three bottles of wine, which Moishe gladly accepts, although Moishe is the village's most desirable "poor" guest for Shabbat dinner, and just by accepting the invitation to dinner "Moishe behaves as though he were conferring a favor."[44] The significance of three bottles may be reflective of the additional "act of beneficence" bestowed on him by Michael as symbolized by the Hebrew letter *gimel*.[45]

Other examples of three appearing in the narrative include Michael's employment as a Hebrew tutor for three lessons and the three slips back to the present in the prison in "Second Prayer."[46] Despite including conversations between them throughout the narrative, Michael finally narrates meeting Pedro in "Third Prayer." It is at this point that the reader learns that Pedro specifically defines for Michael the three-day period: "In case you're arrested [. . .] try to hold out three days. Enough time for the guides to cross the border or disappear."[47] In striving to fulfill Pedro's wishes, Michael is attempting to bestow a kindness upon his friend: he wants to repay Pedro for his help in making the journey to Szerencseváros by ensuring that Pedro is not also arrested.

Gimel may also represent the "divine flow of goodness that pours down to the universe from on high," which can be exemplified in Kalman and his two disciples, Hersh-Leib and Menashe, who together form a three-character grouping.[48] These characters have been proclaimed mad and dangerous by the village, and Michael must fight his father for the ability to enter their society. In this case, by seeking them out despite the cautions of the village, Michael becomes the recipient of the reward of divine knowledge: knowledge that flows down through studying with the master and his disciples, who in turn bestow their mystic wisdom upon him.

3 + 1

The addition of Michael to Kalman's two existing students represents the addition of one more person to their existing group of three. Just as gematria provides a hermeneutic for ascribing meaning to the number three through the Hebrew letter *gimel*, 3 + 1 is "a number cluster that signals the fulfillment of God's plans."[49] Though what plan this addition is fulfilling is not immediately apparent, it is clear from the narrative that the time spent studying with Kalman as a child provides a spiritual foundation for Michael, who will return to and rely upon the wisdom and knowledge he received through this study, even subconsciously, throughout his life.

The structure of the narrative also exemplifies this 3+1 idea. We know that Michael intends to last three days in order to save Pedro, and we know through his narration that he has survived three Prayers toward this end. Nonetheless, at the end of "Third Prayer," after the introduction of the third officer signaling the completion of twenty-four hours, Michael finally collapses. And yet, his collapse does not signal the end of narration. More specifically, after the three chapters representing the three "Prayers," there is a fourth and final section: "The Last Prayer."

In "The Last Prayer," with little indication other than his collapse, Michael awakes to "a sad-faced man [. . .] shaking him frantically."[50] He is now in a cell with three other prisoners, having effectively survived the Prayers in the temple. Again, he is one man added to the existing three in the group. The three prisoners Michael meets in the cell are in varying stages of madness. And here, in the cell, Michael's own madness becomes clearer.

Michael as Madman

Several scholars read *The Town Beyond the Wall* as a narrative of friendship and of hope, one in which Michael successfully evades a descent into madness in the end.⁵¹ These themes of friendship and hope are certainly present in the text; however, it is also clear that Michael is, in fact, struggling against madness from the very beginning. As a Holocaust survivor, it is reasonable to expect Michael has seen things inaccessible to others, even if his wartime experiences are not specifically narrated within this text. Thus, a component of mystical madness can be ascribed to Michael from the beginning. Notwithstanding this leap to extradiegetic factors, the progression of his narrative itself reflects that he does not actually evade but ultimately succumbs to madness. It is only through his efforts in "The Last Prayer" to draw the Silent One out of the confines of his madness that Michael himself begins to emerge from madness as well.

Wiesel initiates the reader into his storyworld by offering a quote from Dostoevsky as the epigraph: "I have a plan—to go mad."⁵² This paratextual information keys the reader into madness as a primary theme of the novel right from the very start. A series of analepses and hallucinations directs the reader along Michael's path and reveals his struggles against madness. According to Felman, madness is "blindness blind to itself, to the point of necessarily entailing an illusion of reason."⁵³ We can see this feature clearly as evidence of Michael's madness appears early in the text and persists throughout. Indeed, in the "First Prayer" we learn that Hersh-Leib is "the first of *three* students to lose his mind," and less than three months later it was Menashe's turn.⁵⁴ Michael, we know, is Kalman's third student. The narrative suggests "the Germans saved [Michael]" from sharing their mad fate.⁵⁵ In actuality, Michael is indeed the third of Kalman's students to descend into madness, it just takes the reader longer to work that out. This knowledge is effectively veiled by Michael's narration.

Still, it is not an intentional obfuscation of Michael's reality. Instead, the narration simply and clearly follows Michael's descent into madness, becoming more imaginative, perhaps even more unreliable, the further into the tale we go. It is only through retrospect that the reader can identify all the indicators of madness. The time and space of the narrative are constantly at issue, as Michael notes, "These jumps from one world to another had killed all sense of time."⁵⁶ Michael begins in "First Prayer" by fairly rapidly navigating between the present in the prison, the memories of his past, and his imagined conversations with Pedro. The speed and ease with which the narrative shifts are altered in "Second Prayer," with Michael lingering much longer in the world of his imagination: he slips back into the present only three brief times and his two conversations with Pedro remain centered on Michael's struggle with madness and divine will. In "Third Prayer," when he finally narrates his meeting with Pedro, conversations between the two appear solely in the analepsis, not in italicized conversations, suggesting that it is actually a memory that Michael is recalling, unlike the conversations thus far. As the narrative progresses into "Third Prayer," the stories Michael, the character-narrator, relays become more and more convoluted, and with increasingly blurred boundaries, and the italicized conversations with Pedro are nonexistent. Examination of Michael's narrative analepses, as well as his conversations with Pedro, support the idea that he has been slipping deeper into madness all along, losing contact with the present and effectively incapable of functioning within it.

Familiarity with Dostoevsky will afford the reader another bit of received wisdom to consider: *only the mad can see ghosts*. We can recall the words of Svidrigaïlov, who noted, "They say, 'You are ill, so what appears to you is only unreal fantasy.' But that's not strictly logical. I agree that *ghosts only appear to the sick*, but that only proves that they are unable to appear except to the sick, not that they don't exist."[57] During their times of italicized conversation, Michael *sees* Pedro, both in the temple during the Prayers and in the cell when he is no longer subjected to torture. Initially the conversations are easily read as another form of analeptic moment. However, in "The Last Prayer" when the italicized conversations return, Michael again sees Pedro, no longer presumed as memory or flashback but present in the cell and commenting on the current events taking place there. This cannot be possible unless Michael is hallucinating in a fit of madness.

From the very first of their italicized conversations, Michael and Pedro discuss God and madness:

> "You like to talk about God?"
> "You know I do."
> "Then go on. Go on, Pedro. Talk to me about God."
> "God, little brother, is the weakness of strong men and the strength of weak men."
> "What about men? Do you like to talk about men too?"
> "You know I do?"
> "Then talk to me about men."
> "Man is God's strength. Also His weakness."[58]

In the beginning, Pedro speaks to Michael about God, and Michael, in turn, explains to Pedro that madmen are beloved by God, noting, "they're the only ones he allows near him."[59] In the end, Pedro encourages Michael to save The Silent One: "re-create the universe. Restore that boy's sanity. Cure him. He'll save you."[60] Carole J. Lambert suggests that "Wiesel's novel ends without showing Michael daring to communicate, one on one, to God."[61] On the contrary, however, the ongoing conversations that Michael imagines with Pedro throughout the narrative can be read as his attempts to communicate with God. Michael reveals through his third-person narration that he once had the urge to ask Pedro if he is God, and his conversations and questions throughout would seem, by extension, to represent his attempts to communicate with God during his darkest moments at the wall.[62] Nonetheless, throughout the novel, Pedro is shown as a reliable vehicle for conversations pertaining to matters of faith. Through his relationship with Pedro, Michael is taught that no one really walks alone and that there must be a connection to others. Pedro serves as his guide from darkness to light, isolation to community, pain and brokenness to recovery and a road to healing.

In prison, Michael clings to his loyalty to Pedro in order to stay silent during the prayers. Pedro is Michael's reason to survive in prison—he will not betray Pedro, he must keep the promise he made. It is when he is moved to the cell with the other three prisoners, however, that he truly begins to look beyond himself. Menachem, the only other prisoner in the cell whose name is offered, consistently urges Michael to be vigilant and serves as a reminder to Michael that he must return to faith, saying he would rather blaspheme than be without God. Menachem is a clear example of Wiesel's approach to his *din torah*—always with God. While Menachem signals a return to faith for Michael, his characterization is one of the God-intoxicated prophet afflicted with moral madness.

Shortly after these urgings from Menachem, Michael resumes conversations with Pedro. When The Impatient One tries to kill Menachem, Michael saves his life, but barely avoids taking The Impatient One's life in the process. Later, at Pedro's urging, Michael reaches out to The Silent One to draw him from his silence. Pedro teaches Michael that he must reach out to others, and Michael ultimately becomes for The Silent One what Menachem and Pedro had been to him: a chance to move out of the darkness and toward the path of healing. In the end, Michael learns that to redeem himself from madness he must try to save the *other* madman in the cell with him.

The Town Beyond the Wall features madmen representative of each of the types and roles discussed thus far. The prisoners, The Impatient One and The Silent One, were perhaps the clearest echoes of the people that Wiesel would have encountered in the camps during the Holocaust, each representative of the mystical madness experienced by those who have seen things inaccessible to others. The prisoners join the many other madmen in the text: the God-intoxicated Kalman, who guides adolescents to and through questions of faith; Moishe, himself a mystical madman who not only represents the "other" but encourages dialogue with and identification of the other in ourselves; and Menachem and Pedro, who provide an ongoing link to matters of faith and a reminder to look outside ourselves. Although Wiesel has said that no one character defines him—rather, he suggests, "all the characters together define me"—Michael, with his struggle against madness, certainly embodies the paradoxical position Wiesel proposes in his preface to *Night*: Michael not only struggles against madness, he touches it and ultimately begins to find his way back through the wisdom of all the other madmen he met along the way.[63] *The Town Beyond the Wall* clearly reflects Wiesel's affection for madmen and the complicated place they hold in the post-Holocaust world. No matter the role they play, Wiesel embraces madmen and encourages the reader to do the same.

Notes

1. Elie Wiesel, *Night*, trans. Marion Wiesel (New York: Hill and Wang, 2006), vii. For a discussion of *Night* as memoir, see the introduction to this volume.

2. While the term "madman" is inherently gendered male by the suffix "-man," its use in this essay is not intended to convey any meanings or expectations of gender. Wiesel utilized both male and female mad characters, but he regularly referred to them as *madmen*. This essay follows his lead in using the term.

3. See Mary Catherine Mueller, "The Role of the Four Prophet Figures in *Night*," chapter 3 in this volume.

4. Shoshana Felman, *Writing and Madness: Literature/Philosophy/Psychoanalysis* (Paolo Alto: Stanford University Press, 2003), 40–42, emphasis added.

5. Carole J. Lambert, "Friendship and Hope: Elie Wiesel's *The Town Beyond the Wall*," in *The Gift of Story: Narrating Hope in a Postmodern World*, ed. Emily Griesinger and Mark A. Eaton (Waco: Baylor University Press, 2006), 163–64.

6. Robert McAfee Brown, *Elie Wiesel: Messenger to All Humanity* (South Bend: University of Notre Dame Press, 1989), 75.

7. Brown, *Elie Wiesel*, 75.

8. Brown, *Elie Wiesel*, 75.

9. Gary Henry, "Story and Silence: Transcendence in the Work of Elie Wiesel," *PBS*, http://www.pbs.org/eliewiesel/life/henry.html, accessed 30 June 2017.

10. Felman, *Writing and Madness*, 3.

11. Felman, *Writing and Madness*, 37.

12. Susan Salter Reynolds, "Elie Wiesel: Embracing Memory and Madness," *Los Angeles Times*, 22 February 2009, http://www.latimes.com/entertainment/la-ca-elie-wiesel22-2009feb22-story.html, accessed 30 June 2017.

13. Henry, "Story and Silence."

14. Henry, "Story and Silence."

15. In "Stultifera Navis," the first chapter of *Madness and Civilization*, Foucault begins his detailed examination of the history of madness. Significantly, he notes the appearance during the Renaissance of the "Ship of Fools, a strange 'drunken boat' that glides along the calm rivers of the Rhineland and the Flemish canals" (8). Foucault describes the Ship of Fools as a literary composition, which was "probably borrowed from the old Argonaut cycle," populated by a "crew of imaginary heroes, ethical models, or social types [who] embarked on a great symbolic voyage which would bring them, if not fortune, then at least the figure of their destiny or *their truth*" (8–9), emphasis added.

16. "Elie Wiesel," telephone interview by author, 20 March 2013.

17. Wiesel, *Night*, 25.

18. Henry, "Story and Silence."

19. Elie Wiesel, *The Forgotten* (New York: Schocken Books, 1995).

20. Elie Wiesel, *Twilight: A Novel*, trans. Marion Wiesel (New York: Schocken Books, 1995).

21. Wiesel, *Twilight*.

22. Elie Wiesel, *The Time of the Uprooted* (New York: Schocken Books, 2007).

23. Anson H. Laytner, *Arguing with God: A Jewish Tradition* (Lanham: Rowman & Littlefield, 2007), 224.

24. Wiesel's entire body of work constitutes a literary *din torah*, a trial of God. Significantly, Wiesel stressed that his *din torah* comes from inside the Jewish faith: always questioning, and always *for God* or *against God* but never *without God*. As he states in a March 20, 2013, interview, "I may resent God but cannot live without Him."

25. Bill Moyers, "Facing Hate with Elie Wiesel," BillMoyers.com, 27 November 1991, http://billmoyers.com/content/facing-hate-with-elie-wiesel/, accessed 30 June 2017.

26. Colin Davis, *Elie Wiesel's Secretive Texts* (Gainesville: University Press of Florida, 1994), 110.

27. Elie Wiesel, *The Town Beyond the Wall* (New York: Avon Books, 1964), 8.

28. Wiesel, *The Town Beyond the Wall*, 11–12.
29. Wiesel, *The Town Beyond the Wall*, 12.
30. Wiesel, *The Town Beyond the Wall*, 7, 8.
31. Brown, *Elie Wiesel*, 75.
32. Wiesel, *The Town Beyond the Wall*, 8.
33. Wiesel, *The Town Beyond the Wall*, 20.
34. Wiesel, *The Town Beyond the Wall*, 20.
35. Wiesel, *The Town Beyond the Wall*, 18.
36. Stanford V. Sternlicht, *Student Companion to Elie Wiesel* (Westport: Greenwood Press, 2003), 62.
37. Wiesel, *The Town Beyond the Wall*, 45.
38. Seymour Chatman, *Story and Discourse: Narrative Structure in Fiction and Film* (Ithaca: Cornell University Press, 1978), 212.
39. Chatman, *Story and Discourse*, 212.
40. Wiesel, *The Town Beyond the Wall*, 112.
41. Wiesel, *The Town Beyond the Wall*, 47.
42. Geoffrey W. Dennis, *The Encyclopedia of Jewish Myth, Magic and Mysticism* (Woodbury: Llewellyn, 2007), 105.
43. Dennis, *The Encyclopedia of Jewish Myth, Magic and Mysticism*, 105, 108.
44. Wiesel, *The Town Beyond the Wall*, 18.
45. Dennis, *The Encyclopedia of Jewish Myth, Magic and Mysticism*, 108.
46. Wiesel, *The Town Beyond the Wall*, 66.
47. Wiesel, *The Town Beyond the Wall*, 135.
48. Dennis, *The Encyclopedia of Jewish Myth, Magic and Mysticism*, 108.
49. Dennis, *The Encyclopedia of Jewish Myth, Magic and Mysticism*, 188.
50. Wiesel, *The Town Beyond the Wall*, 143.
51. Lambert, Sternlicht, and others have published essays to this end.
52. Wiesel, *The Town Beyond the Wall*.
53. Felman, *Writing and Madness*, 36.
54. Wiesel, *The Town Beyond the Wall*, 51–52, emphasis added.
55. Wiesel, *The Town Beyond the Wall*, 52.
56. Wiesel, *The Town Beyond the Wall*, 7.
57. Fyodor Dostoevsky, *Crime and Punishment*, Gutenberg.org, 28 March 2006, https://www.gutenberg.org/files/2554/2554-h/2554-h.htm, part 4, chapter 1, emphasis added, accessed 30 June 2017.
58. Wiesel, *The Town Beyond the Wall*, 13.
59. Wiesel, *The Town Beyond the Wall*, 24.
60. Wiesel, *The Town Beyond the Wall*, 182.
61. Lambert, "Friendship and Hope: Elie Wiesel's *The Town Beyond the Wall*," 163.
62. Wiesel, *The Town Beyond the Wall*, 123.
63. "Elie Wiesel," telephone interview by author, 20 March 2013.

Works Cited

Brown, Robert McAfee. *Elie Wiesel: Messenger to All Humanity*. South Bend: University of Notre Dame Press, 1989.

Chatman, Seymour. *Story and Discourse: Narrative Structure in Fiction and Film*. Ithaca: Cornell University Press, 1978.

Davis, Colin. *Elie Wiesel's Secretive Texts*. Gainesville: University Press of Florida, 1994.

Dennis, Geoffrey W. *The Encyclopedia of Jewish Myth, Magic and Mysticism*. Woodbury: Llewellyn, 2007.

Dostoevsky, Fyodor. "Crime and Punishment." Gutenberg.org. 28 March 2006. https://www.gutenberg.org/files/2554/2554-h/2554-h.htm. Accessed 30 June 2017.

Felman, Shoshana. *Writing and Madness: Literature/Philosophy/Psychoanalysis*. Palo Alto: Stanford University Press, 2007.

Foucault, Michel. *Madness and Civilization: A History of Insanity in the Age of Reason*. New York: Pantheon Books, 1965.

Henry, Gary. "Story and Silence: Transcendence in the Work of Elie Wiesel." PBS. http://www.pbs.org/eliewiesel/life/henry.html. Accessed 30 June 2017.

Lambert, Carole J. "Friendship and Hope: Elie Wiesel's *The Town Beyond the Wall*." In *The Gift of Story: Narrating Hope in a Postmodern World*, ed. Emily Griesinger and Mark A. Eaton, 149–64. Waco: Baylor University Press, 2006.

Laytner, Anson H. *Arguing with God: A Jewish Tradition*. Lanham: Rowman & Littlefield, 2007.

Moyers, Bill. "Facing Hate with Elie Wiesel." BillMoyers.com. 27 November 1991. http://billmoyers.com/content/facing-hate-with-elie-wiesel/. Accessed 30 June 2017.

Reynolds, Susan Salter. "Elie Wiesel: Embracing memory and madness." *Los Angeles Times*. 22 February 2009. http://www.latimes.com/entertainment/la-ca-elie-wiesel22-2009feb22-story.html. Accessed 30 June 2017.

Sternlicht, Sanford V. *Student Companion to Elie Wiesel*. Westport: Greenwood Press, 2003.

Wiesel, Elie. *The Forgotten*. New York: Schocken Books, 1995.

Wiesel, Elie. *Night*. Trans. Marion Wiesel. New York: Hill and Wang, 2006.

Wiesel, Elie. *The Time of the Uprooted*. New York: Schocken Books, 2007.

Wiesel, Elie. *The Town Beyond the Wall*. New York: Avon Books, 1964.

Wiesel, Elie. *Twilight: A Novel*. Trans. Marion Wiesel. New York: Schocken Books, 1995.

5

The Bystander in Elie Wiesel's *The Town Beyond the Wall*

CHRISTIN ZÜHLKE

Elie Wiesel is most publicly recognized as an Auschwitz survivor, an outspoken commentator on genocide and remembrance, and—as chair of the President's Commission on the Holocaust—one of the most vocal and visible gatekeepers of Shoah memory. His memoir, *Un di velt hot geshvign* (And the World Remained Silent), later adapted as *Night*, focuses specifically on a direct experience of the Shoah.[1] Many of his novels, however, encircle rather than enter the death camps. The destruction of European Jewry is, as Alan Berger argues, "the framing event for all his observations."[2] Wiesel's past as a prisoner and his survival have informed, even if indirectly, the substance of his fiction.[3] One such example is the novel *The Town Beyond the Wall* (hereafter referred to as *The Town*).

In their press release, the Nobel Prize committee described Wiesel as a "messenger"—he was a witness who gave voice to those who cannot speak for themselves.[4] Stressing the importance of Wiesel for the development of Holocaust literature, the scholar Alan Astro notes: "Wiesel took part in the shift of the universalizing paradigm, from one that subsumed—nay, drowned—the Holocaust in a sea of Nazi crime to another wherein the specifics of the Jewish tragedy were presented before a universal audience."[5] With his memoir of his own story of survival, Wiesel imbued the countless victims of the Nazi killing project with an identity and a voice.[6] His work grapples with the tension between historical truth and fiction—between a simple description of what he saw and the wider philosophical and sociological implications of those events.[7] One such figure who sits at the fault line between the specific event and its broader implications is the bystander.

The purpose of this chapter is twofold. First, I seek to detail and contextualize Wiesel's depiction of the bystander in *The Town*. By drawing from his own experience, I argue, Wiesel's description of the bystander presents the failure to intervene as an immoral act. The text itself does not resolve this problem, however; by the end of the novel the bystander's motives remain opaque. The bystander represents an ethical question, which the text, by design, fails to resolve. The second purpose of this chapter, then, is to explain this contradiction. In an attempt to understand the phenomena Wiesel describes, I turn to recent studies that suggests that bystanders choose not to intervene, first, because they do not see victims as a member of their group and, second, because inactivity is not, itself, seen as an action—to allow an event to occur is seen as morally distinct from causing an event to occur. This research might point a way toward resolving the central question of *The Town*, and yet understanding the psychology of the bystander does not necessarily allow us to overcome the problem that such a figure poses.

The Town

To understand Wiesel's preoccupation with the bystander, this chapter begins before the Shoah, in another town. Elie Wiesel was born in a town called Sighet in Northern Transylvania, where he lived until his deportation to the concentration camp Auschwitz in 1944. The northwestern part of Transylvania was reannexed from Romania by Hungary after the Second Vienna Award on August 30, 1940. This shift in Sighet's national affiliation had an impact on the political decisions about the Jewish population during the Shoah; the Jews in Sighet were Orthodox and many of them followed the Hasidic movement. According to the race-focused census of the National Socialists (which maintained a definition of "Jew" that did not wholly correspond with that of European Jewish communities), there were up to 206,000 Jews in Transylvania before the Shoah. Even though Transylvania's rule rotated between Hungary and Romania in the nineteenth and twentieth centuries, the Jewish population identified themselves as Hungarians. The shifting rule of Transylvania made the situation of the Transylvanian Jews during the

Shoah even more precarious: in Romania they belonged to the unwanted minorities of Hungarians and Jews, while the Hungarian citizens accused the Jews of collaboration with the Romanian government. Furthermore, they had no protection from either state, because both countries were allies of the Nazi regime. Until 1944, Prime Minister Miklós Kállay and the conservative government protected the Jewish population in Hungary and refused to turn them over to the Nazis for deportation. However, the Jews were still subject to prejudices and discrimination.[8] As Randolph Braham contends, "The fate of Jews during the Holocaust differed country by country, region by region. What evolved slowly in Germany over twelve years or in Poland over three took less than three months in Hungary."[9]

The Hungarian Jews remained the largest Jewish community in the occupied European territory until German soldiers invaded Hungary on March 19, 1944. Within a month the Jews were ghettoized and the deportations began July 8. After fifty-four days Hungary was, in Nazi terminology, *judenrein* (free of Jews). As Braham contends, none of the other countries processed the isolation, ghettoization, and deportation of the Jews "with as much barbarity and speed as in Hungary."[10] Before the Shoah approximately 825,000 Jews lived in Hungary. The Nazis deported and murdered 565,000, the majority of whom were killed at the moment of their arrival in Auschwitz. The Nazis transported about 120,000 victims from the region of Transylvania and the culturally rich Jewish community was destroyed. As Elie Wiesel himself asserts: "Never before had the abominable Final Solution been implemented with such efficiency. The average daily transport was twelve thousand." The speed and efficiency of the deportation of the Hungarian Jewish population was unique and very different from the case in Poland.[11]

The plot of *The Town* therefore, which takes place after the Shoah, clearly draws, in part, from Wiesel's own experiences. It describes Michael, who, like Elie Wiesel himself, is a Holocaust survivor. Michael wishes to return from his current country of residence, France, to his former hometown of Szerencseváros.[12] However, reaching Szerencseváros from France proves to be dangerous—the town is behind the Iron Curtain as Soviet-controlled territory after the end of World War II.[13] Wiesel continues the narrative in Szerencseváros, to which Michael returns. While Michael is walking around the town, he finally understands that his main goal was to meet somebody from the time of the Shoah, or to be more specific, to return to the site that has been burned into his memory: at the place and moment during which Jewish residents were being deported. The individual he seeks is a bystander who watched on as the deportations occurred. Michael meets and confronts the unnamed bystander but fails to elicit an explanation from the man as to why he watched as Jews were beaten. Michael walks away, the bystander calls the police, and Michael is put into prison, accused of being a spy. The police torture him in order to make him talk about his alleged spying activities. To resist this torture he mentally transports himself in his memories to the time before the Shoah, telling the reader about different people he knew from Szerencseváros, none of whom returned. Michael also reveals the details of his deportation, when Jewish victims had to wait in the old synagogue, on a Saturday, Shabbat, the Jewish holy day of rest. Families were already separated and the people awaited their impending deportation.[14]

Among his memories, Michael has attached great significance to the moment when he saw a man watching a scene of violence occur: "The police beat women and children; he did not stir. It was no concern of his. He was neither victim nor executioner; a spectator, that's what he was."[15] The bystander is at once a part of the event and yet separate from it. The passivity of the bystander is placed into stark contrast with the movement occurring around him: "they averted their faces; the more sensitive bowed their heads."[16] The bystander, instead, watched on.

What shocks Michael the most about the bystander is that he could have, at little personal risk, averted the suffering of the Jewish victims. Wiesel writes: "[The bystander] could have interrupted the game. If he had simply gone down to the courtyard of the synagogue and alerted the Jews: 'Good people! Listen to me! Don't be fooled! Be careful! It's not a game!' He hadn't done it."[17] When they meet once more, Michael addresses this lack of intervention directly:

> "Coward!" I shouted, and crashed my fist down on the table. "You're a shameful coward! You haven't got the courage to do either good or evil! The role of spectator suited you to perfection. They killed? You had nothing to do with it. Children were thirsty? You had nothing to do with it. Your conscience is clear. 'Not guilty, your honor!' You're a disgusting coward!"[18]

In *The Town*, as in the Shoah as a whole, there are, of course multiple bystanders. Michael remembers "all those neutrals in the feature of a single face: the spectator across from the synagogue." The one bystander looms largest of all for him, however: "The others were only reflections of him. Copies."[19] The inaction of many seems to be crystalized in the one moment where a single man watched and did nothing. Wiesel writes: "His face, empty of all expressions, followed me for long years. I have forgotten many others; not his."[20] What Michael already implies with "the others" who were only copies of the "face behind the window" is that the bystander was not a single person but a phenomenon, an entire group of people who observed the violence without seeking to intervene. Victoria J. Barnett asserts:

> The genocide of the European Jews would have been impossible without the active participation of bystanders to carry it out and the failure of numerous parties to intervene to stop it. The Holocaust did not occur in a vacuum. There was general failure—among individuals, institutions, and the international community to acknowledge and stop the genocide. Moreover, the genocide was preceded by the years of intensifying anti-Jewish persecution, which much of Europe's non-Jewish population either witnessed or participated in.[21]

The Shoah, then, did not happen in a bubble. It was part of daily life in Nazi-occupied territories. In *The Town* (as in reality), many deportations occurred publicly, in full view of the local population. The events of the novel went on for an entire week. When we look back upon the widespread ghettoization and deportations all over the occupied European territory, we understand that it was not possible for the Nazis to hide the destruction of the Jewish people.[22] Indeed, the killing project required the tacit acceptance of humiliation, violence, and murder on the part of the gentile population of the annexed country. As Barnett asserts: "At the most fundamental level, the *relationship* between the bystanders and victims was betrayed: neighbors, colleagues, and friends were suddenly divided into victims, bystanders, and perpetrators."[23]

For Michael, the crucial mystery of the bystander, and the mass of humanity that he represents, is his decision not to intervene. He understands the bystander, in other words, as one with agency, who chooses to allow violence to take place. The question of agency is key here: unlike the bystander, the victims faced a situation the historian Lawrence L. Langer called "choiceless choice"—any action they chose would lead to an undesirable outcome and so they were frozen in passivity.[24] But, as Tony Kushner asserts:

Choices *were* there for the bystanders. Of course, these need to be placed in their specific contexts, recognising their own particular specific limitations, throughout the Nazi era. Yet there is a danger that, rather than confronting the ambivalence, contradictions and ambiguities of contemporaries, we either increasingly take refuge in the creation of plaster saints or retreat, as with the obsessive interest in the western intelligence world and its knowledge of the Holocaust, into the comfortable fiction that only the privileged few knew of its existence during the war or that nothing at all could be done to stop mass murder.[25]

Not every individual, of course, was, like the bystander in *The Town*, afforded the opportunity to intervene without personal risk. The nature and degree of this agency depended on specific circumstances such as location, political status of the country, and political status of the person his- or herself. Not every bystander had unlimited options, and many who did not intervene were driven by fear despite a desire to help. A large number seem to have been driven by greed—the desire to possess the abandoned belongings of the victims, for example. Not every one of those who did intervene was wholly or necessarily altruistic—some only helped for as long as their protection yielded payment. Some helped for as long as their bravery held. The facets of motives and choices of people helping are as broad as those of the bystanders. The question remains, however—as Michael insists—why populations as a whole failed to protect their neighbors and why a large number of bystanders, who were able to help, at apparently smaller personal risk than the victims, chose not to.

The Psychology of the Bystander

As Philip Zimbardo, a professor of psychology, argues, "Every act of intervention in the life of an individual, a group, or an environment is a matter of ethics [. . .]."[26] It is dictated, in other words, by the moral systems in which the individual is immersed. Along these lines, Barnett offers one possible explanation for the bystander's passivity. She defines the bystander as "someone immediately present, an actual witness, someone for whom involvement was an option."[27] Barnett's description of the bystander rhymes with Wiesel's: "The bystander is not the protagonist [. . .] nor is the bystander the object of the action. In a criminal case, the bystander is neither victim nor perpetrator; his or her legally relevant role is that of witness."[28] The bystander is the third option within the scope of action, besides victims and perpetrators.[29]

The bystander's behavior is predicated upon, and facilitated by, physical distance—he is at once close enough to observe an event but far enough away to avoid being immersed or involved in it. It is noteworthy, then, that Wiesel's bystander is a "face in the window across the way."[30] The window functions as a physical separation between the victims and the bystander. It not only divides them physically but also builds an emotional wall, so that the bystander is not touched by the suffering he observes. In *The Town* Michael describes the separation as follows: "A spring day, sunny, the day of punishment, day of divorce between good and evil. Here, men and women yoked by misery; there, the face that watched them."[31] The violence is emphasized by the incongruously pleasant weather, as though the bystander exists in a space that is climatologically separated from the violence he witnesses. There are several references in Wiesel's work, not only in *The Town*, but also in *Night*, in which the suffering of the Jewish victims stands in contrast to the bystander's safe place behind the window.[32] The window separates the worlds of the victims and the onlooker symbolically and physically, which serves as a metaphor for Barnett's explanation of the "parallel worlds":

> The phenomenon of "parallel worlds" depicts a fundamental reality of the Holocaust, in which the bystanders and perpetrators deliberately constructed and cultivated the illusion that the victims had disappeared from their universe. In one part, people suffered horribly in the other, people continued to live normal lives, pursue careers, and raise their children.[33]

Jennifer N. Gutsell and Michael Inzlicht contend that this apparent indifference is rooted in the neuropsychology of prejudice. They demonstrate that if one person is observing another, the second person's body language will activate parts in the first person's brain to show the same expressions and movements. But this connection between observing and copying of body language seems to be influenced by sympathy of the observer with the observed person.[34] Gutsell and Inzlicht argue that this process, called "perception-action-coupling," might be impaired in response to disliked outgroups. Such a fundamental bias, would not only make it difficult to empathize with outgroup member's suffering, but also to understand their actions and intentions, potentially hampering smooth intergroup interactions and communication.[35]

According to Gutsell and Inzlicht, if prejudice against the outgroup leads to a lower level of empathy, this might, from a neuroscientific point of view, explain why people felt less sensitive about expressions of suffering of Jewish victims. The racially determined Nazi ideology assigned the Jews the status of a member of an unwanted outgroup, and anti-Semitism is deeply rooted in European history and cultural memory motivated by Christianity.[36] In order to help somebody who does not belong to the ingroup, the moral grounding of the observer needs to be unaffected by negative influences. This research may suggest, then, a neuropsychological context for the phenomenon of the bystander grounded in a sense of group identity.

Researchers Bibb Latané and John M. Darley reach similar conclusions. They tested the conditions under which people will help others and the influence that witnessing a stranger offering help had on others:

Even if our observer [in the psychological experiment] has noticed an event and identified it as an emergency, this does not automatically mean that he will assume responsibility for helping. Several things determine whether the observer will feel a responsibility to handle the situation himself. Among these variables are whether the victim "deserves" help, the competence of the bystander, the relationship between the bystander and the victim, and whether responsibility is shared among a number of bystanders.[37]

According to Latané and Darley, a bystander will only intervene when several factors weigh in favor of the victim, among them being the individual's perception of the victim.

Along similar lines, Zimbardo argues that ideological apparatus, particularly a sense of an outgroup as deserving of suffering, can complicate and disrupt empathy:

Motives and needs that ordinarily serve us well can lead us astray when they are aroused, amplified, or manipulated by situational forces that we fail to recognize as potent. This is why evil is so pervasive. Its temptation is just a small turn away [. . .] leading to disaster.[38]

Zimbardo explains how moral terms can be changed. Even though his theory is focused on perpetrators, we can learn universal aspects from his research. His Stanford Prison Experiment does not justify the perpetrators' actions but helps us understand why people can act in a certain way, a way that is generally understood to be "immoral" or "evil," as Zimbardo calls it. Nazi propaganda was one way to manipulate people's often already anti-Semitic perception of Jews, which led to even more powerful prejudices.

The research suggests, then, that the bystander described by Wiesel did not intervene because he did not recognize the victims as a members of his "tribe." His failure to act was informed, no doubt, by the depiction of Jews in Nazi propaganda, which further enforced his sense of separation from the victims. When Michael finally has his meeting with the man behind the window from all those years ago, his exasperation lies in his inability to elicit any remorse or shame from the man, this "symbol of anonymity, the average man," who remembers the suffering of the Jews without emotion, as a game between two sides, of which he belonged to neither.[39]

The Ethics of the Bystander

The psychology of inaction in the face of atrocity intersects with and is informed by the philosophy of ethics. Seumas Miller argues that the "bystander is *individually* morally responsible for failing to individually intervene in order to effect the rescue [. . .]."[40] In Wiesel's novel, Michael similarly argues that the bystander did not see himself as responsible for the victims: He is "just" observing but not involved. By choosing this attitude, the bystander rejects his or her moral responsibility. The moral compass, influenced by Nazi ideology, had in many cases a direct impact on personal choices during the Shoah, as Lawrence L. Langer claims: "Since responsibility is directly related to choice, one can make this charge only by ignoring or denying how radically the Holocaust disrupted the equilibrium of our moral and spiritual universe."[41] This is the real reason Michael returns: to confront the bystander with what he did, or to be more precise, what he did not do. Michael is not only speaking for himself but for all the victims who cannot speak for themselves anymore. He is the messenger who has to ask the questions and to accuse the bystander of being a coward, a leaf in the political wind.

The bystander represents a moral paradox, which Michael struggles to resolve. The bystander's indifference, and the implications of that indifference for all of humanity, have remained imprinted in Michael's memory. The ethical questions are raised indirectly: How can you stay indifferent when another human being is suffering? Is it not our responsibility to do something? This point of indifference questioned in *The Town* comes from the author's struggle with the same issue. Wiesel was haunted by the bystander's behavior for his whole life and spoke publicly against remaining silent:

> This, this was the thing I had wanted to understand ever since the war. Nothing else. How a human being can remain indifferent. The executioners I understood; also the victims, though with more difficulty. But the others, all the others, those who were neither for nor against, those who sprawled in passive patience, those who told themselves, "The storm will blow over and everything will be normal again," those who thought themselves above the battle, those who were permanently and merely spectators—all those were closed to me, incomprehensible.[42]

The psychological experiments and research of Zimbardo, Latané and Darley, Gutsell and Inzlicht provide some understanding of why a bystander may not intervene; his or her inaction is often motivated by a sense of difference—the bystander in *The Town* stood by because he felt no affiliation with the Jewish victims. They were not a part of his group and so he felt no moral obligation to save them. His choice was also informed by a (perhaps artificial) sense of his not being involved—of being physically and morally separate from the events he witnessed. The violence he observed did not rely upon his taking action, and so he felt he was separate from what he saw.

Understanding the "why" of the bystander, however, may provide little to no solace for Michael and those like him. We may be able to identify the psychological mechanisms that inform their choice, but it brings us no closer to resolving the moral gulf that the bystander opens. As Barnett asserts:

> This is one reason why the behavior of *bystanders* during the Holocaust haunts us. In our awareness of what they failed to do then, we are compelled to reflect on our responsibilities today. Like them, we move along a continuum of human behavior. How and in what direction we move is shaped by the kind of people we are and the circumstances in which we find ourselves.[43]

The Town, too, offers no resolution to the problem of the bystander. During his life, Wiesel spoke bravely and unceasingly against inhumanity and injustice. In a speech at the memorial of the former concentration camp Buchenwald, he said, "But the world hasn't learned. When I was liberated in 1945, [. . .] somehow many of us were convinced that at least one lesson will have been learned—that never again will there be war; that hatred is not an option, that racism is stupid [. . .]."[44] The issue of the bystander, it seems, was a recurring problem, which he, like the researchers described earlier, recognized but could never resolve. It was a never-ending story interwoven with his personal background as a survivor. In *The Town* Wiesel shows the bystander from the perspective of the victim. He urges his reader, perhaps in vain, not to remain silent but to understand and embrace our moral responsibility for each other, for humankind. As Barnett asserts: "As human beings present in the world, we bear responsibility for what happens in it."[45]

Notes

1. See the introduction to this volume for a discussion of the contested status of *Night* as literary memoir.
2. Alan L. Berger, "Faith and God during the Holocaust: Teaching *Night* with the Later Memoirs," in *Approaches to Teaching Wiesel's "Night,"* ed. Alan Rosen (New York: The Modern Language Association of America, 2007), 48.
3. Cf. Ellen Merritt Brown French, "Archetype and Metaphor: An Approach to the Early Novels of Elie Wiesel," PhD diss., Middle Tennessee State University, 1981, 21.
4. French, "Archetype and Metaphor, 12.
5. Alan Astro, "Revisiting Wiesel's Night in Yiddish, French, and English," *Partial Answers: Journal of Literature and the History of Ideas* 12, no. 1 (2014): 143.
6. Because of the focus of this chapter is on Elie Wiesel, who was Jewish, I will focus on Jewish victims.

7. Simone Gigliotti, "*Night* and the Teaching of History: The Trauma of Transit," in *Approaches to Teaching Wiesel's "Night,"* ed. Alan Rosen (New York: The Modern Language Association of America, 2007), 38.

8. Sources for this paragraph: Holly Case, "The Holocaust and the Transylvanian Question in the Twentieth Century," in *The Holocaust in Hungary: Sixty Years Later*, ed. Randolph L. Braham and Brewster S. Chamberlin, East European Monographs, vol. 678 (New York: Rosenthal Institute for Holocaust Studies, 2006), 19ff.; Alan Rosen, "Instructor's Library," in *Approaches to Teaching Wiesel's "Night,"* ed. Alan Rosen (New York: The Modern Language Association of America, 2007), 8; Menahem Schmelzer, "Personal Recollections," in *The Nazis' Last Victims: The Holocaust in Hungary*, ed. Randolph L. Braham and Scott Miller (Detroit: Wayne State University Press, 1998), 183–84; Wiesel Elie, "Keynote Address," in *The Holocaust in Hungary: Sixty Years Later*, ed. Randolph L. Braham and Brewster S. Chamberlin, East European Monographs, vol. 678 (New York: Rosenthal Institute for Holocaust Studies, 2006), xv; Zoltán Tibori Szabó, "Transylvanian Jewry during the Postwar Period, 1945–1948," in *The Holocaust in Hungary: Sixty Years Later*, ed. Randolph L. Braham and Brewster S. Chamberlin, East European Monographs, vol. 678 (New York: Rosenthal Institute for Holocaust Studies, 2006), 291.

9. Randolph L. Braham and Scott Miller, *The Nazis' Last Victims: The Holocaust in Hungary* (Detroit: Wayne State University Press, 1998), 9.

10. Braham and Miller, *The Nazis' Last Victims*, 38.

11. Sources for this paragraph: Braham and Miller, *The Nazis' Last Victims*, 9; Schmelzer, "Personal Recollections," 177–84; Szabó, "Transylvanian Jewry during the Postwar Period, 1945–1948," 293; Wiesel, "Keynote Address," xv.

12. Elie Wiesel, *The Town Beyond the Wall* (New York: Bergen-Belsen Memorial Press, 1967), 12.

13. Elie Wiesel found himself in the same situation while he lived in France until the mid-1950s, before he moved to the United States. Writing *The Town* was Wiesel's way to return to Sighet, which belonged to Romania at the time, something he was only able to do physically in 1964. The title of the book refers to the location of Michael's and Elie Wiesel's hometowns behind the Iron Curtain.

14. Wiesel, *The Town Beyond the Wall*, 148.
15. Wiesel, *The Town Beyond the Wall*, 150.
16. Wiesel, *The Town Beyond the Wall*, 150.
17. Wiesel, *The Town Beyond the Wall*, 158.
18. Wiesel, *The Town Beyond the Wall*, 158.
19. Wiesel, *The Town Beyond the Wall*, 149.
20. Wiesel, *The Town Beyond the Wall*, 150.

21. Victoria J. Barnett, *Bystanders: Conscience and Complicity during the Holocaust* (Westport: Greenwood Press, 1999), 11.

22. A lot of people from the occupied territories were also involved. This was one way information could spread about the Holocaust. "To carry out the 'Final Solution' across an entire continent, the Germans required the collaboration and complicity of many individuals in every country, from leaders, public officials, police, and soldiers to ordinary citizens. In every country locals participated in a variety of ways—as clerks, cooks, and confiscators of property; as managers or participants in roundups and deportations; as informants; sometimes as perpetrators of violence against Jews on their own initiative; and sometimes as hands-on murderers in killing operations." "Collaboration and Complicity during the Holocaust," United States Holocaust Memorial Museum, https://www.ushmm.org/information/press./press-releases/collaboration-and-complicity-during-the-holocaust, accessed 31 August 2017.

23. Barnett, "Bystanders," 145.

24. "Moreover, this little discredit falls to these victims, who were plunged into a crisis of what we might call 'choiceless choice,' where crucial decisions did not reflect options between one form of abnormal response and another, both imposed by a situation that was in no way of the victim's own choosing." Lawrence L. Langer. *Versions of Survival: The Holocaust and the Human Spirit* (Albany: State University of New York Press, 1982), 72.

25. Tony Kushner, "'Pissing in the Wind'? The Search for Nuance in the Study of Holocaust 'Bystanders,'" in *Bystanders to the Holocaust. A Re-evaluation*, ed. David Cesarani and Paul A. Levine (London: Frank Cass, 2002), 70, emphasis in the original.

26. In the so-called Stanford Prison Experiment Philip Zimbardo conducted in 1971, a psychological study. This study "was a classic demonstration of the power of social situations to distort personal identities and long cherished values and morality as students internalized situated identities in their roles as prisoners and guards." Scott Plous, "Philip G. Zimbardo," Social Psychology Network, https://zimbardo.socialpsychology.org/, accessed 30 July 2017; Philip Zimbardo, *The Lucifer Effect: Understanding How Good People Turn Evil* (New York: Random House, 2007), 232.

27. Barnett, "Bystanders," xv.

28. Barnett, "Bystanders," 9.

29. This is a somewhat reductive breakdown that does not fully encompass all possible relationships within an act of violence, but for this chapter I will focus on the triangle of victim, perpetrator, and bystander.

30. Wiesel, *The Town Beyond the Wall*, 150.

31. Wiesel, *The Town Beyond the Wall*, 148.

32. «מ‹טריפ אונדז דורך די הויפט-גאסן. אין דער ריכטונג פון דער גרויסער שול. די שטייען אמתן דער אין. אזעלכער איינדרוק אן בלויז איז דאס אבער. פוסט זיין צו שיינע שטאט אויפן ווארטן און פענצטער פארמאכטע הינטער—!פריינט געטרייע און גוטע נעכטיקע—גויים די מומענט, וועלן זיי וואון פארמעגן יידיש רויבן און דירות יידישער אין אריינרייסן זיך קענען».

Eliezer Wiesel, אוז די וועלט האט געשוויגן . . . In דאָס פּוילישע ייִדנטום, vol. 117 (Buenos Aires: Central Organization of the Polish Jews in Argentina, 1956), 45. The English translation is in general a shortened version of the Yiddish original. In this passage, the information that the Jewish victims must walk the main street is missing. Also, the impression that the street is left empty, and the people behind the shutters are gentiles, *goyim*, is not translated well, missing nuances that give a more intensive impression. "Our convoy headed toward the main synagogue. The town seemed deserted. But behind the shutters, our friends of yesterday were probably waiting for the moment when they could loot our homes." Elie Wiesel, *Night*, trans. Marion Wiesel (New York: Hill and Wang 2006), 22.

33. Barnett, "Bystanders," 129.

34. Jennifer N. Gutsell and Michael Inzlicht, "Empathy Constrained: Prejudice Predicts Reduced Mental Simulation of Actions during Observation of Outgroups," *Journal of Experimental Social Psychology* 46 (2010): 841–45.

35. Gutsell and Inzlicht, "Empathy Constrained," 842.

36. "Research is not conclusive, but does suggest that this is a distinct possibility. For example, selective attention and motivation seems to favor ingroup members such that ingroups are processed in greater depth than outgroup members, with evidence indicating greater activity in the amygdala, fusiform gyri, and orbitofrontal cortex [. . .]. Similarly, selective attention and motivation might filter for the actions of ingroup members." Gutsell and Inzlicht, "Empathy Constrained," 844.

37. Bibb Latané and John M. Darley, *The Unresponsive Bystander: Why Doesn't He Help?* (New York: Appleton-Century-Crofts, 1970), 33.

38. Zimbardo, *The Lucifer Effect*, 258.

39. Wiesel, *The Town Beyond the Wall*, 153–57.

40. Seumas Miller, "Collective Moral Responsibility: An Individualist Account," *Midwest Studies in Philosophy* 30 (2006): 191, emphasis in the original.

41. Langer, *Versions of Survival*, 87.

42. Wiesel, *The Town Beyond the Wall*, 149.

43. Barnett, *Bystanders*, 167, emphasis in the original.

44. Elie Wiesel, "Remarks by Elie Wiesel," Buchenwald and Mittelbau-Dora Memorials Foundation, https://www.buchenwald.de/en/913/, accessed 22 June 2017.

45. Barnett, *Bystanders*, 168.

Works Cited

Astro, Alan. "Revisiting Wiesel's *Night* in Yiddish, French, and English." *Partial Answers: Journal of Literature and the History of Ideas* 12, no. 1 (2014): 127–53.

Barnett, Victoria J. *Bystanders: Conscience and Complicity during the Holocaust* (Westport: Greenwood Press, 1999.
Berger, Alan L. "Faith and God during the Holocaust: Teaching *Night* with the Later Memoirs." In *Approaches to Teaching Wiesel's "Night,"* ed. Alan Rosen, 46–51 (New York: The Modern Language Association of America, 2007).
Braham, Randolph L. "Keynote Address." In *The Holocaust in Hungary: Sixty Years Later*, ed. Randolph L. Braham and Brewster S. Chamberlin. East European Monographs, vol. 678, xxi–xix. New York: Rosenthal Institute for Holocaust Studies, 2006.
Braham, Randolph L., and Scott Miller. *The Nazis' Last Victims: The Holocaust in Hungary*. Detroit: Wayne State University Press, 1998.
Case, Holly. "The Holocaust and the Transylvanian Question in the Twentieth Century." In *The Holocaust in Hungary: Sixty Years Later*, ed. Randolph L. Braham and Brewster S. Chamberlin. East European Monographs, vol. 678, 17–40. New York: Rosenthal Institute for Holocaust Studies, 2006.
French, Ellen Merritt Brown. "Archetype and Metaphor: An Approach to the Early Novels of Elie Wiesel." PhD diss., Middle Tennessee State University, 1981.
Gigliotti, Simone. "*Night* and the Teaching of History: The Trauma of Transit." In *Approaches to Teaching Wiesel's "Night,"* ed. Alan Rosen, 32–40. New York: The Modern Language Association of America, 2007.
Gutsell, Jennifer N., and Michael Inzlicht. "Empathy Constrained: Prejudice Predicts Reduced Mental Simulation of Actions during Observation of Outgroups." *Journal of Experimental Social Psychology* 46 (2010): 841–45.
Kushner, Tony. "'Pissing in the Wind'? The Search for Nuance in the Study of Holocaust 'Bystanders.'" In *Bystanders to the Holocaust: A Re-evaluation*, ed. David Cesarani and Paul A. Levine, 57–76. London: Frank Cass, 2002.
Langer, Lawrence L. *Versions of Survival: The Holocaust and the Human Spirit*. Albany: State University of New York Press, 1982.
Latané, Bibb, and John M. Darley. *The Unresponsive Bystander: Why Doesn't He Help?* New York: Appleton-Century-Crofts, 1970.
Miller, Seumas. "Collective Moral Responsibility: An Individualist Account." *Midwest Studies in Philosophy* 3, no. 1 (2006): 176–93.
Patterson, David. "Wiesel, Elie (1928–)." In *Encyclopedia of Holocaust Literature*, ed. David Patterson, Alan L. Berger, and Sarita Cargas, 213–16. Westport: Oryx Press, 2002.
Plous, Scott. "Philip G. Zimbardo." Social Psychology Network. https://zimbardo.socialpsychology.org/. Accessed 30 July 2017.
Rosen, Alan. "Instructor's Library." In *Approaches to Teaching Wiesel's "Night,"* ed. Alan Rosen, 8–13. New York: The Modern Language Association of America. 2007.

Schmelzer, Menahem. "Personal Recollections." In *The Nazis' Last Victims: The Holocaust in Hungary*, ed. Randolph L. Braham and Scott Miller. Detroit: Wayne State University Press, 1998.

Szabó, Zoltán Tibori. "Transylvanian Jewry during the Postwar Period, 1945–1948." In *The Holocaust in Hungary: Sixty Years Later*, ed. Randolph L. Braham and Brewster S. Chamberlin. East European Monographs, vol. 678, 291–314. New York: Rosenthal Institute for Holocaust Studies, 2006.

United States Holocaust Memorial Museum. "Collaboration and Complicity during the Holocaust." United States Holocaust Memorial Museum. https://www.ushmm.org/information/press/press-releases/collaboration-and-complicity-during-the-holocaust. Accessed 31 August 2017.

Wiesel, Elie. "Keynote Address." In *The Holocaust in Hungary: Sixty Years Later*, ed. Randolph L. Braham and Brewster S. Chamberlin. East European Monographs, vol. 678, xv–xix. New York: Rosenthal Institute for Holocaust Studies, 2006.

Wiesel, Elie. *Night*. Trans. Marion Wiesel. New York: Hill and Wang, 2006.

Wiesel, Elie. "Remarks by Elie Wiesel." Buchenwald and Mittelbau-Dora Memorials Foundation. https://www.buchenwald.de/en/913/. Accessed 22 June 2017.

Wiesel, Elie. *The Town Beyond the Wall*. New York: Bergen-Belsen Memorial Press, 1967.

Wiesel, Eliezer. געשוויגן האָט וועלט די און . . . In ייִדנטום פּוילישע דאָס vol. 117. Buenos Aires: Central Organization of the Polish Jews in Argentina, 1956.

Yad Vashem. "The Holocaust: Definition and Preliminary Discussion." Yad Vashem. http://www.yadvashem.org/yv/en/holocaust/resource_center/the_holocaust.asp. Accessed 30 July 2017.

Zimbardo, Philip. *The Lucifer Effect: Understanding How Good People Turn Evil*. New York: Random House, 2007.

6

Enduring Anti-Semitic Christian Scripts in Elie Wiesel's *The Gates of the Forest*

Lucas Wilson

In "Script Theory and Nuclear Scripts," Silvan Tomkins proposes his definition of *scripts* as "*sets of ordering rules* for the interpretation, evaluation, prediction, production, or control of scenes."[1] Scripts are the guiding mechanisms that structure individuals' day-to-day conduct and thoughts. They are generally unwritten—and are largely adopted unconsciously—but oftentimes are *informed* by written texts. One such written text, if not *the* foundational text in the West, is the Bible, the Christian version of which details the metanarrative of God's redemption of humanity through the God-man Jesus. As the Gospels present and theologize Jesus's ministry, death, and resurrection—in tandem with the epistles' theological commentaries on Jesus's life—the Bible attempts to recount God's salvific work in human history. It also aims to shape its readership's thoughts and actions, attempting to script followers' lives. Indeed, the biblical script—the ordering set of religious rules and principles—filters and undergirds Christian perceptions of the world and how Christians are to act in it. Of course, it should be noted that Christianity comes in many denominations; adherents observe a variety of doctrines and their attitudes differ depending on said denominations, and the degrees of religiosity and tolerance ranges considerably even within the same denomination. Across all denominations the central ordering script, however, is the Christian Bible itself. And as the Bible details a number of ethical imperatives—including how to pray, how to treat the Other, and so forth—scripture aims to shape the thoughts, life, and conduct of Christian adherents.

I highlight the prescribed "Christian" treatment of the Other, which—despite its exploration by a host of scholars, Christian and non-Christian alike—still raises a number of questions. For some scholars this has become an academic and personal preoccupation, as is the case for one Jewish literary theologian in particular: Elie Wiesel. As Wiesel poignantly articulates in his novel *The Gates of the Forest*, though Christian scriptures instruct readers how to treat the Other—the outcast, the estranged, the sojourner—with an abundance of Christian charity, Christian charity "is different from charity as such."[2] Although many would agree that the Christian Bible's dictum concerning the treatment of the Other is overwhelmingly affirmative and calls for unconditional love on the model of Jesus, there has historically been a major incongruity between Christians' *teachings* and Christians' *treatment* of those who do not look, act, or talk like them. This incongruity is perhaps most evident in how certain groups of Christians have viewed and violently treated Jews over the past two millennia.

Regarding Jews, scripture itself is conflicted—or, at a bare minimum, *interpretations* of scripture are conflicted, as Amy-Jill Levine, E. P. Sanders, John Gager, Adele Reinhartz, Joseph B. Tyson, Lloyd Gaston, and a number of others have demonstrated.[3] Though the Gospels present Jesus carrying a banner of love for *all*, they also code "the Jews" en masse as those who are sick (Mark 2:17), children of the devil (John 8:42–44), and those who collectively accept the responsibility for the death of God (Matt. 27:24–26). The Gospels' defamation of Jews, in concert with Paul's supersessionist theology—most emphatically, albeit ambiguously, detailed in Romans 9–11—can eclipse scripture's competing ethical demand to love and protect human life in the name of Christian charity (1 Cor. 13:4–8). Worded differently, Christianity's anti-Judaic and anti-Semitic teachings assumed primacy as the dominant script certain groups of Christians have historically followed when thinking about and/or interacting with Jews. And this script has been followed since the formation of the early church. Surveying the long history of Christian anti-Semitism that took root shortly after the birth of the Christian faith, Franklin Littell, in *The Crucifixion of the Jews*, explains that, as the early church shifted from a Jewish to a gentile majority, early gentile converts had a "natural resentment of the priority of Israel" and resisted "the authority of events in Jewish history."[4] In "The Birth of Christianity and the Origins of Christian Anti-Judaism," Paula Fredriksen further explains how this resentment indeed "began when Christian Hellenistic Jewish texts, such as the letters of Paul and the Gospels, began to circulate among total outsiders, that is, among Gentiles without any connection to the synagogue and without any attachment to Jewish traditions of practice and interpretation."[5] Certainly, early Church Fathers—Origen, Bishop Gregory of Nyssa, Saint John Chrysostom, for example—and theologians thereafter concretized and amplified these anti-Semitic Christian teachings that have since permeated Western collective consciousness.[6] But it is the Christian Bible *itself*, from which Christian doctrine has arisen, that contains what can be and often has been understood as scripted hatred toward Jews, which has functioned more often than not as the primary theological "justification" for Christian anti-Semitism.

Interrogating this dark underbelly of Christian theology and Christian history, Wiesel's *The Gates of the Forest*, which Robert McAfee Brown describes as "Wiesel's first fictional grappling with Christianity," specifically locates the Passion play and narrative as setting the stage, so to speak, for Christian antagonism and repudiation of Jews during the Holocaust.[7] As few scholars have treated *The Gates of the Forest*'s depiction of the Passion play in detail—with Brown as one of the only notable exceptions—I seek to examine the ways in which Wiesel's novel presents the Passion narrative as the backdrop of the Holocaust. I ought to point out that religious teachings, of course, were not the only means Nazis used to justify the Holocaust—they also drew upon the resources of economics, politics, German mythopoeia, and "biology," but religion (or, perhaps more accurately, the *perversion* of religion) was, undeniably, a significant aspect of Nazi anti-Semitism. In either case, Wiesel's novel explores the Passion narrative's influence on and production of centuries-long anti-Semitic violence that ultimately assisted in leading to the ovens of Auschwitz. As Richard L. Rubenstein posits in *After Auschwitz*, "the death camps were the terminal expression of Christian anti-Semitism. Without Christianity, the Jews could never have become the central victims."[8] Rubenstein further argues that Hitler and his Nazis "did not invent a new villain, but took over the ancient Christian tradition of the Jew as villain and epitome of the darkest evil. Nor did the Nazis create a new hatred. Folk hatred of the Jews is at least as old as Christianity."[9] Indeed, the Third Reich intensified the already present Jew-hatred found in Christian theology. By positioning protagonist Gregor and the other actors on the Passion play stage, *The Gates of the Forest* metaphorizes Christians' scripted performance of anti-Semitic attitudes and behaviors, as well as Jews' roles as passive receivers of such vitriol. And these scripts, which many Christians have performed, though they directly contradict the majority of New Testament teachings, often find their genesis in, or have been supported by, Christian doctrine.

The Larger Historical Context

Before specifically focusing on the Passion play in the context of *The Gates of the Forest*, it bears noting how the persecution that Gregor experiences throughout his life metonymically represents, to borrow the words of Victoria Aarons, "the suffering of all Jews."[10] The text's extended portrait of Gregor, which offers a particularly grave presentation of his childhood, points to the ways in which he is forcibly implicated in the violence that results from Christian anti-Semitism throughout his life. Shedding light on "the suffering of all Jews," Aarons explains: "Individual trauma, in the literature of the Holocaust, is a part of the larger trauma of the specific history of the Jews, the collective experience of trauma and the defining weight of Jewish identity."[11] Along with Aarons, Joyce B. Lazarus picks up on the blurring of time in the novel, where the Holocaust is "an event that forever implicates the future as well as the past and present, and all those associated with it are inextricably part of one's life."[12] As the text illustrates the diffuse cultural anti-Semitism of the time, along with the periodic hatred Gregor faces throughout his life, his childhood walk to school—a seemingly mundane occurrence—assumes grave historical significance. His walk to school not only illustrates the "longstanding historical [. . .] continuation of the self-justifying pathology of scapegoating,"[13] but it also sheds light on the guiding script that, across time and space, underpins Christian hatred of Jews:

> Gregor walked uncertainly toward school, hardly daring to raise his head or even to breathe, because he knew he was on enemy terrain. He was not misled by the apparent peace and quiet, because he knew that the Gang was lying in wait. They would leap on him from the recessed doorway on the corner. [. . .] To beat up a lone Jewish child, to rub his nose in the mud, that was the Gang's idea of amusement. It had gone on for centuries, so that it was more than habit: it had

become a tradition, a law. Without this game there would be no organized life. It had to be played for the good of the community; every generation gave birth to a Gang, and every Gang knew how to stalk its prey.[14]

As he walks on "enemy terrain"—which, for Jews at the time, could be interpreted as the vast majority of Christian Europe, not just Gregor's localized Hungarian milieu—he anticipates facing the "tradition" and "law" that the Gang follows. Here, "tradition" and "law" signal the codification of hatred, the canonization of anti-Semitism in everyday life, that is taken for granted and unquestionably adopted by Christian masses. Without the negative pole of the us-versus-them binary—or, more specifically, the Christian-versus-Jew dichotomy—the very construction of Christian identity would not have cohered as it has throughout Christian history, for there would indeed be no binary of which to speak. Illustrating the necessity for "the Jew" in the Christian-Jewish binary, the narrator includes a song that Stan, a villager, sings in church. This song is at first enigmatic, but, if the "passer-by" it references is understood as a Jew, it becomes clear how the passerby's lack affords the singer's plenitude: "Forget, passer-by, that thanks to you I smile, / That thanks to you I dream and see sights lost to you a while."[15] Here, the singer's happiness (his "smile") and "dream[s]" are a result of the passerby, the one who is in transit, the one who does not reside next to or near the singer, that is, the one who is outside organized Christian life; the good (Christian) life of this individual is a direct function of the *un*happiness, the lack of dreams, and the (spiritual?) blindness of the Jewish passerby. The misery of "the Jew" not only, *via negativa*, highlights the joyous life of the privileged Christian, but it also forms the very basis upon which Christian triumphalism stands. As Jews have been labeled a witness people (cf. Saint Augustine's *City of God*), Christians have historically ensured that Jews survive but, emphatically, do not thrive. As Jews have been viewed by Christians as the negative measure against which Christian godliness is understood—that is, because Jews are said to be carnal, hypocritical, showy, haters of Christ, devilish, and so forth—Jews become in the Christian imagination that which they are *not* and, thus, that which they must *resist*.

Moreover, as laws are intended to facilitate and promote order, the childhood Gang's scripted attacks against Jewish bodies—in this case, Gregor's—reveal how such violence is understood as not only acceptable but as *normal* and *necessary*, a "proper" and "justifiable" response to the existence of Jews in Christian Europe. Further detailing Gregor's walk to school, the narrator continues:

> The Gang, with Pishta at its head, fell upon the two boys, shouting savagely, "Büdos zsido, büdos zsido! Dirty Jews, dirty Jews, go to Palestine! You killed Christ. You'll see what it costs to kill Christ; you're going to pay for his blood." Set phrases picked up at home, in school, at church, in the street, the shouts echoed from house to house and multiplied in number and volume.[16]

The text picks up on the scriptedness of anti-Semitism, referring to the "set phrases"—those that have been premeditated, intentionally selected, and unwaveringly employed and those that have been insidiously spread by the Christian majority. In addition to the attacks on the cleanliness of Jews seen here, the rote memorization and regurgitation of anti-Semitic contempt becomes overwhelmingly clear. Their inherited script is of perennial consistency—accusations of abjection/dirtiness and deicide find expression in most, if not all, anti-Semitic Christian slander. The effectiveness and affectiveness of such libel are twofold: not only does that which is dirty risk contamination of the clean, but also that which is abject ought to be vigorously removed ("go to Palestine!"). And of course, there is no more deadly accusation than that of deicide. These young boys' adoption of the anti-Semitic script is unreflective, as is all hatred that essentializes, totalizes, and demonizes entire groups. Yet, it is this script that enables them to "justify" their violence in the name of the Christian God. Their conduct conforms to the cultural and religious "laws" that, though not (at the time) state-sponsored, operate as official policy. And it is within this historical record of Christian anti-Semitism that the novel—along with the Passion play itself—is situated.

The Passion Play

The Passion play, directed by village schoolteacher Constantine Stefan—a telling name, given the record of Emperor Constantine's ardent disdain for Jews—occurs near the end of chapter 2. The play's performance, its ritualistic enactment, furnishes the villagers with a theatrical depiction and actualization of how to respond to Jews and their putative treachery. But, long before the play is performed in the Romanian village, as noted earlier, the villagers, like most Europeans, are already quite familiar with the scriptural narrative on which the play is based. This familiarity enables them to perceive and evaluate Jews as many before perceived and evaluated them, drawing upon the prototypical image of Jesus's Passion and its accompanying age-old libels that frame Jews as lecherous, murderous, and Other. The text explores how the villagers' enduring perception, evaluation, and control of Jewish life issues forth from these inherited anti-Semitic scripts understood as "Gospel truth."

As is evident in Gregor's interaction with the Romanian villagers, there remains a script that organizes the Christian polis while simultaneously excluding Jews from it. Drawing attention to the stock nature of the villagers, the novel describes them as "village characters."[17] Such diction of villagers qua "characters" gestures toward the idea that these individuals in the village have indeed been scripted into a larger narrative. Within this larger narrative, the triumphalist Christian account rests upon and is made possible by the oppression of Jews, wherein no dissent is tolerated concerning those who allegedly murdered God. As such, the village "characters" recite the tired script passed down from one generation to the next, effectively forfeiting the occasion to think for themselves (which would require the work of critical inquiry—a price too high for anti-Semites and bigots alike). As they follow this script, the "characters"/villagers sacrifice their individual subjectivities. Assuming scripted personas, they abdicate both their will to think for themselves and their agency in the name of the alleged objective truth of the anti-Semitic Christian narrative believed to be synonymous with God's words. For to question the narrative is tantamount to questioning God. Such uncritical abdication of individual subjectivity breeds blind adherence to these hate-inspired scripts, forcing the villagers to step into the larger drama of Christian history as "characters," which has historically come at the expense of Jewish livelihood and dignity. Focusing on abstractions ("the Jews") leads to blindly following scripts, and so too does uncritically following scripts lead to the repeated renunciation of self—a perpetual cycle of self-sacrifice and submission to dominant narratives believed to be of and from God.

As the villagers are described as "characters," the text's description of Gregor, both wearing "his mask" and passing as an Aryan before the play, can be read as his forced acquiescence to self-implicate in the performance of the day-to-day anti-Semitic Christian script.[18] His wearing the mask differs from the blind adherence of the village "characters"; he wears his mask out of necessity, given the precarious time and the place in which the novel is set. His forced participation in the village's daily "performance" thus parallels his forced participation in the Passion play; Gregor's coerced participation in the dramatization of a narrative that has "dramatized" his life, making his life a veritable hell, reveals how Gregor is given a script that attempts to debase his moral character, which compels him to *act* accordingly. The stereotypical roles that "the Jews" are expected to play, however, find no such expression in reality—as has been demonstrated with the dispelling of blood libel myths and the debunking of the inflammatory *Protocols of the Elders of Zion*. Instead, these demonizing roles are only ever actualized in Christian scriptures themselves or on Passion play stages directed by Christian haters of Jews. Nonetheless, as these narratives remain largely unchallenged, they become all the more taken for granted, seen as normal or natural, and just "the way things are," that is, *as a reflection of "reality."* Thus, though Maria emphatically objects to his participation, Gregor is forced to assume the part of Judas Iscariot, *the* treacherous Jew. This is of course wildly ironic given the reality of his absolute powerlessness.

As Gregor can be understood as metonymic of Jews,[19] Constantine's selection of Gregor as Judas, the epitome of Christian antagonism, further emblematizes how he and all Jews have been coded as possessing a common underlying Jewish "nature." That Constantine does not know Gregor is Jewish at the time of his casting renders his selection ironic. Unaware of Gregor's Jewish identity, he blindly characterizes the Jewish person before him as Judas. His characterization is unexceptional in the literal sense of the word, for many Jews in their everyday lives are assigned characteristics supposedly similar to those of the New Testament Judas. Constantine's insistence on Gregor playing this unwanted role profoundly mirrors anti-Semitic insistence that every "Jew" acts like Judas. According to such thinking, all Jews are immutably alike. The narrator offers a portrait of the classical Christian understanding of Judas, the one who "stood for baseness and betrayal," stating:

> The disciple Judas inspired deep-seated mistrust. This was only natural. Almost every Sunday at Christmas and, above all, at Easter the priest stuffed their heads with Judas's irreparable crimes. A coward, a liar, an informer, the symbol of

everything detestable! Had he not, for thirty pieces of silver, sold the Savior of mankind to the Romans? He was impure to the touch and even his name could not be pronounced without spitting on the ground or brandishing the fist in the direction of an actual or imaginary Jew. Take the part of this traitor? No thanks. Too dangerous. Constantine Stefan was at his wit's end. He cursed the Jews; this, too, was their fault.[20]

The so-called "natural[ness]" of their "deep-seated mistrust" is a function of how the villagers repeatedly hear the scriptural narrative of Judas's involvement in Jesus's death. Thus, as the other children do not want to play Judas because of his New Testament portrayal, Gregor becomes the ideal candidate for the theatrical role, a role that he has been forced to assume, even though he cannot fulfill its basic requirements.

Further exposing Jews' forced acquiescence to follow the Christian script passively, Constantine's expectation for Gregor to perform as Judas further reinforces the expectation held by certain Christians for Jews *all* to act as Judases: antagonistic but ultimately subject to Christian rule. Referring to how easy it will be for Gregor to play Judas, Constantine states:

> He won't have to speak or even to move, really. He'll appear on the stage at the appropriate moments of the last act, that's all, without a word, or a gesture, just as a presence; he'll look on and accept what happens. A silent Judas, there's something original for you, a Judas struck dumb by God![21]

The theme of irony continues here, as his suggestion that "a silent Judas" is "something original." From the Christian perspective, *Judas's words* in scripture have become markedly less important and less emphasized than the *words about Judas* (specifically his betrayal of Christ for thirty pieces of silver). This skewed emphasis is most likely a function of Christians' repetition of verses *about* Judas—verses that give him no voice. That verses *about* Judas are better remembered than verses that include Judas's words reveals how many Christians have rejected Judas as a human subject who speaks, a flesh-and-blood person made in the Imago Dei. Instead, Judas is largely remembered as having a hardened heart and thus no subjectivity of his own—a function of scripture's portrayal of him, in concert with the imaginative Christian rendering of this demonized disciple. Constantine highlights this rejection of Judas's humanity in his plans to portray Judas: without movement (emblematic of a lack of agency) and without speaking (symbolic of his inability to express his subjective position, an ability never afforded him by the village). As Judas is not believed to be his own person but a vessel of God's wrath, the association of Jews with him colors all Jews, by extension, as possessing the same stock characteristics. Gregor's coerced performance of the role of Judas thus makes plain the scriptedness of Jewish stereotypes that expect all Jews to act according to the New Testament rendering of Judas.

Vengeance

As the play is performed, the audience's ecstatic collective response reveals how enduring hatred finds fertile ground when members of a group feel, think, and act in collusion. The narrator explains that the audience "found the play highly *impressive*. Every speech won applause, and their faces filled with a mixture of pride and emotion."[22] That the audience's perception of the play is *impressive*—that it makes an impression and/or impresses—signals how the performance impinges upon, touches, and thus changes those in attendance. Through this impression, this transfer of affective energies that register in the audience as "pride and emotion," members of the audience are propelled to position themselves within the narrative. They are to enact vengeance against the one who is said to have betrayed Christ. As the play progresses, the villagers take it upon themselves to mete out God's wrath, believing their responsibility is not just to act *for* God but to act *as* God. Indeed, in fanatical expressions of faith, as demonstrated here with the village mob, practitioners of such faith systems often confuse their role with the role of God; their understanding of God's judgment, as presented in both the Hebrew Bible and in the New Testament, comes to serve as a rubric for their own judgment, where they adopt and communicate to others, what they perceived to be, God's wrath. In the novel, one of the villagers cries: "You thought you could get away? There's no escape from the wrath of God!"[23] Here, "the wrath of God" finds expression through *their* anger, not leaving God the responsibility to avenge but, instead, assuming the mantle of divine fury for and by themselves. Echoing the sentiments of the first villager, another exclaims: "The bastard! Come on, let's show him he can't betray Christ and get away with it!"[24] This villager's imperative to retaliate for the supposed betrayal of Christ directly contradicts Christian teachings, for as Paul states in his epistle to the Roman church: "Beloved, never avenge yourselves, but leave it to the wrath of God, for it is written, 'Vengeance is mine, I will repay, says the Lord'" (Rom. 12:19). Regardless, Christian anti-Semites prooftext and mobilize specific New Testament verses that defame Jews, while disregarding the larger corpus that preaches love and acceptance, especially of the Other. Adding to the univocal chorus of village spectators, an additional man shouts to the boys performing onstage: "Go ahead, boys, hit him. In the name of heaven, hit him, hit him! Do you want us to come up and give you a hand?"[25] Though this man claims such violence is to be done "in the name of heaven," his actions counterpoint the Christian call to pardon and to forgive and thus are in direct opposition to the call of "heaven." Indeed, these spectators, as they propose to "give [the actors] a hand," are taking the wrath of God into their own hands and meting it out according to their *own* sense of justice and necessity, not God's. As these fanatical villagers espouse hatred and violence toward Jews, they disregard the dominant message of the Gospels to love, thus evacuating Jesus's message of its transformative power to liberate the oppressed in the name of maintaining the hegemonic power that comes part and parcel with hatred of and dominance over the Other.

This confusion of divine and human roles is largely effected by the play's production and circulation of toxic affect in the performance hall. In *The Oberammergau Passion Play* Saul S. Friedman offers insight into the evocation and maintenance of affect in the context of the Passion play when he explains that, historically, the Passion play was quite "likely to trigger a wave of negative passions directed specifically against the Jews."[26] Illuminating this concept of affect production and circulation, Teresa Brennan suggests: "The 'atmosphere' or the environment literally gets into the individual."[27] In the context of Wiesel's novel, as the Passion narrative is already embedded in the villagers' collective consciousness, the atmosphere of the performance hall easily implants itself within them, serving to amplify their preexisting contempt directed toward "Judas." Friedman further explains how in many performances of the Passion play, particularly of the Oberammergau variety, those "who held the roles of villains were ostracized like modern-day sin-eaters."[28] Friedman even notes how following one particular performance of the Oberammergau Passion play, spectators shunned and refused to touch the individual who played Judas for over two decades.[29] Thus, it can be surmised that the sight of those on the Passion play stage compounded the preexisting hatred of spectators and helped to create affectively charged performance spaces.

This violent atmosphere is given further expression in *The Gates of the Forest* in how the performance hall is coded as quasi-military space, which thereby spatializes and concretizes the hostility and violence of the Passion narrative and in turn highlights the militancy of Christian anti-Semitism. As it is set in "a long wooden shed resembling a military barracks,"[30] the atmosphere of the play assumes a combative affect, a bellicose energy that is consistent not only with the Holocaust that surrounds them but also with the anti-Semitic narrative that underlays its creation and production. Throughout much of *The Gates of the Forest* the Holocaust constitutes the backdrop of Gregor's lived experience. But as Gregor finds himself in the village, the novel presents how the Passion narrative itself undergirds anti-Semitism writ large, as it provided Nazi ideology anti-Semitic fodder that made the Holocaust and the base treatment of the Jews possible in the first place. Indeed, such a curated decision to house the theatrical production of the Passion play in the barracks-like shed signposts the violent and militant views that will be performed within, views not only communicated onstage but also transformed into physical action and attacks against Gregor qua Judas. As such, Constantine's opening greetings to the audience are gravely ironic, given the literal bloodshed that ensues moments later: "Welcome! Our holiday is a big house, room for everybody."[31] In truth, there is *not* room for everybody, as the play soon illustrates. Only those who are understood to be *humans* by the villagers are welcome, and any who are perceived as less than human are militantly brutalized. The contagion of affect to which the play gives birth incites the crowd's latent mob mentality against Jews. And as the mob of villagers assemble with "Judas" before them onstage, together they begin to enact the age-old script that gives rise to their religious rage.

Collective Action

Before moving on, I want to offer pause to examine *The Gates of the Forest*'s portrayal of the *Christian* mob in the village. I propose that the story of the collective *Christian* mob during the play's performance functions as an inversion of the New Testament narrative that lays the unforgiveable charge of blasphemy against the *Jewish* mob who reportedly calls for Jesus's death as a collective group. The novel's depiction of the Passion serves as a revision of the identity of the mob; Wiesel's text rejects the Christian narrative of "the Jews" as a monolithic group with murderous intentions. Shedding light on this phrase "the Jews" (translated from the Greek *hoi Ioudaioi*), John K. Roth and Richard L. Rubenstein explain that the term "the Jews" implicitly vilifies Jews "as benighted disbelievers who are hostile to God's grace and truth."[32] The inclusion of the definite article "the" has become, more often than not, inextricably tied to Christian descriptions of Jews where Jews are almost unanimously referred to as "the Jews." In striking contrast, Christians are rarely described as "the Christians" and are, instead, referred to as simply "Christians." In *The Gates of the Forest*, we see this diction used by the violently anti-Semitic Yonel—Gregor's family's maid's expired love interest—who refers to Jews as "the Jews" when expressing his desire to report Gregor to local authorities.[33] Though seemingly a minute difference between describing Jews as a group versus Christians as a group, the addition of "the" suggests a defined collective identity, a more *definite* character as the definite article is employed. Such collectivizing rhetoric codes Jews as homogeneous, uniform in nature, and immutable, which has not historically boded well for a group accused of sickness, devilishness, and deicide. The novel rejects this Christian notion of "the Jews"—homogeneous and indeed murderous—as it depicts the Christian villagers as an angry and violent crowd, illustrating how *Christians* have overwhelmingly been the ones to enact ruthless violence against their Jewish neighbors, not the reverse. Such a literary reversal of roles reflects Wiesel's statement that "the Christians betrayed the Christ more than the Jews did."[34] By repositioning Christians as the moblike antagonists and the sole Jewish man as victim, *The Gates of the Forest* offers a corrective to the historical record of Jewish-Christian relations. Not only does the text highlight the marginal position of Jews in Christian Europe—as Gregor faces the mob alone—but it also illustrates the predominant power relations of the Christian majority over and above the Jewish minority, which finds its "justification" in the Christian Gospels' accounts of Christ's crucifixion, along with Paul's ambivalent theological attitudes toward Jews.

The accusations that the mob directs toward "Judas" not only reveal the roteness of Christian anti-Semitism, but such accusations further illustrate the affective nature of scripts when blindly adopted in community. Friedman notes how many audiences of Passion plays, comprised by those who were typically illiterate and ignorant of "papal encyclicals dealing with ecumenism,"

> brought with them to the theater a religious zeal not unlike that of today's football fan. Theirs was a world of good pitted against evil. The evil ones were responsible for the bloodied crucifixes which hung in churches from Europe to Latin America. Many Christians brought with them a "pathological absorption in the physical wounds of Jesus." Now the Jewish merchants, priests, and mob responsible for these hideous torments were reveling before them onstage.[35]

And such is the scene, brimming with "religious zeal" and "pathological absorption," that we see in *The Gates of the Forest*. As Gregor takes the stage, the villagers break the fourth wall and begin to scream at him: "Traitor!"; "You did it for the money!"; "You betrayed the Son of God!"; "You killed the Savior!"[36] The accusations continue: "Why did you betray him? Speak up, you dog; we're listening. Why did you sell him?"[37] The mob does not deviate from the libel of the traditional Christian script, defined by its perennially repeated phrases that speak of betrayal, pecuniary lust, and animalization. Thus, the spectators' affective investment of contempt in the Passion play renders the narrative an "antitoxic script," a script that addresses scenes of toxic affects (like contempt) that are to be "opposed, excluded, attempted to be attenuated or defeated, avoided, or escaped."[38] The Passion narrative qua antitoxic script is indeed effective and affective in its mobilization of contempt, concretizing the spectators' hatred toward Jews and employing the dramatized narrative as a model for "dealing with" them accordingly. The dramatization of the Passion narrative onstage is designed to incite contempt against "Judas" and to push for a celebratory expression of his death in the last scene: "The whole cast, including the Romans, was to take part in the last act, which Constantine Stefan had intended to be an apotheosis of passion: justice triumphant! And at this point the audience began to join the actors. Anything for action!"[39] In tandem with the mob's intimate familiarity with the Passion narrative, the visual of Judas onstage concentrates the mob's focus and offers them an outlet—a physical, tangible body—to receive their fury. By assaulting "Judas" physically on the stage, the mob excises the toxic negative affects of rage and contempt that are aroused by the thought of the treacherous betrayer of Jesus. And this rage and contempt further fuel their brutalization of "Judas." Such brutalization, if completed, would serve to affirm the Christian triumphalist narrative had "Judas" lain dead and had Christ risen triumphantly from the dead—though of course we know that the killing of Gregor qua Judas is never carried out.

This "collective effervescence"—that is, the affective transference of negative energies in the form of contempt and rage—serves to unify the spectators, demonstrating the affective function of how the mythic narrative of Judas's betrayal leads to the foul ritual of communally punishing "Judas" onstage. After describing the crowd as "delirious with an ancient hate, suddenly reawakened,"[40] the narrator continues: "The attack continued and the attackers invested it with all their heart, their passion: they were enacting a rite."[41] The mutual reinforcement of myth (the long history of "ancient hate") and ritual (the "rite") fortifies the villagers' theological convictions; the former bolsters the latter as the latter undergirds the former, a perpetual cycle of nonreflective, though thoroughly affective, self-validation that operates within religious systems defined by unchecked hatred. The text highlights this circular self-validation as it notes that the villagers "feed this lie [the lie of deicide] and are fed by it."[42] Here, the village "feeds" the story of deicide as they dramatize—or, put differently, as they *ritualize*—it onstage. In turn, the villagers are "fed" by hearing and watching the familiar story (again) unfold before their eyes, reinforcing their affective purchase in both the ritual and the myth and thus evoking an even stronger affective response to the antitoxic script, which they already follow.

Shedding light on the New Testament framing of Jews as less than human that the villagers employ during the play, Emmanuel Levinas and Miroslav Volf offer insight into language's role in projects of Othering. Levinas examines how language assists in the taxonomical construction of living beings in ontologically separate geneses. This is to say that Levinas explores how language aids in categorizing those who are considered human and those who are not. "Language," he posits, "accomplishes a relation between terms that breaks up the unity of a genus. The terms, the interlocutors, absolve themselves of the relation, or remain absolute within relationship. Language is perhaps to be defined as the very power to break the continuity of being or of history."[43] Of course, the chimerical construction of Jews as less than human—that is, devilish, predatory, animalistic, and so forth—lays the necessary groundwork to treat them as such, enabling the villagers to disregard Gregor's face, that which Levinas describes as "a moral summons."[44] Volf picks up on this need for exclusionary language in order to disregard the humanity of an individual when he says that such language

> is often a distortion of the other, not simply ignorance about the other; it is a willful misconstruction, not mere failure of knowledge. We demonize and bestialize not because we do not know better, but because we *refuse* to know what is manifest and *choose* to know what serves our interests. That we nevertheless believe our distortions to be plain verities is no counter-argument; it only underlines that evil is capable of generating an ideational environment in which it can thrive unrecognized.[45]

The onstage dramatization of Judas indeed demonstrates the villagers' refusal "to know what is manifest" since the audience is convinced that Gregor is a Christian actor. Yet, in their ecstatic delirium, they treat him as a "Jew." It is the ease by which the spectators are able to switch scripts, which they do at the drop of a hat, that reveals the tenuous nature of scripts in general. Since scripts do not inherently correlate to reality but are, instead, applied to make sense of reality, the arbitrary nature of scripts can be quickly surmised. More specifically, as the anti-Semitic Christian script is based on the flimsy linguistic construction of what does and what does not constitute a human, it flies in the face, in a doubly figurative sense, of the human subject; as the human face "opens the primordial discourse whose first word is [moral] obligation,"[46] it becomes apparent how the stock phrases of these scripts consistently cloud the Christian understanding of Jews' *humanitas*.

Thus, as Gregor reveals his ability both to talk and to hear—which thereby interrupts the play—he "breaks the script," so to speak. This interruption forces the villagers to reevaluate him not as Judas (from their point of view, a *nonhuman*) but, mistakenly, as a Christian subject (or, in their estimation, as a *human*). When the audience profusely apologizes to Gregor after he demonstrates his ability to communicate verbally, they do so not out of sincere regret for the inherent violence of their actions directed toward "Judas." Rather, they beg for forgiveness because they are mortified to have been recognized by a "Christian" individual (for, at the time Gregor first speaks onstage, they do not yet know him to be Jewish).[47] Once the crowd again becomes lucid, snapping out of their vicious mob mentality, only then are they exposed for and ashamed of their actions. However, that shame is only a function of being seen and regarded by a "Christian," by a *human subject* whose presence demands that he be treated according to the standard of civility and love that the mob theretofore does not meet. This, of course, undermines the popular notion of Christian charity, which Wiesel poignantly articulates, as noted earlier, when he argues that Christian charity "is different from charity as such."[48] Yet, once Gregor reveals his Jewishness, no longer does the audience perceive itself to be subject to the gaze of a human person. Conversely, those in the audience revert back to the script of Christian anti-Semitism upon realizing his Jewish identity. The villagers' shame is quelled and their fear of consequence erased upon realizing they are not being looked at by another "human." Another "human" would, if present, reveal the shame of their violent actions, a human whose face, according to Levinas, ought to invite the onlooker to respond in an ethical posture.[49] That Gregor is a Jew, however, evokes not the overwhelming sense of shame from the audience it did seconds before when they believed they were in the presence of a young Christian man. The presence of a Jew, in sharp contradistinction, validates their brutal treatment because of how, in their estimation, their violent treatment was warranted given his status as a dangerous nonhuman.

Conclusion

In truth, *The Gates of the Forest* does not end on the Passion play stage—seeing as Gregor, with the help of the enigmatic mayor Domnul Petruskanu, makes "a miraculous escape"[50]—but the unresolved scene of the Passion play, particularly for Christian readers, leaves a number of lingering questions of how to draw the curtain, as it were, once and for all on the ritualized myth and the mythicized ritual of Jewish responsibility for the death of Christ (which is further complicated because Gregor is presented as something of a Christlike figure who offers himself to the violence of the angry mob). In contrast to how many Passion plays historically ended with spectators being roused to action against Jews and Jewish life, *The Gates of the Forest* offers us a different model of and raises questions about how we ought to respond to the old and theologically repugnant scripts of Jew hatred: How should Christians combat the Christian (script)ures that have galvanized believers against Jews for millennia? How might Christians also interrupt the performance of such violent scripts, as Gregor does even in the face of foaming mouths and gnashing teeth? How might Christians step in, as Petruskanu does, to deviate from scripts of hate when no one else has the moral courage and ethical resolve to follow suit?

Such questions, in addition to and not excluding a host of others, leave the ethical reader disturbed, particularly those who identify within the Christian tradition. *The Gates of the Forest* reminds readers of the violent reality of Christian anti-Semitism, a topic that Rosemary R. Ruether in "The *Faith and Fratricide* Discussion" explains often "remains shrouded in a conspiracy of silence" in many Christian milieus.[51] Ruether extrapolates when she says: "Facts about the long history of Christian persecution of the Jews, well known to their Jewish neighbors, are unknown to Christians" particularly because, as "the victims remember," "the victors forget."[52] Yet, as Wiesel's work offers a necessary reminder of the reality and effects of Christian anti-Semitism, it also furnishes us with the images of Gregor speaking up and of Petruskanu acting out (along with Maria's moral example earlier in the novel). These images of protest attest to the profound power of words and of action when articulated in the face of hatred and injustice. Words and actions of moral resistance are not always received kindly or even heard at all, as is the case with Gregor, whose words fall on deaf ears after revealing his Jewish identity. That Gregor's message is disregarded situates him as one of the many unheard witnesses in the work of Wiesel, as one who speaks truth but whose words are not received, for his words do not fit within his audience's paradigmatic understanding of the world. Nonetheless, as Gregor demonstrates the need to break the script, the text reveals how we too must never make a good audience for Christian Jew hatred or, for that matter, hatred of any sort. We are rather called to speak up, whether or not we, the (potentially) unheard witnesses, are ignored; we must work against the Christian anti-Semitic script that endures today and work on behalf of those who have endured and continue to endure such anti-Semitic hatred. For if we do not, it seems to me that the "Passion play," as it has been scripted throughout the centuries and as it is presented in *The Gates of the Forest*, will continue to be blindly, yet violently, performed.

Notes

1. Silvan Tomkins, "Script Theory and Nuclear Scripts," in *Shame and Its Sisters: A Silvan Tomkins Reader*, ed. Eve Kosofsky Sedgwick and Adam Frank (Durham: Duke University Press, 1995), 181.

2. Elie Wiesel, *The Gates of the Forest*, trans. Frances Frenaye (New York: Holt, Rinehart and Winston, 1964), 17.

3. See Amy-Jill Levine, "Matthew, Mark, and Luke: Good News or Bad?," in *Jesus, Judaism, and Christian Anti-Judaism: Reading the New Testament after the Holocaust*, ed. Paula Fredriksen and Adele Reinhartz (Louisville: Westminster John Knox Press, 2002); E. P. Sanders, "Jesus, Ancient Judaism, and Modern Christianity: The Quest Continues," in *Jesus, Judaism, and Christian Anti-Judaism: Reading the New Testament after the Holocaust*, ed. Paula Fredriksen and Adele Reinhartz (Louisville: Westminster John Knox Press, 2002); John Gager, "Paul, the Apostle of Judaism," in *Jesus, Judaism, and Christian Anti-Judaism: Reading the New Testament after the Holocaust*, ed. Paula Fredriksen and Adele Reinhartz (Louisville: Westminster John Knox Press, 2002); Adele Reinhartz, "The Gospel of John: How 'the Jews' Became Part of the Plot," in *Jesus, Judaism, and Christian Anti-Judaism: Reading the New Testament after the Holocaust*, ed. Paula Fredriksen and Adele Reinhartz (Louisville: Westminster John Knox Press, 2002); Joseph B. Tyson, "Anti-Judaism in the Critical Study of the Gospels," in *Anti-Judaism and the Gospels*, ed. William R. Farmer (Harrisburg: Trinity, 1999); and Gaston Lloyd, "Paul and the Torah," in *Antisemitism and the Foundations of Christianity*, ed. Alan T. Davies (New York: Paulist, 1979).

4. Franklin Littell, *The Crucifixion of the Jews: The Failure of Europe during the Second World War* (New York: Holt Paperback, 1987), 25–26.

5. Paula Fredriksen, "The Birth of Christianity and the Origins of Christian Anti-Judaism," in *Jesus, Judaism, and Christian Anti-Judaism: Reading the New Testament after the Holocaust*, ed. Paula Fredriksen and Adele Reinhartz (Louisville: Westminster John Knox Press, 2002), 28.

6. See Judson Shaver, "New Testament Roots of Christian Anti-Semitism," in Saul Friedman's *The Oberammergau Passion Play: A Lance against Civilization* (Carbondale: Southern Illinois University Press, 1984), xv.

7. Robert McAfee Brown, *Elie Wiesel: Messenger to All Humanity* (Notre Dame: University of Notre Dame Press, 1989), 169.

8. Richard L. Rubenstein, *After Auschwitz: Radical Theology and Contemporary Judaism* (New York: Macmillan, 1966), 43–44.

9. Rubenstein, *After Auschwitz*, 30.

10. Victoria Aarons, "The Trauma of History in *The Gates of the Forest*," in *Elie Wiesel: Jewish, Literary, and Moral Perspectives*, ed. Steven T. Katz and Alan Rosen (Bloomington: Indiana University Press, 2013), 150.

11. Aarons, "The Trauma of History in *The Gates of the Forest*," 150.

12. Joyce B. Lazarus, "Expanding Time: The Art of Elie Wiesel in *The Gates of the Forest*," *Modern Language Studies* 24, no. 4 (1994): 41.
13. Aarons, "The Trauma of History in *The Gates of the Forest*," 148.
14. Wiesel, *The Gates of the Forest*, 28.
15. Wiesel, *The Gates of the Forest*, 95.
16. Wiesel, *The Gates of the Forest*, 29.
17. Wiesel, *The Gates of the Forest*, 70.
18. Wiesel, *The Gates of the Forest*, 73.
19. Aarons, "The Trauma of History in *The Gates of the Forest*," 150.
20. Wiesel, *The Gates of the Forest*, 89.
21. Wiesel, *The Gates of the Forest*, 89.
22. Wiesel, *The Gates of the Forest*, 100, emphasis added.
23. Wiesel, *The Gates of the Forest*, 101.
24. Wiesel, *The Gates of the Forest*, 103.
25. Wiesel, *The Gates of the Forest*, 103.
26. Saul S. Friedman, *The Oberammergau Passion Play: A Lance against Civilization* (Carbondale: Southern Illinois University Press, 1984), 104.
27. Teresa Brennan, *The Transmission of Affect* (Ithaca: Cornell University Press, 2004), 17.
28. Friedman, *The Oberammergau Passion Play*, 103.
29. Friedman, *The Oberammergau Passion Play*.
30. Wiesel, *The Gates of the Forest*, 96.
31. Wiesel, *The Gates of the Forest*, 98.
32. John K. Roth and Richard L. Rubenstein, *Approaches to Auschwitz: The Holocaust and Its Legacy* (Louisville: Westminster John Knox Press, 2003), 44.
33. Wiesel, *The Gates of the Forest*, 67.
34. Wiesel qtd. in Brown, *Elie Wiesel*, 48.
35. Friedman, *The Oberammergau Passion Play*, 107.
36. Wiesel, *The Gates of the Forest*, 101.
37. Wiesel, *The Gates of the Forest*, 102.
38. Tomkins, "Script Theory and Nuclear Scripts," 190.
39. Wiesel, *The Gates of the Forest*, 101.
40. Wiesel, *The Gates of the Forest*, 103.
41. Wiesel, *The Gates of the Forest*, 104.
42. Wiesel, *The Gates of the Forest*, 106.
43. Emmanuel Levinas, *Totality and Infinity: An Essay on Exteriority*, trans. Alphonso Lingis (Pittsburgh: Duquesne University Press, 2005), 195.
44. Levinas, *Totality and Infinity*, 196.
45. Miroslav Volf, *Exclusion and Embrace: A Theological Exploration of Identity, Otherness, and Reconciliation* (Nashville: Abingdon Press, 1996), 76.
46. Levinas, *Totality and Infinity*, 201.
47. Wiesel, *The Gates of the Forest*, 109–10.

48. Wiesel, *The Gates of the Forest*, 17.
49. Levinas, *Totality and Infinity*, 198.
50. Wiesel, *The Gates of the Forest*, 209.
51. Rosemary R. Ruether, "The *Faith and Fratricide* Discussion: Old Problems and New Dimensions," in *Antisemitism and the Foundations of Christianity*, ed. Alan Davies (New York: Paulist Press, 1979), 230.
52. Ruether, "The *Faith and Fratricide* Discussion," 230.

Works Cited

Aarons, Victoria. "The Trauma of History in *The Gates of the Forest*." In *Elie Wiesel: Jewish, Literary, and Moral Perspectives*, ed. Steven T. Katz and Alan Rosen, 146–59. Bloomington: Indiana UP, 2013.

Brennan, Teresa. *The Transmission of Affect*. Ithaca: Cornell University Press, 2004.

Brown, Robert McAfee. *Elie Wiesel: Messenger to All Humanity*. Notre Dame: University of Notre Dame Press, 1989.

Fredriksen, Paula. "The Birth of Christianity and the Origins of Christian Anti-Judaism." In *Jesus, Judaism, and Christian Anti-Judaism: Reading the New Testament after the Holocaust*, ed. Paula Fredriksen and Adele Reinhartz, 8–30. Louisville: Westminster John Knox Press, 2002.

Friedman, Saul S. *The Oberammergau Passion Play: A Lance against Civilization*. Carbondale: Southern Illinois University Press, 1984.

Gager, John. "Paul, the Apostle of Judaism." In *Jesus, Judaism, and Christian Anti-Judaism: Reading the New Testament after the Holocaust*, ed. Paula Fredriksen and Adele Reinhartz, 56–76. Louisville: Westminster John Knox Press, 2002.

Lazarus, Joyce B. "Expanding Time: The Art of Elie Wiesel in *The Gates of the Forest*." *Modern Language Studies* 24, no. 4 (1994): 39–46.

Levinas, Emmanuel. *Totality and Infinity: An Essay on Exteriority*. Trans. Alphonso Lingis. Pittsburgh: Duquesne University Press, 2005.

Levine, Amy-Jill. "Matthew, Mark, and Luke: Good News or Bad?" In *Jesus, Judaism, and Christian Anti-Judaism: Reading the New Testament after the Holocaust*, ed. Paula Fredriksen and Adele Reinhartz, 77–98. Louisville: Westminster John Knox Press, 2002.

Littell, Franklin. *The Crucifixion of the Jews: The Failure of Europe During the Second World War*. New York: Holt Paperback, 1987.

Lloyd, Gaston. "Paul and the Torah." In *Antisemitism and the Foundations of Christianity*, ed. Alan T. Davies, 48–71. New York: Paulist Press, 1979.

Reinhartz, Adele. "The Gospel of John: How 'the Jews' Became Part of the Plot." In *Jesus, Judaism, and Christian Anti-Judaism: Reading the New Testament after the Holocaust*, ed. Paula Fredriksen and Adele Reinhartz, 99–116. Louisville: Westminster John Knox Press, 2002.

Roth, John K., and Richard L. Rubenstein. *Approaches to Auschwitz: The Holocaust and Its Legacy*. Louisville: Westminster John Knox Press, 2003.

Rubenstein, Richard L. *After Auschwitz: Radical Theology and Contemporary Judaism*. New York: Macmillan, 1966.

Ruether, Rosemary R. "The *Faith and Fratricide* Discussion: Old Problems and New Dimensions." In *Antisemitism and the Foundations of Christianity*, ed. Alan Davies, 230–56. New York: Paulist Press, 1979.

Sanders, E. P. "Jesus, Ancient Judaism, and Modern Christianity: The Quest Continues." In *Jesus, Judaism, and Christian Anti-Judaism: Reading the New Testament after the Holocaust*, ed. Paula Fredriksen and Adele Reinhartz, 31–55. Louisville: Westminster John Knox Press, 2002.

Shaver, Judson. "New Testament Roots of Christian Anti-Semitism." In Saul Friedman's *The Oberammergau Passion Play: A Lance against Civilization*, xv–xix. Carbondale: Southern Illinois University Press, 1984.

Tomkins, Silvan. "Script Theory and Nuclear Scripts." In *Shame and Its Sisters: A Silvan Tomkins Reader*, ed. Eve Kosofsky Sedgwick and Adam Frank, 179–96. Durham: Duke University Press, 1995.

Tyson, Joseph B. "Anti-Judaism in the Critical Study of the Gospels." In *Anti-Judaism and the Gospels*, ed. William R. Farmer, 216–51. Harrisburg: Trinity, 1999.

Volf, Miroslav. *Exclusion and Embrace: A Theological Exploration of Identity, Otherness, and Reconciliation*. Nashville: Abingdon Press, 1996.

Wiesel, Elie. *The Gates of the Forest*. Trans. Frances Frenaye. New York: Holt, Rinehart and Winston, 1964.

Part III

Theology and Tradition

7

Stories Untold

Theology, Language, and the Hasidic Spirit in Elie Wiesel's *The Gates of the Forest*

ARIEL EVAN MAYSE

So much for the language of the words. But, in addition, "there are yet to the Lord" languages without words: songs, tears, and laughter. And the speaking creature has been found worthy of them all. These languages begin where words leave off, and their purpose is not to close but to open. They rise from the void. They *are* the rising up of the void. Therefore, at times they overflow and sweep us off in the irresistible multitude of their waves; therefore, at times, they cost a man his wits, or even his life. Every creation of the spirit which lacks an echo of one of these three languages is not really alive, and it were best that it had never come into the world.

—Hayim Nahman Bialik, "Concealment and Revealment in Language"

Now, in this generation, we have learned at least one lesson: that some experiences lie beyond language, that their language *is* silence. For silence does not necessarily mean absence of language. [. . .] And now we know what it was: an appeal, an outcry to God on behalf of his desperate people, and also on His behalf, an offering to night, to heaven, an offering made by wise old men and quiet children to mark the end of language—the outer limits of creation—a burning secret buried in silence.

—Elie Wiesel, *Somewhere a Master: Further Portraits and Legends*

The novels of Elie Wiesel usher his readers into a world of repercussive silence. The struggle with the limits of language is present throughout his written oeuvre, and Wiesel embraced silence as an evocative literary and pedagogical tool.[1] He offers silence as a possible response to unspeakable pain, a reaction to trauma so inexpressible and dehumanizing that the inadequacy of language is utterly laid bare. Wiesel's silence had the power to reveal, to convey ideas and experiences that, by their very nature, must remain essentially unspoken. But he understood that moral failing may easily be garbed in the facade of silence; he fiercely condemned those who hide cowardice behind quiet inactivity. And he was painfully aware that the confrontation with silence may lead to a state of overwhelming existential loneliness. Humanity's silence is nearly unbearable, but it becomes all the more disquieting when compounded by the silence of God.

Elie Wiesel's novel *The Gates of the Forest* (*Les portes de la forêt*, 1964) pivots on the redemptive power of language.[2] The stirring book explores the capacity of words to deliver human beings from madness and loneliness in a silent world seemingly devoid of God's presence. The book highlights the importance of storytelling, of song and even of laughter as mediums that pierce through this existential silence, thus allowing for a breath of uplift amid the crush of tragedy and God's inscrutable hiddenness.[3] *The Gates of the Forest* grapples with silence both human and divine, reflected in an ineffable, unspoken quality that inheres in Wiesel's prose.

My aim is to examine this work as a return to language, an embrace of the spiritual power of words, songs, and storytelling. I shall argue that a Hasidic conception of language, in which words figure as the sacred nexus between God and man, will provide an important interpretive key to unlocking new dimensions of *The Gates of the Forest*. This point comes into relief as we compare this work to Wiesel's Hasidic stories,[4] which bridge the realms of fiction and nonfiction, as well as the Hasidic sources from which he drew inspiration.

Wiesel uses the ethos of Hasidism to bring his reader on a journey through silence, laughter, song, and storytelling. In Hasidism, as we shall see, one may inhabit different spheres of language simultaneously, shuttling between them in moments of shifting consciousness. Words and silence ebb and flow against one another, producing tidal currents in which the quest for religious and existential meaning is born. And, offering a fluid approach to time as well, *The Gates of the Forest* ventures beyond linear temporality by compressing past, present, and future into a single expansive moment in which the infinite—and the Divine—erupt into being through language.

Hasidism: Silence, Rapture, and Rupture

Elie Wiesel's post-Holocaust portraits of Hasidism, recast in light of his own spiritual struggles, places him within a broad school described as literary neo-Hasidism.[5] He was enamored with these great masters of the spirit, in part, because of his childhood in Sighet in rural Transylvania. Wiesel's family belonged to the community of Vizhnitz Hasidim, and he longed for that world that had been destroyed by the Nazis. But his reasons were largely constructive rather than nostalgic, for Wiesel saw in Hasidism an answer to the spiritual and moral crisis of his day.[6] He interpreted Hasidism's embrace of both silence and song, of joy and exultation as well as gloom and melancholy, as a courageous—if paradoxical—response to tragedy.[7]

Wiesel's complicated relationship with silence and the limits of language in confronting absurdity were the result of his encounter with French existentialist thinkers like Albert Camus (1913–1960) and Jean-Paul Sartre (1905–1980).[8] But the influence of Hasidism is unmistakable in *The Gates of the Forest*, written at a transitional time in Wiesel's own complicated religious journey after the Holocaust. Two friendships with other Eastern European Jews living in New York helped him rediscover the spiritual riches of Hasidism. Abraham Joshua Heschel (1907–1972) showed Wiesel that one could translate Hasidic piety into a contemporary register, drawing from its wisdom without retreating into the ghetto.[9] And Menachem Mendel Schneerson (1902–1994), the seventh Lubavitcher Rebbe, offered an example of a fearless quest for religious meaning and life without ignoring the horrors of Auschwitz.[10]

Wiesel was particularly drawn to a tension, rooted in the heart of Hasidic spirituality, on the question of language. As a path of mystical devotion, the Hasidic masters yearned for an experience of the Divine beyond words. Hasidic descriptions of rapture in its most elevated form refer to becoming enveloped in a sublime illumination in which all descriptions melt away. Yet the Hasidic masters inherited the Kabbalistic tradition in which language is viewed with a sense of deep appreciation and reverence.[11] André Neher has suggested that "silence is the metaphysical form of the cosmos."[12] Hasidism, however, offers a theological vision in which language, both human and divine, is the very essence of being. Creation was accomplished through the divine Word, and God's sustaining utterance endures as the animating force of the cosmos. This primal force of God's sacred Word is the vital source from which all human language is hewn, and uniting with this sublime divine language is the goal of all worship:

> The purpose of all prayer is to uplift the words, to return them to their source above. Just as the world was created by the downward flow of letters.
>
> Our task is to form those letters into words and take them back to God. If you come to know this dual process, your prayer may be joined to the constant flow of Creation—word to word, voice to voice, breath to breath, thought to thought. The words fly upward and come before Him.[13]

Hasidic sources thus offer a robustly positive account of the role of language in religious life.[14] They do indeed refer to an inward realm of creativity and inspiration that lies beyond words. It is into this region that the mystic journeys in contemplative prayer, tracing spoken words back to their roots in the mind, and then the ineffable beyond. Yet this indescribable realm is restricted by its silence, for flashes of insight have no expression until they are brought into language. God too is restrained by silence, and in moments—such as Revelation or Creation—the Divine emerged from the preverbal inner realm and came into existence through the pathways of language. Rather than seeking to transcend language or retreat into meditative silence, the Hasidic masters affirm that language is a divine gift, even describing the faculty of speech as an element of God imbued within humanity. For the panentheistic Hasidic mystics, the world was created through language, and God's immanent presence within the cosmos *is* a form of enduring linguistic vitality that sustains and animates existence itself.

According to the Hasidic masters God's presence in the world—and, by contrast, hiddenness—is intertwined with human language. One early Hasidic source states: "Think that the letters of prayer are the garments of God [. . .]. Enter into every letter with all your strength. God dwells within each letter; as you enter it, you become one with God.[15] And elsewhere, "It is through the letters that the word of God may come to dwell with us."[16] Words create limits and boundaries, but language is the portal—the gateway—through which the Divine flows into the cosmos and the human heart. The pain of divine concealment was known to the Hasidic masters, who offer language as a method for overcoming the experience of God's absence and silence.[17] Human language, a faculty imbued within mankind as a divine gift, restores the link between the human and divine realms. But the inverse is true as well: humanity's silence may lead to the silence of God, whose presence depends on human deeds and language. To speak—in protestation or confrontation—is to draw God into the world, overturning God's hiddenness through the power of the word. And the Hasidic masters taught that laughter and song can provide relief even when specific language cannot. The same holds true for stories, which inspire and illuminate as a type of affective religious discourse found in living examples rather than logical postulates and reasoned arguments.

Key to the Hasidic approach to language is the love of other human beings as expressed in togetherness, words, and songs.[18] Indeed, says Wiesel, "Beshtian Hasidism is founded on solidarity."[19] Introspective contemplation of the Divine, though perhaps sublime, is callous and cold toward others; silence generates solitude and isolation.[20] As we shall see, the lonely forest is a place of security and silence, but "the man that chooses solitude and its riches is on the side of those who are against man, who pay with the blood and tears of others."[21] Only through connecting to others may the forces of meaninglessness and indifference be banished.[22] Wiesel, like Martin Buber and Abraham Joshua Heschel, saw Hasidic spirituality as unbound by the dichotomy of religious duties and ethical obligations.[23] In Hasidism, says Wiesel, "the way to heaven [. . .] the way to God leads through your fellow man."[24] The Hasidic masters summoned us to humility, open-heartedness, and courage, thus lovingly embracing the immeasurable worth of every human being. More than in shared silence, this connection to others and thus to God is forged through songs, words, and stories.

Shrouds of Language and Time

The structure of *The Gates of the Forest* reveals a complicated interweaving of language and time. The arc of the book traces the seasons from spring to winter, each of which is followed by a blank, white page of declarative silence.[25] Many years elapse unannounced, and throughout the novel we are reminded that time, along with language, has melted into absurdity.[26] In this war-torn world of silence, a realm in which words, names, and meaning have become unmoored from their foundations, time is similarly uncoupled from the cosmos.[27]

The novel opens in spring with a cave and concludes in a synagogue, parallel shelters that bookend the narrator's journey. This cave, like the setting of Plato's parable and like the Talmudic legend of Rabbi Shimon bar Yohai's flight from the Romans, provides solace and transformation, but it is also a place of silent helplessness. The narrator, using the assumed name of Gregor, meets a mysterious figure whom he calls Gavriel. Both of these Jews "lost" their onetime names in their flight from the Nazi collaborators. Gregor gives the stranger his original name, blurring the identity of the two throughout the novel. They exchange stories, coming to appreciate each other's words and laughter as a means of healing the silence. Gavriel is sighted after leaving the cave to forage, and he offers himself up to the soldiers in order to save his comrade. Gavriel greets their fearful guns and barking dogs with a heartrending peal of laughter.

In summer Gregor returns to the village of his family's Christian housekeeper, who encourages him to hide as a gentile with this newly adopted name. Pretending to be deaf and mute, Gregor melts into the background. The villagers see him as a confidant, prompted by his silence to reveal their secrets. The ploy unravels when Gregor is forced to take the role of Judas in a town play, and he becomes a Christlike figure of tragic suffering and expiation. He says nothing in the face of the villagers' ancient bloodlust, even when physically attacked, for Gregor has absorbed their sins and become saturated with their confessions. The townspeople seem determined to kill this mute simpleton who bears witness to their hypocrisy, lust, and greed, and the blows of over a thousand years of hatred of Judaism—and Jews—rain down upon him. The Count, a mysterious village patron, silently offers to deliver Gregor in words that nobody else can hear. But the narrator demurs, breaking his silence and calling the peasants to atone for their injustice. Judas, not Jesus, has become the sacrificial lamb to be slaughtered on their altar of iniquity. The villagers' surge forward to cut out his tongue, seeking to inflict a punishment of eternal silence. The Count saves Gregor by seizing his hand and whisking him away—silently—to a partisan camp.

Thus in the twilight of autumn, the third of the novel's quartets, Gregor has once more returned to a forest. Gregor joins the partisan group headed by his childhood friend Leib "the Lion," and, now among his people, the words long restrained begin to gush forth. Gregor tells the partisans about Gavriel and his descriptions of the wholesale destruction of Jewish communities across Eastern Europe. Together they mourn and plot their vengeance, but this communitas is short-lived. Leib is killed in an attempt to rescue Gavriel, and Gregor incriminates—indeed, condemns—himself in regard to the alleged betrayal leading to the partisan leader's death. The narrator sacrifices himself once more, thus making an absurdity of the quest for certainty and justice in a world rife with corruption. Another partisan dies in a failed foraging raid, and the band exacts revenge upon the murderer and recite Kaddish for their fallen comrade. Gregor musters the courage to declare his love for a fellow partisan, giving words to an emotion now rekindled in his heart, but his secret is greeted only with silence.

After this tender moment of openheartedness, followed by another blank page and the final section of winter, many years pass. The war has drawn to a close, for Gregor is attending a Hasidic gathering in Brooklyn, but the narrative silence leaves untold questions in abeyance. The Hasidim at this annual celebration commemorating the death of an early master are singing, drinking, and telling stories. The narrator, however, stands quietly apart, appreciating their enthusiasm but refusing to join their song. Gregor is granted a private audience with the nameless rebbe, a person of melancholy and grace, and their conversation focuses on the possibility of faith—in God and in man—after the horrors of Auschwitz. Gregor argues that continuing to live in an absurd world is perpetuated madness. The rebbe admits God's guilt but underscores that inaction and silence are nonetheless inexcusable. The way beyond the Holocaust, says the rebbe, lies in song and heartfelt words. Gregor is obviously transformed by his disquieting encounter with this man of faith, a spiritual master who wields the power of language and melody. He goes to a little Hasidic synagogue and recites the Kaddish on behalf of the many casualties of the Holocaust, including God. This is a homecoming of sorts, for Wiesel as for the narrator, representing a return to the struggle with God and to the spiritual world of Hasidism.[28] Gregor has come back from the perilous, void solitude, now expressing the inchoate power of silence in language—through laughter, song, and storytelling.

Silence

The Gates of the Forest is suffused with several modalities of silence. For Gregor and Gavriel hiding in the cave, the quiet is an agent of terror and desolation: "The silence was heavy, weighed down by the passage of time. Silence was everywhere, in the trees, the bushes, and the eyes of the dogs."[29] Such quiet is born in fear, in the absurdity of life in a world governed by destruction. "Words kill," says Wiesel, and the retreat into silence is a strategy for self-preservation.[30] The narrator abandons language while hiding in his housekeeper's village:

> Gregor gave up speech. This was no sacrifice at all. Already in the cave he had become used to silence and loved it. Gavriel had told him: "Men talk because they're afraid, they're trying to convince themselves that they're still alive. It's in the silence after the storm that God reveals himself to man. God is silence."[31]

Wiesel alludes to the biblical story of Elijah in the cave, but with a crucial difference.[32] In the theophany in the book of Kings, God speaks to the prophet in a still, small voice, but this passage suggests that silence is the truest vehicle of revelation. Human beings adorn themselves in language in order to pretend to be alive, and in doing so their clamor overpowers the voice of God.

His silence allows Gregor to move unencumbered among the village. The townspeople naturally open their hearts to him, revealing their depravity and speaking about their guilt, turning him into a reservoir for their words. Yet the sound of his mysterious friend endures within him: "The voice of Gavriel vibrated within him, regulating his breathing and giving depth to his silence. He hid himself behind Gavriel's face, beneath Gavriel's star, and this was why he was able, almost without effort, to keep silent."[33] Perhaps it is this quiet but powerful repose that incites the villagers to rise against him. They desire his blood, but they also demand something more: "he must be made to speak."[34] The townspeople are unable to bear his silence, for, as Judas, he is an unmistakable testimony to their sin. Gregor quietly grits his teeth against their onslaught but reclaims the power of language and declares that the Jews are the real sacrifice.

The potent silence of active listening is a key theme throughout the book. Gregor pays close attention to the words of Gavriel and the townspeople, and then, as he tells the story of the botched rescued attempt to the partisans, the roles are reversed: "I have spoken [. . .] and my words have dug a ditch between us. I must now build a bridge between us, that they may share my shame as I share their silence."[35] Words create divisions, whereas silence binds them together. Even the trees of the partisan forest absorb words, soaking them up and preserving them within their verdant ranks.[36]

But silence can also reflect human passivity in the face of escalating and unthinkable tragedy. In the cave Gavriel tells Gregor about a friend of his who "had the power, by the use of words, to dispel darkness."[37] This mysterious person, who could have been the Messiah, came to Gavriel's town but humbly refused to reveal himself. He stays silent, waiting in the face of mounting terror. To unlock the gates of heaven and stop the Nazi death machine would not have taken much: "A single gesture, a word, an outcry; above all, an outcry from you can change everything," says Gavriel.[38] But his silence persisted until his tongue was cut out; the Messiah was quiet evermore, and God too remained silent as the Jews were led to the slaughter.[39] Such quiet is thus filled with shame and insufficiency, a blistering condemnation of human apathy.

Silence features prominently in Wiesel's retelling of Hasidism. Of one Hasidic school characterized by fiery enthusiasm, ascetic piety, and intolerance of compromise, he remarks: "In Kotzk one does not speak; one roars or one keeps quiet [. . .]. Silence in Kotzk is so heavy, so dense that it tears the nights."[40] Rather than the absence of words, silence is a palpable force that isolates and surrounds the worshiper. But there are modes of silence that lead beyond alienation. "In Hasidism," says Wiesel, "everything is possible, everything becomes possible by the mere presence of someone who knows how to listen, to love and give of himself."[41] And he writes, "The *tsaddik* had to know the art of speaking, the better to remain silent, and the art of silence, the better to speak."[42] Cultivating an attentive heart, one that can heal the suffering of others, requires careful attention to silence.

Classical Hasidic teachings rarely refer to silence as an independent spiritual goal. These sources often describe the project of redemption as a process through which human awareness of the Divine is renewed and all language is restored to its source in God. In a homily by an important eighteenth-century master, we read:

> Every one of Israel has to prepare the part of the Messiah belonging to his particular soul [. . .]. This cannot take place absent the passion aroused by Elijah the herald. This is called "Messiah," related to the word *mesiah*, meaning speech [. . .].

> Thus whenever thought and speech are united, the Messiah is restored. But this is not yet constant, as it will be when the Messiah actually comes. Before the arrival of such wholeness, there will need to be a heralding by Elijah, to arouse the passion of Israel.[43]

Redemption is an unfolding process through which humanity's relationship to words is radically transformed. In the time to come *all* language will become sanctified, but this development is anticipated through hallowed speech even in the present world. The task of uplifting language is incumbent upon all; such spiritual labor hastens the arrival of the messianic age, but it also reveals the presence of God amid *this* world.

The silence undergirding Wiesel's *The Gates of the Forest* is a cosmic quiet gesturing toward the absence of God. And the inescapable divine silence is directly linked to the accepting complicity of human beings: "Jews resemble their God. They're always hiding. The world's not only *Judenrein*; it's *Gottrein* as well. Soon there will be no more Jews and no more God. Nobody will hide any longer. That will be hell. We shall be alone."[44] The slaughter of the Jewish people is almost like murdering God, for Whom Wiesel utters a Kaddish at the end of the novel. Without the voice of the Jews to challenge the absurdity of life through their sacred speech, God falls terminally silent. In one collection of Hasidic tales, Wiesel writes:

> When divine silence is answered by human silence—it is tragic for both.
>
> But then—where is hope to be found? The two silences *can* merge, *can* grow one through the other, one in the other. That is sufficient—that *must* be sufficient. One can purify and free the other, and that is sufficient, that must be sufficient.
>
> For ultimately, the choice is a limited one: We can answer God's silence with words—or respond to God's words with human silence [. . . . But] what if the silence of one is the language of the other?[45]

There is redemptive hope in silence, it seems, when it leads to togetherness and interconnectivity rather than isolation. Indeed, our silence has the power to uplift the divine silence, shaping it and giving it meaning. Such is one response to our experience of God's absence. But another possibility, says Wiesel, lies in the deep imbrication of human and divine language. God's resonant voice may thus be present in our silence, and, perhaps, our words may become vessels for expressing God's silence.

The Gates of the Forest seems to conclude with a note of silence, as Gregor meets Gavriel—or a curious doppelganger—once more.[46] This figure, now doubly mysterious, is totally silent, and Gregor is happy that "the power of speech has been taken from him. All friends should be such friends as to have their tongues cut out. Save the world by killing the word. That's the solution. But then we are afraid of silence."[47] It is tempting to abnegate our duties and lapse into silence, pushing forward through destroying the illogical world, rather than seeking its recreation. But Gregor resists Gavriel's allure, reciting the Kaddish for all that he has lost and reawakening to the power of song and stories. Indeed, says Wiesel, the Hasidic masters remind us that tales must be told even amid tragedy and heartbreak: "In our history, this need to communicate, to share, comes close to being an obsession. Of course, all experiences cannot be transmitted by the word. There are those that must be transmitted from being to being, by a whisper or a glance, or—and why not—through laughter.[48] Something infinite cannot easily be contained in a word, nor can the absurd be totally overcome with language. The gesture of silence is thus necessary to communicate the depths of some human experiences too great or too terrible for the spoken word. Laughter, however, holds the keys to an even more expansive realm of communication and redemption.

Laughter

Gregor's return to words happens through laughter, a mode of defiant activism and protest.[49] Laughter, says Wiesel, is a quintessentially Jewish response to suffering. Their tormentors pay heed only to their cries, and the laughter, which goes unnoticed, allows their spirit to endure.[50] At first Gregor is overwhelmed by Gavriel's laughter, assuming that he must be ignoring the calamity around them. But the mysterious stranger replies, "I'm listening to the war and I'm laughing [. . .]. I've decided once and for all not to weep [. . .]. To weep is to play their game."[51] Crying grants victory to their enemies, and only laughter can shatter the absurdity of a world devoid of reason or logic. Only in laughter can one's thoughts turn to God.[52]

Gavriel's laughter fills pages of *The Gates of the Forest*. "His laughter echoed through the cave and mingled with the early morning wind," says Wiesel, "as it blew toward the forest and the mountain, toward all forests and all mountains, as if to shake and uproot them."[53] The intensity and madness of his laughter is overwhelming, but this is precisely why it can overcome the limitations of the world into which mankind has been thrust:

> Do you know what laughter is? It's God's mistake. When God made man in order to bend him to his wishes, he carelessly gave him the gift of laughter. Little did he know that later the earthworm would use it as a weapon of vengeance. When he found out, there was nothing he could do; it was too late to take back the gift.
>
> And as if to illustrate his words he laughed with such passion that Gregor, in order not to scream, refused to hear.[54]

Laughter was a gift bestowed upon us rather than stolen like the Promethean fire, but humanity was thrust out of Eden when it became clear that it mirrors the madness of the world and shatters it. Words cannot contain the horror of this world, but laughter can help one move beyond the mire of sadness and depression. And it can do more, says Gavriel, since laughter may fill the silence left by God's quietude.

Wiesel found in Hasidism a spiritual élan in which laughter is used to confront darkness.[55] The founder of Hasidism, he writes, called his followers to "fight sadness with joy."[56] The Hasid sees existence itself as an unconditional cause for rejoicing, looking to other human beings to share in this passion.[57] This optimism is expressed in the use of laughter to overcome spiritual enemies. Said the Baal Shem Tov: "A person has [moments of] expansive and constricted [consciousness] (*gadlut ve-katnut*). Through joy and laughter (*milta de-bedihuta*) one leaves the state of constriction and attains an expansive mind, studying [Torah] and connecting to the blessed One."[58]

The Hasidic rebbe is thus a *badkhan*, the troubadour or jester whose laughter can effect miracles and transform his disciples without recourse to words.[59] But Hasidic laughter conceals a darker moment, navigating the hair's breadth separating melancholy and exaltation. In Wiesel's Hasidic writings this tension is found in the lives of two important figures who struggled with sadness without relinquishing the power of laughter.

Wiesel suggests that "laughter occupies an astonishingly important place" in the teachings of Rabbi Nahman of Bratslav.[60] Such laughter was far from unbridled jocularity:

> [His was] laughter that springs from lucid and desperate awareness, a mirthless laughter, laughter of protest against the absurdities of existence, a laughter of revolt against a universe where man, whatever he may do, is condemned in advance. A laughter of compassion for man who cannot escape the ambiguity of his condition and of his faith. To blindly submit to God, without questioning the meaning of this submission, would be to diminish Him [. . .]. Revolt is not a solution, neither is submission. Remains laughter, metaphysical laughter.[61]

This Hasidic master, who understood the absence of God and the torments of existence within a void that is seemingly devoid of meaning, taught that a "playful glance" (*panim sohakot*) can even revive the dead.[62] Joy is a consistent theme in Rabbi Nahman's teachings, but his works also describe laughter, comedy, even mockery as connected to our confrontation with the absurd.[63] Wiesel underscores this biting voice found in Rabbi Nahman's sermons, highlighting laughter as a kind of pious rebellion against meaninglessness and divine silence.

Elsewhere Wiesel retells Rabbi Nahman's story about how different conceptions of comedy reveal the essence of each and every community.[64] In this story, he refers to a certain land that includes all others, a city within that contains all cities, and a house that includes all houses. Wiesel continues: "In that room there was a man, and that man personified all men of all countries, and that man laughed and laughed—no one had ever laughed like that before."[65] Closer inspection reveals critical innovation, for although this mysterious figure appears in Rabbi Nahman's story, the fact that he laughed—and did so in an electrifying, unparalleled way—is Wiesel's own introduction. And Wiesel adds a final theological comment: "Who is that man? The Creator laughing at His creation? Man sending Him back His laughter as an echo, or perhaps a challenge? Will we ever know?"[66] Rabbi Nahman's story implies that the person in command of laughter is the tzaddik, the heart of all the worlds, but Wiesel's recasting further blurs the lines between human and Divine. For Wiesel the figure might represent mankind throwing down the gauntlet before the Divine, but his reading suggests that the individual may well be God laughing at humanity.

Wiesel describes Rabbi Naftali of Ropshitz, the second master of laughter and tears, as follows:

> Most Rebbes cried; he laughed. Better yet: he made other people laugh. Most tended to take life seriously, if not tragically; there were few things *he* took seriously. Laughter was one of them. "Why do you laugh while I am crying?" asked Rebbe Mendel of Riminov. "Because you are crying while I am laughing," he replied. For him, laughter performed a philosophical, quasi-religious function. With him, laughter became an integral part of Hasidic experience and its tales.[67]

In Rabbi Naftali's hands, laughter holds the power to redeem and to uplift. Other rebbes used tears and words to transform their disciples, but Rabbi Naftali accomplished these feats by raising laughter to an honored place in the realm of religious service. But Rabbi Naftali's joyfulness and mirth, says Wiesel, concealed a deep inner torment:

> Behind the visible Ropshitzer, there was another, invisible one. The first told stories, teased the great and amused them; the second, withdrawn in his own inner tent, lived in silence and torment, aspiring to some unattainable truth.
>
> [. . .] No matter what the cost, the unhappy Jews in Galicia [. . .] needed to laugh, to rejoice, to hold on to existence. In this respect, the Ropshitzer performed a vital function: his combat against despair was a personal one. He didn't trust disciples or messengers; he came alone wherever communities in distress were in danger of giving in to resignation. His weapons? Song and laughter.[68]

The Ropshitzer used his humor to heal others, but his laughter belied the unspeakable sadness within. Telling the stories of this great leader, says Wiesel, allows the contemporary worshiper to avoid giving in to the crush of depression and to "hold on to existence" even in a world seemingly devoid of meaning. To laugh is one manner of achieving this goal, and the other, of course, is to sing.

Song

Music is another mode of active resistance in *The Gates of the Forest*. To sing, we learn, is to defy the absurdity of existence by linking past to present in a moment of spiritual uplift. Song transforms the human being in ways that laughter cannot; it is an act of mellifluous rebellion against the forces of darkness. Indeed, while in hiding Gregor recalls the power of his pious Hasidic grandfather, "for whom song was an instrument of battle."[69] Wiesel, both in this work and elsewhere, recalls that Rabbi Pinhas of Koretz taught that song draws the Divine down to man—even against God's will.[70] Music brings sacred illumination, overcoming divine silence and the eclipse of God's presence.

God seems to be present in the dance hall of the Hasidim, whose joyful song continues despite a world littered with the ashes of the crematoria. "The hall was stifling as if God filled it; he was the interval that separated the words and then brought them together into prayer or melody."[71] The divine presence is revealed through the collective melody of the community; their song intoned with love and faith, in God and in each other, unbroken even in the wake of unspeakable tragedy.

At this celebration, the nameless rebbe stops his homily midsentence, perhaps sensing that words have carried him as far as they can. He calls for a peasant song in Hungarian, which an old man volunteers, and the community begins to sing without fear. The crass words of folksong fade away, their coarseness is transcended, and the community moves beyond language, as "the soul has no need of words to sing."[72] Gregor gazes longingly upon the Hasidim, admiring their courage but unable to join their song.

In his private audience, the narrator asks the Hasidic leader to help him to cry. The rebbe, formerly ensconced in reposeful silence, replies that he will teach Gregor to sing instead. Crying is defeat before tragedy and trauma; the tears of sadness paralyze the soul until it hardens into a pillar of salt. The rebbe, bursting through his once-calm exterior, exclaims:

> A song on the lips is worth a dagger in the hand. I take this song and make it mine. Do you know what the song hides? A dagger, an outcry [. . .]. You've [God] taken away every reason for singing, but I shall sing. I shall sing of the deceit that walks by day and the truth that walks by night, yes, and the silence of dusk as well.[73]

Music is a sign of vital protestation. Like Gavriel's laughter, song brings one to meet absurdity and inhumanity with jubilation, perhaps greeting even death with a weapon of triumph. Elsewhere Wiesel remarks: "I try to imagine my grandfather in the train that carried him away. They tell that some danced, others sang and still others prayed—fervently, joyously, as though they anticipated a celebration, a reunion. [. . .] I shall never know whether my grandfather, Dodye Feig, the Vizhnitser Hasid, went to his death singing or dancing for a man, for a child, or for a tale he will never tell."[74] Through music one confronts tragedy with honor and dignity.

Wiesel drank deeply from the well of Hasidic teachings on the power of song and the transformative capacity of music.[75] He tells us that the Baal Shem Tov understood that "song is more precious than words," a mode of spiritual devotion beyond language.[76] A melody reaches across the generations, for, like a story, it connects the singer to great personalities of long ago.[77] But music is crucial for cultivating attention to the present moment: "Tomorrow the Hasidim will lose every reason for hope, or even to go on living, but today, rooted in the present, they are carried by a powerful song of solidarity."[78]

Many Hasidic melodies express mystical exaltation and joy, but the Hasidic masters also bequeathed songs of longing and heartbreak. These follow the example of the Song of Songs, a ballad of unrequited yearning for God. "It is a song of endless waiting and faithfulness, it is majestic and moving but marked by tragedy. God waits for Israel while Israel is waiting for God [. . .]. And yet—beyond sadness, beyond despair, there *is* love, and there always will be."[79] The seeker and the Beloved may never consummate their passion, but song underscores the power of longing in the never-ending quest to find one's lover. Such a journey includes sweetness and desire in addition to brokenness.

But Wiesel understood that song, like language, is deeply intertwined with silence in the Hasidic imagination.[80] Rather than oppositional or mutually exclusive forces, many Hasidic sources present melody and silence as complementary forces propelling spiritual growth. In a sermon by Rabbi Shneur Zalman of Liady, we read:

> The service of the Levites is in song, to arouse such [emotional] qualities as love, awe, and joy. Their arousal below brings about their arousal above. This is also the quality of *binah* or contemplation (*hitbonenut*), since the emotions arise from the contemplative self.

> But *kohen* ("priest") refers to the aspect of mind (*hokhmah*) that lies beyond all these qualities, since they do not exist on the rung of "there is nothing else [but God]" (Deut. 4:35). When you see that there is nothing but God, and all existence is truly negated, then there is no one to love, no one before whom to stand in awe, nor any other emotion. This is "priest of the heart's desire," beyond all such qualities (Zohar 3:39a). This is the meaning of "Silence is a guard for mind" (m. Avot 3:13). Silence reaches higher than sound, which is the Levites' song. Here you cannot raise your voice, since your existence itself has been negated.[81]

Such Hasidic teachings underscore the power of music to illuminate the mind and heart, but they envision melody as closely linked to contemplative silence. Both are integral to the spiritual journey beyond the confines of a human language that cannot stretch to encompass the catastrophic scope of the Holocaust.

Gavriel tells the narrator that the Messiah will one day reclaim his name and destiny, but Gregor inherited a different vision from his own family: "The Talmud says of the Messiah that he knows how to sing. To Gregor's father he was something rather than someone. 'The Messiah,' he used to say, 'is that which makes man more human, which takes the element of pride out of generosity, which stretches his soul towards others.'"[82] The Messiah's true gift, says Wiesel, is a song that grants victory over dehumanizing pain and sadness by opening the self to others. But the eruption of this messianic song is a process rather than a historical moment, one that is firmly rooted in the service of the present: "The Messiah isn't one man [. . .] he's all men. As long as there are men there will be a Messiah. One day you'll sing, and he will sing in you. Then for the last time, I'll want to cry. I shall cry. Without shame."[83] The ability to sing returns after one has overcome silence, and with it, catharsis in the face of tragedy. Rather than tears of depression, the weeping that accompanies this melody lifts the singer out of doldrums of absurdity, sadness, and passivity.

Storytelling

The Gates of the Forest has the effect of a narrative-cum-prayer. The tale concludes with a Kaddish, but throughout the novel storytelling reveals its life-giving power. Gavriel and Gregor are sustained in the cave by exchanging tales; this links them to the immortal eternity that stretches beyond their tragic present. Gavriel listens to the narrator describe his deceased father, then adds that, as long as the tale continues, "he is still alive."[84] Stories, it seems, animate the storyteller as well as the subject. Like names and memories, they persist long after death.

Rather than growing stale, stories of the past are enriched with new power and emotion each time they are retold. Gregor persistently recalls the events leading up to Leib's death, and yet, "Every one of his sentences translated a portion of an infinite evil, of a murderous truth."[85] Repetition grants stories new vitality, a potency that is embedded in all language:

> The power of repetition, Gregor thought. Perhaps the mystics are right in choosing to repeat a single sentence or prayer all their life. A thousand times one still makes one. Yet one multiplied by a thousand differs from one multiplied by ten or by one. In taking a single word by assault, it is possible to discover the secret of creation, the center where all threads come together.[86]

The power of a mantra, plucked from the realm of ordinary language and imbued with spirit through constant repetition, inheres in stories as well. Repeated storytelling allows for the simultaneous coexistence of multiple narratives, which may contradict one another or fail to cohere as a single portrait of historical events. But this for Wiesel, signals the unique importance of storytelling in the wake of the indescribable tragedy of the Holocaust.[87]

Hasidim come together in order to celebrate life through telling the tales of bygone masters, anticipating the future by connecting their present struggles and spiritual quests to the past.[88] Stories return the listeners to the deepest wells of human spirit and creativity, transcending the constraints of time and space. Through Hasidic tales, says Wiesel, "we are linked to the most fervent moments of Jewish imagination and Jewish soul; without them our history would be poorer, much poorer, for it would be a dreamless history, devoid of nostalgic legend."[89] Tales connect us to the untold riches of hope and elation found in the past, and which, through the power of storytelling, extends to the future. Indeed, says Wiesel, "God makes us remember the past so as to break our solitude."⁹⁰ Time unwinds into eternity, and the tale shatters the forces of absurdity and sadness that accost the present moment.

Storytelling enables human beings to look beyond the paradoxes of existence. Rather than grasping for answers, we are encouraged to awaken the soul by venturing on a narrative quest into the past.⁹¹ The goal is not to recall ancient miracles and thus reinforce our belief in the possibility of such supernatural deliverance from contemporary tragedies. "A good story in Hasidism," writes Wiesel, "is not about miracles, but about friendship and hope—the greatest miracles of all."⁹² These wonders are all the more magnificent—and all the more necessary—in a world after Auschwitz.

Wiesel opens *The Gates of the Forest* with a famous story about the Baal Shem Tov. When danger threatened the Jewish people, he would go off to the woods, kindle a fire, and recite a prayer to ward off the misfortune. Hasidic leaders of later generations, says Wiesel, gradually forgot the details of this ritual. Eventually a master emerges who can only tell the story, but even the tale is enough to prevent the tragedy. "And it was sufficient," writes Wiesel, presenting his belief in the power of stories to transform the world even as we are cut loose from the enchantments of the past.⁹³

The same story appears in Wiesel's *Souls on Fire*.⁹⁴ In this later account, however, Wiesel follows the concluding "and it was sufficient" with an italicized comment that changes the picture entirely. "*It no longer is,*" he says. "*The proof is that the threat has not been averted. Perhaps we are no longer able to tell the story. Could all of us be guilty? Even the survivors? Especially the survivors?*"⁹⁵ Ghastly attestations of mankind's cruelty abound; the possibility of near-instant descent into terrible brutality against others is poised like the sword of Damocles. Maybe the Holocaust has made storytelling impossible. But perhaps Wiesel intends to spur survivors, who are obligated to recount their experiences to prevent future cruelty, to begin to speak once more. *Souls on Fire* is, after all, filled with stories about the Hasidic masters and their spiritual, existential struggles. While our tales may lack the effectiveness of the Baal Shem Tov's story ritual, our stories surely have their own power and vitality.

Wiesel was a storyteller with a particular love for Hasidic tales.⁹⁶ He explains that he was "seduced by the idea of bringing back to life some of the characters that peopled his universe, the universe of his childhood. They fascinate and haunt him [i.e., Wiesel] still, ever more."⁹⁷ But his purpose was more constructive than nostalgic. Wiesel understands that all tales reveal the inner world of one storyteller, who weaves his present spiritual situation together with the deeds of a bygone master. In this, he says, we are all followers of the Baal Shem Tov, a storyteller who has

> but one motivation—to tell of himself while telling of others. He wishes neither to teach nor to convince, but to close gaps and create new bonds. Nor does he try to explain what was or even what is; he only tries to wrest from death certain prayers, certain faces, by appealing to the imagination and the nostalgia that make man listen when his story is told.[98]

The storyteller illuminates the hearts and minds of his listeners by sharing of his own soul. Such openheartedness is, of course, miraculous in its beauty.

In the afterword to *Somewhere a Master*, Wiesel explains that he is retelling the stories, with admiration and love, in order to stop the entropy of a mad world rent asunder by the tragedy of the Holocaust. Through stories the Hasidic masters overcame their own calamity, torment, and exile, and in reclaiming their tales Wiesel turns the Hasidic mystics into living examples of how to overcome God's absence through language, narrative, and song. "Somewhere," says Wiesel, "a Master is singing, and we feel compelled to join him and learn his song."[99] These songs of times past, of the spiritual struggles, of tragedy and hope, are resurrected through telling stories.

L'esprit de l'escalier and *Trepverter*

Wiesel's novels and Hasidic writings invite readers to consider the twentieth century as a world of paradoxes and incongruities, a Gordian knot of unspeakable events, narratives, and experiences that cannot be untangled. Grasping the historical processes behind the horrific examples of the bloodlust, hatred, atrocity, and genocide is difficult enough. But making sense of the silence of God and humanity in the midst—and aftermath—is simply imponderable. Wiesel forces the reader to explore his discontent with this moral passivity, leading us into the forest of absurdity and back again. "Happy is the one who knows how to enter [the sacred mystery] and to leave," declares the Zohar in a line often attributed to the Hasidic masters.[100] Such is the journey into and return from the silent heart of language, the quest through the gates of the forest.

What are the "gates" from which the novel draws its name? Wiesel's forest is a place of enigma, where silence and protection, isolation and repose, safety and danger enjoy a meaningful, if tense, coexistence. Perhaps the portals are apertures through which we see beyond the knotted wood of our existence, twisted and rendered absurd by the tragedies of modernity.[101] The forest may also be the woods into which the Baal Shem Tov would venture, leaving behind the company of men to ward off impending violence.

And yet, perhaps Wiesel has once more followed the Hasidic masters and employs the forest as a symbol of the tangled thicket of language. The following homily from Rabbi Nahman of Bratslav, rooted in clever wordplay, illustrates this point:

> "Make a portal (or 'illumination') in the ark" (Gen. 6:14).[102] A person may become surrounded on all sides [by forces of darkness]. Even if he tries to arouse his spirit and return to the One, it is difficult to pray and to speak words before God; such a person feels set upon from all sides [. . .]. The prayers that he utters are unable to break through the barriers and veils that separate them [from God, preventing them] from ascending higher and higher [. . .]
>
> These utterances remain trapped until he speaks words fitting to be accepted, in love and awe, from the depths of his heart [. . . Such prayer] will shatter all boundaries, illuminating the veils and raising up all fallen prayers [. . .]. God's illumination shows him the way to find a way out of the darkness and exile in which he had been imprisoned. For, in truth, these many gateways were always there [. . .] and only "the fool walks in darkness" (Eccl. 2:14) without seeing the doors through which he might leave.[103]

The existential darkness surrounding us is ultimately only a mirage. The absurdity of the void is an illusion, a veil preventing us from seeing exits, and to pierce through it we need only to find the portals of language.

Through these gateways, hewn from words uttered with attention and open-heartedness, we depart from our self-made prison.

S. Y. Agnon offers a strikingly similar image, drawn from a story attributed to the Hasidic master Rabbi Hayyim of Tsanz:

> A man had been wandering about in a forest for several days, not knowing which was the right way out. Suddenly he saw a man approaching him. His heart was filled with joy. "Now I shall certainly find out which is the right way," he thought to himself. When they neared one another, he asked the man, "Brother, tell me which is the right way. I have been wandering about in this forest for several days."
>
> Said the other to him, "Brother, I do not know the way out either. For I too have been wandering about here for many, many days. But *this* I can tell you: do not take the way I have been taking, for that will lead you astray. And now let us look for a new way out together."[104]

The way through the forest is utterly unknown, but the task of the Hasidic teacher is to share his wisdom and experience with others. Neither a miracle worker nor an unfailing messenger of divine instruction, the rebbe simply tells others about the dead ends in his own spiritual journey. Masters and disciples walk the same path, but the teacher is the one with the courage to open his heart and share the journey.

But Wiesel's forest is more than a symbol of alienation, solitude, and loneliness. The verdant labyrinth teems with life; it has a voice of its own. People steal away to the woods in order to hide from the world, surely, but they come also to absorb something beyond language:

> to listen and tremble, to tremble as they listen to this roaring voice which, before creation, before the liberation of the word, already contained form and matter, joy and defeat, and that which separates and reconciles them, from all of which the universe, time, and their own secret life were fashioned [. . .]
>
> Outside the voice of the forest is drowned out by the chattering and lamentations of those who traffic in their future and in anxiety, their own and that of others.[105]

In the forest we reclaim the voice of Gavriel, the mirthless man of laugher whose protest against divine injustice has never died down. His murmurs joined the wind and the leaves, his presence is revealed through the rustle of the breeze through the trees. We are overcome by worry, anxiety, sadness, and doubt outside of this sheltered world. The incessant chatter of humanity further dulls our attunement to this sacred roar of the woods. Rather than looking for exits, then, Wiesel may also wish for his readers to step into the forest and thus remember the silent rush of eternity amid the madness of language.

Wiesel has spun *The Gates of the Forest* from the gossamer of Hasidism and its devotional approach to language and the spirit. The author threads together silence and song, the eruption of laughter and storytelling amid absurdity, winding them into a powerful story of redemption. These different avenues of communication, each modes of overcoming tragedy, are gateways through which the novel's protagonists and readers are invited to enter the forest of stillness—and to return to the world once more. Wiesel offers the teachings of the Hasidic masters and their tales as a living link to the eternal struggles of the spirit. These contests—with words, and with God—brook no resolution. But the stories give us a foothold in the paradoxical simultaneity of silence, song, and laughter. Wiesel's tale is a window, a portal into the enduring power of narration to open the heart and mind to a radiant silence that shimmers with illuminated words.

Notes

1. On the constructive role of silence, see Simon P. Sibelman, *Silence in the Novels of Elie Wiesel* (New York: St. Martin's Press, 1995), 17.

2. The English version appeared as *The Gates of the Forest*, trans. Frances Frenaye (New York: Holt, Rinehart and Winston, 1966).

3. See Victoria Aarons, "The Trauma of History in *The Gates of the Forest*," in *Elie Wiesel: Jewish, Literary, and Moral Perspectives*, ed. Steven T. Katz and Alan Rosen (Bloomington: Indiana University Press, 2013), 146–59; Sibelman, *Silence in the Novels of Elie Wiesel*, 85–102; Irving Halperin, "From *Night* to *The Gates of the Forest*: The Novels of Elie Wiesel," in *Responses to Elie Wiesel: Critical Essays by Major Jewish and Christian Scholars*, ed. Harry James Cargas (New York: Persea Books, 1978), 45–82; and Joyce B. Lazarus, "Expanding Time: The Art of Elie Wiesel in *The Gates of the Forest*," *Modern Language Studies* 24, no. 4 (1994): 39–46.

4. Of particular relevance are his *Souls on Fire* (1972) and *Somewhere a Master* (1982), the first of which appeared some eight years after *The Gates of the Forest*.

5. See also Nicham Ross, *A Beloved-Despised Tradition: Modern Jewish Identity and Neo-Hasidic Writing at the Beginning of the Twentieth Century* (Beer-Sheva: Ben Gurion of the Negev Press, 2010; Hebrew). On Wiesel's interpretation of Hasidism, see the studies by Arthur Green, Gershon Greenberg, Steven T. Katz, and Nehemia Polen in *Elie Wiesel: Jewish, Literary and Moral Perspectives*, ed. Steven T. Katz and Alan Rosen (Bloomington: Indiana University Press, 2013); and Lothar Kahn, "Elie Wiesel: Neo-Hasidism," in *Responses to Elie Wiesel: Critical Essays by Major Jewish and Christian Scholars*, ed. Harry James Cargas (New York: Persea Books, 1978), 45–82.

6. See his remarks in Elie Wiesel, *Souls on Fire: Portraits and Legends of Hasidic Masters* (New York: Simon & Schuster, 1972), 256.

7. Wiesel, *Souls on Fire*, 83.

8. See Mary Jean Green, "Witness to the Absurd: Elie Wiesel and the French Existentialists," *Renascence* 29, no. 4 (1977): 170–84. See, for example, Jean-Paul Sartre, *What is Literature? And Other Essays* (Cambridge: Harvard University Press, 1988), 52: "Thus, from the very beginning, the meaning is no longer contained in the words [. . .] the literary object, though realized *through* language, is never given *in* language. On the contrary, it is by nature a silence and an opponent of the word."

9. See Elie Wiesel, *All Rivers Run to the Sea: Memoirs* (New York: Alfred A. Knopf, 1995), 353–55; cf. Wiesel, *Souls on Fire*, author's note (unpaginated).

10. Nehemia Polen, "Bridging the Abyss Three Rabbinic Luminaries and Their Influence on Elie Wiesel," in *Lifelines: The Jewish Testimony of Elie Wiesel Offered to a World in Need*, ed. David Patterson and Alan Rosen (forthcoming). See also Wiesel, *All Rivers Run to the Sea*, 402–5.

11. The approach to language in Kabbalah has generated an expansive scholarly literature too lengthy to recount here, but the reader is invited to turn, inter alia, to the studies of Gershom Scholem, Elliot R. Wolfson, Moshe Idel, Joseph Dan, and Eitan Fishbane.

12. André Neher, *The Exile of the Word: From the Silence of the Bible to the Silence of Auschwitz*, trans. David Maisel (Philadelphia: Jewish Publication Society, 1981), 9.

13. *Or Torah* (Brooklyn: Kehot Publication Society, 2011), *ki tissa*, no. 105, 145–47. Translation based on Arthur Green and Barry W. Holtz, *Your Word Is Fire: The Hasidic Masters on Contemplative Prayer* (Nashville: Jewish Lights, 2018), 51.

14. See Ariel Evan Mayse, "Beyond the Letters: The Question of Language in the Teachings of Rabbi Dov Baer of Mezritch," PhD Dissertation, Harvard University, 2015, 227–45.

15. *Tsava'at ha-RiVaSH* (Brooklyn: Kehot Publication Society, 1998), no. 108, 50. From Green and Holtz, *Your Word Is Fire*, 44.

16. *Shemu'ah Tovah* (Warsaw: 1938), 73b, based on Green and Holtz, *Your Word Is Fire*, 43.

17. Elie Wiesel, *Somewhere a Master: Further Portraits and Legends of Hasidic Masters* (New York: Simon & Schuster, 1984), 21: "God may be hiding, but you know it. That ought to be sufficient." Such knowledge changes one's suffering, though it does not alleviate it entirely.

18. Michael Berenbaum, *The Vision of the Void: Theological Reflections on the Works of Elie Wiesel* (Middletown: Wesleyan University Press, 1979), 57, argues: "Gregor discovered that Hasidism is a way of combating despair by sharing it. It is a way of finding hope by living in hope. It is a way of overcoming mourning by demanding joy. The Hasid is one whose rebellion is found in his fidelity. He is a man who cries with song and mourns with joy and who disobeys by remaining obedient."

19. Wiesel, *Souls on Fire*, 20; and cf. *Souls on Fire*, 208: "What was Hasidism in the beginning? One man—and then many—who knew how to restore to the individual a sense of sacredness and confidence in his ties with the community."

20. Wiesel, *Souls on Fire*, 87: "The spoken word's function is to humanize thought." For an example of a Hasidic master struggling with silence, see Arthur Green, *Speaking Torah: Spiritual Teachings from Around the Maggid's Table*, vol. 1 (Woodstock: Jewish Lights, 2013), 125.

21. Elie Wiesel, *The Gates of the Forest*, trans. Frances Frenaye (New York: Holt, Rhinehart and Winston, 1966), 221; cf. Wiesel, *The Gates of the Forest*, 21, 135, 195.

22. Wiesel, *Somewhere a Master*, 108, offers the following as a teaching of the early master Moshe-Leib of Sassov: "Learn to listen. Learn to care. Learn to be concerned, to be involved. The opposite of love is not hate but indifference; the opposite of life is not death but insensitivity."

23. See especially Martin Buber, "Love of God and Love of Neighbor," in *Hasidism and Modern Man* (Princeton: Princeton University Press, 2016), 108–29.

24. Wiesel, *Somewhere a Master*, 151.

25. Sibelman describes these startling white pages, found in many of Wiesel's works, as "le grand silence typographique-respiratoire."

26. Wiesel, *The Gates of the Forest*, 8–9; and Wiesel, *Souls on Fire*, 181. Wiesel's treatment of time also recalls the opening lines for T. S. Eliot's 1943 classic *Four Quartets*.

27. See especially Wiesel, *The Gates of the Forest*, 31–35, on the fabled but hidden Messiah who resides in the tranquil origin of eternity.

28. Halperin, "From *Night* to *The Gates of the Forest*," 51, notes an increased willingness in returning to the Jewish tradition, a marked development since Wiesel's earlier novels.

29. Wiesel, *The Gates of the Forest*, 43.
30. Wiesel, *The Gates of the Forest*, 147.
31. Wiesel, *The Gates of the Forest*, 63.
32. I Kings 19.
33. Wiesel, *The Gates of the Forest*, 83.
34. Wiesel, *The Gates of the Forest*, 103.
35. Wiesel, *The Gates of the Forest*, 165.
23. See Wiesel, *The Gates of the Forest*, 119.
37. Wiesel, *The Gates of the Forest*, 26.
38. Wiesel, *The Gates of the Forest*, 47–48.
39. Cf. Gregor's confession in Wiesel, *The Gates of the Forest*, 173–74.
40. Wiesel, *Souls on Fire*, 248.
41. Wiesel, *Souls on Fire*, 257.
42. Wiesel, *Souls on Fire*, 66.
43. Green, *Speaking Torah*, vol. 2, 59–60. See also *Speaking Torah*, vol. 1, 269–70: "It is good to hope for the salvation of God [i.e., that God is saved], while being silent about oneself. By bringing yourself into silence, you merit to bring about the salvation of Y-H-W-H, which is the emergence of the divine Word."
44. Wiesel, *The Gates of the Forest*, 154.
45. Wiesel, *Somewhere a Master*, 200.
46. Wiesel, *The Gates of the Forest*, 204–5.
47. Wiesel, *The Gates of the Forest*, 205.
48. Wiesel, *Souls on Fire*, 257.
49. See Halperin, "From *Night* to *The Gates of the Forest*," 72–73. On the theme of laughter, protest, and awakening, see Jacqueline Aileen Bussie, *The Laughter of the Oppressed: Ethical and Theological Resistance in Wiesel, Morrison, and Endo* (New York: T & T Clark, 2007), 29–76; Anne Greenfeld, "Laughter in Camus' *The Stranger, The Fall*, and *The Renegade*," *Humor* 6 (1993): 403–14; and Jean Le Bitoux, "At the Source of Thought, Silence, and Laughter," *Critical Inquiry* 37, no. 3 (2011): 381–84.
50. Wiesel, *The Gates of the Forest*, 58, where the narrator suggests that Jesus was crucified because "he never learned how to laugh." Had the Nazarene done so rather than asking God why he had been forsaken, his laughter—even if mirthless—would have triumphed.
51. Wiesel, *The Gates of the Forest*, 7.
52. Wiesel, *The Gates of the Forest*, 11.
53. Wiesel, *The Gates of the Forest*, 20.
54. Wiesel, *The Gates of the Forest*, 21.
55. Wiesel, *The Gates of the Forest*, 12.
56. Wiesel, *Souls on Fire*, 26.
57. The Baal Shem Tov explained the merit of two jesters mentioned in the Talmud as "worthy of the World to Come" in the following manner: "They

would cheer [a sad] person up with [humorous] words until he became joyous, and then they could connect to him. Thus all become attached to the Divine." See *Toledot Ya'akov Yosef* (Korets: 1781), *tetsaveh*.

58. *Ben Porat Yosef* (Korets: 1781), *toledot*.

59. Martin Buber, *Tales of the Hasidim* (New York: Schocken Books, 1991), 118, retells a story about a Hasid coming to the Rebbe of Apt and tearfully explaining that he had atoned for his sin with pious penance. The rebbe only laughs, but "the laughter robbed him of his speech [. . .] then his very soul held its breath and heard that which is spoken deep within." This moving tale was surely known to Wiesel.

60. Wiesel, *Souls on Fire*, 198.

61. Wiesel, *Souls on Fire*, 198.

62. *Sihot ha-RaN* (Beitar Illit: 2010), no. 43, 43–44. On his religious personality and struggles with depression, see Arthur Green, *Tormented Master: The Life and Spiritual Quest of Rabbi Nahman of Bratslav* (Woodstock: Jewish Lights, 2004).

63. Rabbi Nahman is remembered as having once desired to travel far away from the world together with his wife, emerging from time to time to gaze upon it and laugh at its senselessness; see *Hayyei Moharan* (Jerusalem: 1996), no. 19, 295. The Yiddish version of this saying, preserved in *Kokhevei Or* (Jerusalem: 2009), *hokhmah u-vinah*, no. 39, 148, is even pithier: "lakht oys der gantser velt."

64. The word in Rabbi Nahman's Yiddish tale is *katoves*, a term of obscure origin that connotes comedy, joking, and jesting but also a sardonic or dark humor. See Judah A. Joffe, "The Etymology of *Davenen* and *Katoves*," *Proceedings of the American Academy for Jewish Research* 28 (1959): 77–92. For a more literal translation of the tale, see Arnold Band, *Nahman of Bratslav: The Tales* (New York: Paulist Press, 1978), 117–19.

65. Wiesel, *Souls on Fire*, 200.

66. Wiesel, *Souls on Fire*, 200.

67. Wiesel, *Somewhere a Master*, 159.

68. Wiesel, *Somewhere a Master*, 172.

69. Wiesel, *The Gates of the Forest*, 11.

70. Wiesel, *Souls on Fire*, 42; and *The Gates of the Forest*, 189; and *Imrei Pinhas ha-Shalem*, vol. 2, no. 186 (Benei Berak: n.p., 2003), 444: "If I was a singer, I would not allow Him to dwell in the supernal worlds—I would force Him to dwell with us here."

71. Wiesel, *The Gates of the Forest*, 189.

72. Wiesel, *The Gates of the Forest*, 203.

73. Wiesel, *The Gates of the Forest*, 198.

74. Wiesel, *Souls on Fire*, 167.

75. See *Torah Or* (Brooklyn: 2001), *bereshit*, 7c: "Whenever something rises from one state of being to another, for example when [a soul] ascends from the lower to the higher Garden of Eden, this comes about through song,

for song allows one to surrender existence," based on our translation in Green, *Speaking Torah*, vol. 1, 83. My thanks to Nehemia Polen for his insight regarding the word "surrender" in this context. On music in Hasidism, see also Yaakov Mazor, "The Power of Song in Hasidic Thought and Its Role in Religious and Social Life," *Yuval: Studies of the Jewish Music Research Center* 7 (2002): 23–53 (Hebrew); Yaakov Mazor, "Hasidism: Music," in *YIVO Encyclopedia of Jews in Eastern Europe*, vol. 1, ed. Gershon D. Hundert (New Haven: Yale University Press, 2010), 676–79; and see the expanded version with multimedia at www.yivoencyclopedia.org/article.aspx/Hasidism/Music; Chani Haran Smith, *Tuning the Soul: Music as a Spiritual Process in the Teachings of Rabbi Nahman of Bratzlav* (Boston: Brill, 2010).

76. Wiesel, *Souls on Fire*, 26; and cf. Wiesel, *Somewhere a Master*, 30.
77. Wiesel, *Souls on Fire*, 21.
78. Wiesel, *Somewhere a Master*, 61–62.
79. Wiesel, *Somewhere a Master*, 93.
80. *Likkutei Moharan* I:64; and see Alon Goshen-Gottstein, "Speech, Silence, Song: Epistemology and Theodicy in a Teaching of R. Nahman of Breslav," *Philosophia* 30, nos. 1–4 (2003): 143–87.
81. Green, *Speaking Torah*, vol. 2, 35.
82. Wiesel, *The Gates of the Forest*, 33.
83. Wiesel, *The Gates of the Forest*, 225.
84. Wiesel, *The Gates of the Forest*, 24.
85. Wiesel, *The Gates of the Forest*, 161.
86. Wiesel, *The Gates of the Forest*, 166.
87. Wiesel, *The Gates of the Forest*, 169: "There are many truths. Each one denies the others."
88. Wiesel, *The Gates of the Forest*, 193–94.
89. Wiesel, *Souls on Fire*, 81.
90. Wiesel, *Somewhere a Master*, 15.
91. Wiesel, *Somewhere a Master*, 11.
92. Wiesel, *Somewhere a Master*, 12.
93. Wiesel, *Somewhere a Master*, iv. On the development of this tale, see Levi Cooper, "'But I Will Tell of Their Deeds': Retelling a Hasidic Tale about the Power of Storytelling," *The Journal of Jewish Thought and Philosophy* 22, no. 2 (2014): 127–63.
94. Wiesel, *Souls on Fire*, 167–168.
95. Wiesel, *Souls on Fire*, 168.
96. See Rosemary Horowitz, ed., *Elie Wiesel and the Art of Storytelling* (Jefferson: McFarland & Co., 2006).
97. Wiesel, *Souls on Fire*, 255.
98. Wiesel, *Souls on Fire*, 259.
99. Wiesel, *Somewhere a Master*, 205.

100. Zohar 2:213b and 3:292a; and cf. *Likkutei Moharan* I:6.
101. See Wiesel, *The Gates of the Forest*, 43.
102. *Teyvah*, the biblical term for "ark," can also mean "word" in rabbinic Hebrew. And *tsohar* can mean an "opening" or a window, but it can also refer to something that gives light. Similar teachings on this verse are common in early Hasidic literature. See Green and Holtz, *Your Word Is Fire*, 41–42.
103. *Likkutei Moharan* I:112.
104. S. Y. Agnon, ed., *Days of Awe: A Treasury of Jewish Wisdom for Reflection, Repentance, and Renewal on the High Holy Days* (New York: Schocken Books, 1995), 22.
105. Wiesel, *The Gates of the Forest*, 119–20.

Works Cited

Aarons, Victoria. "The Trauma of History in *The Gates of the Forest*." In *Elie Wiesel: Jewish, Literary, and Moral Perspectives*, ed. Steven T. Katz and Alan Rosen, 146–59. Bloomington: Indiana University Press, 2013.

Agnon, S. Y., ed., *Days of Awe: A Treasury of Jewish Wisdom for Reflection, Repentance, and Renewal on the High Holy Days*. New York: Schocken Books, 1995.

Band, Arnold. *Nahman of Bratslav: The Tales*. New York: Paulist Press, 1978.

Berenbaum, Michael. *The Vision of the Void: Theological Reflections on the Works of Elie Wiesel*. Middletown: Wesleyan University Press, 1979.

Bialik, Hayyim Nahman. "Revealment and Concealment in Language." In *Revealment and Concealment: Five Essays*. Trans. Zali Gurevitch. Jerusalem: Ibis Press, 2000.

Buber, Martin. *Tales of the Hasidim*. New York: Schocken, 1991.

Cooper, Levi. " 'But I Will Tell of Their Deeds': Retelling a Hasidic Tale about the Power of Storytelling." *The Journal of Jewish Thought and Philosophy* 22, no. 2 (2014): 127–63.

Goshen-Gottstein, Alon. "Speech, Silence, Song: Epistemology and Theodicy in a Teaching of R. Nahman of Breslav." *Philosophia* 30, nos. 1–4 (2003): 143–87.

Green, Arthur. *Speaking Torah: Spiritual Teachings from Around the Maggid's Table*. Woodstock: Jewish Lights, 2013.

Green, Arthur. *Tormented Master: The Life and Spiritual Quest of Rabbi Nahman of Bratslav*. Woodstock: Jewish Lights, 2004.

Green, Arthur, and Barry W. Holtz. *Your Word Is Fire: The Hasidic Masters on Contemplative Prayer*. Nashville: Jewish Lights, 2018.

Green, Arthur, Gershon Greenberg, Steven T. Katz, and Nehemia Polen. "Part 2. Hasidism." In *Elie Wiesel: Jewish, Literary and Moral Perspectives*, ed.

Steven T. Katz and Alan Rosen, 51–102. Bloomington: Indiana University Press, 2013.

Green, Mary Jean. "Witness to the Absurd: Elie Wiesel and the French Existentialists." *Renascence* 29, no. 4 (1977): 170–84.

Halperin, Irving. "From *Night* to *The Gates of the Forest*: The Novels of Elie Wiesel." In *Responses to Elie Wiesel: Critical Essays by Major Jewish and Christian Scholars*, ed. Harry James Cargas, 45–82. New York: Persea Books, 1978.

Horowitz, Rosemary, ed. *Elie Wiesel and the Art of Storytelling*. Jefferson: McFarland & Co., 2006.

Joffe, Judah A. "The Etymology of *Davenen* and *Katoves*." *Proceedings of the American Academy for Jewish Research* 28 (1959): 77–92.

Kahn, Lothar. "Elie Wiesel: Neo-Hasidism." In *Responses to Elie Wiesel: Critical Essays by Major Jewish and Christian Scholars*, ed. Harry James Cargas, 45–82. New York: Persea Books, 1978.

Lazarus, Joyce B. "Expanding Time: The Art of Elie Wiesel in *The Gates of the Forest*." *Modern Language Studies* 24, no. 4 (1994): 39–46.

Mayse, Ariel Evan. "Beyond the Letters: The Question of Language in the Teachings of Rabbi Dov Baer of Mezritch." PhD Dissertation, Harvard University, 2015.

Mazor, Yaakov. "Hasidism: Music." In *YIVO Encyclopedia of Jews in Eastern Europe*, vol. 1, ed. Gershon D. Hundert, 676–79. New Haven: Yale University Press, 2010.

Mazor, Yaakov. "The Power of Song in Hasidic Thought and Its Role in Religious and Social Life." *Yuval: Studies of the Jewish Music Research Center* 7 (2002): 23–53.

Neher, André. *The Exile of the Word: From the Silence of the Bible to the Silence of Auschwitz*. Trans. David Maisel. Philadelphia: Jewish Publication Society, 1981.

Polen, Nehemia. "Bridging the Abyss Three Rabbinic Luminaries and Their Influence on Elie Wiesel." In *Lifelines: The Jewish Testimony of Elie Wiesel Offered to a World in Need*, ed. David Patterson and Alan Rosen (forthcoming).

Ross, Nicham. *A Beloved-Despised Tradition: Modern Jewish Identity and Neo-Hasidic Writing at the Beginning of the Twentieth Century*. Beer-Sheva: Ben Gurion of the Negev Press, 2010.

Sartre, Jean-Paul. *What Is Literature? And Other Essays*. Cambridge: Harvard University Press, 1988.

Sibelman, Simon P. *Silence in the Novels of Elie Wiesel*. New York: St. Martin's Press, 1995.

Smith, Chani Haran. *Tuning the Soul: Music as a Spiritual Process in the Teachings of Rabbi Nahman of Bratzlav*. Boston: Brill, 2010.

Wiesel, Elie. *All Rivers Run to the Sea: Memoirs*. New York: Alfred A. Knopf, 1995.

Wiesel, Elie. *The Gates of the Forest*. Trans. Frances Frenaye. New York: Holt, Rinehart and Winston, 1966.
Wiesel, Elie. *Somewhere a Master: Further Portraits and Legends*. New York: Simon & Schuster, 1984.
Wiesel, Elie. *Souls on Fire: Portraits and Legends of Hasidic Masters*. New York: Simon & Schuster, 1972.

8

Testifying, Writing, and Putting God in the Dock
Elie Wiesel and the Crisis of Traditional Theodicy

FEDERICO DAL BO

This chapter will address the works of Elie Wiesel in terms of the crisis of traditional theodicy before the destruction of European Jewry during the Second World War. Elie Wiesel never stopped questioning traditional metaphysics. Nor did he stop exploring new ways of testifying, writing, fictionalizing, and thinking of that which he would eventually call by many names—Holocaust, Tragedy, Destruction, and, latterly, the Event. Wiesel's early life—he was deported at a young age to a concentration camp from which he barely survived—provided him with a sort of epistemological duty neither to indulge in classical theodicy nor to ever stop looking for theological answers. This required Wiesel to face the permanent intellectual challenge of negotiating between his Jewish Orthodox education and the traumatic experience of the emergence of evil. He never stopped asking himself what the better opportunity would be—testifying or writing?

I would like to thank Colin Davis (Royal Holloway University of London) and Naomi Seidman (Graduate Theological Union) for reading a first draft of my chapter and providing me with useful observations.

Testifying or Writing? On Wiesel's Aesthetics of Memory

Scholarship has generally gravitated toward Wiesel's works from *Night* onward while neglecting his first, less accessible text, *Un di velt hot geshvign*. Scholars have also tended to downplay the intellectual process that transformed this voluminous text, written in Yiddish, into a significantly shorter one, written in French. Put in simple terms, scholars working on Wiesel—for instance, authors such as Ellen Fine and, more recently, Ruth Franklin, who were published by prominent academic publishing houses—still generally conclude that the former had been "translated" or "reduced down" into the latter.[1] Only relatively recently has Naomi Seidman addressed this process from the perspective of translation studies. She argues that Wiesel has not simply "translated" his previous Yiddish text into a shorter French one but rather that he has embarked on a general transformation of his general theological attitude toward his experience in concentration camps:

> The Yiddish text may have been only lightly edited in the transition to French, but the effect of this editing was to position the memoir within a different literary genre. Even the title *Un di velt hot geshvign* signifies a kind of silence very distant from the mystical silence at the heart of *Night*. The Yiddish title indicts the world that did nothing to stop the Holocaust and allows its perpetrators to carry on normal lives; *La Nuit* names no human or even divine agents in the events it describes. From the historical and political specificities of Yiddish documentary testimony, Wiesel and his French publishing house fashioned something closer to mythopoetic narrative.[2]

Seidman's insistence on the "mythopoetic" nature of Wiesel's *Night* allows one to understand why his second work was received as if it were his first one. The apparently pedantic question on the genesis of Wiesel's most famous book actually hides a deeper one, whether Elie Wiesel had effectively decided between two options—testifying as a survivor or writing as a writer.[3] Those who addressed this question in too simplistic a set of terms would be tempted to conclude that one might either write as a witness or as a writer; any other option would then be a fraud.[4] Colin Davis argues that one can distinguish different phases in Wiesel's work: a first one, dominated by "storytelling"; a second one, characteristic of his early works and progressively "conversing to ambiguity"; a third, characteristic of his later fiction, when he experienced a significant "crisis of narration."[5] Davis concludes that Wiesel's work implicitly answers Adorno's famous ostracism against any form of poetry after Auschwitz, fearing that it might become "art." Davis argues that, had he lived longer, Wiesel would have followed a more complex, almost imperceptible solution—adopting an "aesthetics of secrecy" that would eventually prevent him from choosing between two rigid options: either testimony or fiction. There is indeed a powerful passage from Wiesel's memories that perfectly describes the complex dialectics between these two options: "You spend your time to mask reality, divine or human, by words created for other purposes. In other terms, you write lies [. . .]. Certain events happen but they are not true. Others, on the other hand, are, but they never happen."[6] Wiesel negotiated a *third way* between the trite, now outdated, options between witnessing reality and writing fiction—a "deconstruction" of both. If Davis is right in claiming the importance of the death of Wiesel's father, this might be regarded as a sign for a deeper epistemological crisis involving the art of writing in general.[7] In resonance with some presuppositions from Jacques Lacan's psychology, one could also assume that "the death of the Father"—abundantly present in Wiesel's work—exactly designates the end of an art of writing that is "masculine," assertive, normative, and positively divine. One should then conclude that the art of the writer has dramatically changed in Wiesel's opinion. Adorno was probably right in claiming that the abysmal experience of the Shoah would ultimately escape any aesthetics and that writing poetry on it would be "barbaric" (*barbarisch*).[8]

Wiesel appears then to opt for a complication of modern aesthetics: after the Shoah, testimony and writing cannot be separated. Removed from the reassuring perimeter of a fatherly narrative, Wiesel would then have opted for a different art of writing, resonating with the assumption that the "language of the Father" is predated by a more disordered, emotional language, proceeding from the subject of meaning—what the French writer and psychologist Julia Kristeva would call *chora*.[9] In Jewish terms, one could argue that Wiesel eventually departed from the rigid dimension of *halakhah* and ventured in *aggadah*—that is the "emotional" dimension of Jewish thought, as the Hebrew poet Hayim Bialik said.[10] In other terms, Wiesel would have left the dry, objective dimension of writing as witness to the subjective, emotional dimension of a writer—someone who engages in storytelling, a secular *maggid*, a "preacher," "storyteller," and "exegete." This change in style would also have a serious epistemological impact on the dimension of history and verifiability.

Only those who followed ordinary, traditional historiographical coordinates would assume that that the dimension of reality and truth would idealistically converge: what *happened* can simultaneously only be *true*; if not, it would then never have happened. And yet Wiesel seems to object to the argument that the Shoah opened up an unprecedented experience in history—the impossibility of fully testifying to what happened, because whoever has experienced the extreme of what occurred has died and been reduced to ashes.[11] In other terms, those who have experienced the extreme in history would object that *reality* and *truth* can depart the one from another and result in a paradox: writing fiction that is truer than testifying events that are not as true as fiction. This would indeed be a sort of "barbarism"—the disruption of ordinary concepts of literacy and culture.

Writing would then involve far more than the act of assuming several identities and then creating fantasies, as Wiesel writes, speaking through one of his characters: "Writer. Novelist." "What's that?" "Someone who writes. Someone whose life is writing. Then, man is a book: all the stories can be contained inside. It's a world that exists in your head, inhabited by all men. Words that make one sing."[12] Writing on the Shoah would also be different from any traditional storytelling—when "images rise up from ancient midrashic and mystical sources, crowding [Wiesel's] brain and memory."[13] On the contrary, writing on the Shoah simultaneously as a witness and an author of fiction would necessarily be something different entirely. Before deportation, Wiesel divided his pious existence—between day and night, Talmud and Kabbalah, normative and mystical, masculine and feminine:

> By day I studied Talmud and by night I would run to the synagogue to weep over the destruction of the Temple [. . .] And so we, the Jews of Sighet, waited for better days that surely were soon to come. I continued to devote myself to my studies, Talmud during the day and Kabbalah at night.[14]

But night has suddenly become the time when personal security, morality, and theology collapsed all at once:

> Never shall I forget that night, the first night in camp, that turned my life into one long night seven times sealed. Never shall I forget that smoke. Never shall I forget the small faces of the children whose bodies I saw transformed into smoke under a silent sky. Never shall I forget those flames that consumed my faith forever. Never shall I forget the nocturnal silence that deprived me for all eternity of the desire to live. Never shall I forget those moments that murdered my God and my soul and turned my dreams to ashes. Never shall I forget those things, even were I condemned to live as long as God Himself. Never.[15]

To write on the Shoah would be to perpetually resonate with the most secret Face of God, "for, believe me, night has a face,"[16] with the secret hope that these stories could eventually be transformed into prayers. Such prayers might provide sanctity for those who, like Wiesel himself, were no longer able to address God properly. They rhyme with the words of Rabbi Nahman of Bratslav: "and in spite of myself, a prayer formed inside me, a prayer to this God in whom I no longer believed."[17]

Writing as Disseminating Memory

Wiesel's writing begins only with the Shoah and entirely depends on it:

> After the war I absorbed. I absorbed not only the suffering, which was not mine alone—suffering everywhere in the camps—but I absorbed, unwittingly, perhaps unconsciously, the obsession to tell the tale, to bear witness that every single person shared and nourished and had to put forward. I knew that anyone who remained alive had to become a storyteller, a messenger, had to speak up.[18]

The duty of remembering and perpetuating memory of the past is a well-known biblical prescription, eloquently associated with the request not to forget the evil deeds of Amalek, the eternal enemy of Israel: "You shall remember what Amalek did to you on the way, when you went out of Egypt [. . .] you shall obliterate the remembrance of Amalek beneath the heavens. You shall not forget!" (Deut. 25:17 and 19). Whereas the original biblical commandment is to remember and simultaneously to obliterate this memory, it is the ordinary event of *forgetting*, as the mere disappearance of memory, that Wiesel appears to fear: "That is why I am forgetting other things now. Can there be anything worse than that? Yes, there was worse, there is worse: to forget that one has forgotten."[19] In contrast to this biblical commandment that prescribes, in a somewhat convoluted manner, both memory and forgetfulness before the divine salvation from Egypt, Wiesel's duty to write and bear witness is self-imposed. There is no longer any salvific God who had rescued His people from Destruction and then asked them to bear memory of salvation. Therefore, Wiesel's prose cannot be a "good story (*bonne histoire*)" that his father, "a good storyteller (*un bon conteur*)" might have narrated.[20] Faced with a decisive crisis of paternal—both divine and human—authority, Wiesel's prose suffers from a fundamental hermeneutical paradox. On the one hand, God has ostensibly failed in salvaging His people; on the other hand, the Jewish people had somehow survived. Therefore, there is no metaphysical support for the traditional Jewish mandatory task of bearing witness of history; testimony—either objective or fictional—appears to live on the emergence of death, suspended on failure. And yet memory can only be a monotheistic task, as it is nested in the very belief that *the only God* has decided to lead *His* people in history. Therefore, forgetfulness can only be a *Jewish curse*:

> "Wasn't forgetfulness a gift of the gods to the ancient world? Without it, life would be intolerable, wouldn't it?" Yes, but the Jews live by other rules. For a Jew, nothing is more important than memory. He is bound to his origins by memory. It is memory that connects him to Abraham, Moses and Rabbi Akiba. If he denies memory he will have denied his own honor. "So you insist on keeping all your wounds open?" Those wounds exist; it is therefore forbidden and unhealthy to pretend that they don't.[21]

Wiesel seems to admit that writing on the Shoah essentially means disseminating testimony on death and yet claiming for survival, despite the epochal discovery that God has not helped. More radically, as claimed by the Jewish orthodox rabbi Irving Itzhak Greenberg and often resonated by Wiesel himself, it was God who had unilaterally broken His alleged perpetual alliance with Jewish people and humanity.[22]

In an autobiographical remark on his own activity as a writer and a novelist, Wiesel addresses the issue of constantly writing *post festum*, or in consequence of the Shoah, and revises his own production with some clear words:

> My very first works of fiction are set not during the Event, but after. Why? Why? In *Dawn*—about the clandestine struggle of the Jews against the British army in Palestine—a survivor of the death camps is ordered to execute a British officer. In *Day*, a young journalist is run over by a taxi in New York. Accident or attempted suicide? *The Town Beyond the Wall*? A book on man's fascination with madness. *The Gates of the Forest*? An homage to friendship, and the story of a young orphan who pretends to be deaf and mute and who is given the part of Judas in a Passion Play at school. I often think of these entirely fictional works, losing myself in an elusive elsewhere, searching for my inner compass [. . .]. *A Beggar in Jerusalem*—I shall bring the title character along when I appear before the celestial Tribunal as a witness for my defense. I had met him in front of the Wall during the Six-Day War. [. . .] *The Testament* represents my attempt to unmask communism—in particular, the liquidation of the great Jewish novelists and poets during the Stalin era. Begun as a messianism without God, invented as a marvelous message of comradeship, a noble concept of brotherly humanism, communism was transformed by Stalin into a gigantic laboratory for deception, torture and murder.[23]

Wiesel seems to admit that the awareness of the Shoah both in experiential and theological terms might be too strong a demand for a single individual. The epochal assumption that God has not helped His people, has broken His eternal promises, and yet delivered the survivors the task of perpetually testifying the truth requires existential help.

No one can really provide such support, as if no one could really bear the lack of providence alone. Therefore, it is not surprising that Wiesel's aesthetics multiply his lives and identities, with an endless play of masks or doppelgängers. While being neglected by God, it is only the desperate dissemination of someone's own identity that might provide the necessary support for testifying. Besides, Wiesel candidly asks himself about the eventual conflation between surviving and having the duty of bearing witness—as if the one could not be separated from another: "I'm here to remember what my father has forgotten. But do I live only to remember? Suppose life were only your ancestors' imagination, or a dream of the dead?"[24] It is the awareness that God has broken the same perpetual covenant that He had stipulated with Jewish people and humanity that gives rise to a theological progression that goes from disputing and revolting against Him until a formal accusation against Him.

A Theological Progression: From Disputing to Revolting against God

There was no immediate awareness in Wiesel's texts that God has broken His own promises and that, in the Jewish understanding, He might even be asked to account for this betrayal. It took ten years of silence before Wiesel gained the strength to write and publish his own first report: *Un di velt hot geshvign*. In this long time, Wiesel had to absorb that suffering and "metabolize" it—in the proper sense of the expression: he had to "transform" his tragic experience into words. And yet his accusations were still directed on to the "world," as the title transparently showed. It seems that this work still shares too much theological and linguistic proximity with that community where he had received his Jewish education. Regardless of what he might have begun thinking in his own heart, Wiesel's first text was almost void of references to God and especially to Jewish mysticism—whose more radical version would call God's "Other Side" (*sitra ahra*) as responsible for the evil in the world.[25] But this was too soon. At the time of his first work, Wiesel still focused his attention on the "world"—which the Gnostics have always believed to be God's greatest adversary.

A radical process of revision, especially the passage from Yiddish to French, helped Wiesel to respect another agenda—directly addressing the question of theodicy and facing the challenge of atheism. It is at this point that he introduced the Jewish Kabbalah as a possible, still latent reservoir of alternative theology, different from Jewish Orthodoxy and yet still falling within the perimeter of Jewish faith. Whoever could not indulge in the easy solution of ordinary faith might find in a theological complexion of several sources—Talmud, Kabbalah, memories, and literature—the very means for asking radical questions with the awareness that one might put God in the dock but cannot expect Him to truly answer. Regardless of the imposing tone of His believers, God would never have shown up in any court and therefore should have been processed in His absence.

Besides, even God's traditional agents seemed to have been transformed into secular entities. Those angels that populated Wiesel's stories were nothing but Hasidic ghosts:

> "The angels, who are they?" I once asked my grandfather, whose Wizsnitzer melodies overwhelmed me, so violent and tender was the joy they expressed. By way of response, he leaned toward me and whispered into my ear a secret which has remained with me to this day: "The angels, my child, the angels are all of us sitting around this table—and other tables like it—covered with a white cloth and transformed into an altar."[26]

Even God's angels have lost their prominence, as there is a much more reliable figure—whose wicked promises have yet been fulfilled: "I have more faith in Hitler than in anyone else. He alone has kept his promises, all his promises, to the Jewish people."[27] Devoid of biblical promises, Jewish people are deserted by God—whom they may now put in the dock. A Talmudic mind does not understand God's inability to deliver providence and salvation as a sign of a deeper mystery in the divine life. There is only one passage in Wiesel's works that would encourage one to read God's weakness as a sort of Christian kenosis:

> Behind me, I heard the same man asking: "For God's sake, where is God?" And from within me, I heard a voice answer: "Where He is? This is where—hanging here from this gallows . . ." [. . .] Every fiber in me rebelled. Because He caused thousands of children to burn in His mass graves? Because He kept six crematoria working day and night, including Sabbath and the Holy Days? Because in His great might, He had created Auschwitz, Birkenau, Buna, and so many other factories of death?[28]

Whoever is familiar with Talmudic phraseology would hardly fail to note how crucifying and hanging are often conflated—due to legal, procedural, and theological reasons. For instance, Jesus is called the "hanged one" (*taluy*).[29] It is not implausible that this Christianizing theological pondering—truly unusual for a young Jewish student in 1944 who divided his time between Talmud and Kabbalah—was ultimately inspired by the French editor of Wiesel's *Night*: the novelist and 1952 Nobel Prize laureate François Mauriac. In his foreword to *Night*, Mauriac sees the episode of the hanging of a child in the concentration camp as resonant with a latent Christological nature:

> And I, who believe that God is love, what answer could I give my young questioner, whose dark eyes still held the reflection of that angelic sadness which had appeared one day upon the face of the hanged child? What did I say to him? [. . .] All is grace. If the Eternal is the Eternal, the last word for each one of us belongs to Him. This is what I should have told this Jewish child. But I could only embrace him, weeping.[30]

Yet Wiesel will never indulge again on exalting the theological sense of suffering. Two years later after publishing *Night*, he will ask himself, doubtful, in his next novel, *Dawn*: "So many questions obsessed me. Where is God to be found? In suffering or in rebellion? When is a man most truly a man? When he submits or when he refuses? Where does suffering lead him? To purification or to bestiality?"[31] One year later, in his novel *Day*, he will more explicitly argue that suffering cannot be a way for meeting God, as it only brings out the worst in man:

> Suffering brings out the lowest, the most cowardly in man. There is a phase of suffering you reach beyond which you become a brute: beyond it you sell your soul—and worse, the souls of your friends—for a piece of bread, for some warmth, for a moment of oblivion, of sleep. Saints are those who die before the end of the story. The others, those who live out their destiny, no longer dare look at themselves in the mirror, afraid they may see their inner image: a monster laughing at unhappy women and at saints who are dead . . .[32]

One should look carefully at this progression since *Night* (1958), *Dawn* (1960), and *Day* (1961) were eventually published together as a trilogy—therefore suggesting a sort of narrative and theological continuity between them. In a few years, Wiesel appears to have rejected even the suspicion that the suffering of the Jews in the Shoah could resonate with any Christology and implicitly objected that God might have hidden Himself but this had been an incommensurably darker event than the evangelical kenosis. Wiesel evidently accepted Ignaz Maybaum's assumption that the Shoah would represent a third epochal "Destruction" (*hurban*) in the Jewish history, together with the Destruction of the First Temple (586 BCE) and the Destruction of the Second Temple (70 CE).

Yet Wiesel would hardly accept Maybaum's definition of "Auschwitz [as] the pagan Golgotha of our time."[34] On the contrary, he would eventually follow another path and accurately avoid any ambiguous treatment of the question of God's hiding before the Shoah. Wiesel would rather amplify his Jewish understanding of God's silence and refrain from simply appealing to a mystery that no one would ever be able to solve. If there was a divine hiding, this would necessarily have had a different, sinister nature—showing the "Other Side" of the divinity, engine and cause of the deepest evil. It should hardly be surprising to see that Wiesel treated God's inability to fulfill His promises and stop the Shoah as legitimation for arguing with Him and eventually escalating a theological dispute—from accusations to protests as to the point of repudiating Him.

At first, the prisoners lament in almost biblical terms, still believing in being tested and asking to endure a temporary suffering:

> Akiba Drumer would break our hearts with his deep, grave voice. Some of the men spoke of God: His mysterious ways, the sins of the Jewish people, and the redemption to come. As for me, I had ceased to pray. I concurred with Job! I was not denying His existence, but I doubted His absolute justice. Akiba Drumer said: "God is testing us. He wants to see whether we are capable of overcoming our base instincts, of killing the Satan within ourselves. We have no right to despair. And if He punishes us mercilessly, it is a sign that He loves us that much more . . ." Hersh Genud, well versed in Kabbalah, spoke of the end of the world and the coming of the Messiah.[34]

But these biblical terms would soon cease to be relevant. Outdated theodicy could not rationalize the tests the prisoners were experiencing, if they chose to view their experience as a test, and eventually the pressure they faced brought about a tragic failure of faith:

> I knew a rabbi, from a small town in Poland. He was old and bent, his lips constantly trembling. He was always praying, in the block, at work, in the ranks. He recited entire pages from the Talmud, arguing with himself, asking and answering himself endless questions. One day, he said to me: "It's over. God is no longer with us." And as though he regretted having uttered such words so coldly, so dryly, he added in his broken voice, "I know. No one has the right to say things like that. I know that very well. Man is too insignificant, too limited, to even try to comprehend God's mysterious ways. But what can someone like myself do? I'm neither a sage nor a just man. I am not a saint. I'm a simple creature of flesh and bone. I suffer hell in my soul and my flesh. I also have eyes and I see what is being done here. Where is God's mercy? Where's God? How can I believe, how can anyone believe in this God of Mercy?" Poor Akiba Drumer, if only he could have kept his faith in God, if only he could have considered this suffering a divine test, he would not have been swept away by the selection.[35]

In time, Wiesel remembers him progressively revolting against God, whom he no longer believed to be the Merciful and the Compassionate: "For the first time, I felt anger rising within me. Why should I sanctify His name? The Almighty, the eternal and terrible Master of the Universe, chose to be silent. What was there to thank Him for?"[36] In the end, Wiesel would protest overtly against God, deliberately transgressing fasting at Yom Kippur—not for self-preservation, as already prescribed by Jewish law, but out of anger and revolt: "as I swallowed my ration of soup, I turned that act into a symbol of rebellion, of protest against Him."[37]

This protest would then materialize in almost blasphemous description of the Divinity that bore no similarity to the one depicted in Wiesel's books of study. One of these doppelgängers would eventually dare to mystify God who had "created men in a drunken moment" and to assume, with some Nietzschean undertone, that Creation itself had been only a gigantic fraud, a dark joke.[38]

> The greatest shame is to have been chosen by destiny. Man prefers to blame himself for all possible sins and crimes rather than come to the conclusion that God is capable of the most flagrant injustice. I still blush every time I think of the way God makes fun of human beings, his favorite toys [. . .]. Yes, God needs man. Condemned to eternal solitude, he made man only to use him as a toy, to amuse himself. That's what philosophers and poets have refused to admit: in the beginning there was neither the Word nor Love, but laughter, the roaring, eternal laughter whose echoes are more deceitful than the mirages of the desert.[39]

And yet this blasphemous passage was hardly conclusive. In this tirade Wiesel was not simply rejecting some central Christian beliefs—"in the beginning there was neither the Word nor Love"—but especially objecting that there was something demonic at the very center of Creation: an Event that would have caused or forced God to *be absent* from the scene of the world and therefore prove unable to morally govern His creatures. This sort of ontological inability—God's lack of surveillance upon His Own Creation—would constitute a crime to a Talmudic mind that would exclaim His awareness and responsibility. Therefore, God could be persecuted and judged. And yet a question would arise: if a lawsuit was addressed against God for His inability to stop evil, which parties would be involved in this process? Who would accuse Him and who would dare to defend Him?

The Trial: Putting God in the Dock

The assumption that God could be accused of neglecting the very pact that He had stipulated with the Jewish people suffered from foundational difficulty. Some Talmudic legends had elaborated on the assumption that God was somehow subjected to His Own Law, in the very sense that He would participate in rabbinical assembly and even be put into minority during a discussion, if pertinent and necessary.[40] There was no difficulty, in principle, in imagining that the Jewish people, as second party of a biblical covenant, might address God and call Him to account for breaching the terms that had been stipulated. Yet there was a crucial question: if any procedure in court would require, as legal preliminary, to summon God, how would He *be present* at the dock, while *being absent* from the scene of history?

Most of Wiesel's work seems to answer to this question that is simultaneously legal and metaphysical. God's absence during the Shoah should not be dismissed easily as proof that there is no supernal power in the skies but rather that the traditional Jewish notion of God has irreversibly expired as an untimely concept that cannot make reason of the actual events. In other terms, there was a time when "God still dwelt in our town," but it has passed.[41] There was no longer a survivor from the camps protesting in Yiddish against "the world" but only a survivor—or one of his many masks—believing that God has turned into a sort of hallucination and could no longer be remembered when He did actually speak:

> "No," I answered. "I'm crying because I just saw God." Strange dream. I had gone to heaven. God, sitting on his throne, was presiding over an assembly of angels. The distance which separated Him from me was infinite, but I could see Him as clearly as if He had been right next to me. God motioned to me and I started to walk forward [. . .]. Then God talked to me. The silence had become so total, so pure, that my heart was ashamed of its beating. The silence was still as absolute, when I heard the words of God. With Him the word and the silence were not contradictory. God answered all my questions and many others [. . .]. That is when I woke up. Dr. Sreter was leaning over me with a smile. I wanted to tell him that I had just heard the words of God, when I realized to my horror that I had forgotten them. I no longer knew what God had told me [. . .]. The doctor burst into a friendly laugh: "If you want I can put you back to sleep; and you can ask Him to repeat . . ." [. . .]. I didn't see God in my dream. He was no longer there.[42]

Yet, the Nietzschean touch in the doctor's laughter is hardly conclusive. Wiesel does not indulge in the trite assumption that "God is dead," maybe hanging from the gallows, as uniquely maintained in *Night*. Wiesel seems to admit that God might still exist but has been absent from the scene of history and He should be accountable for it, although he seems to suspect that even a trial might only be a practical comedy that requires everyone to play his own part:

> That's just it. Trials are like theater. All those who participate in them are playing a part. In England, the judges wear wigs. In France it's robes. When the lawyer says, in his client's name, "we plead guilty or not guilty," it's as if he himself were guilty or not guilty, too. It's theater, I tell you. In a criminal trial, especially with a jury, there's always suspense and drama. That's why the readers are interested in it.[43]

Nevertheless, a Talmudic mind would see no difference in taking to trial a person or the supreme moral and ontological authority in the universe, regardless of whether it is a farce, a comedy, or a true procedure. In any case, a trial had to fulfill specific requirements—an accusation, a prosecutor, a defender, and a final judgment.

The *accusation* is clear, as Wiesel maintains in almost all his works: God was unable to act, either out of moral or ontological inability. More subtly the accusation begins when one acknowledges that God has limited Himself by attributing man free will. At first, one could assume that this is the greatest gift that God could have ever given to man, since He would prefer willing servants rather than slaves:

> We must also consider the tragic situation of God Himself. He can only give His commandments to free men, to people with free will. But in considering the past and their future, men and women no longer demand that freedom which only God can grant. So they give it back to Him, and there is God dealing with people who are no longer free: is it to the greater glory of God if He rules, is obeyed by, a mankind diminished and enslaved?[44]

Yet Wiesel soon questions this moral arrangement of the world. He objects that freedom is not really tempered by judgment and when transgressions take place, *nothing* really happens: "When one denies God, it is the first step that matters; one transgresses a law and realizes that nothing has changed. The heart beats as before, the blood circulates, people come and go, the universe remains the same. That is the beginning of separation."[46] Again, Wiesel has chosen his words carefully. He does not argue that transgression will be punished with some delay, as substantial as it might be. "Separation" is indeed a Kabbalistic term that describes an inner movement between the divine potencies—the *sefirot*—that progressively lose unity and are then taken apart the one from another.[47] Human transgression plays an important role in effecting this "separation," as Wiesel candidly maintains, but this event is probably subtler and alludes to a metaphysical mystery—an *absent* God.

As God's absence from history has mostly affected the Jewish people, who had stipulated a covenant with Him, it is hardly surprising that Wiesel considers himself and any former Talmud student to be the best candidate for acting as *prosecutor* in this imaginary trial:

> But now, I no longer pleaded for anything. I was no longer able to lament. On the contrary, I felt very strong. I was the accuser, God the accused. My eyes had opened and I was alone, terribly alone in a world without God, without man. Without love or mercy. I was nothing but ashes now, but I felt myself to be stronger than this Almighty to whom my life had been bound for so long. In the midst of these men assembled for prayer, I felt like an observer, a stranger.[47]

The act of *accusing* God is indeed the first step for overcoming the sense of guilt from which every survivor suffers just because he has dared to exist, when most of his fellows have been murdered. At first, a pious survivor would be requested to feel guilty just for *being* after the Shoah, "because otherwise it would mean that God does not know what He's doing, and does not do what He wants"; then rises the awareness that this process of "separation" is a metaphysical event within God Himself; therefore, none should feel guilty for the mere fact of surviving and existing.[48] On the contrary, this pious attempt of excusing God from His duties can be reverted into a clear accusation, especially by the one who

> studied the Talmud, not because he saw it as a holy and immutable document, but because he found correspondences and points of reference in it that related to his curiosity about

some officially marginalized or concealed book that didn't have the good fortune of being included in the canon.⁴⁹

While alluding to the extra-canonical books from Jewish tradition, Wiesel seems to argue that canonical text—Scripture, Mishnah, and Talmud—cannot really account for the mystery of God's absence. Even Jewish mysticism hardly appears to be conclusive when arguing that a truly monotheistic God has to empower both Good and Evil—that the two are only symmetrical parts of a same, mysterious Whole:

> "God Himself likes an argument," Elhanan told his son. "But what is an argument? It is an admission of conflict and separation; these God creates and destroys, by His presence as much as by His absence. All is possible with Him; nothing is possible without Him. But the opposite is equally true. Never forget what the ancients taught us: God exists in contradictions, too. He is the limit of all things, and He is what extends the limit."⁵⁰

And yet the classical statement would no longer provide Wiesel with any justification but rather would point to another, more radical question, as he protested in his most recent work, *Open Heart*:

> When I was a child, I situated God exclusively in all that is Good. In all that is sacred. In all that makes man worthy of salvation. Could it be that for God, Evil represents just another path leading to Good? In truth, for the Jew that I am, Auschwitz is not only a human tragedy but also—and most of all—a theological scandal. For me, it is as impossible to accept Auschwitz with God as without God. But then how is one to understand His silence?⁵¹

There was a time when the Jewish prophets could claim and maintain that God is the source of everything, both of Good and Evil, the One who "makes peace and creates evil" (Isa. 45:7). And yet that time has passed because the evil brought about on earth has nullified God's promises and His agents—God's new prophets—are madmen and demons.⁵²

In his *Trial of God*, Wiesel elaborates on an event that allegedly took place in Auschwitz—a trial against God supported by three rabbis—on account of several Talmudic and mystical presuppositions. While transporting this event in the imaginary Central European town of Shamgorod—whose name sinisterly resonates with the Hebrew word *shem* (name) and the English word *shame*—in the seventeenth century during a pogrom, Wiesel imagines a Jewish community that attempts to put God in the dock, accusing Him of failing to protect His people. The occasion for such enactment is the festival of Purim, a carnivalesque celebration of the salvation of Persian Jews from a lethal persecution, as reported in the book of Esther. One should recall that this short biblical book never mentions once the name of God and therefore has traditionally been read as a primary source for Jewish negative theology: God would be present and yet only in disguise, "hidden" within His own providential acts.[53] While arguing against this traditional, reassuring, reading of biblical theology, Wiesel objects that God has actually failed to save His people from the Shoah. Therefore, God was not simply "hiding" during the Shoah but absent, turning the festival of Purim into a massacre, the celebration of God's hidden action in history into an accusation for His absence.

It is indeed for these reasons that Paolo De Benedetti—a prominent Jewish-Christian Italian theologian—has argued that Wiesel's *Trial of God* advances a *radical* theological proposition:

> If God exists, today He needs more than ever . . . not of the defenders modeled on the Satan from [Wiesel's] *Trial of God*, but of critical believers (*credenti critici*) who despise His imperial mask and show His wounds . . . We are looking for another God (*un altro Dio*), who does not boast in this so unhappy world. We need to change God in order to keep Him (so that He will keep us). Perhaps this only means changing our way of thinking about God. Or maybe not.[54]

Whereas many are willing to accuse God and act as prosecutors, there is only a mysterious figure, a stranger who wants to be called Sam—"call me Sam [. . .]. Just Sam [. . .]. No family"—who offers to defend Him in front of the jury and make the case for God, trying to persuade the community "to take the side of the Creator [. . .] explain His mysteries [. . .] love Him in spite of everything, and love Him enough to defend Him against His accusers."[56] This stranger is the only one who speaks on God's behalf. He argues well, uses Jewish tradition, "cool logic," and yet in the end he is revealed to be Satan.[56]

Wiesel's work, of course, features the recurring figure of the mad prophet who warns against disaster and whose insight is only apparent after that disaster has struck (see Mary Catherine Mueller and Jennifer Murray's chapters in this collection for more on this). Such a figure suggests a form of benevolent divine intervention. However, when proposing a radical reading of Wiesel's *Trial of God*, as De Benedetti suggests, the power of the madman in his novels would virtually be nullified when contrasted with some other representation of Wiesel's relationship to God—as exemplified in the many Kabbalistic concepts that appear in his novel *A Beggar in Jerusalem*.[57] While resonating with the work of other Jewish authors, especially André Neher's seminal works,[58] De Benedetti implied that the fact of the Shoah requires that modern interpreters revise the original meaning of a rabbinic dictum that celebrates God's indignant "silence" against blasphemy. There is indeed a famous passage from the Babylonian Talmud that suggests that the biblical apostrophe "Who is like you among the gods?" (Exod. 15:11) should rather be read as "Who is like you among the mute ones?"[59] One should treat carefully this famous rabbinic interpretation and distinguish between the text's original intention and the interpretation of the latest commentators. While following the passage, it is clear that the Talmud intended to celebrate God's indignant silence against blasphemies of His archenemy—the Roman emperor Titus, the destroyer of Jerusalem. Yet one might argue, more subtly, that the rabbis intended to rely on Scripture—even thought of changing its wording—in order to theologically justify what seemed incomprehensible: "who is strong and indurate like You, since You hear the abuse and the blasphemy of that wicked man and remain *silent?*" Yet Paolo De Benedetti and most of the recent Jewish Christian theologians have argued differently. Regardless of the traditional intention of this rabbinic reading, one might learn from Wiesel's warning and *refrain from* "satanically" defending God with easy speeches and acknowledge that He was actually "silent" during the Shoah, failing to biblically save His people.

Wiesel's *Trial of God* is not conclusive—at least not in the sense that one should take the final revelation that the stranger defending God actually was Satan himself as a sort of admonition not to "defend" God. A subtler dynamic is at work here, especially considering that the assumption of putting God in the dock resonates with several Talmudic assumptions. At first, Wiesel seems to argue that conventional, traditional theodicy is an obsolete, if not deceptive, way to understand the enigma of God's absence during the Shoah. As he himself and many of his masks have eloquently protested, classic theodicy cannot really respond to the abysmal event of the Destruction of European Jewry—the third one after the Destruction of the First Temple (586 BCE) and the Destruction of the Second Temple (70 CE).

From this perspective, the revelation from *The Trial of God*—that the only defender of God actually was Satan—should be interpreted according to the same Talmudic logic that allows God to take part in legal discussions and to be a minority when necessary. This logic would also justify the assumption that God can be put in the dock and summoned for neglecting His people. With respect to this, the discovery that God's defender actually is Satan would reflect the same procedural phraseology and designate a more complex transformation of traditional assumptions. Far from assuming that whoever might defend God would be no better than a demon, Wiesel's fantasy of depicting the stranger taking the side of God as Satan actually is an *inversion* of a classical rabbinic figure: Satan is no longer the "accuser" of Israel in front of God, but His "defender." Accordingly, Satan has never changed sides. Just as he previously served as the "accuser" of Israel from the Left Side, now he is the "defender" of God from the Left Side. In other terms, Satan still shares the same location—the Left Side of God—and participates in the divine life, albeit in a controversial and mysterious way.[60] Therefore, whoever defends God is not "demonic" but still participates in the same logic that would suggest that the Shoah could be interpreted as a sort of "punishment" of Israel. Both acting as accuser (of Israel) or defender (of God), Satan would still cast his judgments from inside the perimeter of the divine life—from the Left Side that emanates evil.

Wiesel seems then to argue that whoever takes seriously enough the theological challenge posed by the Shoah should rather depart from a conventional biblical economy—accusing or defending God—and embark in the much more radical task of *questioning* Him, possibly resonating with a poignant epigram of Rabbi Moshe Leib of Sassov: "Do you want to find the fire? Search for it in the ashes."[61]

Notes

1. See for instance: Ellen Fine, *Legacy of Night: The Literary Universe of Elie Wiesel* (Albany: State University of New York Press, 1983), 150, and Ruth Franklin, *A Thousand Darknesses: Lies and Truth in Holocaust Fiction* (Oxford: Oxford University Press, 2011), 73. This thesis is also maintained in

the authoritative *The American Zionist* (Bloomington: Zionist Organization of America, 1969), 40.

2. Naomi Seidman, "Elie Wiesel and the Scandal of Jewish Rage," *Jewish Social Studies* 3, no. 1 (1996): 5.

3. The oversimplifying expression "survivor-writer" is used, for instance, in Isabel Wollaston, "Post-Holocaust Interpretations of Job," in *The Oxford Handbook of the Reception of the History of the Bible*, ed. M. Lieb, E. Mason, and J. Roberts (Oxford: Oxford University Press, 2011), 491.

4. Seidman's brilliant article has been misquoted and deformed in the anti-Semitic blog "Elie Wiesel Tattoo" by the controversial journalist Carolyn Yaeger. On this unfortunate reception, see also Peter Manseau, "Revising *Night*: Elie Wiesel and the Hazards of Holocaust Theology," *Cross Currents* 56, no. 3 (2006): 387–99.

5. Colin Davis, *Elie Wiesel's Secretive Texts* (Gainesville: University Press of Florida, 1994).

6. Elie Wiesel, *Entre deux soleils* (Paris: Éditions du Seuil, 1970). This does not feature in the English edition. I am quoting from the original French edition. The translation is mine.

7. Davis, *Elie Wiesel's Secretive Texts*, 141–74.

8. Theodor W. Adorno, *Prismen: Kulturkritik und Gesellschaft* (Frankfurt am Main: Suhrkamp, 1955), 30.

9. Julia Kristeva, *La revolution du language poetique* (Paris: Éditions du Seuil. 1974).

10. Chaym Bialik, "Halakhah we-Haggadah," in *Kol Kitvey Chaiim Bialik* (Tel Aviv: Dvir, 1951).

11. Giorgio Agamben, *Quel che resta di Auschwitz. L'archivio e il testimone* (Turin: Bollati & Boringhieri, 1998).

12. Elie Wiesel, *The Sonderberg Case* (New York: Knopf, 2010), 9.

13. Elie Wiesel, *Open Heart* (New York: Schocken, 2012), 23.

14. Elie Wiesel, *Night* (New York: Bantam Books, 1982), 1, 8.

15. Wiesel, *Night* 32.

16. Elie Wiesel, *Dawn* (New York: Hill and Wang, 1961), 12.

17. Wiesel, *Night*, 91.

18. Robert Franciosi, *Elie Wiesel: Conversations* (Jackson: University Press of Mississippi, 2002), 61.

19. Elie Wiesel, *The Forgotten* (New York: Knopf Doubleday, 1992), 38.

20. Wiesel, *Night*, 22. See also: Davis, *Elie Wiesel's Secretive Texts*, 46–48.

21. Wiesel, *The Forgotten*, 63.

22. Irving Greenberg, *The Third Great Cycle of Jewish History—Voluntary Covenant: The Third Era of Jewish History, Power and Politics* (New York: CLAL, National Jewish Center for Learning and Leadership, 1981).

23. Elie Wiesel, *Open Heart*, 26–27.

24. Wiesel, *The Forgotten*, 11.

25. The "Other Side" is a euphemistic Aramaic expression designating the Left Side of the divine emanation that is impure and produces evil.

26. Elie Wiesel, *One Generation After* (New York: Schocken Books, 2011), 12–13.

27. Wiesel, *Night*, 80.

28. Wiesel, *Night*, 65, 67.

29. For a general treatment of this expression in Talmudic literature, see for instance Peter Schäfer, *Jesus in the Talmud* (Princeton: Princeton University Press, 2008).

30. Wiesel, *Night*, x–xi.

31. Wiesel, *Dawn*, 11.

32. Elie Wiesel, *Day* (New York: Hill and Wang, 2006), 37.

33. Ignaz Maybaum, *The Face of God after Auschwitz* (Amsterdam: Polak & Van Gennep, 1965), 80.

34. Wiesel, *Night*, 44.

36. Wiesel, *Night*, 76–77.

36. Wiesel, *Night*, 32.

37. Wiesel, *Night*, 69.

38. Wiesel, *Open Heart*, 22.

39. Wiesel, *Day*, 31–32.

40. This Talmudic legend is to be found in the Babylonian Talmud, tractate *Baba Metzia*, 59b.

41. Elie Wiesel *Dawn*, 5.

42. Elie Wiesel *Dawn*, 54–55.

43. Elie Wiesel *Day*, 35.

44. Wiesel, *The Forgotten*, 196.

45. Wiesel, *The Forgotten*, 173.

46. The Kabbalistic notion of "separation" (*havdalah*) enjoys a complex connection with the ritual of the Shabbat that manifests the most comprehensive unity within the Godhead. It derives from the act of "separating" the secular, unholy days of the week from the Shabbat with the consequence of letting demonic forces spreading into the world. See for instance: *Zohar*, 1:14b.

47. Wiesel, *Night*, 68.

48. Wiesel, *One Generation After*, 187.

49. Wiesel, *The Sonderberg Case*, 8.

50. Wiesel, *The Forgotten*, 196.

51. Wiesel, *Open Heart*, 37–38.

52. Wiesel, *Night*, 60.

53. The theological issue raised by the circumstance of canonizing a book that actually never mentions God is well reflected in many Talmudic discussions. The traditional explanation to this theological conundrum is that the name *Ester* itself would be an allusion to the fact that God hides Himself.

This famous reading is based on a verse from Scripture: "and I will surely hide My face in that day" (*we-anokhi haster astir panay ba-yom ha-hu*) (Deut. 31:18). While elaborating on the redundant Hebrew expression *haster astrir* (literally, "hiding, I will hide"), the rabbis argue that it is an allusion to the name of Esther and therefore dismiss the ingenuous assumption that the book of Esther never mentions God. See: the Babylonian Talmud, tractate *Chagigah* 5b. For a similar treatment, see also: tractate *Chullin* 139b.

54. Paolo De Benedetti, *Quale Dio? Una domanda nella storia* (Brescia: Morcelliana, 1996), 9–10. The work of Paolo De Benedetti (1927–2016) is unfortunately poorly received outside of Italy. See: Pierluigi Cattani, *Dio sulle labbra dell'uomo: Paolo De Benedetti e la domanda incessante* (Trento: Il Margine, 2006).

55. Elie Wiesel, *The Trial of God*, trans. Marion Wiesel (New York: Schocken Books, 1979), 113, 109.

56. Wiesel, *The Trial of God*, 122, 115.

57. In his *A Beggar in Jerusalem* (New York: Schocken, 1970), Wiesel tries to distance himself (and his work) from the Shoah, as the most traumatic and formative event in his life. See in particular the introduction to this novel in Sanford V. Sternlicht, *Student Companion to Elie Wiesel* (Westport: Greenwood Press, 2003), 79–84.

58. André Neher (1914–1988) was a prominent French Israeli scholar of Jewish studies. Particularly notable is his famous *The Exile of the Word: From the Silence of the Bible to the Silence of Auschwitz* (Philadelphia: JPS, 1981), dealing with the notion of "silence" in Scripture and especially mentioning Elie Wiesel, whom he calls "a diviner of silence" (217–18). A throughout examination of the relationship between André Neher and Elie Wiesel is a desideratum of scholarship.

59. The Babylonian Talmud, tractate *Gittin* 56b. This interpretation—ascribed to the early Jewish school of Rabbi Ishmael—plays on the modification of the original term *ba-'elim* (among the gods) into *ba-'elmim* (among the mute ones) by inserting the letter *mem*. A similar reading is therefore to be found also in the rabbinic *Mekhilta de-Rabbi Ishamel* 8 (on Exod. 15:11).

60. Rabbi Arthur Segal writes that Satan "is not an opposite of God, but part of God. He is the left side of the Tree of the Ten Sephirot. Satan is not a 'he,' but an adversarial thought in God's mind. Satan is God's *yetzer ha-ra*, His evil inclination." Arthur Segal, *A Spiritual and Ethical Companion to the Torah and Talmud* (Charleston: BookSurge, 2008), 395.

61. Wiesel, *Conversations*, 60.

Works Cited

Adorno, Theodor W. *Prismen: Kulturkritik und Gesellschaft*. Frankfurt am Main: Suhrkamp, 1955.

Agamben, Giorgio. *Quel che resta di Auschwitz: L'archivio e il testimone.* Turin: Bollati & Boringhieri, 1998.
The American Zionist. Bloomington: Zionist Organization of America, 1969.
Bialik, Chaym. "Halakhah we-Haggadah." In *Kol Kitvey Chaiim Bialik,* 207–14. Tel Aviv: Dvir, 1951.
Cattani, Pierluigi. *Dio sulle labbra dell'uomo: Paolo De Benedetti e la domanda incessante.* Trento: Il Margine, 2006.
Davis, Colin. *Elie Wiesel's Secretive Texts.* Gainesville: University Press of Florida, 1994.
De Benedetti, Paolo. *Quale Dio? Una domanda dalla storia.* Brescia: Morcelliana, 1996.
Fine, Ellen. *Legacy of Night: The Literary Universe of Elie Wiesel.* Albany: State University of New York Press, 1983.
Franciosi, Robert. *Elie Wiesel: Conversations.* Jackson: University Press of Mississippi, 2002.
Franklin, Ruth. *A Thousand Darknesses: Lies and Truth in Holocaust Fiction.* Oxford: Oxford University Press, 2011.
Greenberg, Irving. *The Third Great Cycle of Jewish History—Voluntary Covenant: The Third Era of Jewish History, Power and Politics.* New York: CLAL, National Jewish Center for Learning and Leadership, 1981.
Kristeva, Julia. *La revolution du language poétique.* Paris: Éditions du Seuil, 1974.
Manseau, Peter. "Revising *Night*: Elie Wiesel and the Hazards of Holocaust Theology." *Cross Currents* 56, no. 3 (2006): 387–99.
Maybaum, Ignaz. *The Face of God after Auschwitz.* Amsterdam: Polak & Van Gennep, 1965.
Neher, André. *The Exile of the Word: From the Silence of the Bible to the Silence of Auschwitz.* Philadelphia: JPS, 1981.
Schäfer, Peter. *Jesus in the Talmud.* Princeton: Princeton University Press, 2008.
Seidman, Naomi. "Elie Wiesel and the Scandal of Jewish Rage." *Jewish Social Studies* 3, no. 1 (1996): 1–19.
Sternlicht, Sanford. *Student Companion to Elie Wiesel.* Westport: Greenwood Press, 2003.
Wollaston, Isabel. "Post-Holocaust Interpretations of Job." In *The Oxford Handbook of the Reception of the History of the Bible,* ed. M. Lieb, E. Mason, and J. Roberts, 488–501. Oxford: Oxford University Press, 2011.
Yaeger, Carolyn. "The Shadowy Origins of 'Night' II." Eliewieseltattoo.com. http://www.eliewieseltattoo.com/the-evidence/wiesels-writings/the-shadowy-origins-of-night-ii/. Accessed 26 October 2017.
Wiesel, Elie. *A Beggar in Jerusalem: A Novel.* Trans. Lily Edelman and Elie Wiesel. New York: Schocken Books, 1985.
Wiesel, Elie. *Dawn.* New York: Hill and Wang, 1961.
Wiesel, Elie. *Day.* New York: Hill und Wang, 2006.

Wiesel, Elie. *Entre deux soleils*. Paris: Éditions du Seuil, 1970.
Wiesel, Elie. *The Forgotten*. New York: Knopf Doubleday, 1992.
Wiesel, Elie. *Night*. New York: Bantam Books, 1982.
Wiesel, Elie. *One Generation After*. New York: Schocken Books, 2011.
Wiesel, Elie. *Open Heart*. New York: Schocken Books, 2012.
Wiesel, Elie. *The Sonderberg Case*. New York: Knopf, 2010.
Wiesel, Elie. *The Trial of God*. Trans. Marion Wiesel. New York: Schocken Books, 1979.

9

The Importance of Memory
Jewish Mysticism and Preserving History in Elie Wiesel's *The Forgotten*

ERIC J. STERLING

> I needed to help perform a transfusion of memory; as Elhanan's diminished Malkiel's would be enriched.
>
> —Elie Wiesel, *And the Sea Is Never Full*

Introduction

Elie Wiesel was an enormously talented and sophisticated writer who explored various genres, including fiction. Colin Davis notes that because of scholars' and students' focus on his nonfiction, "Wiesel's fiction remains curiously unexplored despite an apparent consensus in France and the United States that Wiesel is one of the most important novelists of the post-Holocaust period."[1] Although Wiesel's complex novel *The Forgotten* (1992, published first in French as *L'oublié*, 1992) is a work of fiction, it shares much in common with his memoir *Night* (1960).[2] In both works, memory, survivor guilt, faith, and father-son relationships play significant roles. Wiesel accepts that he resembles the protagonist of *The Forgotten*, Elhanan Rosenbaum: in his autobiography *And the Sea Is Never Full*, Wiesel admits, "Like Elhanan in *The Forgotten*, I am afraid of forgetting."[3] For Wiesel, art (fiction and the novel) and historical fact both effectively provide testimony to future generations. Wiesel never claims that his novels are historical truth, and he clearly demarcates fiction from memoir, but both inform readers about the atrocities inflicted by the Nazis upon their innocent victims.

Wiesel wrote and published *Night* not only in order to share his story and provide his testimony to the world but also to honor the memory of the dead who did not live to provide their own accounts. Wiesel claims in *Legends of Our Time* that "writing is a *matzeva*, an invisible tombstone, erected to the memory of the dead unburied."[4] Alvin H. Rosenfeld asserts, "Surely that is one of the major functions of Holocaust literature, to register and record the enormity of human loss."[5] Wiesel employs this function in *The Forgotten* when Holocaust survivor and now elderly New York psychotherapist Elhanan Rosenbaum wants to share his testimony with his son Malkiel in order to preserve his account of the suffering he witnessed and endured, and to perpetuate the memory of the victims for future generations.

The Importance of Memory

Elhanan feels miserable because his function as a repository of memory to survivors and future generations is threatened by an unnamed disease, most probably Alzheimer's disease, that gradually destroys his mind. Given his preoccupation with memory, Wiesel himself had a strong fear of Alzheimer's, even asking rhetorically in his autobiography, "Is there a disease worse than Alzheimer's? It is a cancer of identity, of memory."[6] The mind and memory disintegrate while the body stays comparatively intact. As a psychotherapist, Elhanan can no longer help survivors heal when he cannot remember past events he witnessed or recent conversations with patients. (Listening to survivor stories is an important and generous but emotionally painful deed, a *mitzvah*, which I know because that was the job of my grandfather, Gunter Kamm, a Buchenwald survivor who, after the war, became the director of the United Restitution Organization in New York). Elhanan prays to God for relief from his debilitating disease, yet his memory continues to decline. It does not occur to him that perhaps God declines to help him because his illness is divinely designed to incite his son Malkiel's visit to Romania and bring closure to Elhanan's guilt for failing to help a woman who is being raped during the war. Elhanan prays for relief for his failing memory, yet he does not correlate his disease with Jewish mysticism and God's higher purpose. He cannot apologize in person for his past cowardly inaction—choosing not to intervene when Zoltan the Nyilas's wife, Madame Calinescu, was being raped—because he is too old and sickly to travel and track down the woman, but he hopes that his son's visit to his former town can help make amends for and bring closure to his past failure. In his father's hometown of Feherfalu, Romania, Malkiel meets the two elderly Jews in the village who survived the Holocaust and remain there; Hershel the gravedigger and Ephraim the caretaker remember Malkiel's heroic grandfather and the obliteration of Jewish culture in the region, and they send Malkiel on a path toward faith and a concomitant understanding of his father's preoccupation with memory. Malkiel's physical journey to Feherfalu initiates his spiritual journey that stimulates his lukewarm faith, ultimately leading to a stronger bond with his father, his Jewish heritage, and God.

In *The Forgotten*, Wiesel stresses the significance of memory, heritage, and faith. Memory is important to many survivors of the Holocaust, for they often remember and honor those who were mercilessly and senselessly murdered during the Shoah and thus cannot speak for themselves. Although the preservation of Jewish history and culture is generally important, personal testimony about the Holocaust is unique and particularly important. Regarding the Holocaust, Simon Sibelman says, "Jewish consciousness appeals to that dimension of its being that could certainly be said to characterize its spiritual attitude: namely, memory."[7] As Sibelman has also pointed out, the title of Wiesel's novel in French (the language in which the author first penned the novel) is not *l'oubli* (forgetting or forgetfulness), but rather *oublié* (the past participle of *oublier*), meaning being forgotten: "as Elhanan forgets, he too is forgotten, tragically and ironically erased from his own memory until he will cease to exist for himself. A second reading, more importantly, would refer to . . . some episode that has been forgotten, or that has been transformed into an unmentionable event that strenuously resists all efforts of voluntary memory to bring it to the conscious surface."[8]

Sibelman makes an excellent point about Wiesel's verb usage; Elhanan has repressed his decision, long ago, not to stop his best friend Itzik from raping Calinescu, partly because he understands the desire for revenge. Although Calinescu herself is innocent, her husband is a mass murderer. Elhanan's shock in witnessing and failing to stop the rape is traumatic for him. Calinescu is not a major character but rather more of a plot device that Wiesel employs to show Elhanan's cowardice when he should have helped the woman; the fact that Elhanan, a strong man (a partisan), proves unable to come to the aid of a vulnerable woman makes him feel ashamed and makes the incident traumatic not only to her but also to him. He never forgives himself for his cowardice but is so traumatized that he can never fully recall the event. Cathy Caruth notes that when one suffers from posttraumatic stress disorder, "the overwhelming events of the past repeatedly possess, in intrusive images and thoughts, the one who has lived through them. This singular possession by the past extends beyond the bounds of a marginal pathology and has become a central characteristic of the survivor experience of our time."[9] Elhanan feels that his inaction defines him shamefully and permanently stains his character. He knows he has sinned but has successfully suppressed the details of his inaction from his memory. Caruth adds that trauma "does not simply serve as record of the past but precisely registers the force of an experience that is not yet fully owned. [. . .] Perhaps the most striking feature of traumatic recollection is the fact that [. . .] while the images of traumatic reenactment remain absolutely accurate and precise, they are largely inaccessible to conscious recall and control."[10] Elhanan's memory resists his strenuous and prayerful efforts to recall the rape partly because the psychotherapist feels so shamed by his inaction that he unconsciously hinders his ability to recall that inaction. Elhanan is forgetting memories not only about other people but also about his own past and identity. Being a keeper of memory requires remembering all events, even the ones of which one is ashamed. Elhanan has hidden his traumatic memory from others and himself but wants to make amends, so he sends Malkiel to Feherfalu.

Memory forges bonds between generations of European Jewry, linking those slain during the Holocaust to those who survived and to second-generation Jews—children of the survivors. When writing *The Forgotten*, Wiesel asked himself, "Is there a tenderness more profound, more intense, more human than the one that links the survivor to his child?"[11] Wiesel's novel portrays familial bonds that have both a linear progression and a cyclical genealogy. In World War II, Malkiel Rosenbaum (the grandfather) serves as the reluctant leader of the Feherfalu ghetto in Romania (then under Hungarian control and German occupation), who is tortured and then executed by a Nazi officer. His son Elhanan survives the war as a partisan and immigrates to the United States. Elhanan's son

Malkiel is born and raised in New York City, blissfully unaware—unlike his father—of an upbringing under Nazi control. Yet Malkiel shares his grandfather's name, just as Elhanan shares his grandfather's name, symbolizing an unbreakable connection between ancestors of multiple generations. Sternlicht believes that in this novel:

> Wiesel returns to the theme of the importance of remembering. Young Jewish people now and in the future must know the story of their ancestors, who underwent the greatest trauma of the twentieth century. In not forgetting, they will maintain the continuity of the Jewish people. In not forgetting, they may be armed to prevent a holocaust from happening to Jews again, or, indeed, to any beleaguered ethnic or racial minority.[12]

Malkiel learns about his father's world and the significance of preserving the past so that it will never be forgotten. Learning his father's past during the Holocaust is part of Jewish tradition. Sibelman points out that in *Célébration Hassidique* (*Souls on Fire: Portraits and Legends of Hasidic Masters*), Elie Wiesel wrote, "'In Hebrew *massora*—tradition—comes from the verb *limsor*—to transmit; being a Jew means putting oneself into the tradition in order to transmit.'"[13] Despite his rapidly failing memory, Elhanan attempts valiantly to transmit his memory and legacy to Malkiel so that his story and his eyewitness accounts pass down communally to the next generation and are not lost forever.

Memory is important to Elhanan because he considers remembrance of Holocaust atrocities to be his duty, particularly since he is most fortunate to survive when the vast majority of the inhabitants in his village perished. Reflecting upon his days as a partisan, Elhanan confesses to Malkiel, with much guilt in his heart, "'Without even knowing it, I must have walked across their graves.'"[14] Elhanan expresses guilt because the dead cannot be properly mourned or identified, having been tortured and then buried unceremoniously in piles in unmarked graves—bloodied bodies existing beneath the surface in unconsecrated ground with nothing above the earth to indicate the carnage that lies below. Elhanan's commitment to memory and his desire to memorialize the dead from his village and from his days as a partisan help somewhat to mitigate his survivor guilt and make him feel more humane and sensitive.

Malkiel

Elhanan most probably suffers from survivor guilt and considers his fortuitous survival of the Shoah to be a miracle from God, so he feels engaged in a meaningful mission to preserve the memory of those who were less fortunate and cannot tell their own accounts of the suffering they endured. Therefore, after he realizes that he suffers from memory loss, he frequently testifies to his son. But his son, not having lived in Eastern Europe, visited Feherfalu, or been hurt directly by the Holocaust (his mother died during childbirth, not at the hands of the Nazis or the Nyilasok), listens politely but emotionlessly. This lack of passion and motivation concerns Elhanan, who wants to ensure that his eyewitness accounts are not lost forever; Wiesel has the same goal, which is why he wrote *Night*. Malkiel is initially shocked and unprepared to learn his history. To demonstrate this fact, Wiesel describes Malkiel's shock and confusion upon seeing his grandfather's (and namesake's) grave, a sight that should not prove unsettling to a man who serves, as Malkiel does, as the obituary editor of the *New York Times*:

> The shock was so violent that he lost his balance and almost fell to the damp soil; the name on the tombstone, tilted as if under the weight of its weariness, was his own. Malkiel ben Elhanan Rosenbaum. A wild notion crossed his mind: could he already be dead? He could not remember living through his death. [. . .] Who's to say that the dead carry their memories into the other world?[15]

This relevant quotation focuses on memory and whether it can be shared after death. Upon spotting his name on the tombstone, Malkiel feels afraid, forgetting momentarily that he is alive and that this is his grandfather's grave. This confusion, which occurs at the beginning of the novel, shows Malkiel's lack of preparation for the spiritual journey upon which he is to embark, and how much he must learn spiritually and mentally to be worthy of the memories his father wants to impart.

Malkiel is quite moved by visiting his namesake's grave, even more so when the gravedigger informs him that Malkiel the grandfather (the martyr) allowed himself to be horrifically tortured during the Holocaust rather than sacrifice the life of any of his townspeople. Malkiel the martyr acted heroically and selflessly, unlike his son Elhanan, who proves unable, in a moment of cowardice, to behave nobly. Malkiel (the grandson) and the reader discover the cyclical nature of the family bonds. The word *ben* (son of) in their names indicates that they are not only individuals but also part of a larger community and are related inextricably to their family. When Elhanan declines to come to the aid of the woman being raped, he shames not only himself but also his father, who acted as a martyr and who shares his name (Elhanan ben Malkiel). Wiesel makes this connection clear by also naming Malkiel's grandfather Malkiel. Elhanan is the name of both the son and the father of Malkiel. He thus implies the lineage of four generations of the Rosenbaum family. Wiesel's novel is rich in tradition, including the significance of family through generations, which is why it is important that the nonpracticing Jew Malkiel (the grandson) atone for the sin of his father and meet his grandfather (by visiting his grave and learning about his Eastern European Jewish heritage).

Malkiel falls far short of the noble legacy of his grandfather, a man blessed by his community for his honor, integrity, and self-sacrifice after choosing to be killed to spare the lives of others. Ephraim, an elderly Jew who lives in the old Feherfalu graveyard and is the embodiment of memory itself, knew Malkiel's grandfather and mocks the younger Malkiel for being far less noble than his namesake. Angered that a second Malkiel son of Elhanan Rosenbaum has appeared before him in Feherfalu, Ephraim taunts Malkiel, "'I knew him. He was a martyr. By what right do you usurp his name?'"[16] Instead of calling him "Malkiel," Ephraim repeatedly mocks him by calling him "Malkiel son of Elhanan." Ephraim employs the word "usurp" because he comprehends that the younger Malkiel lacks the faith and moral integrity of his grandfather (and his father) and is thus unworthy of the name. The younger, American Malkiel, unlike his grandfather, lacks a noble spirit and even chastises himself for caring more about his affairs with women (even with a Jew-hating member of the PLO) than being concerned with strengthening his relationship with this father, honoring the memory of those who died during the Holocaust, and living his faith.

Wiesel suggests in the novel that second-generation Holocaust survivors inevitably seem to have less faith in God and Jewish mysticism than their parents, primarily because they have not endured the same struggles and ethical dilemmas as their parents and have not been raised in the devoutly religious Jewish communities in Eastern Europe that were destroyed irrecoverably during the Shoah. Philip Smith notes that

> due to the moral and logistical immensity of their subject, as well as recurring themes in the depiction of the Holocaust in popular culture, many members of the second and third generations do not feel that they are able to take ownership of, or see themselves as a part of, their family. [. . .] A member of the second generation [. . .] lack[s] the authority of an eyewitness, and yet the Holocaust has invaded their life to an extent that they cannot be considered wholly separate from the events they seek to describe.[17]

Living in the post-Holocaust era, Malkiel is divorced from Eastern European Jewish culture and the Yiddish language, which had been spoken by millions of Jews yet became all but forgotten after the war. The Nazis wanted to do more than murder eleven million Jews in Europe; they also wanted to obliterate the Jewish culture, customs, and language (Yiddish). Malkiel cares little about Eastern European Jewish customs but transforms, however, when his father contracts Alzheimer's disease and starts to lose his memory. Malkiel's guilt for having focused primarily on worldly and epicurean pleasures causes him to want to learn more about Elhanan's past—a past to which he had previously listened indifferently—and to become his father's repository of memory.

Faith

Faith plays an integral role in *The Forgotten*. Faith in God and Jewish mysticism is intertwined with memory of suffering and loss during the Holocaust. Marcel Dubois points out that, in his writings, Wiesel

> has given a tragic but incontestable expression to the Jewish faith. The singular value of his work is that it objectively puts the question of the impossibility of a faith that is not seared and traumatized by the catastrophe. He shows us that the *Shoah* forces us to reconsider the human being's relationship to God. Despite the darkness and silence, the remembrance of Auschwitz brings us the theological memory that reminds

Israel, because of the Election and Covenant, of God's presence among His people. At a deeper level than that of the psychological or historical faculty of recalling, there is what could be called the ontological memory, the act of presence to oneself or to God.[18]

In his novel, Wiesel contests Martin Buber's statement about "the eclipse of God" and Richard Rubenstein's assertion in *After Auschwitz* that the enormity of the Holocaust tragedy indicates the termination of God's covenant with the Jewish people and of an omnipotent, active God that protected the good and the innocent. Wiesel's works are more optimistic, with the author finding a horrific tragedy compatible with a benevolent, loving, and omnipotent God that rules the universe and is the holder and source of memory. Elhanan, Hershel, and Ephraim never lose faith or stop loving God. Despite losing his memory, Elhanan prays to God—without anger—and asks the Lord for assistance. His love for God and belief in God's ability to protect him never wavers.

Memorializing the dead murdered during the Shoah is also essential to Elhanan because memory derives from God. As Wiesel claimed in his 1978 lecture "Let Him Remember":

> When Jews remember, they turn to God and they ask Him to remember. When Jews remember, they say, "Yizkor Elokim— Let Him remember" [. . .]. Let Him remember Majdanek and Ponar and Treblinka and Dachau. Let Him remember all those we can't remember because we are too weak [. . .]. If we stop remembering, we stop being.[19]

In this quotation, Wiesel links memory both to God and human existence. Memory serves as an integral part of Elhanan's existence and brings him closer to God, the ultimate keeper of memory. Elhanan fears, therefore, that the loss of his memory separates him not only from his family, friends, patients, and students, but also from God. His disease detracts from his purpose as someone whose function is to provide testimony of the Holocaust and speak for those unfortunates who cannot. The more time passes and eyewitnesses perish, the more vital his role, yet his Alzheimer's disease prevents him from continuing to perform his role as a witness and from listening to and counseling those who want to bear witness to him of the atrocities that devastated them. Being a psychotherapist is not merely Elhanan's secular job; because it is a spiritual role, he feels that God has selected him to perform it. When he believes that God has allowed him to lose his memory, he therefore feels confused and punished, for bearing witness is the primary role of the survivor. In his "Memory—And Building a Moral Society" speech, delivered upon accepting the 1978 Prize for Human Rights, Wiesel states, "All survivors are witnesses and we take our role seriously. [. . .] We have learned that words transcend writer and reader, speaker and listener; their impact—good or bad—may be felt beyond their realm."[20] Thus, memory, to Wiesel and to his protagonist Elhanan Rosenbaum, possesses a metaphysical and spiritual quality. It is natural, therefore, that in a novel in which a Holocaust survivor fears that he is losing his memory, the character turns to God for assistance, which is why *The Forgotten* begins with a heartfelt prayer.

Elhanan prays to God for the capacity to continue sharing his testimony, asking Him, the keeper of all memory, not to forget him. Elhanan adds:

> You well know, You, source of all memory, that to forget is to abandon, to forget is to repudiate [. . .]. Do not abandon me, God of my father, for I have never repudiated You [. . .]
>
> God of my ancestors, let the bond between them and me remain whole, unbroken.
>
> God of Auschwitz, know that I must remember Auschwitz. And that I must remind You of it.
>
> . . . let me not cut myself off from my past. [. . .]
>
> You spared me in time of danger and death, that I might testify. What sort of witness would I be without my memory?[21]

Elhanan prays to God, the keeper and dispenser of all memory, to continue being a witness. Elhanan's memory is a gift bestowed upon him by God, so when his memory deteriorates, he ponders whether he has committed a sin for which God is punishing him. In his prayer, he suggests that God has abandoned him. Perhaps he is being punished because he abandoned Madame Calinescu in her time of need. God has preserved his life so that he can hold and spread his memory to members of the next generation and console his patients, so the greatest punishment inflicted upon him would be a loss of that purpose, to become a bearer of memory who has, ironically, lost his memory. He is in the process of becoming a man without a past and separated from God, and thus without a purpose.

Ephraim

During his spiritual journey, Malkiel encounters Ephraim, a blind caretaker of memory. Ephraim cries every day whenever he sees Jewish suffering until the day the Nazis occupy Feherfalu. He ceases to cry when he goes blind. Knowing that memory comes from God and is essential, Ephraim goes blind, hoping that losing his sight will enable him to increase his capacity to remember. God needs him to be a purveyor of memory of Jewish suffering, so He allows Ephraim to use Kabbalah, employing "the art of making myself invisible by pronouncing the names of certain angels."[22] By using Jewish mysticism to render himself invisible, Ephraim survives to share his memory with others. Wiesel chooses the name Ephraim for the Jewish mystic (Kabbalah master) and keeper of memory. The name derives from Genesis 41:52: "God has made me fruitful in the land of my affliction" when Joseph has been in prison in Egypt. After being released upon interpreting Pharaoh's dream, he fathers two children, Ephraim being the second. To Joseph, Egypt is the land of his affliction (and the name portends the famine and harsh years of Jewish slavery to come). Most people interpret "fruitful" to mean having children, but being fruitful could signify maintaining and continuing the flow of memory from one generation to the next. Ephraim lives solely to keep memory alive, and his memory derives from God: He prays, "Others have sealed my lips; it is for You to open them. [. . .] Do not touch my memory [. . .] I cling to my memory as I cling to my life, I cling to it because it is my life."[23]

Ephraim informs Malkiel that his grandfather and namesake declined the opportunity to escape the Nazis by being rendered invisible. When Ephraim offered to teach Malkiel's grandfather the Kabbalistic words to become invisible, the noble man declined Ephraim's offer because he knew that the SS officer would murder innocent Jews in retaliation: "'Since all are to die, I will be the first,' he told me. I recall his last words; they were about your father. 'Tell him the date of my death so that he can recite Kaddish.'"[24] The last words of Malkiel the grandfather thus concern his son and a holy prayer to God. Ephraim claims that he is the caretaker of "what people throw away, what history rejects, what memory denies. The smile of a starving child, the tears of its dying mother, the silent prayers of the condemned man and the cries of his friend: I gather them up and preserve them. In this city, I am memory."[25] Malkiel considers Ephraim to be insane, but he still seems moved and feels that Ephraim makes him remember being a child on the eve of Yom Kippur, being blessed by his father.

Hershel and the Great Reunion

An integral mystical element of the novel's theme of memory and testimony is the Great Reunion section, in which Hershel the gravedigger shares his story of the sadness and inaction of the great rabbis of the past. The mysterious, almost mystical Hershel serves as Feherfalu's sole gravedigger for half a century; he has buried everyone who died in Feherfalu before, during, and after the Holocaust (including Malkiel's grandfather). Hershel shares with Malkiel his memory of the burial of the noble ghetto leader, his namesake, Malkiel Rosenbaum. When Hershel reports to Malkiel that he witnessed the rabbi and elders of the town bless and praise his grandfather for his altruistic self-sacrifice that led to his torture and death, followed by them reciting a special Kaddish, Wiesel writes, "'I must tell all that to my father,' Malkiel was thinking. 'He deserves to know everything.'"[26] Here the memory transfusion works the other way, from son to father, so that Elhanan will know what a great man his father was.[27] A multilevel memory transfusion also exists between the Holocaust victims in Feherfalu, Hershel, the rabbis of the village, and Malkiel. Hershel lives on because he must do so; he has no choice. He cannot retire or die because he is the soul of memory and a permanent connection between the living and the dead, the present and the past, the Holocaust and the aftermath, and the village Jews and the *tzaddikim* (tzaddiks; righteous men who perform great deeds and serve as intermediaries between God and human beings).

Wiesel implies the power of Jewish mysticism in the Great Reunion scene when Malkiel is moved upon hearing of his namesake's great courage. Malkiel also listens to (but fails to perceive the significance of) the story involving the tzaddiks. Early one morning Hershel leads Malkiel the martyr and the other renowned dead rabbis of the past on a spiritual procession through Feherfalu. Although Malkiel is skeptical of Hershel's story, the poignant and spiritual account affects him nonetheless. Malkiel the grandson recognizes that his faith must be restored and be sincere in order for him to achieve spiritual closure—and thus healing—for his father. The mystical Great Reunion story serves as the key Malkiel the grandson needs to help his father, for "with the right key, you could unlock the doors of memory."[28]

The novel operates on multiple levels, as with the character of Hershel the gravedigger. Readers are told by the somewhat irreligious and skeptical Malkiel that Hershel is merely an annoying drunk, and Wiesel frames the scenes with Hershel solely from Malkiel's perspective. Consequently, readers mistakenly believe that Hershel is merely an overbearing man who creates fictional stories in exchange for alcohol. Hershel is a human being, the last Jewish survivor (along with Ephraim) of the town, yet he represents Jewish mysticism and seems as much an allegorical figure as a person. Hershel, like Elhanan and Ephraim, plays the role of keeper of memory, but he differs from Elhanan by remaining in his Romanian village after the war and by not sinning grievously. When Hershel considers leaving Feherfalu with the transports to the concentration camps, a mystical, disembodied voice stops him. Hershel informs Malkiel, "I was ready to give it all up and run to the Jews who were dying all day and all night, but some unknown voice held me back: Hershel, it said, don't abandon us; we need you, too."[29] The ethereal voice belongs to the deceased tzaddik Rabbi Zadok. The gravedigger provides Malkiel with valuable historical information and memories not only about his grandfather, Malkiel the martyr, but also about the collective past of his village and how the townspeople suffered mightily during the Holocaust. Hershel's collective memory of the Holocaust ultimately binds together father and son, just as, historically, the experiences of Elie Wiesel and his father Shlomo in concentration camps help forge a strong relationship between them in *Night*.

When all the Jews in the village have been either murdered or rounded up to be sent to Auschwitz, Hershel is miraculously left untouched. The gravedigger thinks to himself, "You disgust me Hershel; you ought to be with the living on their way to death, not with the dead."[30] He fails to realize that he is being kept alive for a higher mystical purpose—his testimony that he can provide to future generations. It is unsurprising, then, that he can walk freely in the town after it has been liquidated but some Nazi soldiers remain. When he fears walking through the town at night, Rabbi Zadok, who has been dead for four hundred years, assures him that he will keep the gravedigger safe.

Rabbi Zadok, the reb of Feherfalu 350 years before the Holocaust, summons Hershel and requests that he wake up the other great, deceased rabbis of the village. Malkiel believes that this event never occurred, that Hershel must have been hallucinating or suffering the effects of a drunken stupor because the account lacks verisimilitude. Malkiel requires realism in a Holocaust account, which manifests his lack of faith in God and Jewish mysticism. Malkiel fails to consider how Hershel miraculously survived the liquidation of the ghetto and remained when all of the other Jews were either murdered or deported in cattle cars to Auschwitz. Malkiel does not realize that God has preserved Hershel because someone (he and Ephraim) must remain in the village to tell the stories of the atrocities and murders on behalf of those victims who unfortunately cannot. Wiesel implies that God ensures that somehow the accounts of the Holocaust victims survive, despite—and long after—their deaths.

Sometimes God's instrument is not necessarily the kind of highly respectable, wealthy person that one would expect God to entrust with important and sacred memories. Similarly, in *Night*, Moishe the Beadle, an unremarkable outcast shunned by the community of Sighet, heroically and altruistically returns to the village to provide testimony about the mass murder of the Jews who have been deported from Sighet; his testimony, like that of Hershel, is disregarded and mocked, foolishly taken to be the lies of a madman. God has chosen Hershel to be the keeper of memory and the conduit between Elhanan and Malkiel, and between the renowned rabbis of the past and the Jews in the present day. How else would the tzaddik Rabbi Zadok know Hershel and speak to him from the grave, where the reb has been buried for 350 years? Zadok requests that Hershel walk to Rabbi Malkiel Rosenbaum's house and obtain a cane that possesses mystical powers and then employ it to wake up all the other deceased rabbis buried in Feherfalu for a 3:00 a.m. meeting in the graveyard to discuss the current Jewish suffering in the village. When Hershel thinks to himself that it is too dangerous to leave the graveyard because Nazi soldiers remain in town, Zadok miraculously reads his mind and reassures him: "'Don't be afraid, Hershel. You'll be safe, I promise.'"[31] Zadok keeps his word, for Hershel walks unimpeded to Malkiel's grandfather's house; the gravedigger admits, "'The dead protected me.'"[32] Hershel finds the cane exactly where the rabbi claims it is (in the closet, on the left), despite never having been in the house and having been buried underground for three and a half centuries. Hershel uses the cane to tap on the gravestones, miraculously and literally waking up the dead. Hershel, now tired, drifts off to sleep but is awakened by a mystical force at exactly 3:00 a.m.; he confesses that "something woke me, and I don't know what it was. A strange sound, or the feel of a hand tugging at my arm."[33] Something supernatural clearly wakes him up, and he serves as the beadle at this spiritual meeting of the rabbis, just as Moishe served as the beadle in the Sighet synagogue in Night.[34]

Zadok informs the other rabbis that the Jews are currently suffering; yet he knows few details and has no idea of the extent of the genocide. In fact, that is why he calls the meeting. Zadok says that he wants to know what the enemy is planning (as if the tragedy is coming soon), not realizing that the enemy (the Nazis) has already liquidated the ghetto and the last cattle car has just left Feherfalu, leaving only Hershel and Ephraim. Zadok believes that the attacks are in the future, not realizing that they have already occurred and that his intercession is too late. The rabbis, like God Himself, are supposed to watch over and protect the Jews but have been remiss and neglectful. Even Rabbi Israel asks, "Are we guilty? Could we have prevented this shame?"[35] These rabbis, like God, possess the mystical power to save the Jews but have failed to act. Zadok uses his power to protect Hershel but not the thousands of other Jews. In *The Forgotten*, as in *Night* and his other works, Wiesel demonstrates his struggles with faith. The author clearly believes in God's existence and he loves God, yet through his works of nonfiction and fiction he expresses his frustration with God's indifference to the suffering and the genocide of Jews during the Shoah. Alan L. Berger notes, "What Wiesel seeks is a way to account for theodicy and to find an acceptable image of deity. [. . . Wiesel's fiction is] simultaneously a protest against—and an affirmation of—God.[36] Wiesel believes that he has "risen against His justice, protested His silence and sometimes His absence, but my anger rises up within faith and not outside it."[37] Despite his faith, Wiesel harbors feelings of protest and rebellion. Wiesel ponders why a benevolent God would refuse or decline to act now, when He frequently interceded in the past, as with Moses. Moses delivered Jews from great suffering. God played an active role in that deliverance, in juxtaposition to God's passivity and seeming indifference during the Holocaust. Where was God's benevolent intercession during the Holocaust? Wiesel manifests his frustration with God when Rabbi Zadok angrily asks, "'God of our fathers, there will be no more prayers to You from this city! The voices of children reading Torah will never again be heard within these walls! The hearts of these people will never again yearn for their Redeemer!

Is that what You wished?"[38] Zadok implies that God Himself will be punished for His inaction. The inhabitants of Feherfalu will no longer adore or pray to Him. God, like Elhanan, has seen evil but failed to act.

Conclusion

In the end, the memory transfusion from Elhanan to Malkiel is largely successful yet incomplete. Elhanan relates many of his memories of the atrocities and the suffering during the Shoah to his son, and Malkiel becomes a repository of this information and a more thoughtful, selfless, and caring human being. Sternlicht notes:

> In *The Forgotten*, as the generation of Holocaust survivors is dying off, the father-son relationship, again central to a Wiesel narrative, revolves around the concept of stewardship. [. . .] Regardless of the pain and emotional cost of recollection, the shame of misdeeds or cowardice, the loss of faith, the fearsome dreams in the night, or action-freezing depression, the generations to come must know the story of the truly lost generation of European Jews. Their memory must survive too. The father-son theme in Wiesel's fiction often ends with the death of the father, coming after reconciliation and understanding. In a way, Wiesel's sons become their fathers upon the death of the elders.[39]

Just as Malkiel becomes the caretaker of his father, he becomes the caretaker of his father's memory. Malkiel even discovers some information regarding Itzik's vengeful rape of Madame Calinescu that Elhanan does not know (her perspective of the incident that she shares with the son and Lidia the translator) or has repressed forever. However, Wiesel manifests in his novel that a memory transfusion, whether it be from Elhanan to Malkiel or Wiesel to his vast readership, can never be comprehensive. Some memories of the Holocaust will inevitably be lost. When survivors die, they often take their memories to the grave or lose them. Wiesel demonstrates this unfortunate fact at the conclusion, when Elhanan, in his advanced stage of Alzheimer's, complains that he forgot his most important memory. He laments in a message to his son, "They say that before dying a man sees his whole past. Not I. All

I see is bursts and fragments. But perhaps that is because I am not yet going to die, not physically, at any rate. Is that why I still cannot recall the essential thing that I want so much to pass on to you, Malkiel?"[40] Elhanan realizes that he has yet to share with Malkiel his most important testimony, and now it is too late because of the ravages of his disease, which systematically erases what is most important to him: his memory, which derives from God and which has previously connected him to his family, friends, patients, and other Holocaust survivors, is fading quickly.

But Wiesel wants to end his poignant novel with a ray of hope. He mentions in *And the Sea Is Never Full*, "To defeat injustice and misfortune, if only for one moment, for one victim, is to invent a new reason for hope. I needed to help perform a transfusion of memory; as Elhanan's diminished Malkiel's would be enriched."[41] Because of Malkiel's transformation, aided by the help of Hershel, Ephraim, and Madame Calinescu, there is hope that the memory transfusion will prove successful. Simon Sibelman has stated that by accepting the responsibility to venture to Feherfalu and help preserve Elhanan's fragile memory, "Malkiel not only places himself within the Jewish tradition of recording and transmitting, already shown to be of paramount importance for Wiesel and for the Jewish people, but he concurrently projects himself upon his distinctive pilgrimage into his father's world, an existence destroyed by the Holocaust, and yet which remains vital in his father's faltering recollections."[42]

The Forgotten manifests Wiesel's optimistic attitude about the testimony of eyewitnesses and memory of the Holocaust. Although Elhanan is permanently losing his memory because of Alzheimer's disease, his testimony continues through the medium of his son. It is a mental transfusion of memory from one generation to the next. Wiesel claims that Malkiel, Elhanan, and Tamar "will proceed with a memory transfusion just as patients are treated with blood transfusions. In the end Malkiel will remember even an episode his father had repressed."[43] Sibelman notes, "While his [Elhanan's] memory and mind are imperceptibly silenced, Malkiel assumes the responsibility to gather together the traces and shards of that fading memory in order to incorporate them into his personal and communal tradition."[44] The legacy will continue. Elhanan's stories still exist in his confused mind, some intact while others appear as fragments, like the story of Calinescu that Malkiel miraculously puts together. The headnote of Wiesel's novel derives from the Talmud and reads, "Respect the old man who has forgotten what he learned. For broken Tablets have a place in the Ark beside the Tablets of the Law."[45]

Broken pieces of knowledge still have value, particularly if someone else can piece them together.

Elhanan maintains hope, and he might be rewarded because of Malkiel's devotion, which is demonstrated by his visit to Feherfalu: "Even as I speak to you I tell myself that you will discover in your own way what my lips cannot say."[46] Although Wiesel states in *Legends of Our Time* that in Auschwitz, "not only man died but also the idea of man," Rosenfeld asserts that Holocaust literature is our record of that dying [in Auschwitz]—a double dying—and, at the same time, "our hope for what might still live on or be newly born."[47] Elhanan knows that because of memory transfusions like his transfusion to Malkiel, much of his accounts will survive, which comforts him: "God cannot be so cruel as to erase everything forever. If He were, He would not be our father, and nothing would make sense." Yet the novel concludes in truncated form, in midsentence, "And I who speak to you cannot say more, for," indicating that his memory is mercilessly leaving him and providing the reader with a disturbing and foreboding feeling that seems to undercut Elhanan's hope.[48]

Notes

1. Colin Davis, *Elie Wiesel's Secretive Texts* (Gainesville: University Press of Florida, 1994), 3.

2. First published in Yiddish as *Un di velt hot geshvign* (And the World Remained Silent) (1956) and then in French as *La Nuit* (1958). While Wiesel described *Night* as memoir, the term is somewhat contested. See the introduction to this volume for an overview of present debates.

3. Elie Wiesel, *And the Sea Is Never Full: Memoirs, 1969–*, trans. Marion Wiesel (New York: Alfred A. Knopf, 1999), 410.

4. Elie Wiesel, *Legends of Our Time*, trans. Steven Donadio (New York: Holt, Rinehart and Winston, 1968), 8.

5. Alvin H. Rosenfeld, *A Double Dying: Reflections on Holocaust Literature* (Bloomington: Indiana University Press, 1988), 27.

6. Wiesel, *And the Sea Is Never Full*, 362.

7. Simon P. Sibelman, *Silence in the Novels of Elie Wiesel* (New York: St. Martin's, 1995), 166.

8. Sibelman, *Silence in the Novels of Elie Wiesel*, 164, his translation.

9. Cathy Caruth, introduction to *Trauma: Explorations in Memory*, ed. Cathy Caruth (Baltimore: Johns Hopkins University Press, 1995), 151.

10. Caruth, *Trauma*, 151.

11. Wiesel, *And the Sea Is Never Full*, 22.
12. Sanford V. Sternlicht, *Student Companion to Elie Wiesel* (Westport: Greenwood, 2003), 109.
13. Sibelman, *Silence in the Novels of Elie Wiesel*, 164, his translation.
14. Wiesel, *The Forgotten*, trans. Stephen Becker (New York: Schocken Books, 1992), 103.
15. Elie Wiesel, *The Forgotten*, 12.
16. Wiesel, *The Forgotten*, 255.
17. Philip Smith, "Holocaust Trauma and Jewish Identity across Generations in Alison Pick's 'Far to Go,'" *Literature Compass* 13, no. 9 (2016): 530, 532.
18. Marcel Dubois, "The Memory of Self and the Memory of God in Elie Wiesel's Jewish Consciousness," in *Elie Wiesel: Between Memory and Hope*, ed. Carol Rittner (New York: New York University Press, 1990), 62.
19. Elie Wiesel, "Let Him Remember," in *Against Silence: The Voice and Vision of Elie Wiesel*, ed. Irving Abrahamson (New York: Holocaust Library, 1985), 1: 368.
20. Elie Wiesel, "Memory—And Building a Moral Society," in *Against Silence: The Voice and Vision of Elie Wiesel*, ed. Irving Abrahamson (New York: Holocaust Library, 1985), 1: 369.
21. Wiesel, *The Forgotten*, 9–10.
22. Wiesel, *The Forgotten*, 257.
23. Wiesel, *The Forgotten*, 253–54.
24. Wiesel, *The Forgotten*, 258.
25. Wiesel, *The Forgotten*, 255.
26. Wiesel, *The Forgotten*, 118.
27. Elhanan does not know his father's fate because he is chosen to escape the ghetto to ascertain whether the Nazis are advancing toward them and are actually committing mass murder. Some members of the ghetto find it hard to believe that the Nazis are committing genocide. After being unable to return to the ghetto, Elhanan joins the partisans.
28. Wiesel, *The Forgotten*, 149.
29. Wiesel, *The Forgotten*, 119.
30. Wiesel, *The Forgotten*, 119.
31. Wiesel, *The Forgotten*, 120.
32. Wiesel, *The Forgotten*, 118.
33. Wiesel, *The Forgotten*, 122.
34. These are allusions and similarities. I am not equating Hershel with Moishe the Beadle.
35. Wiesel, *The Forgotten*, 124.
36. Alan L. Berger, "The Storyteller and His Quarrel with God," in *Elie Wiesel and the Art of Storytelling*, ed. Rosemary Horowitz (Jefferson: McFarland & Co., 2006), 72.

37. Elie Wiesel, *Memoirs: All Rivers Run to the Sea* (New York: Alfred A. Knopf, 1995), 84.
38. Wiesel, *The Forgotten*, 127.
39. Sternlicht, *Student Companion to Elie Wiesel*, 110.
40. Wiesel, *The Forgotten*, 316.
41. Wiesel, *And the Sea Is Never Full*, 403.
42. Sibelman, *Silence in the Novels of Elie Wiesel*, 165.
43. Wiesel, *And the Sea Is Never Full*, 364.
44. Sibelman, *Silence in the Novels of Elie Wiesel*, 164.
45. Wiesel, *The Forgotten*, 7.
46. Wiesel, *The Forgotten*, 316.
47. Wiesel, *Legends of Our Time*, 190; Rosenfeld, *A Double Dying*, 5.
48. Wiesel, *The Forgotten*, 316.

Works Cited

Berger, Alan L. "The Storyteller and His Quarrel with God." In *Elie Wiesel and the Art of Storytelling*, ed. Rosemary Horowitz, 71–89. Jefferson: McFarland & Co., 2006.

Caruth, Cathy. Introduction to *Trauma: Explorations in Memory*, ed. Cathy Caruth. Baltimore: Johns Hopkins University Press, 1995.

Davis, Colin. *Elie Wiesel's Secretive Texts*. Gainesville: University Press of Florida, 1994.

Dubois, Marcel. "The Memory of Self and the Memory of God in Elie Wiesel's Jewish Consciousness." In *Elie Wiesel: Between Memory and Hope*, ed. Carol Rittner, 61–77. New York: New York University Press, 1990.

Rosenfeld. Alvin H. *A Double Dying: Reflections on Holocaust Literature*. Bloomington: Indiana University Press, 1988.

Sibelman, Simon P. *Silence in the Novels of Elie Wiesel*. New York: St. Martin's, 1995.

Smith, Philip. "Holocaust Trauma and Jewish Identity across Generations in Alison Pick's 'Far to Go.'" *Literature Compass* 13, no. 9 (2016): 530–37.

Sternlicht, Sanford V. *Student Companion to Elie Wiesel*. Westport: Greenwood, 2003.

Wiesel, Elie. *The Forgotten*. Trans. Stephen Becker. New York: Schocken Books, 1992.

Wiesel, Elie. *Legends of Our Time*. Trans. Steven Donadio. New York: Holt, Rinehart and Winston, 1968.

Wiesel, Elie. "Let Him Remember." In *Against Silence: The Voice and Vision of Elie Wiesel*, 3 vols., ed. Irving Abrahamson, 1: 368. New York: Holocaust Library, 1985.

Wiesel, Elie. *Memoirs: All Rivers Run to the Sea.* New York: Alfred A. Knopf, 1995.
Wiesel, Elie. "Memory—And Building a Moral Society." In *Against Silence: The Voice and Vision of Elie Wiesel*, 3 vols., ed. Irving Abrahamson, 1: 369–72. New York: Holocaust Library, 1985.
Wiesel, Elie. *Night.* Trans. Marion Wiesel. New York: Hill and Wang, 2006.
Wiesel, Elie. *And the Sea Is Never Full: Memoirs, 1969–.* Trans. Marion Wiesel. New York: Alfred A. Knopf, 1999.

Part IV

Later Works

10

Transcultural Networks of Holocaust Memories in Elie Wiesel's *The Time of the Uprooted*

Dana Mihăilescu

Cultural studies scholar Astrid Erll argues that literature of the two World Wars has been fundamental in developing the notion of "generation"—the belief that a group of people born within a similar time period have a shared experience distinct from that of their parents and children. She identifies the post–World War I period as the time when generationality and genealogy emerged as concepts of cultural memory and praxis discussed in relation to the broader horizon of society via such coinages as the "war generation" or the "lost generation," in which war, violence, hunger, and death functioned as this generation's defining experiences.[1] During this time, the highly successful, translated, and adapted literary work of Erich Maria Remarque *In Westen nichts Neues / All Quiet on the Western Front* (1929) was a significant "node around which transnational and transmedial discourses about the 'lost generation' emerged or were amplified or streamlined," showing how literary images of generational identity can travel across media, nations, and time.[2] Erll further notes how "after the Second World War the familial frame emerged as a central focus of interest [for discussing generationality] in

---

Research for this chapter was supported by a grant of the Romanian National Authority for Scientific Research, UEFISCDI, for grant PN-III-P1-1.1-TE-2016-0091, Transcultural Networks in Narratives about the Holocaust in Eastern Europe.

the face of family histories disrupted or destroyed by the Holocaust," including issues of transgenerational transmission from first-generation survivors, to 1.5-generation survivors (those who were children during the war), and second-generation survivors (their children born after the war's end), which finally branched out toward affiliative and not only familial configurations, especially thanks to Marianne Hirsch's concept of postmemory—the ways in which an individual's experiences can impact the lives of his or her children.[3]

In the aftermath of the Holocaust the nexus between immigration and generation also presents a significant framework for analysis, as most of the survivors left their countries of birth for new places, most often after some sojourn in a European Displaced Persons camp.[4] This coupling of generation with family (understood as both a biological and affiliative unit) and immigration has created a form of entangled generationality, which literary works have particularly underscored. Literature has blazed this path in the attempt to make an intervention into discourses about the Holocaust, generationality, and migration, carving out alternative spaces for thinking of generations beyond mere genetics or familial genealogy and showcasing how "generation is not a given, but a discursive constellation, or assemblage" that transcends boundaries of nation and culture. In this equation, literature functions as an important catalyst for nuanced reflections of what generation means and how it can be used, one in which the category of the transcultural has proved to be especially productive of late.[5]

Erll's identification of World War II as instrumental for coupling scholars' interest in generations of war survivors with their interest in generations of immigrants for which the focus has usually fallen on issues of acculturation to the host country in a family made up of first-generation migrants (usually bearers of the different culture of their original country left behind), second-generation children (as beings between two cultures, using code switching and drawing on different cultural repertoires), and third-generation grandchildren (usually the bearers of the culture of the country of residence) have played a significant role in literary works like those of Elie Wiesel via their technique of foregrounding transcultural networks of Holocaust memories. Wiesel offers a straightforward transcultural biographic trajectory, which he retraced in his memoir *Tous les fleuves vont à la mer* (1994) / *All Rivers Run to the Sea* (1995). He was born into a Jewish family in Sighet, Transylvania, in 1928, then belonging to Romania, where his family continued a more or less normal life until the spring of 1944 when Hungary took possession of the area and they were deported to Auschwitz, where his parents and youngest sister perished. An orphan at the end of the war, Wiesel became a refugee in France, where he studied French language, literature, and philosophy and then relocated to the United States, choosing to continue using French as his main literary language in works that mostly dealt with "the survivor's struggle in the aftermath of the Holocaust," as Steven Katz and Alan Rosen argue in the introduction to their 2013 collection dedicated to Wiesel's oeuvre.[6] Yet, they also go on to indicate that Wiesel's mode of novelistic storytelling evolved over time, following "a shift of focus from the struggle of Holocaust survivors in the wake of the war [in his early works] to that of their children a generation later," especially in his post-2000 works.[7] In this chapter, I will argue that Wiesel also engaged a broader pattern of Holocaust representation in his literary universe, the transcultural stakes of Holocaust memories for present-day Jewish life and identity, as reflected in his novel *Le Temps des déracinés* (2003) / *The Time of the Uprooted* (2005).

In arguing this thesis I continue in the direction of recent theoretical works foregrounding transcultural memory networks as conduits by which scholars "share a common agenda: how to map the circulation of memory and memory practices across national or other borders, and how to explain the impact of these on the constitution of identities" due to "mnemonic mobility: the transmission, circulation, mediation, and reception of memory between and beyond ethnic, cultural, or national groups."[8] I will trace the input of transcultural networks characterizing Holocaust survivors' memories in Wiesel's *The Time of the Uprooted* in which positively acknowledging and inhabiting one's vulnerability takes center stage.

Exile

The novel is the story of Gamaliel Friedman, born in 1936 to a Jewish family from Czechoslovakia, who in 1939 flees to Budapest, Hungary, in search of relative safety and finally survives the Holocaust after his mother decides to leave him with young Christian cabaret singer Ilonka, at whose side he passes as a gentile while his parents die. After the war's end, Gamaliel moves to France in 1956 to escape communism and finally settles in the United States. In Gamaliel's case, the transcultural dimension of memory is immediately associated with the Shoah in Hungary for a Jewish child from Czechoslovakia in which he has to pass as a gentile boy in order to survive, an experience that ties Gamaliel to other characters' equally painful experiences, about which he learns in later encounters. Such characters are gentile Hungarian Ilonka, who serves as his surrogate mother and who accepts sexual advances from various Nazis to save the boy; Bolek, a Jewish survivor from a Polish ghetto; Diego, a hero of the Resistance in the war in Spain; Gad, a Mossad agent; Iasha, a former victim of Stalinist anti-Semitism; Lili Rosenkrantz, a psychiatrist living in New York who was born in Romania toward the war's end, whose father died in a Transnistrian ghetto, and who has her own traumatic life trajectory.

The Time of the Uprooted is not a travel book since its main topic does not revolve around recounting the narrator-protagonist's journey, which would define it as travel writing.[9] Instead, the book most clearly belongs to the tradition of Holocaust-centered writing, which Elie Wiesel considers to be a literature of testimony due to the generation of Holocaust survivors and notes: "If the Greeks invented tragedy, the Romans the epistle, and the Renaissance the sonnet, our generation invented a new literature, that of testimony."[10] Michael Bachmann contends that even though this literature of testimony does not discard the role of imagination, Wiesel "insists on the survivors' sole possession of that experience and its literature," suggesting that the writer of Holocaust literature can only be someone who was a witness of events during World War II.[11] This follows Alan Rosen's claim that Wiesel's "remarkable oeuvre centers on the situation of the victim, on the perils and possibilities of solitude, friendship, testimony, and madness."[12] Yet, the novel also fits the category of "travelling memory-literature," following Erll's concept of "travelling memory," which implies that "memory lives in and through its movements," its mnemonic forms being "filled with new life and new meaning in changing social, temporal and local contexts."[13] Erll most recently scaled down the concept of traveling memory to discuss what she calls "travelling memory-film," that is, films that "address Europe and its transcultural memories through the depiction of performance of movement, through 'travel' on various levels."[14] Similarly, *The Time of the Uprooted* is a novel that addresses the transcultural memory of the Holocaust by foregrounding the performance of movement via various forms of travel. These include, just as in the case of films, the representation of physical travel or movement across space of the protagonist Gamaliel, which presents the multi-sites where he has carried his Holocaust memories; travel in the novel's structure following its montage of various characters' trajectories and memories and how they construct a transcultural network of the Holocaust; travel as social circulation of the novel, suggested by the use of ghostwriting as an allegoric figure. In examining the transcultural memory of the Holocaust in *The Time of the Uprooted*, I therefore look at it as a traveling-memory novel and explore whether its use of various forms of travel promotes its ethical underpinnings or might equally point to nefarious coordinates.

Representation of physical travel or movement across space undoubtedly functions as a major building block of this novel since the protagonist's movement across borders is an essential part of the plot structure. From the outset Wiesel introduces the main protagonist, Gamaliel, in relation to travel, remembering how as a four- or five-year-old child, alongside his parents in Czechoslovakia, he was fascinated by "a wanderer." This wayfarer referred to himself as "a crazy wanderer" when he came to his parents' house to test their hospitality and was positively impressed by how Gamaliel's father welcomed him on Shabbat to the family, offering food and full-hearted company. Associating this man to the figure of the Jewish prophet, Gamaliel notes how in the wake of that encounter "I delight in madmen. I love to see their crazed, melancholy faces and to hear their bewitching voices, which arouse in me forbidden images and desires."[15] And ironically, Gamaliel becomes such a figure of the perpetual wanderer, the eternal stranger, being first introduced as an uprooted old "exile" living in New York, whose life is characterized by loneliness and uncertainty whether this condition belongs to the past or the future.[16] He is not just uprooted from life but also from family; his wife committed suicide and he became estranged from his twin daughters as a result. He is further referred to as an exiled man and a refugee, having four other exiled, refugee friends (Bolek from Poland, Diego from Spain, Iasha from Israel, Gad from the former Soviet Union) who by and large share a similar outlook on the surrounding world.[17] These characters' existence in relation to movement across space because of World War II leads to a multi-sited ethnography of Holocaust memory in Wiesel's novel. These "five once-stateless men" first met in Paris in the early 1960s at an annual reunion of Jewish refugees talking about how to get an extension to residence permits as displaced persons in France, how to obtain working papers and to apply for visas to Canada and the United States, and they continue to meet in New York, on the Lower East Side near the Yiddish daily *Forward* building to discuss their concerns over the increased level of anti-Semitism that is still high in contemporary times.[18] When meeting his future wife Collette in France, Gamaliel further states, "a refugee is a different kind of being, one for whom all that defines a normal person has been amputated. He belongs to no nation, is welcome at no one's table. A leper. He can achieve nothing unless others help him."[19] Here we encounter a negative definition of the refugee as opposed to a "normal person" who seems to be co-referent with the idea of "nation" or family that correspond to a fixed, bounded, restrictive sense of self. The refugee from World War II is thereby constructed in Wiesel's novel as the bearer of what Erll calls "memories [that] are carried along 'on the road' and that may merge with or transform ideas of the past encountered *en route*," the person depending on others' help, be they ethnic, national, religious, generational or other types of others.[20] Initially such a Holocaust survivor refugee seems to be defined negatively in comparison to the "normal person" characterized by an existence bounded especially by national borders, since he seems to be bodily disabled as an "amputated" being and diseased by being defined as a "leper." Yet, his very vulnerable position of obvious dependence on others is gradually turned in the sequel of the novel into an asset that permits such individuals to create positive solidarities of mnemonic relationality by being aware of differences and relying on their empathy for the sufferings of others and by the need to vigilantly try to fight any threats waged against humanity. In a similar vein, the regular students in a New York campus near which Gamaliel goes to a dinner do not share his or other refugees' or exiles' concerns but instead simply comment on sports and political news, only interested in their immediate present.[21] As a result, people like Gamaliel have a marginal position in the mainstream US society in which they live.

Memory

Within a dozen pages, Gamaliel is the wanderer, the uprooted, the exiled, and the refugee, figures par excellence for identifying vulnerable beings tried by history. In these cases, travel is not the journey featured by travelogues, namely, a journey voluntarily undertaken by a narrator/protagonist for all sorts of reasons. Instead, travel stands for forced movement and migration that made Gamaliel and his friends traverse various locations because of traumatic events impinged upon them by others and specific histories at specific times. In response, what seems to unite these people of the temporary is their permanent alertness and incessant concern for new possible catastrophes that might affect them or others, since we read that Gamaliel's as well as his refugee friends'

> gloomy thoughts turn to the events that are threatening the world at the end of the century. In the name of the fatherland, supposedly civilized countries send to death young people who would rather be dancing the frenzied dance of desire. Under the noble pretext of advancing science, man becomes a slave to machines. There is a risk that those who claim to be honoring their people's past in fact may do it to discredit. They talk themselves into saying nothing. The gods of hate hide behind slogans of brotherhood; they fool everybody, including themselves.[22]

Indeed, when Gamliel meets an old man at the New York hospice where he is asked to assist in the identification and potential healing of an old woman who may have been the saintly maternal figure who saved him in Nazi-occupied Hungary, a man that proves to be himself an inmate of the asylum even if he claims he is here to see his ailing wife, we learn that Gamaliel has "met too many people, in too many lands, not to sense a warning signal."[23] Therefore, when the old man decries his wife's and other institutionalized elderlies' fears about being confined to their beds and the electroshock procedures they have to undergo in New York hospitals, the omniscient narrator foregrounds the huge difference that exists between such concerns of America's typical elderly who have always known freedom of movement and those who have gone through the Holocaust, like Gamaliel, for whom fear has taken transcultural forms, seeming to be a completely inescapable fate:

> The old man talks of fear but what can he know about it, this solid citizen, well dressed, free to go where he wants when he wants? As for Gamaliel, the accused refugee, it would take very little for the ground to slip out from under his feet. Should I tell this harmless well-meaning chatterbox that I've known every kind of fear? He wonders. Fear in Budapest. Fear of the Nyilas, the Hungarian Nazis, of the local police, of the German soldiers, and later, in Vienna, the fear of the unknown,

> the physical fear when confronted by a border guard, the fear felt by the refugee, the exiled, the hungry, the person who's been uprooted and is living clandestinely, the fear of showing one's afraid.[24]

The realization that the Hungarian-speaking woman in the hospital could be Ilonka, the Hungarian gentile who took care of him during the war, prompts Gamaliel to revisit many questions: Who denounced his mother? How was she dressed on deportation? Who tortured his father? When and how did he die? Could he have benefited from some sense of solidarity from comrades or was he completely alone? Meanwhile Gamaliel is aware that these bits of information belong to "a memory not his own," but his meeting Ilonka would stimulate his willingness to remember a distant and painful past.[25] As he becomes more and more reflexive about his past, Gamaliel views Ilonka as standing beyond the level of a saint, as a perfect illustration of what it means to be "admirably human," "a brave woman, a noble and passionate one," "a heroic figure," placing her in contrast to "all the intellectuals of Europe [who] are not worth the loving grace of this unschooled woman who did so much to save one human life, his own."[26] All these episodes that contrast Gamaliel's position with that of typical American citizens highlight the novel's double structure as to the experience of transcultural memory and mnemonic relationality. For Gamaliel and his fellow refugees who experienced World War II, the Holocaust is a trigger for reflexive existence in relation to possible genocides and human existence in general, but for the regular American citizens of both young and old generations, the Holocaust is a distant event they never experienced and about which they remain nonreflexive, just as they are not interested in any possible conundrums for the future of humanity.

Similarly, the psychiatrist feels the sudden need to tell to Gamaliel how her happiness was unexpectedly curtailed a year before when one morning her husband, Al, informed her and their two daughters that he would go away and did not know if he would ever return as he felt he was "not worthy of [their] love," he did not like who he was or his life, and needed a complete change.[27] In response to her confession and tearful outburst, Gamaliel presents his own problematic past as if he were talking of another person characterized by fear and who is no longer looking for pleasures but for the reality and the sense of things he has been running away from. He does that by mentioning:

I used to know a man who had no home and no family. Life knocked him about. He ran into one roadblock after another; the ground would give way under his feet. To make a living, he spent his time helping imbeciles who were slaves to their own vanity write nonsense that would win them a false fame, a counterfeit image. He was full of fears and complexes that he'd learned to hide, yet he felt strangely free because, being bound by no social constraints, he could take in everything and explain it all—though in fact he didn't understand anything. He'd read everything, remembered everything, but it was all on the surface. Nothing moved him deeply. Perhaps he was afraid, afraid of revealing himself, of commitment, of giving up his freedom. Without wanting to, without even being aware of it, he was sowing unhappiness all around him. Those he loved and who loved him always became his victims.[28]

To her query if he is still searching for happiness, he answers hesitantly, "I no longer know," and "Perhaps I'm seeking the reality and meaning of what I'm running from."[29] He later learns that the psychiatrist, Lili Rosenkrantz, also had a sad past; she was born in Romania, her family was deported to Transnistria, her father was killed in a ghetto near Moghilev, and then her mother found refuge in Budapest and married an American journalist, coming to the United States.[30] By using such contrasting scenes, Wiesel's novel demonstrates that the state of mnemonic relationality can be a positive case of reflexive engagement with the problems of the world for only few people, those who escaped genocides like World War II or empathetically became imbricated with such events, while most often it is merely the case of a transcultural memory that is nonreflexive or even denied for most individuals that remain mired in trivial details of life, like Lili's husband, Al.

Bolek further foregrounds transcultural conduits of Holocaust experiences when recounting the specifics of the Polish town of Davarowsk where, in the summer of 1942, as he was bringing food from the Aryan side to his parents, after the creation of the ghetto where he hid them in a barrack belonging to some neighbors—shelter from which he thought nobody could find them—he saw the Nazis take them out and kill them in a forest.[31] As he makes his recollection in 1990s New York, Bolek asks Gamaliel not to look at him, as if afraid of "giving himself away, of bursting into tears" or "of taking his confession too far."[32] He especially recalls how he then became aware of a previously unbelievable situation, the existence of "informers in the ghetto," "Jewish scoundrels who were helping the Germans"—this is how his parents were discovered and killed alongside others hiding in the ghetto.[33] The "stool pigeon" was one Horowitz, the son of a wealthy and respected Jewish realtor and commerce dealer.[34] Being part of the Jewish Resistance, Bolek and his friends try to find young Horowitz guilty of betrayal, condemning him to death and executing him while Horowitz remains silent throughout. Bolek's Holocaust experiences from Poland add to Gamaliel's situation of surviving thanks to the care given to him by a good Gentile like Ilonka in Hungary, who made him take a fake, non-Jewish identity, in case of the complicity of some Jews with the Nazis that occurred especially in Poland. During the trial of Horowitz, Bolek functioned as the prosecutor who brought forward witnesses that testified to having seen the young man talk pleasantly with the Nazis after denouncing some of the Jews in hiding while they were taken away. In light of this comes Bolek's conscious and determined decision to have young Horowitz, punished by death despite old Horowitz's plea to be allowed to punish his son himself. The old man feels responsible for what the son did, for having neglected him over business and material success, and for failing to teach him about principles and values. Gamaliel feels that, as a result, Bolek and the other Resistance comrades-in-arms have a killing on their consciences, by which they might "fear that in punishing one of their own they would come to resemble their executioners."[35] As a result, Bolek feels that his hatred toward the Nazis fueling his thirst for revenge does not help his parents, the loss of whom he will forever weep.[36]

The Politics of Memory

Further to Gamaliel's plea that Bolek should write down these experiences, Bolek decries the historiography of the Holocaust, pleading how memorialization and narratives of the event should not only concern empirical matters such as numbers, dates, and orders but should also engage with the victims' truths. To this effect, Bolek bemoans:

> Who knows about my father's heroic dying, my mother's silent tears? Where is their truth? And where is the truth of my brothers and sisters when they were being driven to their

mass grave? We seem to know the murderers better than their victims! And they call that serving history. Well, that history isn't my history, because my truth isn't their truth.³⁷

He therefore asks for the truths of victims to come out from testimonies by survivors like Gamaliel and himself. In response, Gamaliel adds another issue, that of survivors whose status has been trivialized and rendered insignificant by being claimed by anyone and for anything:

Didn't they realize that if everyone is a potential or virtual survivor, then no one is a true survivor? How to explain to them that, confronted with such deception, those who did indeed survive come to be ashamed of having really been there? How to tell them to let "remembrance" rest in peace, because the dead took its key with them when they disappeared in smoke?³⁸

In this exchange, Bolek and Gamaliel decry the primary characteristics of highly coveted "celebrity survivors" of the Holocaust, a crash, a personal crisis, or a reality TV show fostered by post-1990s American movies and TV shows, with whom viewers are encouraged to identify, so that the survivor of any situation becomes the center of attention, telling everyone how he or she survived a Hitler-like figure, while exuding pride, success, and the accomplishment of survival beyond victimization.³⁹

Debarati Sanyal explains how such popular culture depictions of survivors are reproduced in current theorizations of the Holocaust in which "the apparently fluid exchange of guilt and innocence in the gray zone (and we should remember that this symmetry was a deadly fiction) is currently deployed as the *paradigm* for an ongoing contamination that implicates secondary witnesses—that is to say, the readers, listeners, and viewers who issued forth in the aftermath of the Holocaust—within a general web of traumatic culpability," fixing everything in "the rigid plot of trauma and a universal affect of shame," which paralyzes ethico-political engagements.⁴⁰ This is particularly significant for discussing Wiesel's oeuvre especially in light of such other important studies as Anne Rothe's book *Popular Trauma Culture: Selling the Pain of Others in the Mass Media*, which decries the problematical ethics of the Holocaust promoted by mass media in misery memoirs, films, and talk shows. In her book, Rothe particularly singles out the special May 24, 2006, episode of the *Oprah Winfrey Show* as representing the "culmination" moment for the exploitative specifics of popular trauma culture, one depicting the host and Elie Wiesel at Auschwitz, on a pilgrimage-like trip to the most paradigmatic World War II death camp. Rothe identifies the most problematic aspect of the broadcast in its putting forth "a dissonant fusion between his [Wiesel's] quasi-religious understanding of the Holocaust as an incomprehensible mystery of suffering and redemption and her [Oprah's] self-help platitudes of trauma and recovery," simultaneously pointing toward "Holocaust sanctification" and "trauma-and-recovery kitsch" by bringing any kind of survivor figure at the level of a hero to the detriment of the victims who died in the tragedy via an ahistorical melodrama script not dwelling at all on the complex sociopolitical history of the Nazi agendas during World War II.[41] Rothe is right in underscoring the problematics of Wiesel's participation in this *Oprah* show trip to Auschwitz, which sustained mass media's commodification of the Holocaust as an ahistorical event. Yet, Wiesel's novel shows that the pride associated with the image of survivors is not necessarily given at the expense of those who died in the Holocaust, as decried by Rothe, but remains very much ridden with the survivor's guilt of continuing to live or being part of complicit structures. In *The Time of the Uprooted*, Gamaliel precisely dismantles contemporary American culture's impulse toward everyone's identification with the suffering of Holocaust survivors that blurs various subject positions via the stance of surrogate victimhood and transforms it into a universal paradigm for any subject's position in relation to history by which the Holocaust becomes the matrix for interchangeable traumas. This understanding creates fixed paradigms disregarding the particularities of various individuals' positioning in relation to the Holocaust and erodes the difference between those who lived through World War II and the multiple gaps separating them from outside readers, spectators, viewers, among others. As a result, "Gamaliel preferred the word *orphan* to *survivor*."[42] This episode bespeaks of the quality of Wiesel's writing to preserve "the mystery and full complexity of human action and volition," including various degrees of responsibility and guilt that involve the "brutalization" of some Jews putting forth "the fated and pitiable wretchedness of their condition," indicated as well by John Silber.[43] This is achieved by the incorporation of travel in the novel's structure via the multidimensional montage of various survivor refugees' Holocaust experiences that are constantly overlaid. These experiences are rendered as allegories, literary figures that have the power to energize ethical and political commitments as they, according to Sanyal, "enable comparative analysis of violence and the political work of memory" just as "they can also foster nonredemptive forms of connection, solidarity, consolation."[44] These Holocaust trajectories of the various refugee characters of the novel are therefore presented and crosscut in such a way as to make them resonate to each other. They open up mnemonic relationality, articulating different histories of suffering and animating contestatory possibilities.

Through Bolek's allegoric rendering of his Holocaust experiences, for example, Wiesel highlights complicity as a sign of commitment to ethical action at the foundation of responsibility as far as Holocaust survivors are concerned, given their recognition and involvement with the effects of their actions or lack of action on others' fate. The novel therefore underscores that transcultural memory is not intrinsically progressive or inclusive; following Bolek's experience and renderings presented earlier, it can produce differentiated solidarities and affiliations across sociocultural lines in the case of Holocaust survivors from various borderlands, like Bolek and Gamaliel or Gamaliel and Lili Rosenkrantz, but it can also easily deepen divisions and occlude a productive use of the Holocaust by freezing it into paradigms that especially follow the narrow, trivializing depiction of survivors offered by American entertainment culture.[45]

At the end of the novel, as Gamaliel becomes aware of the death of the Hungarian woman he was meant to assist, learning she carried two candles with her, he realizes she might actually be his mother, who used to carry two candles with her and use them for the Sabbath blessing. He realizes that

> it was his mother that he had been so desperately seeking. It was she who knew him best and she whose love was true. She could with a caress or a glance confer the happiness he sought. His mother gave him life and comfort. And Ilonka? She has done the same, but in a different way. His mother had left him too soon, taking with her the promise she had not been able to keep. Her tender, gentle touch, her bedtime stories, her smile, her tears—he had found their traces in other women; they, too, had vanished, their traces scattered on faces that came and went. And, he saw, he had never ceased wondering in his heart of hearts whether he would find her before he died.[46]

After taking part in a Jewish ceremony for burying the dead patient, he and Lili Rosenkrantz go home together, realizing that their being together is not about the hard ways of how to "go on" with life with all its trouble but with the intention to "begin again."[47] The enigma of the identity of the dying woman is here finally illuminated. It is not merely a quest to be settled for good, but the trope of an ethically assumed exposure and responsibility for the other, an identity aware of trauma and its dangers and, yet, capable to continue living and transmit an alternative reality of happiness and a desire for justice to the following generations. In other words, Wiesel's novel finally celebrates mnemonic relationality between Holocaust survivor Gamaliel and the second generation, empathetic Lili as the means to survive after the Holocaust and forever connect the individual with the others. The emotional memory shared by Gamaliel and Lili, one that tries to reconcile one's duty to the past with one's responsibility for the future, is the one that the novel singles out as resonating with other people and their experiences, allowing them to get a glimpse of traumas' lived dimension and to try to find a way out by social conscience.

Memory and Authenticity

All these episodes from Wiesel's novel demonstrate Dirk Moses and Michael Rothberg's point that the transcultural dimension of memory studies primarily encompasses the comparative scope of (particularly traumatic) memories, highlighting "the palimpsestic overlays, the hybrid assemblages, the nonlinear interactions, and the fuzzy edges of group belonging."[48] This could either lead to problems and constraints of transcultural memory as identified by Michael Rothberg, for instance, a form of "competitive assertion that seeks to seize the ground of recognition from people with other experiences of suffering," or productive directions of transcultural memory, putting forth "visions of history that opt for a *differentiated* solidarity—that is, that allow us to distinguish different histories of violence while still understanding them as implicated in each other and as making moral demands for recognition that deserve consideration."[49]

The Time of the Uprooted further underscores travel in the novel's structure in relation to travel as social circulation of the novel by including ghostwriting in the novel's construction and using it as an allegoric figure throughout, showing that for survivors themselves the productive forms of transcultural memory are only achieved in time. Ghostwriting has been scarcely used by Holocaust survivors, since those who were moved to write were most often highly literate and well educated. Only a small number of Holocaust survivors (especially those who immigrated to the West as adults and did not feel they mastered the English language well enough to express themselves in writing) have used this technique for getting their memoirs of the Holocaust published, thereby offering hybrid testimonies to readers that facilitate survivors' and new generations' growing awareness of meta-issues of narrating and various, complex mediations actually making up World War II events, memories, and our hindsight relation to them.[50] Wiesel doesn't use ghostwriting in this literal sense but as an allegoric figure for highlighting the gradual uptake of a reflexive view of the Holocaust on the part of the survivor-protagonist as a result of transcultural encounters and the moral input triggered by the others' presence. In Wiesel's novel, Gamaliel the Holocaust survivor is not the one who is helped to get his autobiography published via a professional ghostwriter. Instead he is the ghostwriter writing for untalented people. We learn that he started doing this job in order to pay the rent, thinking of the "silly narratives he used to dream up for amateur writers who wanted to be thought professional. That was how he paid the rent. Love stories for shop girls, Kiplingesque adventures in exotic settings, financial conspiracies, gritty detective stories: scribbling, not writing."[51] He began ghostwriting as a displaced person in Paris, when a professor of history, Bernard Murat, approached him to help finish a book about a medieval heretic, a Spanish monk, because he was in bad health, but he thought his career and reputation depended on its publication; yet the book Gamaliel produced was finally returned to him as too fictional.[52] Then, following Bolek's pleas as they struggled to pay the rent, Gamaliel became the ghostwriter for one Georges Lebrun. A man without talent, Lebrun wanted recognition and retained Gamaliel to write what he considered a bad novel because it was a "kitsch," "a tearjerker" filled with "cheap emotions" and errors in syntax and spelling. The novel immediately made Lebrun a success, "hailed by *le tout* Paris as the most promising writer of the postwar years."[53] From that moment on, Gamaliel started to get some nice sums of money by writing easy pieces for others, feeding their vanity to be known and admired in exchange for money that would allow him a decent lifestyle and comfortable lodgings. The work allowed him to bypass responsibility in case it was not well received or to have it published if it was good, since he would otherwise not be able to find a publisher willing to put forth an unknown name, following Bolek's insights.[54]

As the novel continues, however, Gamaliel's attitude to ghostwriting becomes ethical in relation to one of his lovers' critical responses. Gamaliel initially explains to Eve that he ghostwrites to make a living as a refugee even if for her this remains a form of lying.[55] Later on, when he embarks on writing the political-philosophical autobiography of a public official who had studied law and become a promising aide to the mayor, he gives it up when she asks if he is absolutely sure the man has a clean record and whether he would not feel "morally obliged to make a public apology" if he found out he did something bad. So Gamaliel gives back the twenty thousand dollars to the politician.[56] He also rejects getting involved in a quarrel between two rabbis when one asks him to write a book that would refute the other's ideas, even if it would have paid the rent for six months. Later on, as he speaks with Lili Rosenkrantz after coming three times on the same day to see the Hungarian patient, he considers writing a new book for Lebrun that includes his own musings about aging:

> the next novel I sell to Georges Lebrun could be about the many challenges an old man faces; about all the ways he is doomed to failure. I would rage against his inevitable defeats: all those women he will no longer be able to seduce; all the voyages he will no longer undertake; all these projects that will fail or be abandoned. I'd recount his sterile dreams, the ways he's found wanting, his complexes—in a word, his impotence.[57]

As such, thanks to his exchanges with others, Gamaliel becomes more and more self-aware and engaged with the problematics of life even in what concerns his writing ethics.

Conclusion

This chapter has explored Wiesel's novel as traveling memory-literature, which uses the representation of physical travel or movement across space, travel in the novel's structure, and travel as social circulation of the novel as transcultural conduits transmitting ethical responsibility about Holocaust memories for the new generations, articulating a contemporary Jewish identity for Holocaust survivors at the heart of which one finds the resorts of transcultural memory practices. To this end, I have shown how the various locations referenced in the novel (Hungary, Poland, France, the United States) have formed a transcultural network to debunk survivors' charged Holocaust memories and to foreground their ethically minded contemporary identity. All this suggests that *The Time of the Uprooted* has occasioned Wiesel's becoming cognizant of unprocessed sore points for his own community, a reflective stance of transcultural networks that belongs to Holocaust survivors who have become uprooted refugees of history, highlighting "the palimpsestic overlays, the hybrid assemblages, the non-linear interactions, and the fuzzy edges of group belonging."[58] These formations come in contrast to nonreflexive forms of mnemonic relationality for regular individuals that have only encountered trivial problems of life, in the United States or elsewhere, and which have been largely reproduced in US popular culture and theorizations of history.

Notes

1. Astrid Erll, "Generation in Literary History: Three Constellations of Generationality, Genealogy and Memory," *New Literary History* 45 (2014): 386.
2. Erll, "Generation in Literary History," 395.
3. Erll, "Generation in Literary History," 397, 400.
4. Erll, "Generation in Literary History, 401.
5. Erll, "Generation in Literary History," 404.
6. Steven T. Katz and Alan Rosen, eds., *Elie Wiesel: Jewish, Literary and Moral Perspectives* (Bloomington: Indiana University Press, 2013), 2.
7. Katz and Rosen, *Elie Wiesel*, 5.
8. Ann Rigney and Astrid Erll, Introduction, *Image [&] Narrative* Special Issue on "Audiovisual Memory and the (Re)Making of Europe," 18, no. 1 (2017): 2; Lucy Bond, Stef Craps, and Peter Vermeulen, Introduction, *Memory Unbound: Tracing the Dynamics of Memory Studies* (New York: Berghahn Books, 2016), 3.
9. Carl Thompson, *Travel Writing* (London: Routledge, 2011), 1.
10. Elie Wiesel, "The Holocaust as Literary Inspiration," in Elie Wiesel, Lucy Dawidowicz, Dorothy Rabinowitz and Robert McAfee Brown, *Dimensions of the Holocaust* (Evanston: Northwestern University Press, 1977), 9.
11. Michael Bachmann, "Life, Writing, and Problems of Genre in Elie Wiesel and Imre Kertész," *Rocky Mountain Review* 63, no. 1 (2009): 83.
12. Alan Rosen, Introduction, *Celebrating Elie Wiesel: Stories, Essays, Reflections* (Notre Dame: University of Notre Dame Press, 1998), xvii.

13. Astrid Erll, "Travelling Memory in European Film: Towards a Morphology of Mnemonic Relationality," *Image [&] Narrative* 18, no. 1 (2017): 11.
14. Erll, "Travelling Memory in European Film," 6.
15. Elie Wiesel, *The Time of the Uprooted*, trans. David Hapgood (New York: Alfred A. Knopf, 2005), 4.
16. Wiesel, *The Time of the Uprooted*, 6.
17. Wiesel, *The Time of the Uprooted*, 15.
18. Wiesel, *The Time of the Uprooted*, 124.
19. Wiesel, *The Time of the Uprooted*, 170.
20. Erll, "Travelling Memory in European Film," 8.
21. Wiesel, *The Time of the Uprooted*, 17.
22. Wiesel, *The Time of the Uprooted*, 14–15.
23. Wiesel, *The Time of the Uprooted*, 65.
24. Wiesel, *The Time of the Uprooted*, 67.
25. Wiesel, *The Time of the Uprooted*, 68.
26. Wiesel, *The Time of the Uprooted*, 117–18.
27. Wiesel, *The Time of the Uprooted*, 98.
28. Wiesel, *The Time of the Uprooted*, 99.
29. Wiesel, *The Time of the Uprooted*, 100.
30. Wiesel, *The Time of the Uprooted*, 112–13.
31. Wiesel, *The Time of the Uprooted*, 177–85.
32. Wiesel, *The Time of the Uprooted*, 183.
33. Wiesel, *The Time of the Uprooted*, 187.
34. Wiesel, *The Time of the Uprooted*, 191.
35. Wiesel, *The Time of the Uprooted*, 195.
36. Wiesel, *The Time of the Uprooted*, 197.
37. Wiesel, *The Time of the Uprooted*, 200.
38. Wiesel, *The Time of the Uprooted*, 201.
39. Anne Rothe, *Popular Trauma Culture: Selling the Pain of Others in the Mass Media* (New Brunswick: Rutgers University Press, 2011), 36.
40. Debarati Sanyal, *Memory and Complicity: Migrations of Holocaust Remembrance* (New York: Fordham University Press, 2015), 26.
41. Rothe, *Popular Trauma Culture*, 3, 39.
42. Wiesel, *The Time of the Uprooted*, 201.
43. John Silber, "From Thebes to Auschwitz: Moral Responsibility in Sophocles and Wiesel," in *Celebrating Elie Wiesel: Stories, Essays, Reflections*, ed. Alan Rosen (Notre Dame: University of Notre Dame Press, 1998), 173, 178.
44. Sanyal, *Memory and Complicity*, 49.
45. For a thorough exploration and explanation of the contrast between narrow depictions of Holocaust memory by freezing it into paradigms versus productive depictions of Holocaust memory by the use of strategies of complicity in aesthetic discourse, applied to French literature and film, see Sanyal's *Memory and Complicity*.

46. Wiesel, *The Time of the Uprooted*, 299.
47. Wiesel, *The Time of the Uprooted*, 300.
48. Dirk A. Moses and Michael Rothberg, "A Dialogue on the Ethics and Politics of Transcultural Memory," in *The Transcultural Turn: Interrogating Memory Between and Beyond Borders*, ed. Lucy Bond and Jessica Rapson (Berlin: De Gruyter, 2014), 32.
49. Moses and Rothberg, "A Dialogue on the Ethics and Politics of Transcultural Memory," 33.
50. Dana Mihăilescu, "The Thrusts of Ghost-Writing Eastern European Survivors' Memories of the Holocaust in Post–Cold War Western Societies," in *After Memory: Rethinking Representations of World War II in Contemporary Eastern European Literatures*, ed. Matthias Schwartz, Nina Weller, and Heike Winkel (Berlin: De Gruyter, forthcoming).
51. Wiesel, *The Time of the Uprooted*, 11.
52. Wiesel, *The Time of the Uprooted*, 20–22.
53. Wiesel, *The Time of the Uprooted*, 24.
54. Wiesel, *The Time of the Uprooted*, 23.
55. Wiesel, *The Time of the Uprooted*, 218.
56. Wiesel, *The Time of the Uprooted*, 228.
57. Wiesel, *The Time of the Uprooted*, 267.
58. Moses and Rothberg, "A Dialogue on the Ethics and Politics of Transcultural Memory," 32.

Works Cited

Bachmann, Michael. "Life, Writing, and Problems of Genre in Elie Wiesel and Imre Kertész." *Rocky Mountain Review* 63, no. 1 (2009): 79–88.

Bond, Lucy, Stef Craps, and Pieter Vermeulen, eds. *Memory Unbound: Tracing the Dynamics of Memory Studies*. New York: Berghahn Books, 2016.

Erll, Astrid. "Generation in Literary History: Three Constellations of Generationality, Genealogy and Memory." *New Literary History* 45 (2014): 385–409.

Erll, Astrid. "Travelling Memory." *Parallax* 17, no. 4 (2011): 4–18.

Erll, Astrid. "Travelling Memory in European Film: Towards a Morphology of Mnemonic Relationality." *Image [&] Narrative*. Special Issue on "Audiovisual Memory and the (Re)Making of Europe." 18, no. 1 (2017): 5–19.

Katz, Steven T., and Alan Rosen, eds. *Elie Wiesel: Jewish, Literary and Moral Perspectives*. Bloomington: Indiana University Press, 2013.

Mihăilescu, Dana. "The Thrusts of Ghost-Writing Eastern European Survivors' Memories of the Holocaust in Post–Cold War Western Societies." In *After Memory: Rethinking Representations of World War II in Contemporary Eastern European Literatures*, ed. Matthias Schwartz, Nina Weller, and Heike Winkel. Berlin: De Gruyter, forthcoming.

Moses, Dirk A., and Michael Rothberg. "A Dialogue on the Ethics and Politics of Transcultural Memory." In *The Transcultural Turn: Interrogating Memory Between and Beyond Borders*, ed. Lucy Bond and Jessica Rapson, 29–38. Berlin: De Gruyter, 2014.
Rigney, Ann, and Astrid Erll. Introduction. *Image [&] Narrative*. Special Issue on "Audiovisual Memory and the (Re)Making of Europe." 18, no. 1 (2017): 1–4.
Rosen, Alan, ed. *Celebrating Elie Wiesel: Stories, Essays, Reflections*. Notre Dame: University of Notre Dame Press, 1998.
Rothe, Anne. *Popular Trauma Culture: Selling the Pain of Others in the Mass Media*. New Brunswick: Rutgers University Press, 2011.
Sanyal, Debarati. *Memory and Complicity: Migrations of Holocaust Remembrance*. New York: Fordham University Press, 2015.
Silber, John. "From Thebes to Auschwitz: Moral Responsibility in Sophocles and Wiesel." In *Celebrating Elie Wiesel: Stories, Essays, Reflections*, ed. Alan Rosen, 173–202. Notre Dame: University of Notre Dame Press, 1998.
Thompson, Carl. *Travel Writing*. London: Routledge, 2011.
Wiesel, Elie. *All Rivers Run to the Sea: Memoirs*. New York: Schocken Books, 1995.
Wiesel, Elie. "The Holocaust as Literary Inspiration." In Elie Wiesel, Lucy Dawidowicz, Dorothy Rabinowitz, and Robert McAfee Brown, *Dimensions of the Holocaust*, 5–8. Evanston: Northwestern University Press, 1977.
Wiesel, Elie. *Le Temps des déracinés*. Paris: Seuil, 2003.
Wiesel, Elie. *The Time of the Uprooted*. Trans. David Hapgood. New York: Alfred A. Knopf, 2005.

11

Wiesel's Political Vision in *Dawn*, *The Testament*, and *Hostage*

Rosemary Horowitz

Elie Wiesel's novels have been studied from various literary perspectives. To date, however, they have been underappreciated as captivity narratives. That is an oversight because some of his works may be situated within that genre, a form that yields insights into an author's political beliefs, as well as the those of his or her society. As the scholar Dahia Messara notes, studying the genre requires a multilevel approach because captivity is "the act of physical imprisonment of individuals by a hostile group who may be motivated by various political, social, or religious reasons."[1] Thus any analysis of the text must consider the representation of the captivity experience, as well as the ideology of the captors and captives, since in addition to their literary merit captivity stories serve various societal functions.

Although captivity narratives, especially the American ones of the seventeenth, eighteenth, and nineteenth centuries, have been widely analyzed, not as much attention has been paid to those of the twentieth and twenty-first centuries. For example, considering the American frontier tale as the ideal type, Roy Harvey Pearce writes about the decline of the genre, stating that the "cultural 'need' for it is gone, or almost gone."[2]

I would like to thank my colleague Colin Ramsey of Appalachian State University for information about captivity narratives.

However, given the many kinds of captives and captors, interest in the genre has not declined over the years. Instead, its scope has increased. The modern genre includes a wider range of stories than the classical genre. Today's captivity narrative often blends modern with traditional elements to explore the concerns of contemporary readers and writers. About that, in her definition of the genre, Lorrayne Carroll writes that the early accounts tend to emphasize redemption and conversion, whereas the later ones tend toward the secular and political. Despite these tendencies, the focus on power and powerlessness remains a constant feature.[3] Questions of identity, including the ways that captivity changes people, are another enduring feature, as are those related to religion. Also, while traditional captivity stories, for example Indian or slave narratives, are often based on true events, the modern stories may be fictional, factual, or some combination of the two. In his definition of the genre, Gordon M. Sayre points out that the interaction between captor and captive "may be portrayed as racial, religious, or broadly cultural, but in any case, it is profound enough that each side regards its own ways as superior to the other's, and captivity forces this prejudice to the surface, either to be defended or abandoned."[4] Thus, the framework of confinement permits an author to expose each side's ideology.

Like many writers, Wiesel is interested in the subject of captivity. Even *Night* may be read as a captivity account, since the core of the text is the imprisonment of Jews in Nazi-occupied Eastern Europe. In fact, captivity is a feature of Wiesel's early fiction. *Dawn* (1961), his first novel, examines the interaction between a captured officer in the service of the British in Palestine and a Holocaust survivor ordered to kill him. The fate of captives appears in several of his later books, notably *The Testament* (1981) and *Hostage* (2012). *The Testament* centers on a Jewish man held by Bolsheviks, whereas *Hostage* tells of a Jewish man held by a Palestinian and a sympathizer. While the accounts involve different circumstances, the through line of captivity in *Dawn*, *The Testament*, and *Hostage* provides glimpses into Wiesel's political vision. A similar point is made by Jonathan Drucker, who finds "coherence" in Wiesel's life and work.[5] Even if the three novels are not in total alignment with Wiesel's thinking, coupling each with his life experiences deepens the reading of the works. Taken together, the three novels are Wiesel's literary response to the significant twentieth-century events of his time.

Jews and the British in Pre-State Israel

In the preface to the 2006 edition of *Dawn*, Wiesel wonders whether he would have joined a resistance group to fight, or perhaps even kill, for a Jewish homeland. He goes on to say that he wrote the novel in order to consider that question.[6] However, that same year, in an interview with Joseph Lowin of *Midstream*, perhaps with hindsight, Wiesel seems more confident in his answer:

> You know that the execution of two British sergeants, after the killing by the British of three Jews—Dov Gruner and two others—was at the hands of the Irgun, not LEHI. I came to Israel for the first time in 1949 and stayed only a few months. If I had been in Palestine at the time [of the execution], I would have joined LEHI, because it had a certain purity and was suffused with poetry. Things happened, but I wrote a different story.[7]

The killing of the three Jews Wiesel mentions took place in 1947. Understanding his references to the Irgun and LEHI requires some knowledge of the Jewish resistance organizations established in pre-state Israel to fight for Jewish liberation. The Irgun Zvai Le'umi (Irgun; National Military Organization) and the Lohamei Herut Yisrael (LEHI; Fighters for the Freedom of Israel) emerged in the 1930s and 1940s. An earlier group, the Haganah (Defense), was formed in 1920. These groups attacked convoys, sabotaged buildings, set fires, killed British soldiers, and carried out other such operations.[8]

In addition to understanding the history of Jewish armed resistance, some knowledge of modern Zionism and British colonialism is helpful in reading the novel. Briefly, the economic hardships and pogroms suffered by Eastern European Jews in the late nineteenth century helped crystallize the modern Zionist movement, an ideology shaped by religious influences as well.[9] After the collapse of the Ottoman Empire in 1918, Britain and France divided a portion of the Ottoman territory into sections, which the British and the French administered. The British Mandate of Palestine was one area. All these historical influences undergird the novel.

More information regarding what "things happened," as Wiesel says, may be found in *All Rivers Run to the Sea*, where he reminisces about the circumstance that led him to the life of a writer, not a fighter. He remembers his own indecision when his friend Kalman left France for Palestine. At that point, Wiesel decided to resume his studies, even while regretting the decision to remain behind. However, through a series of encounters, Wiesel ends up working on behalf of the movement as a journalist, which fulfilled his desire to help the resistance.[10] Later on, writing fiction provides him with the opportunity to explore the war for Israel and its consequences. In *Dawn*, he addresses various religious, ideological, and psychological facets of the fight for Israel from the point of view of the captor.

Dawn is a commentary on Jewish paramilitary activities in the British Mandate of Palestine. Set between 1945 and 1947, the story looks at the words and actions of an unnamed clandestine Jewish paramilitary group in the region. The novel explores the interdependency between an English prisoner and his Jewish jailer. Elisha, the protagonist, is an eighteen-year-old Holocaust survivor recruited to join the resistance group. The main plot is that the Jewish fighter David ben Moishe is scheduled to be killed by the British, and in retaliation, the resistance group captures the English captain John Dawson and plans to kill him. Elisha is chosen as the executioner.

Even though one frequent motif in the captivity narrative is the religious life of the captive, *Dawn* focuses on that of the captor. Elisha's decision to join the clandestine group challenges his Hasid values, as well as his understanding of Zionism. When Gad, the recruiter from the resistance movement, talks about the creation of a Jewish state, Elisha is somewhat puzzled. As a religious Jew, he thinks: "It was the first time that I had heard of any of these things. My parents had not been Zionists. To me Zion was a sacred ideal, a Messianic hope, a prayer, a heartbeat, but not a place on the map or a political slogan, a cause for which men killed and died."[11] As a boy, he only learned about the sacredness of the Messiah. As a result, his upbringing did not teach him about the secular side of Zionism.

The twelfth principle of the Jewish faith as codified by Maimonides is the belief in the Messiah and the messianic era.[12] Elisha remembers that once when he was younger he and a friend performed a number of rituals that they believed would bring the Messiah to earth more quickly. The two friends did so despite knowing that their ability to affect the coming was impossible. Elisha also remembers learning about the Meshulah, a mysterious figure in the Hasidic tradition who walks the world delivering messages. Taken together, these factors help explain why Gad seems like a divine messenger to Elisha and why Elisha is drawn to Gad's charisma and compelling speeches. However, Elisha's upbringing also creates dissonance for him because of the belief that humans cannot force God to establish the Jewish homeland. Thus, a level of discord exists between Elisha's view of Zionism and the behavior required of him by the resistance group. Eventually Elisha comes to believe that "in order to change the course of history we have to become God, we shall become Him."[13] Fundamentally, he knows that he should wait for the Messiah rather than fight for the state of Israel. At the same time, he is fascinated by the thought that Jews do not have to be passive any longer. Instead, they could defend themselves.

The sixth commandment, "thou shall not kill," creates more dissonance for Elisha as he ponders Dawson's pending execution. He needs to reconcile the age-old dream of the establishment of Israel with the reality of the violence needed to create the homeland. With the biblical injunction against killing in mind, Elisha must find an acceptable rationale for his violent actions. Jonathan Drucker makes a similar observation about Elisha's ambivalence:

> Elisha seems not to disagree with the sentiment that the commandments must sometimes be violated to advance collective political aims, but he is nevertheless distressed by the role that circumstance has forced upon him, especially because he has suffered personally at the hands of SS men who believed that they too, were engaged in a difficult and bloody job at the behest of a state that would ultimately improve the world.[14]

The comparison between the SS and the members of the Jewish resistance points to the depth of Elisha's distress. Elisha eventually concludes that he will choose to honor his commitment to his comrades in the resistance group because he reasons that the living have more rights than the dead. The fight for a Jewish state seems to justify murder because the state is an existential Jewish cause.

In a dialogue that takes place in his cell, Dawson complicates Elisha's conflict with an observation that further upsets Elisha's worldview. After Elisha explains that his name is the same as the disciple of the prophet Elijah who resuscitated a dying boy, Dawson made the following comment: "You're doing the opposite."[15] By comparing Elisha's actions to the disciple's action, Dawson is highlighting Elisha's discomfort, increasing Elisha's doubt about his part in the Englishman's captivity. Captors must assign meaning to their actions to justify their behavior, and Bernard Avishai understands Elisha's dilemma as follows: "The arguments for mercy, the quality denied to him in the concentration camp, clash with the argument for ruthlessness in pursuit of the (implicitly just) national cause."[16] Although acting against his self-image, Elisha ultimately kills in defense of Israel, which for him is the righteous decision.

However, not all captors are distressed about their actions. Unlike Elisha, for example, Gad, and Ilana, another member of the resistance group, do not seem ambivalent. As the radio broadcaster who hosts a program called the *Voice of Freedom*, Ilana literally speaks for the group and expresses the group's philosophy. In one broadcast, she tells her listeners that David ben Moishe's death has meaning; John Dawson's does not. She suggests that the Jewish fight for a country is more significant than the British fight against the country. Ilana also asserts that the members of the British Cabinet are actually Dawson's murderers because Britain created the enmity between the British and the Jews. Off the air, she expresses the same sentiments. For example, she explains to Elisha that while the Jews call their fight a holy war, they are actually fighting for survival. Therefore, their violence is justifiable. Elisha is also looking for a meaning to the imprisonment of Dawson so that the action is not "done in vain."[17] Elisha's answer to the question in the following exchange may provide a rationale: "Why do you hate me?" John Dawson asked again. "In order to give my action a meaning which may somehow transcend it."[18] The use of the word "transcend" suggests that Elisha is hoping for a divine source to justify his actions. He is trying to synthesize Zionism's secular and sacred components.

This encounter with Dawson forces Elisha to evaluate his own identity. Unlike his comrades, Elisha questions his role in the resistance because Dawson's imprisonment makes Elisha confront the interplay between captive and captor. Recognizing the dependency between himself and Dawson forces Elisha to reevaluate his sense of self because the prisoner has turned the jailer into a murderer. His need to spend time with Dawson reveals the intertwined connection between the two men. Face-to-face with Dawson, Elisha reflects on the timelessness of the killer-victim relationship. One cannot exist without the other. Elisha needs to hate Dawson and make Dawson into an enemy in order to hate him. As a Holocaust survivor, Elisha has witnessed so much killing. Thus, he finds it hard to accept the fact that he too will become a murderer. When Dawson dies saying Elisha's name, Elisha feels that he has killed himself. To an extent, he has killed himself psychically, since the self before a killing can never be the same as the one afterward. At the end of the novel, Elisha's face is transformed to reflect his new image.

The following summarizes Elisha's and, perhaps, Wiesel's rationale for why Jews must fight for Israel:

> Their tragedy, throughout the centuries, has stemmed from their inability to hate those who have humiliated and from time to time exterminated them. Now our only chance lies in hating [. . .]. Otherwise [. . .] our future will only be an extension of the past, and the Messiah will wait indefinitely for his deliverance.[19]

Whatever the doubts, the suggestion here is that opposing Jewish resistance is not an option. Rather, fighting is the only alternative to establish the state of Israel, which will redress all the humiliation and extermination to which the Jews have been subjected over the millennium.

Jews and Soviet Communism

In a *New York Times* interview dated April 7, 1981, Wiesel spoke to the writer Michiko Kakutani about the Jewish attraction to communism. Calling communism a "distorted utopia," Wiesel says that although he understood the pull of the ideology, he was not drawn to it himself. He mentions that Stalin's anti-Semitism resulted in the purging of Jews from the party.[20] Published the same year as this interview, *The Testament* is Wiesel's exploration of Jews and communism. In his 1997 memoir, *All Rivers Run to the Sea*, Wiesel recalls that he wrote *The Testament* to understand why religious Jews were drawn to Stalin and Marx. Although he is not sympathetic to communism, he imagines that if he were born earlier in the twentieth century, he might have been tempted by its messianic message.

The Testament is an extended critique of communism as articulated by a prisoner in the Lubyanka jail. The novel acts as a lens through which readers may gain insights into Wiesel's stance on that ideology. The central story follows Paltiel Kossover, the protagonist of the novel, from his childhood home in Russia before the revolution through his life and work in Germany, France, Spain, and Russia during the 1920s, 1930s, 1940s, and 1950s. The novel imagines the fate of the Jews as communists by following the involvement between Eastern European Jews and the Soviet Union during those four decades. In the novel, Paltiel is killed during the period when Stalin orders the execution of actual Jewish writers on August 12, 1952. Through his nuanced development of Paltiel's character, Wiesel explores the attraction to and disillusionment with communism of one religious Jew. While critical of the ideology, Wiesel tries to understand the motivation of those Jews for whom communism was appealing. Paltiel is transformed from an observant Jew to an adherent of communism and then back to identifying with Judaism after he realizes that he was betrayed by the regime.

Even though Wiesel is primarily interested in the behavior of observant Jews, historically part of the draw to communism among some religious Jews, as well as some secular ones, was the influence of a number of prevailing conditions during the first half of the twentieth century in Eastern Europe. The historian Jaff Schatz delineates some of the conditions that made the communist movement appealing to Jews of the period.[21] These include the changing Jewish workforce, Jewish poverty, the economic crisis within the region, discriminatory practices against the Jews, ethnic tensions, anti-Jewish violence, and Jewish ideologies. Given all these conditions, some Jews were attracted to the communist promise of a better world.

The document in the title refers to the fictional memoir that Paltiel is permitted to write after he is arrested and placed in prison. Writing the document in confinement allows Paltiel to reflect on his rising power and then its subsequent loss within the party structure. In the document, Paltiel discusses his attraction to and then his disillusionment with communism. His testament, divided into nine parts, is interspersed with the story of his son Grisha. At the beginning of the novel in a letter written to Grisha, Paltiel recounts his own political trajectory:

> Let me at least tell you this: Don't follow the path I took, [sic] it doesn't lead to truth. Truth, for a Jew, is to dwell among his brothers. Link your destiny to that of your people; otherwise you will surely reach an impasse. Not that I am ashamed of having believed in the Revolution. It did give hope to the hungry, persecuted masses. But seeing what it has become, I no longer believe in it. The great upheavals of history, its

dramatic accelerations [. . .] all things considered, I prefer mystics to politicians.[22]

So from the start, Paltiel offers an assessment of communism. Although he still remembers the original appeal of the movement, the party's anti-Semitism eventually destroys him.

One common motif of the captivity narrative is the impact of religion on the captive. *The Testament* explores that by comparing and contrasting Judaism and communism as belief systems. One shared value is the emphasis on social justice. From his studies of Torah and Talmud, Paltiel would have found a commonality between the ideals espoused in party manifestos and those in Jewish texts. For example, the obligation to treat people justly is enshrined in Jewish texts, such as Deuteronomy. *Tsedakah*, or the act of giving to others, is another obligation in the Jewish tradition.

In addition to the seemingly shared value of social justice in Judaism and communism, communism might have been appealing to Jews, like Paltiel, because of other similar beliefs, such as *rakhmones* and *tikkun ha-olam*. *Rakhmones*, defined as compassion, guides the manner in which Jews are encouraged to show empathy toward others. The novel suggests that possibility. In one scene, Paltiel displays compassion toward others at his sister's wedding when he notices the class differences between the distinguished guests and the charity guests. Moreover, he thinks, "The seeds of my future Communist sympathies were planted at that wedding."[23] He describes the conditions of the charity guests in this fashion:

> The table for the poor was set up in a long spacious room. It was stifling in there. Pitiful, grotesque men and women scurried about trying to snatch a piece of fish, a little white bread. Here and there quarrels broke out. People spat, yelled, exchanged insults, came to blows. It was to be expected—they were hungry, these children of poverty.[24]

Paltiel observes the ways in which poverty turns people against each other and distorts their outlook. In retrospect, he sees the genesis of his turn to communism in these observations of the behavior of the poor guests at the wedding celebration.

At his bar mitzvah, which takes place a few months after the wedding, Paltiel reflects on the experience of poverty. In his *d'var torah*, he relays his beliefs to the congregation:

> Long ago, it was thought that if a Jew was poor it was because of society; if he suffered it was because of Exile; people forgot that it is also our fault, mine and yours. And I concluded: If it is given to man to commit injustices, it is also up to him to repair them; if the creation of the world bears the seal of God, its order bears the seal of man.[25]

In his challenge to the audience, Paltiel references Jewish writings, such as the Babylonian and Jerusalem Talmud, as well as Jewish thinkers, such as Nahmanides, Menahem Harecanati, the Maharal of Prague, the poets of the Golden Age, and the Vilna Gaon, to make his case that the congregants attending his bar mitzvah should act on behalf of the poor. By using the word "repair," Paltiel may be alluding to the notion of *tikkun ha-olam*, which is defined as the repair of the world. He implies that *tikkun ha-olam* is the responsibility of all Jews. The practice of *tikkun ha-olam* has a long history. According to Gilbert S. Rosenthal, the idea started as a narrow rabbinical norm based on the teachings of the prophets of Israel, such as Jeremiah.[26] The prophets actively helped the vulnerable members of society. However, over the centuries, the concept has become wider in its religious application and has also been adapted by the secular world. In its broadest sense, the notion extends to working for all types of social justice. On some level, this long-standing Jewish concept seems compatible with a number of communist goals, such as combating inequity and overcoming oppression.

Ironically, Elisha's indoctrination into the teachings of communism started in the House of Prayer by Ephraim, a fellow student who, according to his reputation among the villagers, was destined to be a rabbinical judge not a political agitator. Ephraim is rebelling over his anticipated future role in the community. During many of their study sessions, Ephraim speaks about his impatience with the Messiah and his desire to save the world through revolution. Interestingly, Ephraim's discussions of communism are grounded in Jewish texts and teaching, which was one reason that Paltiel becomes convinced of the merits of the party. Gradually, he engages in illegal activities, meets party members, and takes on numerous assignments.

Paltiel's father expresses his opposition to communism, which may be similar to Wiesel's. The father understands his son's fervor but nevertheless believes revolutionary activity must be grounded in Judaism. As he tells his son:

> I don't know your Communist friends [. . .] I only know that their aim is to diminish unhappiness in the world. That is what counts, that is all that counts [. . .]. You're a Jew, a Jew first and foremost; it is as a Jew that you will be helping mankind. If you care for others to the detriment of your brothers, you will eventually deny everyone.²⁷

In Paltiel's father's worldview, *rakhmones* is superior to politics. Compassion must always emanate from Judaism. Therefore, if Paltiel's actions do not stem from his religious convictions, he will harm his own community despite all his good deeds. In fact, as his prominence in the movement grows, Paltiel struggles with his religious convictions. Throughout it all, Elisha never totally abandons Judaism.

Like other Jews at the time, Paltiel assumes that the Communist Party will live up to its ideals. He sees evidence of that in some of the party's policies. For example, he is impressed with the creation of the Anti-Fascist Committee, artists' and writers' clubs, publishing houses, Jewish theaters, and other institutions that value Jews. The party's defense of Zionism is another good sign. For Paltiel, the positive attitude toward the Jewish in Soviet cultural affairs and foreign affairs lulls him into supporting the party and its positions. Over time, Paltiel achieves a measure of power as a communist for himself. He likes his growing reputation, as well as the benefits he gains from associating with communists. He feels important as he is brought into party affairs.

Despite its seeming compatibility with several tenets of Judaism, communism eventually turns against its Jewish followers. For many of the Jews and fellow travelers, communism turns out to be a false Messiah. Instead of bringing about the hoped-for redemption attributed to the Messiah, the belief of the Jews in the party had tragic consequences. In his testament, Paltiel comments on his growing vulnerability as he begins to recognize the undermining of Soviet ideals by the party members. At first, when an event seemed incongruent with the party platform, he explains the incongruity by rationalizing that party administrators must have confidential information to justify their actions. Eventually, Paltiel realizes what is happening. In the testament, Paltiel addresses the prosecuting judge. He mentions his confusion at the print shop when cases of type, manuscripts, and books are destroyed by party workers. The destruction shatters Paltiel's trust in the party. Ultimately, by returning to Judaism, Paltiel affirms Wiesel's position that communism's values are short-term, whereas Judaism's are eternal. Ultimately, the similarities between Judaism and communism prove to be superficial.

Jews and the Palestinians

As a Diaspora Jew, Wiesel hesitates to criticize Israel. He explains his position in an interview with Ekkehard Schuster and Reinhold Boschert-Kimming.[28] He says that since he does not live in Israel, he feels the need to withhold his judgment on Israeli policies, even though he disapproves of the country's militarism. As a result of his total faith in the Jewish people, Wiesel believes that Israel's problems will ultimately be solved to the satisfaction of all parties. In a response to a similar question about his reluctance to speak of the Israeli-Palestinian conflict posed by Ted L. Estess, Wiesel says: "Occasionally, I have spoken. But for me, because I am here, in diaspora, and because of my past, I have felt that I cannot condemn or instruct Israel from abroad, even if I am greatly pained by what might be happening there."[29] However, he goes on to say that when something terrible is done by Israelis, he does speak up.

Over the years, Wiesel's point of view on the Palestinians has remained fairly constant. He criticizes them for their relentless attacks on Israel, as well as on Jewry worldwide. Wiesel makes this point in "A Letter to a Young Palestinian Arab." He writes as follows: "From Munich to Maalot, from Lod to Entebbe, from hijacking to hijacking, from ambush to ambush, you have spread terror among unarmed civilians and thrown into mourning families already too often visited by death."[30] This list of violent actions outlines the scope of the Palestinian's reach as of the date of the letter: the 1972 massacre of Israeli athletes at the Olympic games in Germany, the 1974 massacre in the Galilee region of Israel, the 1972 massacre at the airport outside of Tel Aviv, and the 1976 capture of an airplane in Uganda, as well as other unnamed acts of violence. Wiesel blames Palestinian leaders, along with their followers, for the ongoing violence against the Jews. In his estimation, all terrorist events are related through the shared hatred of the Jews. Since 1978, there have been other terrorist attacks on Jews that Wiesel has criticized. Additionally, he regularly speaks out against the suffering of people in Bosnia and other places.

Hostage is a treatise on the Israeli-Palestinian conflict as expressed through a kidnapping incident. Set in 1975, the novel centers on

Shaltiel Feigenberg, a child survivor of the Holocaust from the town of Davarowsk who is kidnapped in a neighborhood in Brooklyn, New York, by a Palestinian, Ahmed, and an Italian, Luigi, members of a fictitious revolutionary organization. The kidnappers abduct Shaltiel simply because he is a Jew. Held in a cellar of a warehouse in Brooklyn during a four-day ordeal, Shaltiel is used by Ahmed and Luigi to secure the release of three Palestinian prisoners. Rather than developing the characters of Shaltiel, Luigi, and Ahmed, Wiesel chooses to reveal their beliefs through a series of debates between the three men. These debates offer a lens through which to glimpse Wiesel's position on the Palestinian cause. Shaltiel is quite bold in his conversations with his captors. His adamancy about expressing his beliefs is surprising given his vulnerability as a prisoner. The exchanges between the characters may reflect Wiesel's own beliefs, since like Wiesel, Shaltiel will not condemn Jews or Israel. One example is Shaltiel's refusal to sign a declaration condemning Israel for crimes "committed against the unfortunate Palestinians."[31] He cannot betray the Jewish people.

Not surprisingly given Wiesel's life, the debates between the three men are slanted toward the Jewish experience. An illustration is that the debates regarding Israel start with 1947, the year of the United Nations partition. There is no mention of the history of modern Zionism or of Theodore Herzl, Ahad Ha'am, Chaim Weizmann, or others of the movement. There is also no talk about the Balfour Declaration of 1917, when the British government endorsed the establishment of a Jewish homeland in Palestine. Notably, the letter from Lord Balfour to Lord Rothschild has some conditions:

> His Majesty's Government views with favor the establishment in Palestine of a national home for the Jewish people, and will use their best endeavors to facilitate the achievement of this object, it being clearly understood that nothing shall be done which may prejudice the civil and religious rights of existing non-Jewish communities in Palestine, or the rights and political status enjoyed by Jews in any other country.[32]

This statement clearly mentions that the rights of non-Jews in the territory must be respected, and actions that violate those rights are not permitted under the declaration. Perhaps the omission of this agreement from the novel stems from the possibility that the pre-state history runs counter to Wiesel's position on Israeli nationalism. Instead, he focuses on British Palestinian, Holocaust, and modern Israeli history. Usually, the arguments in the novel foreground the life and death of Eastern European Jewry by relating post-Holocaust events to the fate of the Jews during the Holocaust.

When discussing the United Nations' 1947 partition, Shaltiel criticizes the Arab leadership for its rejection of the resolution. He gives Luigi a brief lesson on the history of the partition. About the resolution, he tells Luigi, "The Arabs rejected it and chose violence instead. Had they accepted the partition plan, today Lydda and Jaffa would be part of a Palestinian state living peacefully alongside a smaller, if not weaker, Jewish state. And Ahmed could have grown up and led a peaceful, productive existence instead of devoting his days and nights to murder."[33] Shaltiel imagines the effect on the citizens of the Middle East if the Arab leadership had made a different decision in 1947. If the leaders had accepted the UN resolution, life in the area would have been peaceful. Then perhaps, young Palestinians, like Ahmed, would not have turned to violence.

Since captives are taken from their homes, the concepts of place and displacement are vital to the captivity experience. The idea of home is doubly important in the novel because of historical events. In another exchange, Shaltiel challenges Luigi's contention that the Jews had a place in Europe after 1945, and so they did not need to settle on Palestinian land. Shaltiel argues that the Eastern European Jews had no country to which they could return after the Holocaust. The postwar pogroms made it clear that there was no Jewish future in Poland, Hungary, Romania, or Lithuania. The land of Israel was their only hope. No real alternative existed for Eastern European Jews.

Shaltiel quickly dismisses any comparisons between the actions of Israelis and Nazis. In one exchange, Shaltiel scolds Luigi for comparing Israeli soldiers to German soldiers:

> "How can you compare the sometimes harsh and severe attitude of Israeli soldiers on the West Bank with the atrocities of the Blackshirts and the SS in occupied Europe? The German occupation, do you know what it was like? What was involved? Torture by the Gestapo, roundups, the executions of hostages, absolute terror, the imprisonment of innocent people, ghettos, deportations to Auschwitz. . ."
>
> "Stop talking," said Luigi, walking away.[34]

Luigi has no answers, so he ends the conversation. For Shaltiel, drawing any similarity between Nazis and Israelis is totally unacceptable. By distinguishing Israeli "attitudes" from Palestinian "atrocities," he defines the behavior of the two groups as different matters. Specifically, he asserts that the scale and the consequences of the actions are not equal. By dismissing the claim that Israelis are using Hitler's methods, Shaltiel echoes Wiesel, who foregrounds the Holocaust in his discussions about the Middle East conflict. The Jewish experience is always central to him. For example, unlike the Nazis, Israeli soldiers are not committing genocide. Moreover, in an article first published in the *London Jewish Chronicle*, Wiesel asserts that equivalences are "obscene comparisons, twisted analogies, vile and base and rooted in hate."[35] In his perspective, there is no moral equivalence.

Since captivity narratives also deal with the nature of victimhood, Shaltiel appeals to the thousand years of Jewish history to make his case about Jewish ethical conduct. He notes that even though Jews were victims themselves over the years, they did not victimize others. Interestingly, Shaltiel is a double victim. Embedded with the captivity story is his memory of a childhood spent hiding from the Nazis. As a child of seven years old, he was held in a cellar under the protection of a German count with whom he played chess. The count had discovered Shaltiel's talent as a chess player and decided to keep him safe during the war as a chess partner. Shaltiel's double victimhood connects the Nazi and Palestinian actions toward the Jews. In his public statements, Wiesel also focuses on Jewish suffering and refuses to compare it to the suffering of the Palestinians. For instance, when asked about Palestinian Arab refugees, Wiesel argues for the Jews who were expelled from Arab countries.[36]

The novel judges Ahmed and Luigi by contrasting their beliefs. Shaltiel is more engaged with Luigi perhaps because Luigi's father was pro-Mussolini and pro-Hitler during the war. As a result, Luigi is ashamed of his own father's actions during the war, along with the effects of the Holocaust on Shaltiel's father. The exchanges between Shaltiel and Luigi serve to expose the weaknesses of the Palestinian arguments. Compared to Luigi, Ahmed is more ruthless toward Shaltiel perhaps because he is driven by a greater revolutionary fundamentalism. Overall, Shaltiel has fewer conversations with Ahmed, possibly because, as Shaltiel observes, "There is no point discussing theology, sociology and politics when someone is under the spell of a self-enclosed totalitarian ideology."[37] Thus, no rational argument can persuade Ahmed to rethink his position due to his fundamentalism. At one point, Ahmed briefly questions his actions on behalf of the revolution, which shows some measure of doubt. However, the novel makes it clear that Ahmed's cause is destructive to himself, his family, and even his people. Ultimately, he is wasting his life with an ignoble cause. When asked by Gregory McNamee about the differences between Ahmed and Luigi, Wiesel says:

> Both Ahmed and Luigi are part of the same international terrorist group. Both of them have the same general background. But there's a difference. Luigi is loyal to the cause, but Ahmed is patriotic. He's concerned with the future, but Luigi is part of the past. With one you can talk, with the other you can't. The language of the terrorist is violence, and its expression is also violent. That is the complicity between both of them.[38]

In line with his thinking, Wiesel distinguishes between Ahmed's and Luigi's politics. At the end of the hostage crisis, Ahmed is killed and Luigi is arrested. While both men are responsible for the abduction and mistreatment of Shaltiel, Ahmed's beliefs are more dangerous because they are more dogmatic than Luigi's. According to Shaltiel, even with Ahmed's death, the violence perpetuated by the terrorists will persist.

Strikingly absent from the exchanges between the men is any mention of the Nakba, the Arabic term for catastrophe. Nakba refers to the displacement of Palestinian Arabs from their homes by the Jews during the 1948 Israeli War of Independence. Some historians, such as Benny Morris, and journalists, such as Jo Roberts, want the history of Israel to include a more accurate portrayal of the fate of Palestinian Arabs, arguing that, currently, Israelis tend to gloss over the Palestinian perspective.[39] Some critics, such as the literary scholar Shira Stav, find that Israeli narratives treat the Jewish and Palestinian catastrophes differently too. In her comparison of Noam Chayut's memoir *My Holocaust Thief* and Ari Folman's film *Waltz with Bashir*, she explores the ways in which the Holocaust is given primacy over the Palestinian Nakba in the texts.[40] Also absent from the novel are references to the Palestinian intifadas. Nevertheless, Shaltiel is not depicted as an enemy of Islam. He does not criticize the religion but rather the extremists. Wiesel makes a similar point in his acceptance of the Nobel Prize for Peace: "And then, too, there are the Palestinians to whose plight I am sensitive but whose methods I deplore. Violence and terrorism are not the answer.

Something must be done about their suffering, and soon."[41] In this way, he differentiates between religious and political Islam.

Conclusion

The touchstone for Elie Wiesel is the Holocaust, arguably the most significant event in modern Jewish history. Without comparing the significance of the Holocaust to other events, the rise of modern Zionism, the Russian Revolution, and the establishment of Israel had a major impact on Jewish life too. Although Wiesel's life and work has been analyzed by theologians, philosophers, literary scholars, and other readers, most have glossed over his political side. According to Mark Chmiel, the scholar Colin Davis comes closest to exploring Wiesel's politics.[42] To quote Davis:

> [Wiesel's] concern with general moral issues and the attribution of universal significance to individual instances of suffering lie behind Wiesel's consistent claims to be uninterested in and ignorant about politics. "I distrust politics—moreover I don't understand anything about it" (*Un Juif*, 127); "politics are not my field" (*Qui êtes vous?* 122). He insists that his campaigning is ethical rather than political, and this helps to explain the uncontroversial nature of many of his interventions, at least for the Western readership.[43]

Despite Wiesel's denials in *Un Juif* and *Qui êtes vous?* that he is ignorant about politics, and despite his statement in *The Testament* that he prefers mystics to politicians, Wiesel was a political figure. In that role, he frequently commented on current events and challenged official positions. One significant incident took place in 1985 when he condemned President Reagan's visit to the military cemetery in Bitburg, West Germany. In a speech given during a White House award ceremony, Wiesel expressed his dismay with Reagan's planned trip.[44] Leveraging his prominence, Wiesel conveyed his beliefs to leaders of many countries over the years.

Wiesel used fiction in a similar way. To some degree, his novels are a call to action on the central principles of his life. The dialogues and actions of the characters in *Dawn*, *The Testament*, and *Hostage* express his reactions to the events of his time and their effect on world Jewry. The novels are a means to explain events from a Jewish perspective.

Telling *Dawn* from the perspective of the Jewish captor offers a way to defend the fight for Israel. Narrating *The Testament* and *Hostage* from the perspective of the Jewish captive counters anti-Jewish causes. What guides Wiesel is made clear in this passage from his Nobel Peace Prize acceptance speech:

> Of course, since I am a Jew profoundly rooted in my peoples' memory and tradition, my first response is to Jewish fears, Jewish needs, Jewish crises. For I belong to a traumatized generation, one that experienced the abandonment and solitude of our people. It would be unnatural for me not to make Jewish priorities my own: Israel, Soviet Jewry, Jews in Arab lands.[45]

Although he goes on to enumerate other oppressions that trouble him, such as apartheid, he always foregrounds Jewish concerns. Since for Wiesel, storytelling is a form of activism, the captivity genre lets him express his ideology, lets his readers understand the complexities of the Jewish experience, and, perhaps, lets them act on the lessons in the novels.

Notes

1. Dahia Messara, introduction to *The Captivity Narrative: Enduring Shackles and Emancipating Language of Subjectivity*, ed. Benjamin Mark Allen and Dahia Messara (Newcastle upon Tyne: Cambridge Scholars, 2012), xiii.

2. Roy Harvey Pearce, "The Significances of the Captivity Narrative," *American Literature* 19, no. 1 (March 1947): 20.

3. Lorrayne Carroll, "Captivity Literature," in *The Oxford Handbook of Early American Literature*, ed. Kevin J. Haynes (New York: Oxford University Press, 2008), 165.

4. Gordon M. Sayre, introduction to *American Captivity Narratives* (Boston: Houghton Mifflin Company, 2000), 4.

5. Jonathan Drucker, "Victims, Executioners, and the Ethics of Political Violence," in *Elie Wiesel: Jewish, Literary, and Moral Perspectives*, ed. Steven T. Katz and Alan Rosen (Bloomington: Indiana University Press, 2013), 160.

6. Elie Wiesel, preface to *Dawn* (New York: Hill and Wang, 2006), viii.

7. Joseph Lowin, "A Conversation with Elie Wiesel," *The Free Library* (1 March 2006), n.p.

8. Bruce Hoffman, preface to *Anonymous Soldiers: The Struggle for Israel, 1917–1947* (New York: Alfred A. Knopf, 2105), xi.

9. Colin Shindler, *A History of Modern Israel*, second edition (New York: Cambridge University Press, 2013), 11–12.

10. Elie Wiesel, *All Rivers Run to the Sea: Memoirs* (New York: Knopf, 1995), 149–58.

11. Elie Wiesel, *Dawn* (New York: Hill and Wang, 1961), 22.

12. Jacob Immanuel Schochet, *Mashiah: The Principle of Massiach and the Messianic Era in Jewish Law and Tradition* (New York: Sichos in English, 1992), 17.

13. Wiesel, *Dawn*, 30.

14. Drucker, "Victims, Executioners, and the Ethics of Political Violence," 163.

15. Wiesel, *Dawn* (1961), 77.

16. Bernard Avishai, "Postscript: Elie Wiesel, 1928–2016," *The New Yorker*, 4 July 2016, http://www.newyorker.com/books/page-turner/postscript-elie-wiesel-1928-2016.

17. Wiesel, *Dawn*, 86.

18. Wiesel, *Dawn*, 86.

19. Wiesel, *Dawn*, 86.

20. Michiko Kakutani, "Wiesel: No Answers, Only Questions," in *Elie Wiesel: Conversations*, ed. Elie Wiesel and Robert Franciosi (Jackson: University Press of Mississippi, 2002), 101.

21. Jaff Schatz, "Jews and the Communist Movement in Interwar Poland," in *Dark Times, Dire Decisions: Jews and Communism*, ed. Jonathan Frankel and Dan Diner (New York: Oxford University Press, 2004), 13–37.

22. Elie Wiesel, *The Testament* (New York: Summit Books, 1981), 20–21.

23. Wiesel, *The Testament*, 69.

24. Wiesel, *The Testament*, 69–70.

25. Wiesel, *The Testament*, 70.

26. Gilbert S. Rosenthal, "*Tikkun ha-Olam*: The Metamorphosis of a Concept," *The Journal of Religion* 85, no. 2 (April 2005): 215.

27. Wiesel, *The Testament*, 97.

28. Ekkehard Schuster and Reinhold Boschert-Kimmig, "Elie Wiesel Speaks," in *Elie Wiesel: Conversations*, ed. Elie Wiesel and Robert Franciosi (Jackson: University Press of Mississippi, 2002), 159.

29. Ted L. Estess, "A Conversation with Elie Wiesel," in *Elie Wiesel: Conversations*, ed. Elie Wiesel and Robert Franciosi (Jackson: University Press of Mississippi, 2002), 188.

30. Elie Wiesel, "A Letter to a Young Palestinian Arab," in *A Jew Today* (New York: Random House, 1978), 106.

31. Elie Wiesel, *Hostage* (New York: Alfred A. Knopf, 2012), 40.

32. Jonathan Schneer, *The Balfour Declaration* (London: Bloomsbury, 2010), 341.

33. Wiesel, *Hostage*, 134.

34. Wiesel, *Hostage*, 135.

35. Elie Wiesel, "Voices of Hate," in *Against Silence: The Voice and Vision of Elie Wiesel*, vol. 2, ed. Irving Abramson (New York: Holocaust Library, 1985), 215.

36. Elie Wiesel and Richard D. Heffner, "Religion, Politics, . . . and Tolerance," in *Conversations with Elie Wiesel*, ed. Elie Wiesel and Richard D. Heffner (New York: Schocken Books, 2001), 58.

37. Wiesel, *Hostage*, 41.

38. Gregory McNamee, "'Hostage': A Conversation with Elie Wiesel," *Kirkus* (21 August 2012), n.p.

39. See Benny Morris, *The Birth of the Palestinian Refugee Problem, 1947–1949* (Cambridge: Cambridge University Press, 1987); Benny Morris, *1948: A History of the First Arab-Israeli War* (New Haven: Yale University Press, 2008); and Jo Roberts, *Contested Land, Contested Memory: Israel's Jews and Arabs and the Ghosts of Catastrophe* (Toronto: Dundurn, 2013).

40. See Shira Stav, "Nakba and Holocaust: Mechanisms of Comparison and Denial in the Israeli Literary Imagination," *Jewish Social Studies* 18, no. 3 (Spring/Summer 2012): 85–98.

41. Elie Wiesel, Nobel Peace Prize acceptance speech, Oslo, 10 December 1986, https://www.nobelprize.org/prizes/peace/1986/wiesel/26054-elie-wiesel-acceptance-speech-1986/.

42. Mark Chmiel, *Elie Wiesel and the Politics of Moral Leadership* (Philadelphia: Temple University Press, 2001), 14.

43. Colin Davis, *Elie Wiesel's Secretive Texts* (Gainesville: University Press of Florida, 1994), 118–19.

44. Bernard Weinraub, "Wiesel Confronts Reagan on Trip," *New York Times*, 20 April 1985, n.p.

45. Wiesel, Nobel Peace Prize acceptance speech.

Works Cited

Abramson, Irving, ed. *Against Silence: The Voice and Vision of Elie Wiesel*, vol. 2. New York: Holocaust Library, 1985.

Avishai, Bernard. "Postscript: Elie Wiesel, 1928–2016." *The New Yorker*. 4 July 2016. http://www.newyorker.com/books/page-turner/postscript-elie-wiesel-1928-2016. Accessed 2 July 2017.

Carroll, Lorrayne. "Captivity Literature." In *The Oxford Handbook of Early American Literature*, ed. Kevin J. Haynes, 143–68. New York: Oxford University Press, 2008.

Chmiel, Mark. *Elie Wiesel and the Politics of Moral Leadership*. Philadelphia: Temple University Press, 2001.

Davis, Colin. *Elie Wiesel's Secretive Texts*. Gainesville: University Press of Florida, 1994.
Drucker, Jonathan. "Victims, Executioners, and the Ethics of Political Violence." In *Elie Wiesel: Jewish, Literary, and Moral Perspectives*, ed. Steven T. Katz and Alan Rosen, 160–69. Bloomington: Indiana University Press, 2013.
Estess, Ted L. "A Conversation with Elie Wiesel." In *Elie Wiesel: Conversations*, ed. Elie Wiesel and Robert Franciosi. 174–89. Jackson: University Press of Mississippi, 2002.
Hoffman, Bruce. *Anonymous Soldiers: The Struggle for Israel, 1917–1947*. New York: Alfred A. Knopf, 2015.
Kakutani, Michiko. "Wiesel: No Answers, Only Questions." In *Elie Wiesel: Conversations*, ed. Elie Wiesel and Robert Franciosi, 99–102. Jackson: University Press of Mississippi, 2002.
Lowin, Joseph. "A Conversation with Elie Wiesel." *The Free Library*. 1 March 2006.
McNamee, Gregory. "'Hostage': A Conversation with Elie Wiesel." *Kirkus*. 21 August 2012.
Messara, Dahia. Introduction to *The Captivity Narrative: Enduring Shackles and Emancipating Language of Subjectivity*, ed. Dahia Messara and Benjamin Mark Allen, xiii-xvii. Newcastle upon Tyne: Cambridge Scholars, 2012.
Morris, Benny. *The Birth of the Palestinian Refugee Problem, 1947–1949*. Cambridge: Cambridge University Press, 1987.
Morris, Benny. *1948: A History of the First Arab-Israeli War*. New Haven: Yale University Press, 2008.
Pearce, Roy Harvey. "The Significances of the Captivity Narrative." *American Literature* 19, no. 1 (March 1947): 1–20.
Roberts, Jo. *Contested Land, Contested Memory: Israel's Jews and Arabs and the Ghosts of Catastrophe*. Toronto: Dundurn, 2013.
Rosenthal, Gilbert S. "Tikkun ha-Olam: The Metamorphosis of a Concept." *The Journal of Religion* 85, no. 2 (April 2005): 214–40.
Sayre, Gordon M. *American Captivity Narratives*. Boston: Houghton Mifflin, 2000.
Schatz, Jaff. "Jews and the Communist Movement in Interwar Poland." In *Dark Times, Dire Decisions: Jews and Communism*, ed. Jonathan Frankel and Dan Diner, 13–37. New York: Oxford University Press, 2004.
Schneer, Jonathan. *The Balfour Declaration*. London: Bloomsbury, 2010.
Schochet, Jacob Immanuel. *Mashiach: The Principle of Mashiach and the Messianic Era in Jewish Law and Tradition*. New York: Sichos in English, 1992.
Shindler, Colin. *A History of Modern Israel*. Second edition. New York: Cambridge University Press, 2013.
Schuster, Ekkehard, and Reinhold Boschert-Kimmig. "Elie Wiesel Speaks." In *Elie Wiesel: Conversations*, ed. Elie Wiesel and Robert Franciosi, 146–59. Jackson: University Press of Mississippi, 2002.

Stav, Shira. "Nakba and Holocaust: Mechanisms of Comparison and Denial in the Israeli Literary Imagination." *Jewish Social Studies* 8, no. 3 (Spring/Summer 2012): 85–98.

Weinraub, Bernard. "Wiesel Confronts Reagan on Trip." *New York Times*. 20 April 1985.

Wiesel, Elie. *And the Sea Is Never Full: Memoirs 1969–*. New York: Alfred Knopf, 1999.

Wiesel, Elie. *All Rivers Run to the Sea: Memoirs*. New York: Knopf, 1995.

Wiesel, Elie, and Richard D. Heffner, eds. *Conversations with Elie Wiesel*. New York: Schocken Books, 2001.

Wiesel, Elie. *Dawn*. New York: Hill and Wang, 1961.

Wiesel, Elie. *Dawn*. New York: Hill and Wang, 2006.

Wiesel, Elie. *Hostage*. New York: Alfred A. Knopf, 2012.

Wiesel, Elie. *A Jew Today*. New York: Random House, 1978.

Wiesel, Elie. Nobel Peace Prize acceptance speech, Oslo. 10 December 1986. https://www.nobelprize.org/prizes/peace/1986/wiesel/26054-elie-wiesel-acceptance-speech-1986/.

Wiesel, Elie. *The Testament*. New York: Summit Books, 1981.

12

Allegories of the Holocaust in Elie Wiesel's Late Fiction

The Forgotten, The Sonderberg Case, and *Hostage*

Sue Vice

It is hard to read Elie Wiesel's fiction without thinking of the details of his life, as they appear in his autobiography *All Rivers Run to the Sea*, or in his testimony *Night*, the work for which he is best known.[1] This is certainly the case when considering those novels that are among the last Wiesel wrote, including *The Forgotten* (1992), *The Sonderberg Case* (2010), and *Hostage* (2012). In each instance, a range of similar narrative elements is evident. These include aspects that we might anticipate, following on from the concerns of *Night*, such as emotionally charged father-son relationships, theodicean addresses to God, Hasidic or rabbinical insights, and anxiety about how to remember the past. However, unexpected elements also arise, including unease about the relation of Israel to Palestine and uncertainty about the boundary between a first- and a second-generation Holocaust survivor. In relation to both categories of concern—the expected and the more surprising—in these novels, it is as if the lineaments of Wiesel's own biography have been transformed in oneiric or, to use an epithet that frequently arises in relation to the author's work, poetic ways in his late-twentieth- and twenty-first-century writing.

The Forgotten

The Forgotten's reliance on a single structuring metaphor foreshadows the appearance of this technique in the other two novels under discussion here. As its title seems to suggest, *The Forgotten* centers on the apparently concrete concern of an individual's organic amnesiac condition. However, the memory loss to which Elhanan, the father of the protagonist Malkiel Rosenbaum, is subject in *The Forgotten* is, rather, symbolic, and the novel's title implies not just an individual amnesia but that the fate of a group or collective is in danger of being lost to memory. *The Sonderberg Case* uses its trial setting and *Hostage* that of false imprisonment in an analogous manner, to establish metaphysical and ethical concerns in plot devices, which are foregrounded to the extent that they appear almost generic. Thus in its blurb *Hostage* is described with only partial accuracy as a "thriller" and *The Sonderberg Case*, similarly, as a "mystery."

The Forgotten seems to represent a condition that has appeared in fiction and film with increasing frequency, that of the Holocaust survivor suffering from dementia.[2] Such representations encode contemporary anxieties about the disappearance of the survivor generation, by means of the figure of a still-living eyewitness who can no longer remember, or for whom the past abruptly reappears in the present, abolishing temporal and geographical distance. Yet in *The Forgotten*, the nature of Elhanan's condition is left deliberately vague, despite critics' identification of it as Alzheimer's, in order to emphasize the distressing nature of a lack of diagnosis at the level of the plot as well as the more generally figurative nature of the disease in this case.[3] In a microcosmic example of Wiesel's narrative technique more broadly, the reader's hearing from Elhanan's physician, Dr. Pasternak, in apparently concrete terms that the former has "an extreme case of amnesia" is immediately undercut by the clearly metaphorical words that follow: "Elhanan Rosenbaum has a sick memory; it is dying. Nothing can save it."[4]

If this is a diagnosis, it is not a medical but a cultural one. As a Holocaust survivor, Elhanan embodies the inevitable disappearance of a living memory that is at once precious and tainted. In a complex entwinement, the narrator describes Elhanan's postwar fate in the phrasing often used of the genocide itself: "Thus did Elhanan helplessly witness his own destruction."[5] This is not to liken the "erosion" of memory straightforwardly to the Holocaust.[6] It is, rather, to use the image of the amnesiac survivor as a figure for the complex circumstance described by such commentators as Dori Laub. This is a situation where "there was no one left to witness what was taking place," one in which even the individual subject confronted by the events was unable to "remain a fully lucid, unaffected witness."[7] In this way, as Laub concludes, "there was no witness to the Holocaust, either from outside or from inside the event."[8] Such a logic is indeed one of destruction, one that is invoked in the present case in relation to the experience of an individual undergoing progressive amnesia. Elhanan can only see with "lucidity" the beginning of his own disappearance. Yet in *The Forgotten*, by a version of postmemory made manifest, Elhanan's son Malkiel stands in for a culture attempting to offset this inability to "witness for the witness."[9] As the narrator puts it, "In proportion as Elhanan felt his memory diminish, Malkiel felt his own expand."[10]

Indeed, not only is Elhanan's memory represented in Jewish terms, but Judaism itself is shown to take a definitively memorious form, in a way we are to take as adding to the significance of such a cultural loss. This is apparent in Elhanan's encounter with Inge, a non-Jewish German woman, to whose astonishment at the continued existence of the festival of Tisha b'Av, with its commemoration of the two-thousand-year-old destruction of the Temple, the narrator responds, as if on Elhanan's behalf: "Yes, as if it had happened only yesterday."[11] Such a conception, that "a Jew [. . .] is bound to his origins by memory," that of religious obligation and disaster alike, is repeated in Malkiel's encomium:[12]

> I admired my father not only for his kindness and intelligence, but also for his memory. He could quote long passages of the Talmud and Plato, the Zohar and the Upanishads. He could recall in rich detail his visit to the ghetto in Stanislav, his first skirmish as a partisan, his arrival in Palestine.[13]

Memory here is shown to constitute Jewish identity as both liturgical and historical, composed of Hebrew and other kinds of classical knowledge, alongside the precisely located suffering conveyed by reference to "the ghetto," "a partisan," and "Palestine." This characterization reveals what was lost to Malkiel and his father when Elhanan had to turn to a prayer book to assist his reciting the kiddush. The fact that this is no everyday "gap" in memory is emphasized in Malkiel's description of the incident to his wife Tamar: "For him, forgetting the kiddush is like forgetting my mother's smile, or yours."[14]

The mingling of religious thought with the qualities of temporal human life, including Elhanan's own "kindness and intelligence," in Malkiel's phrasing, and the happiness of his dead wife Talia and daughter-in-law Tamar, makes this specifically Jewish memory all-encompassing. It includes not only religious rites alongside knowledge of world philosophy and secular history, but places emphasis upon family and descent. For this reason, the kind of intergenerational postmemory that is constructed in The Forgotten takes on the form of an element of the plot, in which Malkiel explicitly wishes to absorb the details of his father's past. In this way, it expands upon Marianne Hirsch's definition of Holocaust postmemory as "the relationship of the second generation to powerful, often traumatic, experiences that preceded their births but were nevertheless transmitted to them so deeply as to constitute memories in their own right."[15] Malkiel goes further in overtly identifying himself as the vehicle for the "restoration" of his father's past and seeking out its "transmission" to him.[16] This takes the form of his undertaking a journey to his father's birthplace of Stanislav in Romania and locating there a woman who restores a lost element of Elhanan's past. The same pattern is evident in relation to an apparently everyday remark—Tamar's declaration of her father-in-law, "We'll remember what he used to be"—which is followed by others that transform the psychic phenomenon of postmemory into a geographical one.[17] Malkiel hopes to "rescue Elhanan's memory," since he cannot rescue his father.

Indeed, the rescue of memory is shown to be the only possible filial homage. At first Malkiel doubts the efficacy of returning to his father's birthplace, because "*I can live after you and even for you, but not as you,*" a perception that registers a resistance to the threat of an obliterating or "displacing," in Hirsch's term, merger that a total recall would imply.[18] Malkiel's effort to describe his relationship to his father's story sounds very similar to Shoshana Felman's commentary on the nature of being an auditor to a survivor of this "*event without a witness*," as he puts it:[19] "*I know that whoever listens to a witness becomes one in turn; you told me that more than once. But we are not witnessing the same events. All I can say is, I have heard the witness.*"[20] Malkiel's response to taking on the second-generation witness role goes beyond the usual scope of postmemorial recall, since it is undertaken for the sake of a parent who can himself no longer remember. Partly for that reason, Malkiel's attitude is notably ambivalent and contradictory. For instance, his anxiety that the postmemorial journey to Romania cannot help his father is disproved, as is revealed by his use of the present tense in the very act of his citing the details of what cannot be achieved: "*You told me about your adventures among the partisans; I can see your comrades in arms, and I watch them as they rush into battle against the Germans, I hear the cries of the vanquished.*"[21] On the other hand, this apparently exemplary effort to "witness for the witness" is cast into doubt when Malkiel arrives in Stanislav. Among the events of his father's wartime experience that Malkiel narrates in the present tense are the actions of Elhanan's partisan friend Itzik: "*I see pride on Itzik's face . . . happy to be avenging Jewish honor, happy to be showing that the enemy of the Jews is not godlike but vulnerable.*"[22] Itzik, however, inhabits the novel's most troubling plot element, in relation to an act of postwar vengeance that exceeds the account Malkiel gives here, of Itzik's "*battle against the Germans*," and turns him instead into a perpetrator against those who are already "vulnerable."[23]

Like much of Wiesel's writing, *The Forgotten* is about masculine genealogies. Elhanan's wife Talia died in childbirth, while he was held prisoner in Jordan during the Israeli war of independence. It is hard not to read this plotline as a fictionalized version of Wiesel's own family history, within which his mother, separated from her husband and son, was killed along with her daughter Tzipora in 1944 on arrival at Auschwitz, leaving the teenage Eliezer alone with his father until the latter's death in early 1945. Familial loss and absence of parental figures are elements shared by novel and biography, with differing emphases. However, gender difference takes on a role more characteristic of extreme patriarchal logic in the episode relating to Malkiel's return to Stanislav, where the past takes on embodied form. Malkiel encounters a gravedigger who knew his family, and who shows him the uncanny spectacle of a tombstone bearing his own name, as well as that of his paternal grandfather. As the gravedigger puts it, eliding the difference between generations while also making it sound like a posthumous reminiscence of Malkiel himself: "Malkiel Rosenbaum. I remember him as if he were here, right in front of me, as if he'd asked me to have a drink, like you did."[24] Malkiel encounters another unexpected figure from the past, a woman who turns out to be the custodian of a restorative memory about Elhanan. Yet her own traumatic past has to be "displaced," to repeat Hirsch's caveat about postmemory, in order to validate Elhanan's.

Wiesel's much longer Yiddish original of *Night*, *And the World Remained Silent* (1954), includes a detail about the immediate postliberation behavior of the Buchenwald inmates, "Jewish boys" who "ran off to Weimar to steal clothing and potatoes. And to rape gentile girls."[25] The much shorter *Night* concludes instead with phrasing that implies the women's consent, and in the new translation by Wiesel's wife Marion the term "gentile" has been removed: the young men ran to Weimar "to sleep with girls."[26] Just such an apparently ethical conundrum arises in *The Forgotten*. However, it is not one about the legitimacy of Jewish rage or the nature of what Daniel Magilow calls "revenge fantasies" but rather a question about whether the episode recounted can bear the particular moral weight ascribed to it within the text.[27] Just after the war's end, Elhanan was a bystander at the rape perpetrated by his friend and comrade Itzik against Elena, the young widow of Zoltan, a notoriously brutal leader of the Nyilas, or Arrow Cross. As a bystander to this transgression, Elhanan is aware that the woman is silently "begging" him for help, "as if he were her savior, as if he were almighty" but, as the narrator bluntly concludes, "Elhanan was not."[28] Although he argues with Itzik against the latter's attempt to justify, by reference to her husband's killings, what amounts to a war crime on the part of a survivor, as Elhanan puts it, "I was present and did nothing."[29] Malkiel's meeting with the aged Elena on his visit to Stanislav in the present results in her, perhaps surprisingly, praise for Elhanan as a "man of courage and humanity" despite his failure to rescue her.[30] The use of this episode as a way of shoring up Elhanan's standing might well succeed in making the reader uncomfortable, but not for the reasons implied by its symbolic structure: indeed, it is partly that very act of symbolization that might prompt unease. Elena's fate is represented not for its own sake, but as a way of demonstrating Elhanan's good faith in the past and as a counterpart to his failing memory in the present, as Malkiel sums it up on leaving her: "Thanks to you I've learned something useful and perhaps essential: forgetting is also part of the mystery."[31] The nature of Elena's traumatic experience and its suppression is reduced to being simply a contrast to Elhanan's.

In *The Forgotten*, Malkiel is self-consciously constructed as a version of the implied author. Like Wiesel, he is a journalist whose literary facility has produced, as is implied by the text's alternating passages of first- and third-person narration alongside instances of free direct discourse, the very book we are reading. Elhanan's memory is "rescued" by this means, in what is the only way possible. In this sense, Elhanan resembles a version of Wiesel's own father, whose memory is similarly preserved in textual form in Wiesel's nonfiction works. Rather than witnessing his murder, as the teenage Eliezer did in the case of Shlomo Wiesel, Malkiel sees his father's interiority and identity vanish while his physical being remains. Yet Wiesel's biography also resembles that of Elhanan, as a man who was born in 1926, just two years earlier than the author himself, and as the father of a single beloved son, the equivalent of Wiesel's own son, Shlomo Elisha, equally named for his father. In this way, the author appears in fictional form as split between two generations: as the son grappling with an anguished memory of his father and as the Holocaust survivor beset by incommunicable memories that he fears losing. It is perhaps for this reason that the lineaments of postmemory, including the notion of a return to a vanished shtetl and an encounter with a woman from the wartime past, take on such a literal form, shared as the memories really are between father and son.

The Sonderberg Case

In *The Forgotten*, chronic amnesia appears both diegetically and figuratively, as a way of exploring the transfer of Holocaust memory from a living witness to a member of the second generation. In *The Sonderberg Case*, it is the notion of a trial that similarly takes on both a realist and an allusive role, allowing the plot to raise questions of judgment and guilt in a legal and an existential manner. Yet the novel's denouement depends not on the legal system, but on secrets from the past that emerge for both protagonists by other means. Thus very early on we encounter the protagonist Yedidyah's retrospective questions, which are philosophical versions of those from the trial, as he thinks of the case itself: "Years have gone by, but Yedidyah still can't reach a verdict. Where does a man's guilt begin, and where does it end? What is definitive, irrevocable?"[32] As in the case of Malkiel Rosenbaum, Yedidyah's retrospective aspect shifts into the first person and profession as a journalist, as well as such other hints as his recalling on the opening page, "One day, I thought, I'll turn it into a novel," might make us wonder whether he is the implied author as well as the focalizer of the text we are reading.[33] Yedidyah quotes his father's phrasing, "The journalist defines himself by what he says, the novelist by what he doesn't say," and the novel conforms to this sense of hybrid narrative technique by its strategic alternation of revelations and withholdings.[34] Yet such apparently metafictional gestures also end up redoubling the reader's impression of biographically grounded fiction, with Yedidyah taking on the role of a version of Wiesel himself.

The novel centers on Yedidyah, a journalist and the son of survivors living in New York, who is assigned to cover the trial of the eponymous Werner Sonderberg, a twenty-four-year-old German philosophy student accused of killing his uncle, Hans Dunkelman. Yedidyah also suffers from an apparently terminal illness that goes unidentified, an affliction that this time takes the role of signifying the urgent need for him to tell his story and the uncertain nature of his early youth. The novel's mystery surrounds the death of Dunkelman, which took place during a hiking trip taken by the older man and his nephew in the Adirondacks, over whether it was murder, suicide, or accident. The mystery also concerns Sonderberg's motivation and behavior, since his plea at trial is ambiguous: "Guilty . . . and not guilty."[35]

Following the belated logic of *The Forgotten*, it is over twenty years later that Yedidyah comes to understand the significance of Sonderberg's plea, unresolved during the trial itself since the case was dismissed for lack of evidence. Yedidyah learns that Sonderberg's utterance was not a philosophical statement about human guilt in general, as it might have sounded, but a rather more concrete commentary on his own behavior at a particular historical moment. We learn that Sonderberg's ambivalent plea concerned both the events on the mountainside and his status as a generational representative. Sonderberg seeks out Yedidyah to tell him that Dunkelman had taken the opportunity of the Adirondacks trip to give his nephew what seemed to be an unashamed promulgation of his history as a Holocaust perpetrator and his continued allegiance to Nazi ideology. Sonderberg's repudiation not only of that ideology but also of his and his father's kinship with Dunkelman seems to have led the latter to kill himself by jumping off the mountainside.

Among Sonderberg's revelations to Yedidyah is the fact that Hans Dunkelman, his only living relative, was not his uncle but his grandfather. The older man brings together his familial with his wartime role in his declaration to Sonderberg about his actions: "I felt nothing. I was Death. You're Death's grandson."[36] We learn that the grandson changed his surname from the original, with its negative family associations as well as its ominous German meaning of "dark man," to his own choice of "Sonderberg," or "special mountain." Both phrases give hints at the moral and geographical narrative to come. The apparently small change in Dunkelman's relation to Sonderberg from uncle to grandfather in fact conveys a duality that seems to have preoccupied Wiesel during the composition of this novel. Dunkelman's relationship changes from that of a person of Sonderberg's parents' generation to that of the grandparental era, one that is more distant in generational and historical terms but closer in terms of biological descent. Sonderberg reverses the logic of familial ancestry in his final words to Dunkelman, so that rather than a parent disinheriting a child, the younger person turns his or her back on the older: "I repudiate you. I disown you [. . .]. I extirpate you from my life. I erase you from my memory."[37] In this way, the character of Sonderberg could be viewed as what Lee Chottiner describes as an "homage to those Germans who are genuinely ashamed of their recent history."[38] However, such an estimate overlooks the "ambivalence" of the next generation that the plea of "guilty [. . .] and not guilty" conveys.[39] If Sonderberg believes himself guilty, it is not because he is responsible for those crimes—judging in this vein, a member of the public at his trial noted that, as he was a German, "you can expect anything"—but for fatally pricking a Nazi's conscience.[40]

Just as Sonderberg does in relation to perpetration, Yedidyah hovers between generations in connection to the survivors. Despite his repudiation of the idea that he could be Sonderberg's "double" or appear "in the dock" as the latter did, the two are counterparts.[41] In this parallel narrative, Yedidyah recounts his own unexpected family history. This time, the belated revelation is the result of his narratorial withholding from the reader of a story that transforms him from a second-generation into a first-generation survivor. As Yedidyah puts it over two-thirds of the way through the novel, "It may be time to reveal [. . .] that my parents are not my parents. Mine are dead."[42] Susan Suleiman might describe his newly disclosed status as technically that of the "1.5 generation," which consists of child survivors who are "too young to have had an adult understanding of what was happening to them, and sometimes too young to have any understanding of it at all, but old enough to have *been there* during the Nazi persecution of Jews."[43] Yedidyah's view of survival is in any case ambivalent. Before revealing his own real history, he described his filial love as originating in the fact that his father's "own father was what we now call a 'survivor.'"[44] Yet we learn that, although the grandfather was the only family member to be denounced and sent to a camp, his wife and sons survived the war in hiding. In this way, Yedidyah's apparent transformation of his survivor father into one of the second-generation goes against most official and testimonial definitions of what it is to be a survivor.

However, in this fictional context, Yedidyah's conception that only a former camp inmate can be described as a "survivor" has the effect of dramatic irony rather than that of an exclusive definition. Yedidyah gives voice to an anaphoric collection of rhetorical questions by means of which he outlines what he considers his lack of such an experience: "But what did I know of the concrete experience of that time? Of the denunciations? Of life in the ghetto? Of hunger and crowding? [. . .] Of the hunting down of children?"[45] The final question registers the moment at which what seems to be his distance from these events turns into great proximity: he does know, firsthand, about the "hunting down of children." This question is answered by the memory Yedidyah manages to retrieve, of his biological parents and older brother, all of whom were killed during the war. Rather than being the grandson of a survivor, and thus a member of the third generation, Yedidyah turns out to be one of the first generation, with firsthand experience, in his phrasing: "I thought I was the child of survivors. I'm not; I'm a child survivor."[46] In narrative terms, this abrupt change of ascription has the effect that, instead of its appearing to be the backdrop to "the Sonderberg case," the Holocaust turns out to be foundational to it.

Just as in *The Forgotten*, in *The Sonderberg Case* Yedidyah is able to make a physical return to the past by revisiting his birthplace, the Carpathian village of Davarovsk, where he wishes to encounter the same image of both mortality and continuity that confronted Malkiel in *The Forgotten* in the form of a gravestone for a forebear, one who might share his birth name of Yedidyah Wasserman.[47] Once more, the past is embodied in the form of a significant female figure. This time the non-Jewish woman whose existence enables a male protagonist to recapture a lost realm is Maria Petrescu, Yedidyah's family's "gentle" and "beautiful" peasant maid, who rescued the little boy from the Davarovsk ghetto. Her state is an even more extreme version of posttraumatic stress than that of Elena in *The Forgotten*, since she is described as "silent [. . .]. Gazing into the emptiness."[48] The signs of Maria's allegiance to the past of which Yedidyah learns are small but all-encompassing. Her nephew shows Yedidyah a wartime photograph featuring "a curly-headed little boy [. . .] clinging to [Maria's] skirt," the young Yedidyah whose disappearance has "made her ill."[49] Yet when he departs in the present, Yedidyah is rewarded with a sign from this woman who is almost catatonic as a result of her loss: "A tear appears in her right eye. And in the left one."[50] Although, as Summer Moore argues in a review of the novel, "Yedidyah's connection with his family history [revolves] especially around the men," this female figure plays a crucial but self-denying role.[51] As befits his "1.5

generation" status, and by contrast to the clarity of Sonderberg's recall, Yedidyah's memories emerged "in dreams and in hypnotically prompted memory."[52] His encounter with his rescuer prompts him to try to access his "extinguished" childhood memories by means of hypnosis, allowing him to retrieve both their imagery and affect:[53] "A man and a woman are holding him by the hand as they go down into a dark basement. He knows they love him, and he loves them, but he also knows they'll abandon him. So he starts to cry."[54] The tears of his younger self that Yedidyah recalls are in a sense the hallucinatory counterpart to the tears shed by the mute Maria. Yet their role is quite different, and the ruin of Maria's life exists in the world of the text only to support Yedidyah's. The latter comes to recognize his mother's abandonment as an act of love, whereas Maria's loss of her foster child remains unfilled.

In the case of both Yedidyah and Sonderberg, as Peter Conn argues in a cultural study of adoption, doubt is cast on the importance typically accorded to biological inheritance.[55] While Sonderberg repudiates his own lineage by declaring to his Nazi grandfather that "blood can lie [. . .]. You and I, we don't belong in the same human family," Yedidyah discovers that he has no blood relation to the people with whom he grew up.[56] The fact of adoption does not distance Yedidyah but places him in closer proximity to the events of the Holocaust. Although this might appear a surprising thread of meaning in novels where the significance of descent and family history is so great, particularly in the face of its threatened extinction, the importance given to historical and religious memory, as well as the possibility of affiliative rather than generational postmemory, in this novel and in *The Forgotten*, suggests that a broader conception of family is at play in Wiesel's late writing.

Hostage

Hostage continues the technique evident in both earlier novels of making the realist elements of which the plot is composed do double duty, as symbolic structures too. The scenario of the kidnap accomplishes this duality. Shaltiel Feigenberg is a Jewish man living in Brooklyn where his profession is that of a storyteller, as his wife Blanca describes it: "He's knight of the imaginary, a magician of the word."[57] The plot centers on Shaltiel's being kidnapped; as the narrator puts it, "This tragedy, the very first of its kind, took place in 1975."[58] This omniscient comment reveals the political context within which we are to read the novel: *Hostage* is set in Wiesel's adopted home territory of the United States, a country that, in the era of the Munich massacre of 1972 and Entebbe raid of 1976, as he says in an interview, was the only one "spared hostage-taking and suicide terrorism."[59] In the novel, Shaltiel is held as a hostage by two men, the Italian atheist Luigi and the Palestinian Muslim Ahmed, members of a "small ultra-extremist group" of pro-Palestinians whose goal is to gain the release of three of their number held prisoner in Israel.[60] The act of kidnapping—an apparently chance intrusion into the unexceptional life of "a discreet man with no status or fortune"—is one of the novel's ironies, although Shaltiel turns out to be more of an archetypal figure than at first appears.[61] He is a Holocaust survivor who has foresworn having children as a result of his experiences, and the fact that he is now a kidnap victim turns out not to be random after all. In a version of the wartime notion of a malign chosenness, he is told by his captors, "You're here precisely because you're Jewish."[62]

Shaltiel's captors could only more clearly be avatars of historical positions if Luigi were a German. As it is, he is "a citizen of the complacent European continent that allowed the rise of fascism" in Jason Diamond's phrasing, and the descendant of an Italian fascist who joined the SS and took part in mass murder during the war.[63] This echo of the past within the present is conveyed from the novel's outset, since it is prominently in Shaltiel's mind in his as-yet unidentified setting: "In the basement, his thoughts catapult him into the past. So this is what a man's life is all about? Moving from one shelter to another, both opening out on brutality, remorse and nothingness?"[64] The occasion for this apparently general question about what can seem to be the pointlessness of human existence when faced with chaotic forces, as Darren Richard Carlaw puts it, is not only a philosophical one, since the "shelter" and "brutality" have a double concrete reference: to the underground room in the present where Shaltiel is held captive, and to the wartime basement where he survived in hiding. As he puts it to himself, "Like before?," concluding that his isolation this time makes the situation "possibly worse."[65] His captors allow themselves to fit this palimpsestic temporal role, answering Shaltiel's question about when he will be released by responding, "When we win the war."[66] The self-reflexive mixture of historical and symbolic imagery, evident in all three of Wiesel's novels, reaches a pitch in *Hostage*, as we see in relation to the games of chess the young Shaltiel played during the war with the aristocratic Nazi who provided his basement shelter in return for these tournaments, as the latter puts it: "The world [. . .] is a huge chessboard. And we play for or against fate."[67]

However, such self-reflexivity, by means of which the characters seem to ponder the symbolism of the very novel in which they appear, threatens the text's generic coherence. Readers are likely to agree with such critics as Darren Richard Carlaw and David Ulin in considering the hostage situation itself, and in particular the interactions between the kidnappers and Shaltiel, to be so obviously philosophically inclined that the novel's realist surface is disrupted. This is equally the case for the lawyers' speeches and the dialogue between Dunkelman and Sonderberg in *The Sonderberg Case*, demonstrating Wiesel's faith in a Socratic process of debate to reach particular resolutions, yet one that is imperfectly absorbed into the world of fiction. It also reveals what Ulin calls "the tricky narrative intent" of substituting advocacy for testimony, which characterizes Wiesel's later work.[68] In the case of *Hostage*, Ulin judges the literary quality of the dialogue between the hostage and his captors to be "not very good," while Carlaw considers the conversations between Shaltiel and Luigi as "implausible" and "contrived" in terms of the plot. In relation even to their role as a way of dramatizing debate about Israel and Palestine, the exchanges between hostage and kidnapper are not always entirely successful. Thus when Luigi relates Ahmed's story, one of being born in a Palestinian refugee camp and losing his elder brother to an "Israeli commando," Shaltiel's response is a decision "not to argue"—or even to answer.[69] This episode begs the question of his being tolerated in offering "patronizing" comments to his captors in the first place, in Carlaw's phrasing, as well as appearing tacitly to acknowledge the difficulty of finding a response to such facts. During the same conversation, Shaltiel fails to reply to another of Luigi's assertions, "You Jews have forgotten that your hope is founded on [the Palestinians'] despair"—except to remind his interlocutor of "a few home truths" about the history of Israel and Palestine.[70] Narrative and rhetorical unlikeliness compound each other in this instance.

While such "advocacy" in the two earlier novels under discussion here takes a general form, in relation to reminding readers of the significance of memory and history at a moment of transition, the concern of *Hostage* is with specificities, most notably the Israeli-Palestinian conflict as part of Jewish history. While the novel's fragmentary structure offers an effective representation of its protagonist's mental state during his captivity, with its jump cuts between past and present, and existential musing set against concrete memories, the presence of the dialogues in their rhetorical mode has an uneasy relation to such expressionist fidelity. We learn that Luigi is moved by the photograph of Shaltiel's father with his camp tattoo; yet it is easier to credit the kidnapper's being "thrown" by Shaltiel appearing to be able to work out what his captors look like on the evidence of their voices, because in reality his blindfold has slipped.[71] By contrast, Ahmed declares to his captive, "We're the only people to take you seriously," in an echo of the bitterly ironic insight voiced by one of Wiesel's fellow prisoners in *Night*: "I have more faith in Hitler than in anyone else. He alone has kept his promises, all his promises, to the Jewish people."[72] In both cases, an intellectual and ethical reversal has taken place, in the sense that perpetrators pay malign attention to the victims who are otherwise abandoned by those around them.

The plot of *Hostage* sheds light on a puzzling remark made in *The Sonderberg Case* by an orthodox Jewish man who is considered for jury duty at Sonderberg's trial, and whose claim to objectivity in relation to the German defendant is couched in paradoxically tendentious terms: "Whether German or Muslim, only criminals are guilty; the children of murderers are children, not murderers."[73] While this statement has an uncanny bearing on the solution to the Sonderberg case, it constitutes a different kind of lack of objectivity. The assumption that the Muslims have inherited the Germans' antipathy to the Jews also hangs uncomfortably over the present novel, even as it betrays anxiety about the origins and actions of the Israeli state. Luigi's response to Shaltiel's impassioned plea that he should differentiate between the actions of Nazis and of the Israeli army is to demand that he "stop talking," as if the point cannot be answered.

The Palestinian Ahmed is portrayed throughout *Hostage* as a violent "brute," while the Italian Luigi is a "visionary" idealist.[74] Even if these traits are seen as characterological rather than allegorical, the narration represents Ahmed's convictions as both transparent and immoveable. His particular pathology is inextricable from his politics. Although the narrative voice usually stays close to Shaltiel and his viewpoint, where Ahmed is concerned, ambiguity arises. Thus we read, "All Ahmed knows is how to insult, swear and curse"; since this follows directly after one of Shaltiel's first-person monologues, it appears to be his subjective judgment as he tries to work out Ahmed's motivations. Later, such an impression of free indirect discourse representing Shaltiel's viewpoint

Allegories of the Holocaust in Elie Wiesel's Late Fiction / 275

is undermined by such phrasing about his kidnapper as "In his view" and "Realizing that," which appear to arise from a third-person narrator reporting on Ahmed's inner world.[75] It seems that we are encountering Ahmed's views as envisaged by Shaltiel, in such utterances as "Shaltiel is his enemy and the enemy of his brothers in the desert; he must be denied pity [. . .] the key to his victory is here before him: this pathetic Yid, Shaltiel Feigen-whatever."[76] However, the distinction between this mediated construction of what Shaltiel imagines Ahmed to think and the implied author's construction of Ahmed's actual attitude is perilously thin. For Shaltiel himself, in a manner that is enacted in his discussions with Luigi, it is, rather, public and familial history that underlies his political convictions, as he thinks to himself: "he could not accuse Israel of war crimes or crimes against humanity: His own memory and that of his parents won't allow it."[77] Although it could be said that Shaltiel's partial view of Israel and Palestine is presented solely in terms of his own voice in *Hostage*, and therefore exposed to ironic reflection, it is hard for readers not to imagine that the novel's implied and actual author is responsible for what Carlaw describes as "the oversimplification and dehumanization of [Wiesel's] one Arab character" or even for what Diamond calls its one-sided "propaganda."[78]

Shaltiel's identity as a Holocaust survivor is central to the novel's plot yet represented with a version of the ambivalence we saw in relation to that of Malkiel Rosenbaum in *The Sonderberg Case*. Both hover between generations. Although Shaltiel's childhood was spent in Nazi-occupied Europe, once more in the fictional Carpathian shtetl of Davarovsk, his experience is described as a lesser version of his father's, the true survivor who had been a camp inmate. This uncertainty in Wiesel's later writing about the status of survival seems to arise partly from the increased attention paid to the second generation, to which several of the characters in his later writing belong, and partly from the origins of the fictional individuals in a mixture of Wiesel's own unusual experience, as a teenage Auschwitz inmate, and that of an imagined survival in hiding. Above all, it seems to be a way of paying homage to Shlomo Wiesel, whose death in Buchenwald might seem to make him the true Holocaust victim, as one of the "drowned," in Primo Levi's phrase, in contrast to his son Eliezer, one of the "saved," whose experience was thus secondary. In this way Malkiel in *The Forgotten* belatedly discovers that he is a survivor, not just the son of one, while Shaltiel in the present novel is described in an interpolated press release about the kidnap as "the son of a Holocaust survivor."[79] The experiences that were Wiesel's own, as we know from *Night*, become those of an earlier generation in *Hostage*, and, despite his own survivor status, Shaltiel considers himself "a stranger to the horrors his father witnessed."[80] The death march from Auschwitz at the war's end, so horrifyingly represented in Wiesel's testimony, is an event known only secondhand here, and of which "Shaltiel recalls what his father had recounted."[81] Yet on a more structural level, the connections between Wiesel and his character are clear, as Curt Schleier puts it: "Both are hostages. Wiesel is a prisoner of his memories," just as Shaltiel in the basement is isolated from any environment other than that of his own psyche.[82]

All of Wiesel's writing concerns the importance of transmitting historical lessons to successive generations, whether these lessons are those of Jewish tradition or the facts of the Holocaust. As we have seen in the earlier novels discussed here, the fictive representation of such transmission takes on the form of anxiety about paternity and biological lineage, which is both questioned and lauded. In the present case, we learn that, at first in his basement prison, Shaltiel considers his decision about remaining childless the right one: "Why give life to children when the destiny of men is in the hands of executioners?"[83] Yet Shaltiel's position is altered by his imprisonment, and he starts to think of his fate, "The last living examples of mankind that he would see in his lifetime would be his executioners. And he'd die without an heir."[84] These two sentiments are revealingly linked. The horror of an unwitnessed death would be offset for Shaltiel by an "heir," not just in the usual sense, of a (usually male) descendant who inherits one's estate and worldly goods, but by a figure who could remember on behalf of the earlier generation and for whom the inheritance would be a memorial one. Shaltiel comes even to see the affront of being without a successor to supersede his present circumstances: "The ultimate suffering is that he will leave no heir."[85] If any lesson is learned from this second episode of captivity, it is the "change" in Shaltiel's "convictions" after his release. He learns that his will be important testimony at Luigi's trial, but this witness role is once more transformed into a symbolic one: "Shaltiel nods his head. 'Yes, I will testify. I want to express my gratitude.' Blanca is the only one to smile at him."[86]

As Shaltiel's wife recognizes, "testifying" and "gratitude" here mean the creation of and transmission of life and knowledge to another generation. Such is the novel's denouement, since the reader has known since the opening that Shaltiel will be freed. Some reviewers seemed, understandably, to overlook the brief and allusive flash-forward in which this is predicted—for instance, Weinblatt describes the reader as being "in a constant state of anxiety as to the kindhearted Shaltiel's fate: murder or freedom?"—in which Shaltiel is toasted by officials and family to credit *"the joy of being with someone who was going to lose his life for unacceptable, absurd reasons."*[87] Even here, however, the prediction of successful rescue is subverted by Shaltiel's sense that *"someone is missing"*: as much as any tension over Shaltiel's eventual fate, the novel's mystery concerns this "someone," the protagonist's absent heir.

Conclusion

Primo Levi's science fiction stories, collected in English as *Natural Histories* and *Flaw of Form*, differ from his nonfiction writing about Auschwitz, in such testimonies as *If This Is a Man* and *The Truce*, as well as from his novel about wartime partisans, *If Not Now, When?*, in making the Holocaust "reverberations" subtly subtextual.[88] By contrast, the events of the Holocaust years are close to the surface in the case of the fiction by Wiesel, another writer best known for his testimony. The focus of Wiesel's fiction lies on survivors and their postwar lives, even if the situations and governing tropes of the three late novels I have considered here—amnesia, a murder trial, a terrorist act of kidnapping—appear oblique to those events. Each novel's central concern is with generations and memory, including the development of a second-generation view and of "collective memory."[89] Wiesel's technique of blurring the lines between allegory and realism, and frequently making explicit the parallels on which his symbolism rests, is a distinctive strategy, albeit one that tends to prioritize ideas over their literary incarnation.

In a review of *Hostage*, Adam Parker describes it as Wiesel's "most powerful" novel, "propelled forward less by his skill as a writer than his moral fiber as a human being."[90] This apparent incompatibility between artistry and morality is one that Jason Diamond sees as implicit in Wiesel's persona and his renown, as a "symbol, a public figure and a writer, in that order."[91] However, in the three novels under discussion, notions of autobiography and history are hinted at and refracted through fantasy and invention. In each case, we see versions of a particular and specific family romance: a beloved if beleaguered father, a saintly deceased mother, a devoted if distant spouse, and a precious son. The protagonist, who is invariably a writer, might play the son's part, or himself take the role of the father figure, or even possess elements of both. Such doubling of roles is at the heart of the ambivalence about the nature of the survivor in these works, who is sometimes a child survivor, sometimes a member of the second generation, but never a survivor of Auschwitz itself. Even though Wiesel was such a survivor, it is as if a reticence about fictionalizing this experience has affected the late works. All these elements make Wiesel's late novels resemble versions of autofiction, "a fiction of strictly real events or facts" in which the reader is relied upon to recognize the presence of the implied author as well as of the fictive worlds he has conjured.[92]

Notes

1. See the introduction to this volume for a discussion of *Night* as memoir.

2. See for example such novels as Michel Laub's *Diary of the Fall* (2011), Michael Lavigne's *Not Me* (2005), Harriet Chessman's *Someone Not Really Her Mother* (2004), and Atom Egoyan's film *Remember* (2015).

3. Frederick Busch, "An Endangered Witness," *New York Times Book Review*, 19 April 1992, http://www.nytimes.com/books/99/05/30/specials/busch-wiesel.html; Stanford V. Sternlicht, *A Student Companion to Elie Wiesel* (Westport: Greenwood Press, 2003), 106.

4. Elie Wiesel, *The Forgotten*, trans. Stephen Becker (New York: Schocken Books, 1992), 62.

5. Wiesel, *The Forgotten*, 262.

6. Wiesel, *The Forgotten*, 143.

7. Shoshana Felman and Dori Laub, *Testimony: Crises of Witnessing in Literature, Psychoanalysis, and History* (London: Routledge, 1991), 81.

8. Felman and Laub, *Testimony*, 81.

9. Felman and Laub, *Testimony*, 80.

10. Wiesel, *The Forgotten*, 234.

11. Wiesel, *The Forgotten*, 88.

12. Wiesel, *The Forgotten*, 88.

13. Wiesel, *The Forgotten*, 75.

14. Wiesel, *The Forgotten*, 49.

15. Marianne Hirsch, "The Generation of Postmemory," *Poetics Today* 29, no. 1 (Spring 2008): 103.

16. Wiesel, *The Forgotten*, 221.

17. Wiesel, *The Forgotten*, 47.

18. Wiesel, *The Forgotten*, 194, italics in original.
19. Felman and Laub, *Testimony*, 211, italics in original.
20. Wiesel, *The Forgotten*, 195, italics in original.
21. Wiesel, *The Forgotten*, 194, italics in original.
22. Wiesel, *The Forgotten*, 194, italics in original.
23. Wiesel, *The Forgotten*, 194, italics in original.
24. Wiesel, *The Forgotten*, 116.
25. Quoted in Naomi Seidman, "Elie Wiesel and the Scandal of Jewish Rage," *Jewish Social Studies* 3, no. 1 (Autumn 1996): 6. The Yiddish phrase for the women concerned is quoted here as "daytshe shikses," that is, "German gentile girls," making the element of revenge even clearer.
26. Elie Wiesel, *Night*, trans. Marion Wiesel (Harmondsworth: Penguin, 2006 [1958]), 115.
27. David Magilow, "Jewish Revenge Fantasies in Contemporary Film," in *Jewish Cultural Aspirations*, ed. Ruth Weisberg (Lafayette: Purdue University Press, 2013), 94.
28. Wiesel, *The Forgotten*, 190.
29. Wiesel, *The Forgotten*, 197.
30. Wiesel, *The Forgotten*, 297.
31. Wiesel, *The Forgotten*, 298.
32. Elie Wiesel, *The Sonderberg Case*, trans. Catherine Temerson (New York: Knopf, 2010), 5.
33. Wiesel, *The Sonderberg Case*, 3.
34. Wiesel, *The Sonderberg Case*, 55.
35. Wiesel, *The Sonderberg Case*, 74.
36. Wiesel, *The Sonderberg Case*, 163.
37. Wiesel, *The Sonderberg Case*, 168.
38. Lee Chottiner, "*The Sonderberg Case* Is Less about Plot than Characters," *Jewish Chronicle*, 2010, http://thejewishchronicle.net/view/full_story/10075889/article-The-Sonderberg-Case-less-about-plot-than-characters.
39. Jaclyn Trop, Review of *The Sonderberg Case*, Jewish Book Council, 2010, http://www.jewishbookcouncil.org/book/the-sonderberg-case.
40. Wiesel, *The Sonderberg Case*, 72.
41. Wiesel, *The Sonderberg Case*, 90.
42. Wiesel, *The Sonderberg Case*, 120.
43. Susan Suleiman, "The 1.5 Generation: Thinking about Child Survivors and the Holocaust," *American Imago* 59, no. 3 (2002): 277.
44. Wiesel, *The Sonderberg Case*, 59.
45. Wiesel, *The Sonderberg Case*, 60.
46. Wiesel, *The Sonderberg Case*, 124.
47. Wiesel, *The Sonderberg Case*, 130.
48. Wiesel, *The Sonderberg Case*, 127.

49. Wiesel, *The Sonderberg Case*, 129.
50. Wiesel, *The Sonderberg Case*, 130.
51. Summer Moore, "Wiesel's *Sonderberg Case* Is Tale of Family Ties," NewsOK, 23 August 2010, http://newsok.com/article/feed/184135.
52. Harvey Freedenberg, "*The Sonderberg Case*: A wise work from Elie Wiesel," BookPage, September 2010, https://bookpage.com/reviews/6586-elie-wiesel-sonderberg-case#.WZntRYoo9sM.
53. Wiesel, *The Sonderberg Case*, 142.
54. Wiesel, *The Sonderberg Case*, 137.
55. Peter Conn, *Adoption: A Brief Social and Cultural History* (Basingstoke: Palgrave, 2013), 143.
56. Wiesel, *The Sonderberg Case*, 165.
57. Elie Wiesel, *Hostage*, trans. Catherine Temerson (New York: Knopf, 2012), 20.
58. Wiesel, *Hostage*, 5.
59. Gregory McNamee, "*Hostage*: A Conversation with Elie Wiesel," *Kirkus Review*, 21 August 2012, https://www.kirkusreviews.com/features/hostage-conversation-elie-wiesel/.
60. Wiesel, *Hostage*, 206.
61. Wiesel, *Hostage*, 5.
62. Wiesel, *Hostage*, 89.
63. Jason Diamond, "Blameless and Upright, but Not That Good: Elie Wiesel Is a Better Spokesman than Writer," *Observer*, 7 August 2012, http://observer.com/2012/08/blameless-and-upright-but-not-that-good-elie-wiesel-is-a-better-spokesman-than-writer/.
64. Wiesel, *Hostage*, 4.
65. Darren Richard Carlaw, review of *Hostage*, *Edinburgh Book Review*, 21 December 2012, https://www.edinburghbookreview.co.uk/hostage-by-elie-wiesel/; Wiesel, *Hostage*, 6, 8.
66. Wiesel, *Hostage*, 9.
67. Wiesel, *Hostage*, 51.
68. David Ulin, Review of *Hostage*, *Boston Herald*, 27 August 2012, http://www.bostonherald.com/entertainment/books/2012/08/elie_wiesel%E2%80%99s_%E2%80%98hostage%E2%80%99_captivating.
69. Wiesel, *Hostage*, 133.
70. Wiesel, *Hostage*, 134.
71. Wiesel, *Hostage*, 211, 45.
72. Wiesel, *Hostage*, 142; Wiesel, *Night*, 81.
73. Wiesel, *Hostage*, 78.
74. Wiesel, *Hostage*, 142.
75. Wiesel, *Hostage*, 39.
76. Wiesel, *Hostage*, 40.

77. Wiesel, *Hostage*, 44.
78. Carlaw, review of *Hostage*; Diamond, "Blameless and Upright."
79. Wiesel, *Hostage*, 31.
80. Wiesel, *Hostage*, 205.
81. Wiesel, *Hostage*, 94.
82. Carl Schleier, "*Hostage*: Elie Wiesel's Novel of Kidnapping and Captivity," *Seattle Times*, 26 August 2012, http://o.seattletimes.nwsource.com/html/books/2018968016_br26hostage.html.
83. Wiesel, *Hostage*, 174.
84. Wiesel, *Hostage*, 137.
85. Wiesel, *Hostage*, 205.
86. Wiesel, *Hostage*, 214.
87. Charles Weinblatt, review of *Hostage*, *New York Journal of Books*, 12 August 2012; Wiesel, *Hostage*, 3, italics in original.
88. Jonathan Rosen, "Prisoner of War," *New York Times*, 27 May 2007, http://www.nytimes.com/2007/05/27/books/review/Rosen-t.html.
89. Wiesel, *The Sonderberg Case*, 60.
90. Adam Parker, "Humanity of Hostage," *Post and Courier*, 6 October 2012, http://www.postandcourier.com/features/arts_and_travel/humanity-of-hostage/article_b6e084c8-b24a-5f9b-bfcd-754b01e6689e.html.
91. Diamond, "Blameless and Upright."
92. Serge Doubrovsky, *Fils* (Paris: Gallimard, 1977), 10.

Works Cited

Busch, Frederick. "An Endangered Witness." *New York Times Book Review*. 19 April 1992. http://www.nytimes.com/books/99/05/30/specials/busch-wiesel.html. Accessed 23 July 2017.

Carlaw, Darren Richard. Review of *Hostage*. *Edinburgh Book Review*. 21 December 2012. https://www.edinburghbookreview.co.uk/hostage-by-elie-wiesel/. Accessed 23 July 2017.

Chottiner, Lee. "*The Sonderberg Case* Is Less about Plot than Characters." *Jewish Chronicle*. 2010. http://thejewishchronicle.net/view/full_story/10075889/article-The-Sonderberg-Case-less-about-plot-than-characters. Accessed 23 July 2017.

Conn, Peter. *Adoption: A Brief Social and Cultural History*. Basingstoke: Palgrave, 2013.

Diamond, Jason. "Blameless and Upright, but Not That Good: Elie Wiesel Is a Better Spokesman than Writer." *Observer*. 7 August 2012. http://observer.com/2012/08/blameless-and-upright-but-not-that-good-elie-wiesel-is-a-better-spokesman-than-writer/. Accessed 23 July 2017.

Doubrovsky, Serge. *Fils*. Paris: Gallimard, 1977.
Felman, Shoshana, and Dori Laub. *Testimony: Crises of Witnessing in Literature, Psychoanalysis, and History*. London: Routledge, 1977.
Hirsch, Marianne. "The Generation of Postmemory." *Poetics Today* 29, no. 1 (Spring 2008): 103–28.
Levi, Primo. *The Complete Works of Primo Levi*. Ed. Ann Goldstein. New York: Norton, 2015.
Magilow, Daniel H. "Jewish Revenge Fantasies in Contemporary Film." In *Jewish Cultural Aspirations*, ed. Ruth Weisberg, 88–110. Lafayette: Purdue University Press, 2013.
McNamee, Gregory. "*Hostage*: A Conversation with Elie Wiesel." *Kirkus Review*. 21 August 2012. https://www.kirkusreviews.com/features/hostage-conversation-elie-wiesel/. Accessed 23 July 2017.
Parker, Adam. "Humanity of Hostage." *Post and Courier*. 6 October 2012. http://www.postandcourier.com/features/arts_and_travel/humanity-of-hostage/article_b6e084c8-b24a-5f9b-bfcd-754b01e6689e.html. Accessed 23 July 2017.
Rosen, Jonathan. "Prisoner of War." *New York Times*. 27 May 2007. http://www.nytimes.com/2007/05/27/books/review/Rosen-t.html. Accessed 23 July 2017.
Schleier, Curt. "*Hostage*: Elie Wiesel's Novel of Kidnapping and Captivity." *Seattle Times*. 26 August 2012. http://o.seattletimes.nwsource.com/html/books/2018968016_br26hostage.html. Accessed 23 July 2017.
Seidman, Naomi. "Elie Wiesel and the Scandal of Jewish Rage." *Jewish Social Studies* 3, no. 1 (Autumn 1996): 1–19.
Sternlicht, Sanford V. *A Student Companion to Elie Wiesel*. Westport: Greenwood Press, 2003.
Suleiman, Susan. "The 1.5 Generation: Thinking about Child Survivors and the Holocaust." *American Imago* 59, no. 3 (2002): 277–95.
Trop, Jaclyn. Review of *The Sonderberg Case*. *Jewish Book Council*. 2010. http://www.jewishbookcouncil.org/book/the-sonderberg-case. Accessed 23 July 2017.
Ulin, David. Review of *Hostage*. *Boston Herald*. 27 August 2012. http://www.bostonherald.com/entertainment/books/2012/08/elie_wiesel%E2%80%99s_%E2%80%98hostage%E2%80%99_captivating. Accessed 23 July 2017.
Weinblatt, Charles. Review of *Hostage*. *New York Journal of Books*. 12 August 2012. http://webcache.googleusercontent.com/search?q=cache:O18KnVt_260J:www.nyjournalofbooks.com/book-review/hostage+&cd=1&hl=en&ct=clnk&gl=uk. Accessed 23 July 2017.
Wiesel, Elie. *The Forgotten*. Trans. Stephen Becker. New York: Schocken Books, 1992.
Wiesel, Elie. *Hostage*. Trans. Catherine Temerson. New York: Knopf, 2012.
Wiesel, Elie. *Night*. Trans. Marion Wiesel. Harmondsworth: Penguin, 2006 [1958].
Wiesel, Elie. *The Sonderberg Case*. Trans. Catherine Temerson. New York: Knopf, 2010.

Contributors

Federico Dal Bo is a Marie Curie postdoctoral fellow at the Autonomous University of Barcelona (Spain). His work focuses on Talmud, Kabbalah, Jewish hermeneutics, and translation studies. He holds a PhD in Jewish studies and a further PhD in translation studies. His most recent books in English are *Emanation and Philosophy of Language: An Introduction to Josef ben Abraham Gikatilla* (2018) and *Massekhet Keritot: Text, Translation, and Commentary* (2013).

Yakir Englander, AJR (Academy of Jewish Religion), IAC (Israeli American Council), is a Fulbright scholar and was a visiting professor of Israel studies and religion at Northwestern University, Rutgers University, and Harvard Divinity School. In his academic writings he tries to touch the most sensitive subjects of gender, sexuality, and theology and to create critique with love. His books are *The Male Body in Jewish Lithuanian Ultra-Orthodoxy* (Hebrew) and *Sexuality and the Body in the New Religious Zionist Discourse* (with Avi Sagi) (English and Hebrew).

Rosemary Horowitz joined the faculty of Appalachian State University in 1995, where she teaches in the English Department and is active in ASU's Center for Judaic, Holocaust, and Peace Studies. Her research interests are in literary studies, especially within the Jewish community. Her publications include the edited collections *Memorial Books of Eastern European Jewry: Essays on the History and Meanings of Yizker Volumes* (2011), *Elie Wiesel and the Art of Storytelling* (2006), and *Women Writers of Yiddish Literature* (2015).

Menachem Keren-Kratz is a researcher of Hungarian Orthodoxy and of contemporary Haredi society in Israel. He holds a DMD and two PhDs, one from Bar-Ilan University in Yiddish literature, the dissertation for which is now published under the title *Maramaros-Sziget: Extreme Orthodoxy and Secular Jewish Culture at the Foothills of the Carpathian Mountains* (2013, in Hebrew). Menachem's second PhD, from Tel-Aviv University, is in Jewish history, the dissertation for which will shortly be published under the title *Rabbi Yoel Teitelbaum—The Satmar Rebbe: The Pious, the Zealot and the Politician*. He has published articles and book chapters in publications including *Modern Judaism*, *Contemporary Jewry*, *Modern Jewish Studies*, *Israel Studies Review*, *Dapim: Studies on the Holocaust*, *Tradition*, *Cathedra*, *Identities*, and *Kesher*.

Peppy Margolis is director of community programs for Raritan Valley Community College where she designs the educational programs for the Institute for Holocaust and Genocide Studies. She is assistant to the New Jersey State Holocaust Commission. In 1990 she was the primary author of the first *Curriculum on Prejudice Reduction, Cultural Diversity, Holocaust and Genocide: Caring Makes a Difference K–8*, which is mandated in the schools of New Jersey. She previously served as coordinator of the Holocaust program at the United Jewish Federation of MetroWest. She has produced three films that deal with issues about how the Holocaust has affected families and future generations: *The Second Generation: Ripples from the Holocaust* (2012), *The Other* (2014), and *Margit: Not A23029* (2016).

Ariel Evan Mayse joined the faculty of Stanford University in 2017 as an assistant professor in the Department of Religious Studies, after previously serving as the director of Jewish studies and visiting assistant professor of modern Jewish thought at Hebrew College in Newton, Massachusetts, and a research fellow at the Frankel Institute for Advanced Judaic Studies of the University of Michigan. He holds a PhD in Jewish studies from Harvard University and rabbinic ordination from Beit Midrash Har'el in Israel. Ariel's current research examines the role of language in Hasidism, manuscript theory and the formation of early Hasidic literature, the renaissance of Jewish mysticism in the nineteenth and twentieth centuries, and the relationship between spirituality and law in Jewish legal writings.

Dana Mihăilescu is an associate professor of English/American studies at the University of Bucharest, where she earned her doctorate in 2010 for the thesis "Ethical Dilemmas and Reconfigurations of Identity in Early Twentieth Century Eastern European Jewish American Narratives." Her main research interests include Jewish American studies, Holocaust survivor testimonies, trauma and witnessing, ethics and memory. She has published articles on these topics in *Journal of Modern Jewish Studies, French Cultural Studies, American Imago, European Review of History, Rethinking History, Studies in Comics*, among others. Her most recent book-length publication is a monograph, *Eastern European Jewish American Narratives, 1890–1930: Struggles for Recognition* (2018).

Mary Catherine Mueller obtained her PhD in humanities, studies of literature, with a focus on Holocaust studies, from the University of Texas at Dallas. She holds the position of full-time lecturer in English at Southern Methodist University, where she teaches discernment and discourse (rhetoric), Holocaust literature, and honors humanities seminar courses. In addition to her work appearing in *Shofar: An Interdisciplinary Journal of Jewish Studies*, Mueller, whether presenting in Dallas, Los Angeles, London, Jerusalem, or elsewhere, has presented her research and writings about the Holocaust to scholars, educators, and human rights advocates throughout the world. Her forthcoming publication critically examines how the Holocaust is represented in various literary genres. Her research and writings examine the representations of the Holocaust in pop culture, art, memory, and society; literature as testimony; and the representations of the Holocaust in literature.

Jennifer Murray is a PhD student at the University of Kentucky. Her research interests include multicultural American literature, Holocaust literature, trauma theory, gender studies, and disability studies. Her recent projects include an examination of the representation and transmission of trauma in three generations of women's Holocaust narratives. Her current project interrogates the impact of political conflict and immigration on identity formation and belonging in women's writings at the turn of the twentieth century in the United States.

Victoria Nesfield obtained her PhD on the works of Primo Levi and Elie Wiesel from the University of Leeds. She has previously taught religious studies, conflict and peacemaking, and Holocaust studies and worked as a postdoctoral researcher on Germany's confrontation with the Holocaust in a global context. Her research interests on the Holocaust and responses to the Holocaust include testimony, literature and art, memory, and education. She has published articles and book chapters on these areas in publications, including *Research in Education*, *International Journal of Public Theology*, and *Journal of European Studies*. She works in the Humanities Research Centre at the University of York.

Philip Smith obtained his PhD from Loughborough University. His work has been published in *The American Comic Book*, *The Journal of Graphic Novels and Comics*, *The International Journal of Comics Art*, *Studies in Comics*, *Extrapolation*, *The Journal of Popular Culture*, *Literature Compass*, *Journal of Southeast Asian Studies*, *The Journal of European Studies*, *Asian Theatre Journal*, *Slayage*, and *The International Journal of Bahamian Studies*. He is coeditor of *Firefly Revisited* (2015) and the author of *Reading Art Spiegelman* (2015). He is professor of English at the Savannah College of Art and Design Hong Kong.

Eric J. Sterling earned his PhD in English from Indiana University. He has taught at Auburn University Montgomery since 1994 and holds the title of Ida Belle Young Professor of English. He has also been named Distinguished Research Professor, Distinguished Teaching Professor, and Alumni Professor. He has published four books and more than seventy-five refereed articles. His book entitled *Life in the Ghettos During the Holocaust* was published by Syracuse University Press. Sterling has published on Holocaust literature by Joshua Sobol, Shimon Wincelberg, George Steiner/Christopher Hampton, Jurek Becker, Peter Barnes, Denise Levertov, Martin Sherman, and Arthur Miller. He has also published articles on Holocaust bystanders, the Vilna ghetto in Lithuania, *Schindler's List*, and Janusz Korczak.

Sue Vice is a professor of English literature at the University of Sheffield. Her recent publications include the coedited volume *Representing Perpetrators in Holocaust Literature and Film*, the monograph *Textual Deceptions: False Memoirs and Literary Hoaxes in the Contemporary Era* (2014), and the coauthored study *Barry Hines: "Kes," "Threads" and Beyond*, with David Forrest (2017).

Lucas Wilson, after graduating with his BA in English, summa cum laude, from Liberty University, received his MA in English from McMaster University and his MTS from Vanderbilt University with a Certificate in Jewish Studies. He is currently a PhD student in comparative studies at Florida Atlantic University. Under the supervision of Alan L. Berger, he is writing his dissertation on second-generation Holocaust literature and oral history. The year prior to starting his PhD, he was an assisting faculty member at Lipscomb University in Nashville, Tennessee, while he interned for the Tennessee Holocaust Commission, working specifically with second-generation Holocaust witnesses. Lucas's research focuses on twentieth- and twenty-first-century Canadian and US literatures, second-generation Holocaust studies, Holocaust literature, religion and literature, and evangelicalism.

Christin Zühlke is a PhD student at the Center for Research on Anti-Semitism at the Technische Universität Berlin, Germany. Her doctoral dissertation focuses on "Response to Evil in Nazi Ideology and Practice: The Case of the Sonderkommando and Their Yiddish Writings." She holds a BA in philosophy as well as German literature and linguistics, and an MA in Jewish studies and philosophy. She worked for several years on historical and political education, at an internship at ISHS in Yad Vashem, Israel, and at the Jewish Museum in Berlin. In 2014 she led the Memorial of the Death Marches in the Belower Forest, Germany, part of the Memorial and Museum at Sachsenhausen. Furthermore, she worked with original documents on anti-Semitism and the Shoah at the Wiener Library, and she worked as a research assistant on ritual slaughter at the Buchmann Faculty of Law, both at Tel Aviv University, Israel. In 2016–2017 she was a project manager at the Department of Cognitive Science of the Hebrew University Jerusalem, Israel, while working as a visiting research fellow at the Rothberg International School at the Hebrew University. She is a project coordinator for Jewish religious, cultural, and educational projects at Lauder Yeshurun in Berlin, Germany.

Index

1.5 Generation, xxii, 220, 269

anti-Semitism, xi, 32, 104, 113–134, 222–224, 245–247
All Rivers Run to the Sea, 220
Alzheimer's disease, ix, xxi, 83, 193, 196, 202–203, 210–211, 262
Apshan, Herzl, 18

Basch, Elizer, 18
Bruckstein, Israel Leib, 18
bystander effect, the, 98–112

captivity narrative, 239–260
Christianity, 113–134

Danzig, Hilel, 18
Dawn, 175, 178–179, 239–260
dignity and honor cultures, 25–50

Five Biblical Portraits, 53, 56, 71
Forgotten, The, 195–215, 261–282

Gates of the Forest, The, 113–134, 137–167, 175
God, viii, xvi–xviii, 12–13, 17, 25–50, 52–58, 63–70, 83–84, 89, 91–93, 94fn24, 113–114, 118–119, 122–126, 138, 137–167, 169–193, 196–197, 195–215, 243, 261
Gottlieb, Hirsch Leib, 10
ghostwriting, 232–234

Hirsh, Avraham Mordechai, 7
Holder, Joseph, 7
Humanism, 25–50
humour, *see* laughter
Hostage, 239–260, 261–282

Israel, 16, 18, 60, 69, 114, 145–146, 152, 173, 188, 202–203, 239–260, 261–282
  Israeli-Palestinian conflict, 239–260, 261–282

laughter, 138, 141–143, 147–150, 162fn50, 162–163fn57, 163fn59, 163fn64, 181–182

madness, 54–57, 61–63, 69–71, 79–96, 138, 143, 148, 159, 175, 222
Mark, Nathan, 16–17
memory, 83–91, 104, 170–176, 195–215, 219–238, 261–282
messianism, 38–39, 52, 67, 145–146, 153, 175, 179, 242–245, 248–249

music, *see* song

Night, viii, xi, xiii–xiv, xviii, 13–14, 19, 22fn49, 31, 32–37, 44fn49, 51–76, 79–96, 97, 103, 170, 178, 179, 183, 195–196, 200, 207–209, 240, 261, 265–266, 274, 276

Open Heart, xvi, 185
Oyfgang, 9, 11

Palestine (*see also* Israeli-Palestinian conflict), 7, 16, 118, 175, 239–260, 261–282
Postmemory, 220, 263–267, 271
prophets/prophesy, 34, 51–75, 81–83, 92, 144, 185, 187, 223, 243, 248

Ring, Yechezkel, 7
  Farblondgeter Nigen, 14
  Oyfen Himel A Yarid, 13

Satan, 13, 30, 179, 186–189, 191fn60
Schnabel, Berl, 7
Schwartz, Shlomo, 7
second-generation survivor, 189, 201, 220, 261, 264, 269, 277
Shternberg, Naftaly, 17
Sighet, xviii, 3–24, 59, 82, 98, 108fn13, 139, 172, 208–209, 220
silence, xiv–xv, 12, 36, 56–57, 60–67, 69, 71, 85, 90, 92–93, 106–107, 121, 137–167, 170, 173, 176, 179, 180, 182, 185, 187, 191fn58, 202–203, 206, 209, 211, 228, 266, 270

Sonderberg Case, The, 261–282
song, 7, 15, 52, 117, 138, 139, 141, 143, 147, 151–156, 161fn16, 163–164fn75, 177

Tambur, Wolf, 7
Testament, The, xxii, 175, 239–260
Time of the Uprooted, The, 79–96, 219–238
Torah, the, 29, 38, 52, 57, 62, 148, 209, 247
Town Beyond the Wall, The, 97–112, 175
Trial of God, The, xvi, 13, 94fn24, 185–188
transculturality, 219–238
trauma, ix, xvii, 39, 116, 138, 151, 169, 191fn57, 197–199, 202, 222, 224, 229–232, 256, 264–270, 285

Un Di Velt Hot Geshvigen, 19, 97, 170, 176

Wiesel, Shlomo, vii, 4–6, 10–14, 15–17, 21fn43, 33, 35, 64–68, 171, 174, 176, 207, 210, 261, 266, 275
Weiss, Israel, 11
Witness (*see also* bystander), xiii, 14, 35, 52–71, 83, 97, 101, 97–112, 117, 130, 142, 170–176, 196–206, 211, 222, 228–229, 244, 262–267, 276

Zionism, 4, 6–8, 10, 29, 239–260

Printed in the USA
CPSIA information can be obtained
at www.ICGtesting.com
CBHW031922090924
14022CB00006B/135